good

158

TENNYSON SIXTY YEARS AFTER

TENNYSON

SIXTY YEARS AFTER

By

Paull F. Baum

Chapel Hill

THE UNIVERSITY OF NORTH CAROLINA PRESS

MANUFACTURED IN THE UNITED STATES OF AMERICA BY
THE WILLIAM BYRD PRESS, INC.
RICHMOND, VIRGINIA
A. B.

Preface

THIS book is a critical study of Tennyson's poetry, with the single object of surveying the whole course of his work—neglecting neither the flowers nor the hedges—in order to bring in an interim report on his ultimate position as a poet. Since much of the contemporary criticism remains illuminating, if not always sound, and since much of the verse was influenced by contemporary opinion, a certain amount of material from the reviews has been included; but I have not tried to compile a history of Tennyson's reputation. In fact, most of the book was written without regard to Victorian criticism at all; the illustrations from the reviews were introduced later, I hope without leaving the joinery too rough.

I am well aware of the rashness of attempting to forecast the judgment of posterity. For there is no absolute standard, even for posterity to judge by; and nearly all 'values' are as uncertain as taste. In general I have presumed to apply the æsthetic rather than the moral test (with the admission that they are not quite separable) because it is the fairest for Tennyson. He was an artist above all else. His greater deficiency was in the place where art and spirit merge, a tableland above both 'art' and 'morality,' where criticism in the ordinary sense is nearly helpless.

It might be expected, however, that the critic who attempts to anticipate posterity, or even to speak for the present, should make some statement of his method or principles more than may be discernible from the resultant formulations. Most of all I have relied on perspective, or foreground distance, to separate Tennyson from his enveloping circumstances; for even now a great deal of what is said or thought about him is either an echo of what his contemporaries said and thought about him or of a somewhat violent reaction against their judgments. It is for this reason that I have begun with the Tennyson legend; in order to show the confusion, natural enough perhaps then, which prevented any critical distinction between the permanent literary merits of his poetry and the majestic figure of a man who had for half a century given so much general satisfaction to so many readers of poetry and had somehow become accepted as the poetic voice of England—the Bard.

In the second chapter I intended to sketch so much of Tennyson's life as would show the kind of man he was who wrote the kind of poetry Tennyson wrote. The chapter is ill proportioned because of certain fresh material, principally the fuller details than appear in the *Memoir* or more recent books about the restless decade before his marriage, and about the search for poetic subjects in his later years. The chapter is longer than I could have wished because only by showing, even at the risk of tedium, the bare simplicity and eventlessness of Tennyson's life after 1855 could the want of stimulating experience, emotional and intellectual, which might provoke poetic expression be made convincing. The general character of these years is well enough known; a repetition of the dull details adds the required emphasis on one of Tennyson's great limitations.

The following chapters are almost entirely critical, except perhaps that on the poet as interpreter of his age, which is both critical and discursive. The chapter on the domestic idylls was necessary in order to reveal at full length how far Tennyson shared the ideas of his middle-class followers, and perhaps remind readers to-day how large a proportion of verse was devoted to this sort of writing. The other is really central for our understanding of the Bard's poetical function. Both are rather tedious because they cover a good deal of his inferior work, but they cannot be scamped by the serious student because without them so much, alas so very much, of his lifelong devotion will be missed. There can be no doubt that Tennyson applied himself earnestly to the duty, once it had been revealed to him, of playing demiurge to the *Zeitgeist*. He worked hard at it, after his fashion. His own instincts, as will appear, were at first on the side of art, that is, to create something of beauty. But art, he was soon told, is not enough. For the early Victorians, feeling their way out of the immoralities of the Regency and into the social and political disturbances of Reform, certainly art, in the sense of the ivory tower, was not enough. Life was too real, its confusion too importunate; and presently Matthew Arnold, in his own way equally dissatisfied with British 'culture,' would emphatically tell them that poetry was but an interpretation of life. Could there be a greater or more rewarding mission therefore than to interpret such a multifarious and rapidly growing age to itself? For Tennyson, wanting both through the emotional poverty of his private life and through the absence of inner fire and spiritual energy, here was the very thing, a thrice welcome opportunity. Art, meaning skill and craftsmanship, he already had and he was learning swiftly to improve his native gift; what he needed was matter. His task then was to understand and reveal to his readers the true inwardness of his age. For more than forty years he was its Laureate. It was an impossible task, certainly, for a sensitive and reclusive man, with a strong inherited melancholy, disinclined to face the slings and arrows of the critics, and with only mediocre intellectual endowment.

The outcome would have been more consoling if Tennyson had been able truly and fully to reflect the best of his age. But in social criticism, in politics, he was an innocent. He saw, or heard, that many things were bad; and he had a great gift for saying how bad they were. He had no gift for seeing or saying how they should be improved, save that we should all be better men and women. In religion he clung to simple faith: it was not easy, but there was nothing else. The Church of England and the Chapels and the Church of Rome were somehow wrong, but the individual worker in the vineyard ought to be somehow good. What else? Why of course be sturdy Englishmen with hearts of oak and let freedom slowly broaden down, as of course it will. It was more a judgment on his contemporaries than on the Bard that they encouraged him in propagating these simple truths, and crowned him with their laurel, and though they grumbled continually received him as their prophet. The effect was reciprocal.

In a word, then, the voluntary and to some extent deliberate self-dedication to the interpretation of his age was Tennyson's substitute for poetic energy. It was natural, considering his time; perhaps inevitable; and it betrayed him into writing a large amount of serious popular, even vulgar, poetry. And now, since we are far enough removed to recognize the difference, we are able to separate the "true" from the "false" and to see how, his instinct be-

ing for beauty, the necessity of finding in contemporary life sub-
jects to write about led him to beautify inferior material.

This is the first point. Our judgments are now (as Bacon would
say) less likely to be blooded by the affections. But inevitably our
new judgments are founded on an æsthetic which is of the twen-
tieth century and which may itself be no better than the Vic-
torian. As I have said, the most appropriate test of Tennyson's
poetry seems to me to be the purely artistic one. Whatever the
'subject,' did he succeed in making beauty out of it? It is not
enough to write beautifully about it: that Tennyson could nearly
always do; the power of the winged word and the musical phrase
was his gift. It is enough only when he has created something—a
picture, a mood, an incident, a character—which satisfies our
trained æsthetic sense, and which we recognize as true and honest,
consistent with itself, touching our deeper feelings either with pity
or with exaltation, "springing" our imagination. And this Tenny-
son has done, sometimes in whole poems, oftener in fragments, but
rarely without flaws, flaws which are the more remarkable because
of the fineness of the work in which they inhere. This explains the
peculiar difficulty of criticizing Tennyson: it seems impossible to
commend any poem or even part of a poem without immediately
taking away something of the praise. The excellence of the work-
manship invites and deserves scrutiny, and the scrutiny reveals
blemishes; so that one is involved in a continual meiosis which
can easily become tiresome. But I make no apology for submitting
several of the poems to minute analysis. For a good work of art will
bear any amount of careful examination and stand the sturdier
thereafter. If it does not, we are entitled to know why.

But after all, poetry is to be enjoyed, and it may be no great
matter that there are some who get their enjoyment from a sense
of spiritual and moral improvement—*profit* is the old word for it.
There are however others who hold to a severer standard and who
can unite pleasure with critical intelligence as they read. Each of
us can but give his own opinion, an amalgam of independent and
inherited judgments, and so far as possible 'show cause.' On the
larger question of Tennyson's general successes and failures—what
has he taught us? what does he tell us about ourselves? what does
his poetry reveal of the great passions, what illumination of the

recesses of mind or soul?—we are in a position to come a little closer
to the truth than ever before. His simple beauties and easy answers
are out of fashion with a generation which makes a cult of uncer-
tainty, complexity, and incoherence. Both are temporary and have
their turn on the wheel of fortune. But something more remains.
Tennyson can never expect "all men's suffrage"; for he *was* "of an
age." But a great deal remains which we can admire and praise and
enjoy. Perhaps a still later judgment will be more generous, when
it has become possible both to forget and to forgive, when the
timely part shall have been blown away like the dust which it is.
The dust is even now a little in our eyes.

The quantity of writing about Tennyson is enormous. I do not
pretend to have read all of it, but I have been through a great deal
of it and taken freely whatever I found helpful. All conscious bor-
rowing is indicated in the usual way, with superior numbers re-
ferring to notes at the end of the volume; footnotes properly so-
called (indicated by superior letters) are where they should be.
Many quotations have been left without specific reference, where
the source was fairly obvious. Most of these are from the *Memoir*.

I am particularly grateful to Sir Charles Tennyson for allow-
ing me to make use of the unpublished "Materials" on which the
Memoir (1897) was based. A few details are drawn, with the per-
mission of Messrs. Macmillan, from the Eversley Edition, "An-
notated by Alfred, Lord Tennyson, Edited by Hallam, Lord
Tennyson," 9 vols., with separate titles, Macmillan and Co., 1907.

P.F.B.

Contents

Contents

TENNYSON SIXTY YEARS AFTER

People are almost always silent when one quotes good Tennyson. They prefer it to be awful; and then they can shout "My God!"

G. B. Stern

I think I may safely say that no book in my library remains unopened a year at a time, except my own works and Tennyson's.

Carolyn Wells

Talking it over, we agreed that Blake was no good because he learnt Italian at sixty in order to study Dante, and we knew Dante was no good because he was so fond of Virgil, and Virgil was no good because Tennyson ran him, and as for Tennyson—well, Tennyson goes without saying.

Samuel Butler

. . . before the famous black bust of Antinoüs. Tennyson bent forward a little, and said, in his deep, slow voice, "Ah! this is the inscrutable Bithynian!" There was a pause, and then he added, gazing into the eyes of the bust: "If we knew what he knew, we should understand the ancient world."

Sir Edmund Gosse

Anyhow, Alfred, . . . I feel how pure, noble and holy your work is, and whole phrases, lines and sentences of it will abide with me, and, I am sure, with men after me.

Edward FitzGerald

We express our own age by resisting it, by creating something which will outlast its fears and disillusions.

Laurence Binyon

CHAPTER ONE

Tennyson Dead

THE TENNYSON legend is itself in the way of becoming legendary, for as contemporary judgments harden into tradition they tend to lose their shading. When Tennyson's reputation had supposedly reached its nadir, say about 1910, and it was possible for a bright journalist to say, without apparent disapprobation, that the Arthur of the 'Idylls' was a hero modelled in *blanc-mange,* this state of criticism was understood as a reaction —the inevitable reaction—against the universal adulation which the Bard enjoyed, and suffered from, during the latter years of his long life. The adulation was real, but it was not universal. Hardly a single volume came from the Laureate, that is, after his position was regarded as secure, without some strong dissenting voice being raised, and there were frequent disturbances in the serene atmosphere of his worshippers. Even the obituaries were not altogether unclouded. But obituaries are by convention, almost by definition, laudatory, and Tennyson, if he really enjoyed praise as much as he hated blame, would have been royally content.

The Laureate was taken ill on the 28th of September 1892, as he was planning to leave Aldworth for Farringford. In fact, "the special train in which his lordship invariably travels to Farringford had been requisitioned." But at first no grave danger appeared imminent. At 9:30, however, on Wednesday evening, the 5th of October, a bulletin from Sir Andrew Clark, Tennyson's old friend and physician, and Dr. Dabbs, the family doctor, announced that the poet was only just alive. At 1:35 the next morning Tennyson died. The *Pall Mall Gazette* of 6 October reported as follows:

The morning yesterday rose in almost unearthly splendour over the hills and valleys on which the windows of Aldworth House, where

Lord Tennyson was dying, look out. From the mullioned window of the room where the poet lay he could look down upon the peaceful fields, the silent hills beyond them, and the sky above, which was a blue so deep and pure as is rarely seen in this country.

Lord Tennyson woke ever and again out of the painless, dreamy state into which he had fallen, and looked out into the silence and the sunlight.

In the afternoon, in one of his waking moments, during which he was always perfectly conscious, he asked for his Shakspeare, and with his own hands turned the leaves till he had found "Cymbeline." His eyes were fixed on the pages, but whether and how much he read no one will ever know, for again he lay in dream or slumber, or let his eyes rest on the scene outside.

As the day advanced a change came over the scene, a change almost awful to those who watched the death-bed. Slowly the sun went down, the blue died out of the sky, and upon the valley below there fell a perfectly white mist. The hills, as our representative was told, put on their purple garments to watch this strange, white stillness; there was not a sound in the air, and, high above, the clear, cloudless sky shone like a pale glittering dome. All nature seemed to be watching, waiting.

Then the stars came out, and looked in at the big mullioned window, and those within saw them grow brighter and brighter, till at last a moon, a harvest moon for splendour, though it was an October moon, sailed slowly up, and flooded the room with golden light. The bed on which Lord Tennyson lay, now very near the gate of death, and with his left hand still resting on his Shakspeare, was in deep darkness; the rest of the room lit up with the glory of the night, which poured in through the uncurtained windows. And thus, without pain, without a struggle, the greatest of England's poets passed away.[1]

Dr. Dabbs, who was himself a journalist and a dramatist, gave a slightly different account: "On the bed a figure of breathing marble, flooded and bathed in the light of the full moon streaming through the oriel window"; and he was reminded of the death of King Arthur. Sir Andrew, who was not however in the room at the moment of death, said: "In all my experience I have never witnessed anything more glorious. There were no artificial lights in the chamber, and all was in darkness, save for a silvery light of the moon at its full. The soft beams of light fell upon the bed and played upon the features of the dying poet like a halo of Rembrandt."[2]

Thus nature and journalism collaborated on a brilliant final curtain for the aged and revered Bard. And for the next few days

4

the newspaper readers were regaled with further details and with the various plans for burial: from the howling of Tennyson's favorite wolfhound to the list of those who left cards at the gate of Aldworth, who followed the *cortège* to Haslemere, who accompanied the body to Waterloo station, and who met the procession at Dean's-gate and accompanied it to St. Faith's Chapel, Westminster.

The day of the funeral was very cold for the time of year. It was recalled that three years before, at Browning's obsequies, a yellow fog hung over the city; but now the sky was clear, or nearly so, and though the sun was from time to time obscured, just as the Choir began the Burial Service it "shone out and flooded the church with light." The long procession into the Abbey was led by the clergy in full canonicals. Order was preserved by the boys of the Gordon Home (in which Tennyson had been much interested) in their red uniforms and by a contingent of Highlanders in grey. Another note of color was added by one conspicuous "person" who wore a light grey trailing skirt, a loose blue coat lined with a loud Tartan, and a scarlet toque on the back of her head with a bunch of stiff black quills vertical. And there was also a little Japanese lady in picturesque native attire.

The coffin was covered by a white pall of Ruskin flax linen, woven by the school children of Keswick, embroidered with pink wild roses, the last stanza of 'Crossing the Bar,' a laurel wreath, a baron's coronet, and the initials 'A.T.' There were forty-two flowers for the forty-two years of the deceased's married life and his tenure of the Laureateship. (This pall was brought to Aldworth by the Reverend H. D. and Mrs. Rawnsley.) The pall bearers were Lord Rosebery, Lord Salisbury (who wore a velvet skull cap, which he discarded at the grave), Lord Selborne, Lord Kelvin, the Marquis of Dufferin, the Duke of Argyll, Mr. Henry White (the secretary of the United States legation: the American Minister had sailed for home the preceding Saturday), the Master of Balliol, the Master of Trinity College, Cambridge, and Sir James Paget, each representing some form of public life. (Gladstone had been asked to be a pall bearer, but desired to be excused because of the pressure of public business; he was represented at the ceremonies by his private secretary, the Honorable Arthur Lyttelton.) Then followed Mr. and Mrs. Hallam Tennyson (the Dowager Lady Tennyson was not present in the Abbey), the grandchildren, and other members of the family. Next came Sir Henry Ponsonby carrying the Queen's wreath (Her Majesty was at Balmoral) of laurel, some three feet in diameter, tied with white ribbon, "of the most chaste design," with a holograph card: "A mark of sincere regard and admiration from Victoria, R.I." (The Queen sent also a metallic wreath of laurel with "V.R.I." in monogram.) With Sir Henry was Sir Dighton Probyn, representing the Prince of Wales (who was at Newmarket for the Cesarewitch).[a] Lesser notables were of course very numerous. The Speaker and Mr. Bryce were together. Mr. John Burns was specially invited by the family. Mr. Henry Irving and Sir Charles Tupper walked side by side. (A little later, at the grave, "Mr. Henry Irving, leaning against a pillar, nearly fronting the monument to Chaucer, was a conspicuous figure.")

By 12:45 the body was placed under the lantern—now destroyed *furore teutonico*—and the singing of Psalm XC began. This was followed by the Lesson, the Anthems, and 'Crossing the Bar' specially set by Professor Bridge (opinions were divided on the merits of the music) and 'The Silent Voices,' with music by Lady Tennyson arranged by Professor Bridge. Then while the organ sounded Chopin's Funeral March the body, covered by the Union Jack, was borne to the grave, the space around which was covered with white and violet, because the poet had always disliked black trappings. In silence the coffin, with Her Majesty's wreath on it now, was lowered into the grave, alongside Dryden's. The prayer and collect were read by the Dean, Dr. Bradley, and the whole of the vast assembly joined, congregationally, in singing Bishop Heber's 'Holy, Holy, Holy,'—not a particularly Tennysonian hymn, some thought, but a good vehicle for public emotion. The Dean pronounced the benediction and the organ played the Dead March in 'Saul.'

a The *Times* said that "all that is most illustrious in our land, by birth and rank and position, by gifts and acquired learning, in war and in the arts of peace, in statesmanship and diplomacy, in literature and in science" were at the funeral. No member of the royal family was present, however, and both the Prince of Wales and the Duke of Cambridge, as well as Society, were at Newmarket. The absence of the Prince caused comment in the press, but the *Pall Mall Gazette* defended him for his honesty.

The funerary flowers were profuse. Besides the Queen's wreath there was a beautiful design of arum lilies and stephanotis. Mrs. Gladstone sent a wreath of her own making, with flowers from Hawarden. The Baroness Burdett-Coutts and Mr. and Mrs. Beerbohm Tree sent very handsome crosses; Messrs Macmillan (who had full charge of the ceremonial arrangements) sent a cross of violets and laurels. The Bard's native Somersby sent a wreath with the inscription "We never can forget you." Many of the other wreaths were brightened by the autumn-crimsoned Virginia creeper. Two offerings should be particularly mentioned: a "circlet of Mantuan bays from Virgil's tomb"[b] and, from Alfred Austin, a branch of bay which had been given him by a priest of Delphi. This latter was buried in the coffin. Mrs. Rush, who had been guardian of the Jerusalem Chamber for twenty-five years, was interviewed and said she had never seen so many flowers as at Tennyson's funeral; there must have been between two and three hundred wreaths; they kept coming for three days from every part of England, Scotland, Ireland, and Wales—some even after the funeral. The next day the Poets' Corner was like a flower garden.

Thus was the Laureate buried in the Abbey. It was truly said: "Tennyson is a popular hero, is one of our recognized national glories, hardly less than if he had been a politician or a soldier." And his own famous line on the funeral of Enoch Arden might be appropriately quoted. One sour note, however, must be recorded. On 14 October, two days after the Abbey ceremonies, there appeared in the *Pall Mall Gazette* a letter, signed "F.," which rudely observed that Tennyson's funeral "was not the burial of a man, but of a dead literature and a dead society. The *ci-devants*—the Leckies, the Argylls, the Froudes—who bore the pall, came to bury themselves, not him. He died, I take it, about forty years ago. . . ." And while this was but a part of the truth, it was a sign.

The newspapers, notwithstanding, made capital of the popular interest. A paragraph in one of them, for 20 October, began: "It seems as if the reading public could scarcely hear too much of him." In addition to the news during his illness and the interval between his death and funeral, there were special Tennyson supplements, leading articles, sermons, odds and ends of reminiscence,

[b] It should be recalled that Tennyson died on the 6th and was buried on the 12th.

anecdote, and ana, and the usual precipitate efforts to say clever or final things about his life and work. Curiosity regarding one aspect of his character was met by a statement from Dr. Dabbs: "Yes, I know a great deal has been said about Lord Tennyson having been a morose man. Well, I do not know what he may have been to the outside world, but through all these [twenty-four] years I have known him he has never been anything but friendly and genial. Only, as I said before, he was not a man of many words." *The Hospital* commented on his kindness to his nurses. *The Economist* remarked that he was the poet of his age also "in the practice of material accumulation." The *Times* said that "perhaps the most characteristic feature of Tennyson's work is its serene self-restraint." The *Standard* observed that he employed all literary forms, even satire, "and, though happily he was never expressly and of set purpose didactic, he moralized so much, and was so sensitively in touch with the ethics of his time, that no one would dream of refusing him the title of a didactic poet." The *Daily News* put him down as a scholarly poet, "in spite of his popularity at penny readings." In the *Daily Telegraph* Sir Edwin Arnold spoke of the singular beauty of his hands.—Thus, and a great deal more, the newspapers.

The minor poets hastened forward with their frail tributes, amid the immediate discussion of a successor to the Laureateship; and then the writing world settled down to obituaries in earnest,—in the weeklies, the monthlies, the quarterlies. This required less time than usual because what with Tennyson's advanced age and his serious illness a few years before, the end was not unprepared for. In fact, within a fortnight of the Bard's death one publisher was reported to have six manuscripts on Tennyson sent to him, and another three; and of these nine manuscripts at least four were by "recognized men of letters."

Any attempt to sum up these various early judgments would be both tedious and otiose; but a sampling, with a view to exhibiting their tenor and terms, ought to be of some interest.

The key word of the *Spectator's* article (8 October) on Tennyson's death was adequacy. This was first applied to expression—expression of a general mood, as in trusting the larger hope; or of friendship, as in his tributes to Arthur Hallam; or of love, as in 'Maud'; or of patriotism, as in the 'Light Brigade' and 'The Re-

venge'; or in discussing the position of woman: "there is not in
the language so complete an analysis of the new question. . .";—
and was then extended to his personal life. "So many poets have
been inferior men, but he was the equal of his writing. . . . His
austere pride, which so many thought haughtiness, and which was
not without a trace of ὕβρις added to the sense of his adequacy as
the representative poet of his age." In its next issue the *Spectator*
had four and a half columns on "The Genius of Tennyson." His
most distinctive quality, said the writer, who may have been Hut-
ton, was "the definitely artistic character of his poetry." "He is as
much artist as poet. Nothing that he says seems to be unconscious";
and he frequently erred on the side of over-richness and redun-
dancy, as in 'Enoch Arden.' "His richly jewelled speech . . . some-
times distracted attention from the substance of his narrative."
Yet while this tendency to be "microscopic and elaborate" is a
defect in his poems of pathos, it is the secret of his strength in 'In
Memoriam'—"throwing a glorious rainbow upon the black cloud."

The *Athenæum* came out on 8 October with two black-bordered
pages containing a signed obituary by Theodore Watts, a poem by
Austin Dobson—and three-fourths of a column on The Coming
Publishing Season. Watts' article was devoted more to an exhibi-
tion of his intimacy with the late Laureate and a puff predictive
of the official Memoir than to a critical estimate of the poet. Tenny-
son's charm, he said, "lay in a great veracity of soul—in a simple
single-mindedness so childlike that, unless you had known him to
be the undoubted author of his exquisitely artistic poems, you
would have supposed that even the subtleties of poetic art must be
foreign to a nature so devoid of all subtlety as his." But the in-
cautious statement: "though, of course, he had his share of that
egoism of the artist without which imaginative genius may become
sterile" brought forth a hurt protest, and two weeks later Watts
explained that by egoism he meant nothing offensive. In this same
issue of 22 October there is a recapitulation of a review (by E. D.
Forgues) of the 1842 *Poems* in the *Revue des deux Mondes:*

Tennyson, he goes on to tell his readers, is only a creator of details of
style, a discoverer of words rather than of ideas, and he adds that if
the voluptuous melody and refined archaisms be taken away from his
verse little remains. . . . But he grants freely that Tennyson is an artist,
possessing an impressible mind, and extraordinarily gifted with the

9

power of transmitting his impressions. Tennyson is not, however, a thinker or philosopher, and it seems doubtful if he seeks a meaning in the phenomena which impress him. . . . The moral of 'The Day Dream' is the moral of himself.

It seems significant that the *Athenæum* should now revive this critique without any disclaimer.

The *Academy's* notice (15 October) was by Joseph Jacobs. It began: "The greatest poetic artist of the English-speaking race has passed away," but though generally laudatory, and notable for its admiration of Tennyson's later work, it contained some shrewd touches. It complained both of "the want of depth, want of soul-tone in his earlier work"—his "*Keepsake* period lasted long"—and also of too much high seriousness: "The isolation of the poet must have contributed to this defect." The theology of 'In Memoriam,' said Jacobs, "was from Rugby; it is the voice of the Broad Church, . . . But where is the Broad Church now?" In the 'Idylls' he saw an "absence of the creative rush, the sense of a personality behind the artistic work and greater than it"; and he felt that "the whole conception of Guinevere, and still more that of Vivien, was of the nineteenth-century English gentleman, and something in the spirit of Mr. Podsnap."

I can remember the disastrous effect the epic and dramatic periods had on Tennyson's reputation during the "seventies." We that were interested in the future of English letters had lost all hope in Tennyson: our eyes were turned to Rossetti and Mr. Swinburne. It became the fashion to think and speak slightingly of the great master, who was all the while maturing to a final creative outburst which was to raise him far above any contemporary, far above most of his predecessors in English song, except the two greatest names of all. The fifth act of the drama of Tennyson's poetic career fulfils all, more than all, the promise of the earlier ones. [Witness the *Ballads* volume and the *Tiresias* volume.] . . . There was no want of the rush of inspiration behind the verse; there was rugged vigour, sublime incoherence. . . .

It is in the Tennyson of these later days that we recognize the master —the great poet-soul looming behind the poem, and greater than it.

Nevertheless, "it cannot be said of Tennyson that he has been a great spiritual force in the national development of the last half-century. . . . The pictures of still and cleanly English life in the earlier idylls, of sturdy heroism in the ballads, even the somewhat namby-pamby chivalry of the epical 'Idylls'—these were the teachings of Tennyson, so far as he was a teacher." And in the same tone:

It is no world-poet that England now is mourning with commingled pride and grief. No world-pain throbs through his lines. No world-problem finds in him expression or solution. The sweet domesticities, the manly and refined ideals of English life in the middle period of the nineteenth century—Tennyson was the fluted voice of these. To these he has given immortality while he has gained immortality from them. For us he has helped to form the English ideals which are destined to be an abiding influence in the national life.

The *Open Court* for 17 November published a sort of funeral oration delivered by Moncure Conway in South Place Chapel—the first minister of which, W. J. Fox, had favorably reviewed Tennyson's poems in 1833. One might be suspicious of a statement that 'Demeter and Persephone' is "the grandest literary production ever written by an octogenarian," but under the circumstances one must read the following words as without ironic intent:

He is one man who by his single self has made a fairer, nobler England. He has raised the whole tone of literature; . . . enriched the whole inner life of the nation. And what a response was given by the national heart! . . . He was glad to get ten pounds for his first book; he died in his palace; he was borne to his grave with more homage than any king could hope for, from all classes and all parties.

The Chicago *Dial* for June 1892 contained an omnium-gatherum review, by William Morton Paine, of twenty-one volumes of verse, ranging from 'The Foresters' to Whitman and Burns, Theocritus and Dante. It began:

"The voice grown now to godlike." In this happy phrase Mr. Theodore Watts describes the impression made upon all ears fit to hear by the work of Lord Tennyson's latest years. There is indeed something divinely spiritual, something beyond the ken of mere earthly soul-vision, in such poems as "Locksley Hall Sixty Years After," "Demeter," "Tiresias," and "Crossing the Bar."

The *Dial's* 16 October issue opened with unsigned obituaries of Tennyson and Renan, and proceeded to the usual descriptive and biographical matter. Tennyson was found worthy to rank with Shakespeare, Milton, and Shelley. "Indeed, there is about some of the late poems a beauty that seems almost unearthly, the evidence of a prophetic vision clarified by age, and placing him not only with the artists but with the seers."

The weeklies had not wallowed in adulation. The monthly magazines, drawing a deeper breath, were similarly divided. The November *Bookman* (London) in "A Note on Tennyson" said, forgetting Browning, "He was simply and solely—and he alone of his day—a professional poet." Others had greater gifts, but none cultivated his own so judiciously or made of them "so copious, continuous, varied, and uniformly eloquent" a "stream of song." And after a word on his acting and dressing the part of Laureate, and on his acceptance of the peerage, this writer asked: "We ourselves are no longer the enthusiasts we were. . . . Does Tennyson still enthrall and inspire and purge and glorify the children of their parents?"

Gosse, in the *New Review* for November asked a different but more disturbing question: "What if this vast and sounding funeral should prove to have really been the entombment of English poetry?" "I have found myself profoundly depressed and terrified," Gosse continues, "at an ebullition of popularity which seems to have struck almost everybody else with extreme satisfaction"; and he contrasts the simple funeral of Wordsworth at Grasmere forty-two years ago with "the spectacle of the 12th, the vast black crowd in the street, the ten thousand persons refused admittance to the Abbey, the whole enormous popular manifestation." He expressed a fear, now happily proved to have been groundless, that the personal distinction of the late Laureate might strike a serious blow at the vitality of poetry in England. "Tennyson had grown to be by far the most mysterious, august, and singular figure in English society. He represented poetry, and the world now expects its poets to be as picturesque, as aged, and as individual as he was, or else it will pay no attention." Vain foreboding: for whatever may be the values or the vices of English poetry in the twentieth century, they are, neither the one nor the other, attributable to Victoria's Laureate. Gosse was nearer the truth, however, in saying that "the excitement about Tennyson's death has been far too universal to be sincere."

This article of Gosse's was followed by one from Herbert Paul, praising the dramas and recalling how in the past Tennyson's successive volumes had been attacked by the critics and in turn accepted by the readers of poetry. When 'In Memoriam' first appeared the critics called Arthur Hallam the Amaryllis of Chancery

Bar; but "Nobody ever reads a criticism of *In Memoriam* now. The poem itself is to thousands as sacred as their personal religion, of which it may well form a part." The *New Review's* Special Literary Supplement, by H. D. Traill, was polite, but not enthusiastic.

Early in November the Reverend Stopford Brooke drew an unwontedly large audience in "ugly little" Bedford Chapel for his Sunday morning lectures on Tennyson as artist, as Christian, and as a man. These lectures appeared as a long article in the December *Contemporary Review*. On the first point Stopford Brooke was laudatory and enthusiastic, but with a moral emphasis: "With a few exceptions . . . Tennyson was faithful through his whole life to beauty, writing always of what was worthy of love, of joy, of solemn or happy reverence"; for he "never forgot that the poet's work was to convince the world of love and beauty; that he was born to do that work, and to do it nobly." On the second point Brooke found some difficulty: it was easy to show that the ethics in Tennyson's poetry were admirable, it was another thing to prove that the poet was a Christian. But it was a question hardly worth raising, except by a clergyman perhaps, and Brooke seems to have satisfied himself. On the third point, which was phrased: "What relation did he bear to social politics, if I may use that term?" Stopford Brooke made extensive reservations. "No one has better dwelt on the nobler elements of English character and their long descent from the past, and the sacred reverence we owe to them, than Tennyson"; but his conservatism became extreme: "the main line he takes is the line of careful protection of the old against the onset of the new, . . . of the putting off of the regeneration of society to a period so far off that it may be counted by thousands and thousands of years."

He sometimes got curiously wrong, as on the subject of war. He became curiously and unpoetically hopeless with regard to the future. . . ; having a distant and half *laissez-faire* sympathy with the sorrows of the people, and seeing, and this is the strangest of all, a remedy for their sorrows in the greater growth of commerce as it exists at present, and in the further development of practical science hand in hand with commerce.

Moreover, "He had little sympathy in his poetry with other nations. The only struggles for freedom with which he openly sympathises were those of Poland in his youth, and of Montenegro in his age. The battle of Italy for liberty is scarcely mentioned. The struggle of the North against slavery is never touched." And finally,—

I make no complaint against Tennyson for all this. I only state the case. If he was of this temper, it was because it was mainly the temper of the time in which he grew to his maturity, the thirty years from his first volume to the end of the sixties. He represented the social and political opinions of that time very fairly, but not as a poet who had much prophetic fire and pity in him would be expected to write. . . . He remained for another thirty years in precisely the same position while all the world changed round him. . . . He *is* our poet in the things which he treated poetically; and in those which have to do with Nature and God, and the sweet and honest and tender life of men and women, he will remain our poet as long as the language lasts, but in these social matters not.

The clerical view, from another side however, was equally sincere in reverence. "And, lastly," said Frederic Myers in the *Nineteenth Century* for January 1893,[c] after Homer, Menander, and Vergil—

And, lastly, we have Tennyson penetrating to a still profounder identification; to the sense that what we have held far off and future, that verily is here and now; and that what is in truth the Nameless, that is our world and we; "for we are here in God's bosom, a land unknown."

All men mourn the poet. But those of us who cling to the spiritual aspect of the universe have more than a great poet to mourn. We have lost our head and our chief; the one man, surely, in all the world to-day, who from a towering eminence which none could question affirmed the realities which to us are all. For him we may respect Lucretius' homage to the sage and poet whom that other island "bore within her three-cornered shores;"—that Sicily,

> *Quae cum magna modis multis miranda videtur*
> *Gentibus humanis regio, visendaque fertur,*
> *Rebus opima bonis, multa munita virum vi,—*
> *Nil tamen hoc habuisse viro praeclarius in se,*
> *Nec sanctum magis et mirum carumque videtur.*

c The *Nineteenth Century*, under the editorship of Tennyson's friend Sir James Knowles, gave more space than any of the reviews to the dead poet. Besides this article by Myers and Swinburne's 'Threnody,' which headed the January 1893 issue, it published a group of seven "Poetical Tributes" in November 1892 and a series of seven "Aspects of Tennyson," by various authors in 1893 and 1894. These were all very respectful, but hardly critical in either sense of the term.

In March 1894 the *New Review,* which immediately after Tennyson's death had taken a position well this side of idolatry, contained a somewhat captious article by Francis Adams. The first volume of Tennyson, said he, was "effeminate and factitious," rejecting all the best of Shelley and Keats and adopting the "sicklier side" of their art. "His one instinct is to look nothing in the face." Felicity, said Adams, "is doomed to inferiority"; and apropos of

a downward smoke
Slow dropping veils of thinnest lawn did go

(which had already been a plague to Tennyson during his lifetime) he asked: "Do you call that 'natural magic'? Clearly, it is nothing of the kind. It is the daintily but superficially picturesque." He quoted the "fledged with clearest green" stanza from 'A Dream of Fair Women' and said: "Why, a man who has just begun to be aware that there are such things as art and literature would be delighted with it." He ridiculed Tennyson's treatment of science, "the distressing mental collapse, the insane and incoherent rhodomontade of so much of 'Sixty Years After,' " the caricature of the Frenchman and of the dissenting minister: the Anglican is "that good man," the dissenter "a heated pulpiteer." "King Arthur," said our critic, "is a crucial case because he is Tennyson's deliberate attempt to present to us an ideal figure of social manhood . . . 'the highest and most human too.' " " 'The war of Soul with Sense' is fought and won and lost in the most charming manner all through. . . . We are never allowed to approach reality except with a thousand polite precautions." And in the Guinevere Idyll, when "we are to see what a modern gentleman, a modern English Christian gentleman, has to say . . . to his convicted and humiliated wife. Well, we all know what happens; from the first crude taunt, when he sneers at her barrenness, to the last self-satisfied insult when the squalid and inhuman prig exhorts her to regenerate her life with the consolation that he loves her still . . ." It is not all like this, the article by Francis Adams in 1894, but this is enough to point a direction.

The position of Maga was slightly ambiguous.[3] Christopher North had been supposed an enemy in the earlier days, had ridiculed certain poems in the poet's first two volumes, yet had declared in February 1832: "I have good hopes of Alfred Tennyson. . . . He has—*genius";* and three months later reaffirmed that judgment: "Alfred Tennyson is a poet." Now, sixty years later, "In all reverence, Christopher's poor successor laid a wreath of the poet's laurel, culled in a homely garden, woven by maiden fingers, at Tennyson's head, at Chaucer's feet, amid the sound of the mourning of a mighty nation, the other day when he was laid to his rest." Now Maga could speak of Tennyson as a poet who "has for a long time stood like a tower unassailable, one of the bulwarks of the English name" and "the head, the master, the informing soul of a great period, splendid in literature as in many other achievements." "With Tennyson we stand or fall in the records of the ages." And again the poor successor of "the ever fresh and living Christopher North," said among other fine things this of 'In Memoriam': "Surely no man has ever done more for his world, for his country and tongue, than by opening in it this fountain of grief, and hope, and sympathy, and love eternal—the sorrow that encircles and draws together everything in earth and heaven." And this of 'Maud': "It was his humour to wind this lesson harsh and strong around the most perfect tragic tale of love, like a message wrapped round a swift-flying all-penetrating arrow." Now it is not necessary to find seeds of sarcasm in this grand style of Maga's, undulant and orotund; but it is surely an exaggeration to call Tennyson's Lancelot "one man who will yield to none, as noble a conception as ever human genius has given birth to"; and it sounds like malice to end an obituary thirty-eight columns long with the old question of the Laureate's acceptance of the peerage. "If it was little to Tennyson it was much to the Peers of England that there should be one peerage founded upon nothing ignoble, upon the highest and most elevating of all gifts."

Canon Ainger is the author of the obituary notice in *Macmillan's* (November 1892), a perhaps hurried and plainly unpretentious tribute. Tennyson, he said, was recognized even by the least critical as "something different in kind, as well as in degree" from other poets. There was a bewitching quality in him: "His diction haunts us, and gladdens and purifies while it haunts. . . . Mentem mortalia tangunt." There was something of Shakespeare in his political bias, not so much Shakespeare's aristocratic attitude, as his "insight into the true source of national greatness, freedom based upon moral discipline." And the Canon found it very touching that "as almost the most perfect poem in the little volume of 1830, 'Mariana,' sprang from a single phrase in *Measure for Measure* so Shakespeare was the last volume to fall from his hands when 'life and thought' were ebbing from him." For the rest, Canon Ainger offered a paraphrase of 'Merlin and the Gleam' and pronounced the poet "the wielder of the most wide-reaching, beneficent, spiritual influence in our later literature."

The notice which opened the December *Westminster Review* was written in a hard dogmatic style, and unsigned. "Poet though he be, Lord Tennyson is pre-eminently practical-minded, and so he is characteristically English both in his ideals and in his interpretation of life." In spite of other changes of opinion Tennyson was always an extreme nationalist; he disliked French ideas and showed his contempt for Germany; he might even be charged with provincialism "were it not for his nobility of sentiment, his devotion to truth, his singleness of purpose." 'In Memoriam' is "one of the most remarkable examples of concentrated emotion in the whole range of English literature." The 'Idylls' has "Passages of singular beauty . . . but the treatment of the subject is inadequate." In the dialect ballads "the late Laureate achieved distinct success." And so on. "The characteristics of the dead poet's genius are picturesqueness, a power of portraying the influence of Nature on man's ever-changing moods, a romantic reverence for good women, and a belief in the absolute purity and happiness of the married state. He touched on some of the ethical and psychological problems of his time; but he solved none of them. . . . Nature made him a poet; and culture and a life's devotion made him a consummate artist. . . . He clung passionately to religious forms even after they had ceased to appeal to his reason." In a word, the *Westminster* critic was nothing if not confident, was willing to say yea or nay flatly, and left the whole matter thus: "It remains to be seen whether, as the years go by, he will be regarded as a really great poet; but the words of one who was as different from him as darkness is from light—the ill-fated Edgar Allan Poe—may fittingly be applied to him: he was 'the noblest poet that ever lived.' "

Meanwhile the august quarterlies were pontificating. The *Church Quarterly Review* had at press just as the Laureate died a review article on "The Poetry of To-Day—and To-Morrow," in which it placed Tennyson as the chronological measure and "the typical poet of the Victorian period." The next issue, January 1893, reviewing the last three volumes of Tennyson and the *Works* of 1892, offered a full-dress summary. Tennyson is praised as having enriched the national life and added to the happiness of Englishmen by his landscape poetry, as having taught his countrymen "a rational and dignified patriotism," as having "consistently upheld a lofty idea of purity" and having "passionately forced men to dwell on what is spiritual" in a "sceptical and material age." On the literary side, "what is remarkable in Tennyson is the faultlessness of so great a range of writing. . . . But though Tennyson may sometimes lapse into baldness or pathos, he is never unmeaning or verbose: he is scarcely ever weak." This faultlessness was due to extreme care and this care, in turn,

seems to indicate a certain want of spontaneity and flow, which is a marked characteristic of all his work, with the very important exception of his purely lyric poems. . . . Such a descriptive phrase . . . as

The wide-wing'd sunset of the misty marsh

permanently enriches our sense of the loveliness of the world. But the gain is produced at the cost of ease and rapidity of movement, and even, in many instances, of unity of impression.

There are exceptions, but "taken as a whole, Tennyson's blank verse, indeed his longer poems generally, are wanting in movement and flow, and this is no mere defect of style or literary manner, but springs from a more fundamental characteristic of the poet," namely, a deficiency of imagination, "the imagination which gives to any product of the mind a vital unity, and fuses its various parts into an organic whole." Moreover, "when we ask, what has this incomparable artist to teach us?" the reply is:

Tennyson was not a great original teacher, in the sense in which Wordsworth and Browning—to go no further back—were teachers. . . . He was not an independent creative force in the world of thought. Rather he has been a voice, clear and full-toned and commanding, giving expression to the thoughts and feelings which have inarticulately moved the men of his time, the reflection, in a medium of rich and delicate beauty, of the tendencies, the fears, the hopes, the wishes of the age. They are in his poetry because they were first in the hearts and minds of men; he echoes and reflects and interprets, he does not originate. But a poet, just because he is a poet, stimulates and strengthens by the force of his expression the feelings and thoughts which he expresses, and it is by his sensitiveness to the best tendencies of his age, and by the lasting beauty of the form in which he embodied them, that Tennyson has been a power and an inspiration to men.

And finally, apropos of 'In Memoriam':

That he had no very definite answer to many of our most persistent questionings was perhaps more the fault of his age than of himself; he was vague because he could not but reflect the uncertainty around him, and was haunted by the vastness of the mystery of life. But at least he buoyed men up by his own unconquerable faith in the soul and in God, and his latest message was one of hope—

that is, in 'The Death of the Duke of Clarence and Avondale.'

The *Edinburgh Review,* which had in 1843 printed Spedding's enthusiastic notice of the *Poems,* and in 1849 Aubrey de Vere's of 'The Princess,' and in 1859 Coventry Patmore's of the first 'Idylls,' and had reviewed the 'Maud' volume, 1855, the later 'Idylls,' 1870, 'Queen Mary,' and 'Harold,' 1877, and *Ballads,* 1881, and had a short article on "Tennyson and Browning" in 1890, was silent after the Laureate's death until April 1895. Then it printed a mediocre review of Stopford Brooke's book, favorable to Tennyson and slightly captious towards Brooke whenever he presumed to hint a fault; but it did not pretend to pass judgment as the other reviews had done, though it joined the general voice in saying: "No country or period ever had a truer interpreter than the England of the Victorian age in the late Poet Laureate."

The *Quarterly,* however, girded itself for a triumphant effort and in January 1893 produced the best (it seems to me) of all the attempts to take account of the poet's stock at the time of his death.[4] The article began with a list of twenty-six volumes by Tennyson, and added Waugh's book and Mrs. Ritchie's *Records* but did not mention them later. The first few pages gave particular attention to the 'Death of Œnone' volume and devoted nearly half of the rest of its thirty-seven pages to 'Maud' and the 'Idylls.' The style of old-fashioned eloquence of a large portion of this article gives the impression of laudatory enthusiasm, but the final paragraph strikes a firm judicial attitude:

The excellence and the shortcomings of Tennyson's poetry are displayed in the Idylls. Setting aside his rare moments of inspired elevation, his general work is marred by a certain want of creative originality, of breadth of conception, of vigour of narrative, of dramatic force of presentment. It is characterised by a shrinking from the grander and vaster aspects of Nature, from the profounder depths of human thought, from the most tragic agonies of human passion. It is characterised, also, by a preference for that which is minute and detailed in outward phenomena, for moderation in opinion, for conventionality in thought, for tenderness and grace in the affections of the heart. To say this is to say, in another form, that Tennyson is the true mental representative of an analytic age, that its merits and defects are equally his, and that its special triumphs in the observation of external Nature are his most signal successes. But to the points in which his poetry is truly typical of the century must be added his individual excellences,—his sustained mastery of form and his unsurpassable literary execution, which are the rewards of the conscientious workmanship, and the artistic instinct of an assimilative, reflective, receptive genius. We read his poetry and return to it again and again with unabated zest, for the exquisite perfection with which he has expressed ordinary thoughts and common-place feelings, for the vivid flashes with which he brings before us visual impressions, and for the patient microscopic observation which has revealed to us new beauties of Nature. We do *not* read it to be transported out of ourselves by its play of passions, by its suggestive thought, by its comprehensive grasp of the facts of human life or the outward Universe.

After making due allowance for the variable of the individual critic, one could draw from these attempts to sum up Tennyson at the moment of his death some perhaps useful generalizations on English taste, and these generalizations re-applied to Tennyson's work might yield useful evidence for the final judgment of the poet. For in so far as he reflected his age he was a product of his age and therefore he both reflected and fulfilled its tastes. The most obvious of these generalizations would be the universal satisfaction shown in the morality and nobility of his poetry. Privately the Victorians may have been no better than mankind usually is, but publicly they cherished a fine ideal of high moral tone. Many of them no doubt conformed to it, so far as human nature permits; and Tennyson was one of these. But after all there is the danger of reasoning in a circle, and at present it is better to waive judgment of the obituary critics as themselves the interpreters of the age—the business anyway of social rather than literary history— and notice particularly that with all due piety for the sad occasion dear and the large recompense, with all tribute to the personal qualities of the man and all respect for the monumental legend of the long-cloaked Bard and Prophet, the critics as distinguished from the elegists did not scruple to admit a fault, did not hesitate to declare what they believed to be the shortcomings of their hero. Elegy and eulogy are natural sisters. The melodious tear is expected. It is enough now to recognize that the tear did not altogether blind the critical eye.

In other words, Tennyson was extravagantly lauded at the time of his death and his funeral was made the occasion of national rejoicing that Victorian England had produced such a splendid monument of its own greatness.[d] But the criticism of his poetry—some of it sound and some of it unsound, like all criticism—was never without qualification. The legend was built around Tennyson the interpreter of his age, and of course the greater the age the greater the interpreter. Tennyson's poetry, which is what concerns posterity, was only an adjunct of the legend, not its foundation. The aura surrounded an image of the man, not of the past.

For the legend had, however, another aspect which is but partly reflected in the obituary praise. This can be touched lightly and then passed by. There is no doubt that Tennyson himself both deliberately and by indirection played up to his rôle of *sacer vates*. He dressed the part, he talked it, and to some degree he wrote for it. He helped to create his own legend. But once started, it carried him along with it as *particeps actionum*. And more than this, there gathered about him as pontifex a group of worshippers who flattered him and at the same time gratified themselves as sharers of the glory. They were not insincere or conscious sycophants: they genuinely admired the master, who had many most admirable qualities; but the real enough admiration begat something adventitious, something fictitious even. The strongest evidence of this is the *Memoir*—understandable and perhaps pardonable in a son—and the carefully selected testimonials edited by Hallam under the title of *Tennyson and His Friends*. This was no more than it pretended to be: it was the statue on the pedestal—more than life size, on an eminence which had an element of truth and an element of badness in it. Real filial piety could go no further.

Then came the reaction, reaction (as Mrs. Meynell puts it)—"the paltry precipitancy of the multitude." Yes, and no. Reaction

[d] The *Spectator* (15 October 1892) felt that the mourners in the Abbey "had gathered to honour the memory of a great Englishman, and to thank God for a great achievement": this explained "the spirit of contentment—we had almost said of solemn exaltation—that was abroad in the Abbey on Wednesday."

is a part of the universal pattern. Tastes were changing, had changed; and by the time the centenary of Tennyson's birth came round the new generation could say honestly that "the idol of the Victorian Era is growing dusty in its niche." When the clouds of incense settled Tennyson was seen to be "a very average human man, with few streaks of greatness," who had been "apotheosized because of his perfect accord with Victorian ideals," a man with great musical gifts and an unaffected love of nature, yet a man with a weakness for wealth and rank which was natural but incompatible with his prophetic post, "a man with a limited experience of life, and [who] well content with his domestic ideals, made no effort to widen his point of view by travel, by active service to his generation, by studying how men lived, aside from the narrow circle in which he moved, or even by the strenuous pursuit of studies likely to contribute to the richness of his poetry." "His attitude in general towards the larger world outside his own social circle is represented, perhaps better than he realized, in the prologue to 'The Princess.' "[5]

Yet at the very same time one who had caught "the strange and affronting tone and attitude of a number of captious and erratic critics of late," set the wild echoes flying again with trumpet tones.

What then, do these men mean, who now profess to discover flaws in the well-proved armour of our Tennyson? and who so wildly declaim about his Whitewashing?" It must be, I think, that such "critics" are incapable of quite adequately grasping the full purport and compass of Tennyson's gospel and genius; or, by reason of their own disqualifications, and decadence of faith and morals. . . .

In brief, and emphatically, Tennyson's life rarely accorded with his teachings and gospel; and his character was as solidly based, as his life was well rounded and harmonious. In being, he was English to the backbone—of the pure Berserker type—in intellect, Grecian. . . . His insight and intuition were as profound and impromptu as his perceptions were lively, varied, and illuminative—as the insight and perceptions of genius are, invariably; while his imagery and colouring were (and are still), as beautiful and impressive as his silver notes were (and are, still) delightful.[6]

And all this, let us be sure, is not sarcasm, it is the old flag still flying, the old adulation in autumnal coloring, the silver clarion tones which were (and are, apparently, still) the voice of Tennyson's lovers.

And ten years later, Mr. Brimley Johnson, in the Poetry and Life Series, reminds us: "Tennyson's work is permeated with idealism of the English gentleman, the Victorian Knight-errant, most finally and fully expressed by 'In Memoriam' and the 'Idylls.' We shall find, in studying this work, a fine unity of purpose, an underlying motive, that reveals the man. Thus he lives as a complete, consistent force: with a meaning and value for all time. He sings the message of Victorianism."

And in 1923 the leading article in the *Times Literary Supplement* for 12 April again came to the rescue, apropos of the biographies by Mr. Harold Nicolson and Mr. Hugh Fausset and of the veteran A. C. Bradley's English Association pamphlet. The *TLS* is very severe with Mr. Fausset, both for his contempt of Tennyson— "he fills three-quarters of his three hundred pages with cheap sneers, false innuendoes, and wearisome depreciation"—and for his theory that the moral and metaphysical elements of poetry are more than the poetry itself. It is very firm with Mr. Nicolson for saying that Tennyson suffered "from a lack of intellect and education," though Mr. Nicolson himself had come forward bravely against the Philistines in defence of the great Laureate. And it ends by praising the temperate attitude of Bradley.

Why should the issue be so vigorously taken? Can those who knew the Old Days, and the great Bard, who had seen Tennyson plain, have been so greatly deceived? Can those of a later day, out of sympathy with Victorian Ideals and cherishing a different artistic taste, be so utterly wrong? As it has been said, every century has the Arthur it deserves, can it be that the twentieth century deserves no better Tennyson than the 'reaction' declares? In 1923 Mr. Nicolson and Mr. Fausset were 'young men,' who spoke for a new generation: they were entitled to their point of view, and it betrays the usual impatience of elderly judgment to deny them their privileges. But now a reaction has already set in, it seems, to the earlier reaction.

On one point at least we can claim progress. There was, there must have been, substance in the figure which cast that shadow of legend—"the noble cloaked image with flowing beard and domed forehead"—and there is abundant testimony to its realness. This testimony may be seen in the second volume of the *Memoir* and in the supplementary *Tennyson and His Friends;* and in the many records of which the following, by William Knight, is but one sample. After visiting at Farringford in 1890 Knight, the Scots professor and Wordsworthian, said: "I felt that I sat in the presence of one of the Kings of Men. His aged look impressed me. . . . but his whole bearing disclosed a latent strength and nobility, a reserve of power, combined with a most courteous grace of manner." [7] And if one read carefully the *Memoir* and the *Friends,* it becomes plain that in large part the legend gathered itself about the patriarchal figure of Tennyson the old man, and then by a natural confusion it came to embrace Tennyson's poetry, and in fact found matter of nourishment both in the great man's later verse, wherein he so patently spoke as prophet and seer, and also, when one came to think of it, in the noble doctrine of his earlier poetry. The cloaked and bearded figure in his wide-awake was but the visible confirming image of this nobility. Thus, to put it succinctly, the Tennyson legend represents the prophet rather than the poet; and it is the story of all reputations that the one passes away when his function is finished and the other remains if he have the qualities of permanence. Matthew Arnold is a plain example.

Into the growth of the legend there went also (as I have just said) the memory of Tennyson's early successes. Witness the familiar passage in Alton Locke[e] and all that enthusiasm by which the first

[e] Charles Kingsley, *Alton Locke, Tailor and Poet,* 1850, chapter VI, "Poetry and Poets": "Then, in a happy day, I fell on Alfred Tennyson's poetry, and found there, astonished and delighted, the embodiment of thoughts about the earth around me which I had concealed, because I fancied them peculiar to myself. Why is it that the latest poet has generally the greatest influence over the minds of the young? Surely not for the mere charm of novelty? The reason is that he, living amid the same hopes, the same temptations, the same sphere of observation as they, gives utterance and outward form to the very questions which, vague and wordless, have been exercising their hearts. And what endeared Tennyson especially to me, the working man, was, as I afterwards discovered, the altogether democratic tendency of his poems. True, all great poets are by their office democrats; seers of man only as man; singers of the joys, the sorrows, the aspirations common to all humanity; but in Alfred Tennyson there is an element especially democratic, truly levelling; not his political opinions, about which I know nothing, and care less, but his handling of the trivial everyday sights and sounds of nature. Brought up, as I understand, in a part of England which possesses not much of the picturesque, and nothing of that which the vulgar call sublime, he has learnt to see that in all nature, in the hedgerow and the sand-bank, as well as in the alp peak and the ocean waste, is a world of true sublimity,—a minute infinite,—an ever fertile garden of poetic images, the roots of which are in the unfathomable and the eternal, as truly as any phenomenon which astonishes and awes the eye. The descriptions of the desolate pools and creeks where the dying swan floated, the hint of the silvery marsh mosses by Mariana's moat, came to me like revelations. I always knew there was something beautiful, wonderful, sublime, in those flowery dykes of Battersea Fields; in the long gravelly sweeps of that lone tidal shore;

'Locksley Hall' became a Scripture of young aspiration, "the gospel of buoyant progress," and 'In Memoriam' a Scripture of doubt and mourning and somehow hope. In the *Spectator* for 15 October 1892 a writer expressed soberly some of this feeling.

Those who were growing up, but were not yet grown up, in 1842, can hardly know how much of their ideal of life they owe to Tennyson, and how much to the innate bias of their own character. They only know that they owe him very much of the imaginative scenery of their own minds, much of their insight into the doubts and faith of their contemporaries, much of their political preference for "ordered freedom," and much, too, of their fastidious discrimination between the various notes of tender and pathetic song.

Witness also the statement of Froude:

The best and bravest of my own contemporaries determined to have done with insincerity, to find ground under their feet, to let the uncertain remain the uncertain, but to learn how much and what we could honestly regard as true, and believe and live by it. Tennyson became the voice of this feeling in poetry; Carlyle in what was called prose. Tennyson's poems, the group of poems which closed with 'In Memoriam,' became to many of us what the 'Christian Year' was to orthodox Churchmen.

And witness finally the letter in the *Pall Mall Gazette* for 12 October 1892, signed "The Woman in the Street," undertaking to place on record how much "the womanhood of the world" owed to the late Laureate. "At a time when I was seeking for a meaning and a motive in life," this woman writes, she was accustomed to pass him at dusk in Regent's Park. "He probably never observed me; but I went back to my difficulties strengthened and refreshed by the mere passing sight of one who had told me 'to be strong of will and resolute under wrong.' " Now, recently, during the poet's illness a friend had sent her the news, and she quotes a part of his letter about 'In Memoriam': "This book first opened my mind and

and here was a man who had put them into words for me! This is what I call democratic art—the revelation of the poetry which lies in common things. And surely all the age is tending in that direction: in Landseer and his dogs—in Fielding and his downs, with a host of noble fellow-artists—and in all authors who have really seized the nation's mind, from Crabbe and Burns and Words- worth to Hood and Dickens, the great tide sets ever onward, outward, towards that which is common to the many, not that which is exclusive to the few—towards the likeness of Him who causes His rain to fall on the just and the unjust, and His sun to shine on the evil and the good; who knoweth the cattle upon a thousand hills, and all the beasts of the field are in His sight."

made a man of me. All my life Tennyson has had a great influence
for good over my thoughts . . . and I can never repay the debt I owe
him. He is part of my religion, as he is of yours. We both loved and
reverenced him. We never saw the sunshine or the stars, but he was
with us." At such words it is easy to smile: it is impossible to ques-
tion their sincerity. They reflect, they certify, the Tennyson *charm*,
the spell which he cast, often without knowing, on the minds of his
contemporaries. That this magic was due less to the artistic merit
of his poems than to some other quality is, in a way, irrelevant. It
touched all sorts of people, lowly and lofty, from the Woman in the
Street to the Duke of Argyll and the Queen of England. It was in-
dubitably real and genuine—and by its own nature ephemeral. It
belonged to the man and his generation, the portrayer and ex-
ponent of his age. To us, like the age itself, it is a legend.

CHAPTER TWO

Merlin and The Gleam

WHEN THE Victorians had buried Tennyson and paid due reverence (not altogether uncritical) to the great occasion, what remained? The majestic presence, reclusive in the later years but none the less felt, was withdrawn. The man had vanished, leaving a glowing aura to fade in due course, and his Poetical Works to make their way alone through the devious paths of posterity.

The value and interest of biography are, with a few exceptions, in direct ratio with the value and interest of what the man has done. The life of a philosopher concerns us only in so far as it makes his thought intelligible; the life of a poet only in so far as it supplements or illustrates his poetry. Tennyson's life was to a very unusual degree the story of his poetry; for having devoted, almost consecrated (the word is dangerous but justified here) all his efforts to one purpose, he contributed to history his one talent, in printed verse. Tennyson the man is of interest chiefly for the legend he helped to create: but after his death and the death of his contemporaries the legend can survive only as a curiosity in books. He gave himself to poetry, and therefore he needs no biography except that which illuminates his one great gift.

Is this a hard saying? It is not quite a commonplace and may therefore bear a little examination. In good fiction and drama the most important element is usually said to be character, and secondary to character the story or action which develops or reveals it. From this point of view every human being who possesses 'character' is a fit subject for biography; for though fiction and drama are superior to life in that they are moulded to an artistic pattern, that is, they have design or those qualities of design which produce

27

a more logical and therefore more satisfying unity than ordinary life, which is for most of us determined largely by accident or unintelligent planning, nevertheless, some of the most fascinating developments of character may emerge without the formal design of fiction and drama, or even in spite of any demonstrable design, and may be even more fascinating because they seem accidental and therefore challenge our philosophy to reconcile their apparently inharmonious and contradictory elements. Strangeness becomes an attraction and inconsequence an advantage, for by one theory (at least) nothing is really inconsequent if we can discern the ruling principle. From this it follows that any life, however bizarre, can be interesting; and not even commonplaceness is a limitation, for certain novelists have revealed in the most obvious commonplaces our fundamental humanity. Is this, now, a clear though somewhat circular argument, or a *reductio ad absurdum?* Is the answer in the treatment? meaning that any life can be made interesting, any biography justifiable? A good pragmatic answer, but it leaves some of us unsatisfied.

Tennyson himself was inclined to take a negative position for other reasons. In the sonnet which he wrote as a preface to 'Becket' he said:

> *For whatsoever knows us truly, knows*
> *That none can truly write his single day*

. . . much less his whole life. "Life is a mystery," as he was fond of saying. And so he desired that no biography of him should be written. None has been written. His son Hallam collected first the unpublished 'Materials,' and then issued in 1897 the two-volume *Memoir,* and finally, with exceeding piety the *Friends* in 1911. These are not biographies, but rather collections of raw material; and the other books which bear Tennyson's name are simulacra, interweavings of literary criticism and of details from the *Memoir* —mostly without salt, and conspicuously with "the well-bred discretion of the biographer who knows what 'to leave in the ink-bottle.' "

This suggests another reason for Tennyson's wishing no formal biography: the Victorian standard of reticence. "When I am dead," Tennyson is quoted as saying, "I will take good care they shall not rip me up like a pig." The statement is not quite logical, but the intention is plain. *Caveat filius: vivat biographeus.* "For those who cared to know about his literary history" the poet himself composed a mystical autobiography, showing how he wished to be remembered, 'Merlin and the Gleam,' and Hallam has interpreted it for us.[1] But text and commentary leave the riddle unread. . . . And so, with the helps permitted us, a summary sketch may be undertaken, sufficient (I hope) for an introduction to the poems.

The Tennyson family fortunes began with the marriage, in the middle of the eighteenth century, of Michael Tennyson, a surgeon, with Elizabeth, heiress of the Clayton family of Grimsby. Their son George, later known as "the old man of the wolds," and his wife, a Mary Turner, had two sons and two daughters. The eldest son was George Clayton Tennyson, the poet's father; the second, Charles, inherited the family fortune and became the founder of the Tennyson d'Eyncourt family of Bayons Manor. There was a strain of wildness in George, which accounts perhaps for his rôle of second son though the eldest born; but after a mad adventure in Russia early in 1801, he was ordained priest (December 1802) and settled down, after his marriage (August 1805) with Elizabeth Fytche, daughter of a former vicar of Louth, as rector of Somersby (with a population of about seventy) and Bag Enderby (December 1806) to the life of a country parson and the procreation of twelve children in thirteen years. The first of these died in infancy; the second, Frederick, has a small niche in later memory as poet and letter writer; the third, Charles is known as the sonnet-writer Charles Tennyson Turner; the fourth was Alfred; the fifth, Mary; the sixth, Emily, was engaged to Arthur Hallam; of the remaining four sons and two daughters the eleventh child, Cecilia, became the wife of Edmund Lushington. These all were touched with the paternal moodiness and irritability and general oddness. "Lincolnshire in those days was a sadly barbarous Arcadia," says the poet's grandson,[2] and therefore a natural setting for the hypochondriac family. The mother of these twelve children was a woman of great and simple piety; she is known to us chiefly through the few letters to "Dearest Ally" printed in the *Memoir,* through Alfred's poem 'Isabel' and faintly as Gama's wife in 'The Princess.' The father, however, was clearly a 'character.' In spite of his moods of depression, due partly to physical causes—Frederick said of him at his death that "his soul had been daily wracked by bitter fancies and

29

tossed about by strong troubles"—he seems to have been "a man of considerable imagination, strong personality, active mind and wide interests, who . . . had a touch of the grand style about him." Indeed, after twenty-odd years of isolation in his barbarous Arcadia, in 1830, a year before his death, his early vigor reasserted itself and he made a journey to Italy, where he capped his Russian madness of twenty-nine years before with a final climax of strange adventures.

Alfred, it is important to remember, was his father's son. He shared what he liked to call "the black blood of the Tennysons," and on the night of his father's funeral slept in his father's bed, "in an earnest longing to see once more the spirit of" the departed. But if Somersby and the Somersby life was a natural setting for the father, it seems an odd setting for the man we have just seen buried in Westminster Abbey.

Born on 6 August 1809 at the rectory, Alfred was sent to school in Louth at the age of seven, and at the age of eleven returned home to be taught by his father, the "stern doctor." He did not like school. When he was about eight he "covered two sides of a slate with Thomsonian blank verse in praise of flowers, . . . Thomson then being the only poet I knew. . . . About ten or eleven Pope's *Homer's Iliad* became a favourite of mine and I wrote hundreds and hundreds of lines in the regular Popeian metre,"—and his father complained of their regularity. Next he turned to Scott and "wrote an epic of six thousand lines" in the 'Marmion' manner. "Somewhat later (at fourteen) I wrote a drama in blank verse, which I have still, and other things." And his prescient father said: "If Alfred die, one of our greatest poets will have gone." All this poetic precocity fructified in March 1827 with the publication at Louth of *Poems by Two Brothers,* of which Alfred's share was written while he was between fifteen and seventeen.

For the rest, we know that when he entered Trinity College, Cambridge, later in the same year he had, according to Jowett (thus the *Memoir;* but how could Jowett have known?) "a good but not a regular classical education given him by his father." At the University he remained just three years, without distinguishing himself as a student. In February 1831 he returned to Somersby, about a month before his father's death. He had not cared for school at Louth: he liked it no better at Cambridge. Long afterwards he told the Master of Trinity, "There was a want of love in Cambridge then"; and while he was there he expressed the same feeling in a sonnet:

> *Your manner sorts*
> *Not with this age wherefrom ye stand apart, . . .*
> *you that do profess to teach*
> *And teach us nothing, feeding not the heart.*[a]

Those three years were, however, immensely valuable to him. He missed the discipline of formal learning but he gained his first knowledge of the world outside the domesticity of his barbarous Arcadia of Somersby. He met a group of loyal friends whose enthusiasm strengthened his devotion to the Muses then, and afterwards lent yeoman aid in his battle with the critics. Above all, he met Arthur Hallam, whose friendship there and whose death in 1833 was the one profound emotional experience of his whole long life.

Through Hallam, Tennyson became a member of the Conversazione Society which had been recreated a few years before by F. D. Maurice and John Sterling and which was generally called 'The Apostles' because there were twelve 'brethren.'[3] And of Tennyson's principal friends at Cambridge (as they are listed in the *Memoir*—namely, Spedding, Milnes, Trench, Alford, Brookfield, Thompson, Merivale, Kemble, Charles Buller, Arthur Hallam, Blakesley, Spring Rice, Heath, R. Monteith, and Tennant) all but the last five were Apostles.[b] FitzGerald, who did not know him then, remembered him as looking "something like Hyperion shorn of his beams in Keats' poem"; Thompson, on first sight of him, said at once, "That man must be a poet"; and Fanny Kemble, visiting her

[a] In 1847 he was asked by Whewell, the Master of Trinity, to write the ode for the installation of the Prince Consort as Chancellor. After "some abortive attempts" he declined. " 'Household affection' to my own college," he said, "I have and filial regard towards the University I have—more so perhaps than when I made one among you—neither am I without loyal touches towards Queens and Princes, but for all that, this ode is more than I dare pledge myself to accomplish" (D.A. Winstanley, *Early Victorian Cambridge*, Cambridge, 1940, p. 200 n.)

[b] The distinction of some of these names in later life need not be dwelt upon. Tennyson was not, however, an Apostle in regular standing. He refused to conform with the Society's procedure of reading prepared papers to the brethren, and was made an honorary member and left "sitting in front of the fire, smoking and meditating, and now and then mingling in the conversation." This vignette, which we owe to Douglas Heath, a lesser Apostle, is invaluable because it prefigures Tennyson's whole life. In this instance biographical fact rises to the height of art: no novelist could have imagined a more perfect illustrative detail for his hero's youth.

brother, described him as "our hero, the great hero of our day." Thus he was early marked for fame and wore about him, already recognized, the robes of his priestly office.

Of his friend Hallam, Tennyson said: "he was as near perfection as mortal man could be." This does as much honor to Tennyson's devotion as to Hallam's character; but the element of exaggeration must not be denied. Even the memoir to young Hallam in the *Remains* admits failings; and one may pertinently recall the tribute of Duke Theseus to a very promising young man of earlier times:

> *And certeinly a man hath moost honour*
> *To dyen in his excellence and flour,*
> *When he is siker of his goode name.*[c]

Nevertheless it is something to have stirred a friend's bosom and inspired a friend's worship; it is a very great deal; and it is a better testimonial to Hallam than any tangible evidence which can be now produced. One might almost say that Tennyson created Hallam as a dramatist creates one of his characters: the historical details are corroborative, but they illuminate the poet rather than the mortal.

Arthur Hallam was the one great contribution of Trinity College to Tennyson. There were however two lesser incidents. Before the end of his second year at Cambridge, having meanwhile in June 1829 won the medal with his 'Timbuctoo,' he published his first independent volume, *Poems, Chiefly Lyrical*.[d] which was reviewed with both praise and blame, as it of course deserved, but with enough of the former to encourage a second volume in little more than two years. The other incident is both amusing and significant. It took place during the long vacation of 1830, when his father was returning from his own "neck-break adventures" in

c There is even a suggestion that Hallam was heading down the path of too easy success, like his fellow Apostle Milnes: "he was submitting himself to the influences of the outside world more than (I think) a man of his genius ought to do" (Blakesley to Tennyson, 1830; *Memoir* I, 69). And it will do no harm to repeat, in a footnote, the gossip reported by Oscar Browning *(Memories of Sixty Years,* London, 1910, p. 116). An "old servant of Hawtrey's [where Hallam lived at Eton] told me that he remembered him distinctly, and that he was always called 'Mother Hallam' by the boys. . . . General Fox also told me that he was the most conceited and priggish young man he had ever met."

d It was first planned as a joint product of Tennyson and Hallam. But Hallam withdrew from the project, giving as one reason "the growing conviction of the exceeding crudeness" of his earlier attempts. The other reasons are omitted editorially by Hallam Tennyson from the *Memoir* I, 51.

Italy. The Apostles, it would appear, lent themselves seriously to the cause of the Spanish liberals who were in active revolt against the despotism of Ferdinand VII. Kemble (who was twenty-three) joined the rebels in the south of Spain and had a narrow escape. Alfred Tennyson (who was not quite twenty-one) and Arthur Hallam (a year and a half younger) set out with financial help for the insurgents in the Pyrenees. It looks as though young Tennyson was by way of duplicating his father's incursion, at about the same age, into southern Russia; but the two revolutionary friends of 1830 had nothing more than a pleasant holiday. Hallam wrote back complaining of the heat and Alfred regretted "the impermanence of his impressions in the hurry of travel." His real achievement was part of the first draft of 'Œnone' composed at Cauteretz. When he revisited the valley in 1861 he recalled not the cause of the Spanish liberals but the companionship of Arthur Hallam, then twenty-eight years dead.

After his return to Somersby early in 1831, and his father's death, the Tennysons continued to live at the rectory. Alfred complained of the condition of his eyes, but thought of "the power of 'Tiresias and Phineus, prophets old' " as a possible compensation for blindness. He took to a milk diet, however, and recovered; and throughout his life he enjoyed the double capacity of that well-known myopia which is alleged as the reason for his minute observation of nature and the normal sight which he obtained with "his eye-glass or spectacles." He believed his keenness of hearing was a reward for his shortness of sight. Hallam visited at Somersby, for he was already engaged to Emily, though his father prevented immediate marriage;[4] or wrote frequent letters which Alfred neglected. Or they met in London (where Hallam was now reading law and writing essays) and talked about literature and the Church and "the present race of monstrous opinions and feelings which pervade the age" (so Blakesley), and especially about Alfred's new poems. In April of the next year Hallam opposed the idea of a second volume, but by July, when the two did the Rhine together as far as Bingen, it was nevertheless in preparation, and after their return Hallam was busy seeing it through the press. Moxon, the publisher, he wrote, "is in ecstasies with the 'May Queen'; he says the volume must make a great sensation"; and they were impatient to get it out "before the storm of politics is abroad." But the first Reform Bill was passed with less disturbance than an insurrection, Tennyson's second volume was ready in December (though dated 1833), and disaster came in the literary reviews rather than in an overthrow of the government.

Early in 1833 Tennyson was in Mablethorpe, "a miserable bathing place on our bleak, flat Lincolnshire coast"; in July he was in Scotland; in August he came up to London for a farewell dinner to Hallam, who was leaving for the continent with his father. On 1 October he received word that Hallam had died in Vienna two weeks before. The body—"the mortal part of our dearest Arthur" —was sent home by sea, and did not reach England until the very end of the year. On Monday, 30 December, Henry Hallam notified Tennyson of the vessel's safe arrival and announced the burial at Clevedon for the following Friday. He did not invite Tennyson to be present; in fact, it was not until after the publication of 'In Memoriam,' seventeen years later, that Tennyson, then on his wedding journey, visited the church.

Now the old Tennysonian "black blood" began to show. In March of this year he had written to Aunt Elizabeth: "For myself, I drag on somewhat heavily thro' the ruts of life, sometimes moping to myself like an owl in an ivy-bush, . . . and sometimes smoking a pipe with a neighbouring parson and cursing O'Connell for as double-dyed a rascal as ever was dipped in the Styx of political villainy." The review in the April *Quarterly*—"the sneering savage *Quarterly* attack," his son calls it—twisted and rankled in his morbid sensitiveness,[e] the same feeling which begot the regretted epigram on Christopher North already published (against Hallam's advice) in the 1832 volume, and the regrettable letter to the same Professor Wilson, afterwards published in the *Memoir*.[5] And then Hallam's death added the final stroke of desolation. He began composing 'Thoughts of a Suicide' (which he afterwards finished, with a happy ending, and called 'The Two Voices') and the first passionate songs of grief which grew into 'In Memoriam.' But the Muse is a great consoler, and even the most atrabiliar temperament has its changing moods. Frederick reported, February 1834, Alfred's "health very indifferent, and his spirits variable." The *Poems* of 1832 went tolerably well—at least three hundred copies were

e The review was supposed to have been written by Lockhart, but is now known to be Croker's.

sold and Moxon was eager for another volume; he thought the *Quarterly* attack had "done good." The poet's friends encouraged him, especially the faithful Spedding. Malory's *Morte d'Arthur* is mentioned in their letters. The urgent need of going forward was taking form in a new poem on Ulysses. He told Spedding (1834) "I have written several things since I saw you, some emulative of the ἡδὺ καὶ βραχὺ καὶ μεγαλοπρεπὲς of Alcaeus, others of the 'εκλογὴ τῶν 'ονομάτων καὶ τῆς συνθέσεως ἀκρίβεια of Simonides, one or two epical."[f]

Details of his life now are scanty. The Tennysons continued to live, until 1837, at Somersby. Alfred was there, a sort of head of the family (Frederick was abroad, Charles was ordained in 1835) reading and studying—his private schedule included Greek, Italian, and German; chemistry, botany, animal physiology, electricity, mechanics, and theology—and making verses, many unwritten, many unfinished. His friends occasionally visited him, and from time to time he was away on visits. In February 1835 he wrote to Spedding: "I have sold my medal, and made money, and would visit you"—the Chancellor's medal, which he won with 'Timbuctoo.' The published letters sound not uncheerful, and since there is little gaiety in any of his letters (for there was little in his temperament, though he had a robust peasant sort of humor) one must infer that he was not altogether despondent. But a letter to Spedding reveals one important clue to his state of mind:

John Heath writes me word that Mill is going to review me in a new Magazine, to be called the *London Review,* and favourably; but it is the last thing I wish for, and I would that you or some other who may be friends of Mill would hint as much to him. *I do not wish to be dragged forward again in any shape before the reading public at present,* particularly on the score of old poems, most of which I have so corrected (particularly "Œnone") as to make them much less imperfect, . . .

It has long been a moot point among the critics whether the almost unbroken silence, so far as publication goes, between the volume of December 1832 and the *Poems* of 1842 was the result of

---

[f] These can hardly be identified. The first (sweet and short and magnificent) are of course lyrics, and may be represented by 'Love thou thy land' copied out for Spedding in this same letter. The second, with the word *eclogue* (though in a different sense) and the "minute accuracy of composition," suggests perhaps the domestic idylls. The epical must be the 'Morte d'Arthur," which is mentioned in the same letter.

hurt feelings caused by the strictures of reviewers or of a conscious-
ness of immaturity and previous haste. It was of course neither the
one nor the other, but both. There is no doubt that he resented
criticism, except from a few intimates, and there is no doubt that
much of the criticism was salutary, even though it seemed harsh
and malicious. For the enthusiasm of his friends and his own eager-
ness had forced his talents. He was not quite content, like Sped-
ding, to wait to grow wise. The second volume was really superior
to the first, considering the interval between them, but he knew he
could not confound the critics at once with a third volume which
would be impressively and triumphantly superior to the second.[g]
It was therefore a counsel not of perfection but of simple strategy
to postpone publication until his own confidence was restored and
his muse matured. That he profited by the gibes of Wilson and
Croker can be clearly established from a study of his revisions, but
it cannot of course be proved that most of the improvements might
not have come without the gibes.[6]

In 1835 he was at Spedding's, Mirehouse, in the Lake country,
and FitzGerald was with them. He had "a little red book" of manu-
script poems along and read to them 'Morte d'Arthur,' 'The Day-
Dream,' 'The Lord of Burleigh,' 'Dora,' and 'The Gardener's
Daughter.' Here also he met Hartley Coleridge, thirteen years his
senior, who indited a sonnet beginning—

> *Long have I known thee as thou art in song*

and concluding—

> *Knowing thee now, a real earth-treading man,*
> *Not less I love thee and no more I can.*

The weather was bad, but nevertheless, wrote Spedding, "I think
he [Tennyson] took in more pleasure and inspiration than any one
would have supposed who did not know his almost personal dis-
like of the present, whatever it may be." He refused to meet Words-
worth, though he read 'Michael' with increased admiration. "He

[g] He must have already contemplated a new venture, however, for Frederick wrote to John Frere, 10 February 1834, "Alfred probably will publish again in the Spring." Cf. FitzGerald to W. B. Donne, 25 October 1833: Tennyson "has been making fresh poems, which are finer, they say, than any he has done. But I believe he is chiefly meditating on the purging and subliming of what he has already done: and repents that he has published at all yet. It is fine to see how in each succeeding poem the smaller ornaments and fancies drop away, and leave the grand ideas single. . . ." (*Letters*, London, 1894, I, 24).

would and would not (sulky one), although Wordsworth was hospitably minded towards him."[7] After he and FitzGerald separated at Ambleside, FitzGerald wrote to him teasingly about a French paper called *Le Voleur* in which he was mentioned as a "jeune enthousiaste de l'école gracieuse de *Thomas Moore.*" And just before this FitzGerald had written to John Allen; "the more I see of [Tennyson], the more cause I have to think him great. His little humours and grumpinesses were so droll, that I was always laughing: . . . but I could not be mistaken in the universality of his mind."

In 1837 Tennyson broke silence by publishing in the *Keepsake* his 'St. Agnes'; and this prompted Monckton Milnes to half-promise a Tennysonian poem for a charitable project of Lord Northampton's called *The Tribute.* Tennyson replied with churlish jocularity:

Three summers back, provoked by the incivility of editors, I swore an oath that I would never again have to do with their vapid books, and I brake it in the sweet face of Heaven when I wrote for Lady What's-her-name Wortley. But then her sister wrote to Brookfield and said she (Lady W.) was beautiful, so I could not help it. But whether the Marquis be beautiful or not, I don't much mind; if he be, let him give God thanks and make no boast. To write for people with prefixes to their names is to milk he-goats; there is neither honour nor profit. Up to this moment I have not even seen *The Keepsake*: not that I care to see it, for the want of civility decided me not to break mine oath again for man nor woman, and how should such a modest man as I see my small name in collocation with the great ones of Southey, Wordsworth, R.M.M., etc., and not feel myself a barndoor fowl among peacocks?

Milnes was offended and charged him with "insolent irony." Tennyson's reply, promising a contribution—the little seed called 'Stanzas' from which 'Maud' grew—is one of his liveliest letters:

Why what in the name of all the powers, my dear Richard, makes you run me down in this fashion? Now is my nose out of joint, now is my tail not only curled so tight as to lift me off my hind legs like Alfred Crowquill's poodle, but fairly between them. Many sticks are broken about me. I am the ass in Homer. I am blown.[8]

In the same year, 1837, what remained of the Tennyson family was obliged to leave the Somersby rectory. They settled first in High Beech, Epping Forest; three years later they removed to

Tunbridge Wells; and thence, in 1841, to Boxley, near Maidstone. At High Beech Tennyson was nearer his London friends, but he returned occasionally to visit his brother's vicarage and the Sellwoods at Horncastle. For he was now "quasi-engaged" to Emily Sellwood, whom he had met in 1830 and had apparently fallen in love with when she was a bridesmaid at his brother's wedding in May 1836. In the autumn of 1838 he was at Torquay, writing 'Audley Court.' Meanwhile his friends were urgent: "Do not continue to be so *careless of fame, and of influence.*" They even suggested his living in Prague for the sake of new impressions and stimuli for poetry. He continued to move restlessly from here to there: High Beech and London (where he lived as a semi-bohemian in various lodgings), Warwick, Leicester, Wells, Mablethorpe, Otley, Aberystwyth, Barmouth—but never Clevedon. But it began to be apparent that his friends' exhortations would soon bear fruit. In November 1839 FitzGerald wrote to Bernard Barton:

I want A. T. to publish another volume: as all his friends do: especially Moxon, who has been calling on him for the last 2 years for a new edition of his old volume: but he is too lazy and wayward to put his hand to the business—He has got fine things in a large Butcher's Account Book that now lies in my room: but I don't know if any would take you much.

And in the following February:

When I got to my lodgings [London], I found A. Tennyson installed in them: he has been here ever since in a very uneasy state: being really ill, in a nervous way: what with hereditary tenderness of nerve, and having spoiled what strength he had by incessant smoking &c.—I have also made him very out of sorts by desiring a truce from complaints and complainings—Poor fellow: he is quite magnanimous, and noble natured, with no meanness or vanity or affectations of any kind whatever—but very perverse, according to the nature of his illness—⁹

From Mablethorpe Tennyson wrote to Old Fitz: "You bore me about my book; so does a letter just received from America, threatening, tho' in the civilest terms, that, if I will not publish in England, they will do it for me in that land of freemen." But in October 1841 FitzGerald was rejoiced to hear of him in London "busy preparing for the press"; and in March of the next year FitzGerald wrote to Barton:

Poor Tennyson has got some of his proof sheets: and, now that his verses are in hard print, thinks them detestable—There is much I

have always told him of—his great fault of being too full and compli-
cated—which he now sees, or fancies he sees, and wishes he had never
been persuaded to print. But with all his faults he will publish such
a volume as has not been published since the time of Keats: and which,
once published, will never be suffered to die.

At length the now famous *Poems* of 1842 was ready, in two small
volumes—the first mainly a selection from his earlier verse consider-
ably revised or rewritten (FitzGerald deplored the reprinting of
them), the second mainly new poems. This second volume made
and still largely maintains Tennyson's reputation; it contained not
only pieces which even his admirers now regret (such as 'The May
Queen' and 'The Lord of Burleigh') but also pieces which even his
detractors admire (such as 'Ulysses' and 'Break, break, break').
There were reviews in the *Examiner* and the *Athenæum,* Emer-
son's in *The Dial,* John Sterling's in the *Quarterly,* Milnes' in the
Westminster, and finally, in April 1843, Spedding's in the *Edin-
burgh.* The *Memoir* calls Spedding's review "the most remark-
able." Certainly it sounded a note, besides its praise of individual
poems, which became an organ-point of criticism for years to come:

We cannot conclude without reminding Mr. Tennyson, that highly
as we value the Poems which he has produced, we cannot accept them
as a satisfactory account of the gifts which they show that he pos-
sesses; . . . Powers are displayed in these volumes, adequate, if we do
not deceive ourselves, to the production of a great work; at least we
should find it difficult to say which of the requisite powers is wanting.
But they are displayed in fragments and snatches, having no con-
nexion, and therefore deriving no light or fresh interest the one from
the other. . . . If Mr. Tennyson can find a subject large enough to take
the entire impress of his mind, and energy persevering enough to work
it faithfully out as one whole, we are convinced that he may [is this
Macvey Napier's substitute for Spedding's *will?*] produce a work, which,
occupying no larger space than the contents of these two volumes,
shall as much exceed them in value, as a series of quantities multiplied
into each other exceeds in value the same series simply added to-
gether.[h]

[h] *Edinburgh Review,* LXXVII (1843),
373-391; p. 391. So also the *Examiner* for
28 May 1842 (no. 1791, p. 340) thought
that Tennyson would now "find himself
able to fly a higher flight than lyric, idyl,
or eclogue, and we counsel him to try
it." The *Westminster Review* (XXXVII
(October 1842), 390) commended his mas-
tery of diction and versification and
went on: "he has only to show that he
has substance worthy of these media"
and hoped that "he comprehends the
function of the poet in this day of ours,
to teach still more than he delights, and
to suggest still more than he teaches."

Couched in these gentle terms, because Spedding had on one side of him the withholding hand of the *Edinburgh's* editor and on the other side his acute awareness of Tennyson's hatred of criticism, this exhortation—"If Mr. Tennyson can find a subject . . . and energy persevering enough . . . he may . . ."—was nevertheless a warning, almost a prophecy. It gave the pitch to subsequent criticism; it gave the clue to Tennyson's successive failures. It was also unfortunate in that it goaded Tennyson to efforts for which his genius was ill equipped. It prophetically laid bare the weakness of his subsequent long poems: want of a fit subject and power to forge what materials he came by into a great and justificatory work. This Prince of Promise must ascend his throne or else—and the implication is one half the history of Tennyson's reputation.

Here he was now, however, an acknowledged Prince. By September five hundred copies of the *Poems* had been sold, and "according to Moxon's brother I have made a sensation!" In December Carlyle (whom he had first met in 1840)[10] wrote with "almost surprising" enthusiasm:

I have just been reading your Poems; I have read certain of them over again, and mean to read them over and over till they become my poems: . . . If you knew what my relation has been to the thing call'd English "Poetry" for many years back, you would think such fact almost surprising! Truly it is long since in any English Book, Poetry or Prose, I have felt the pulse of a real man's heart as I do in this same. A right valiant, true fighting, victorious heart; strong as a lion's, yet gentle, loving and full of music: what I call a genuine singer's heart! there are tones as of the nightingale; low murmurs as of wood-doves at summer noon; everywhere a noble sound as of the free winds and leafy woods. The sunniest glow of Life dwells in that soul, chequered duly with dark streaks from night and Hades: everywhere one feels as if all were fill'd with yellow glowing sunlight, some glorious golden Vapour; from which form after form bodies itself; naturally, *golden* forms. In one word, there seems to be a note of "The Eternal Melodies" in this man; for which let all other men be thankful and joyful! Your "Dora" reminds me of the *Book of Ruth;* in the "Two Voices," which I am told some Reviewer calls "trivial morality," I think of passages in *Job*.

He is reminded also of Goethe and of Jean Paul; he quotes three lines from 'Ulysses'; and ends: "Farewell, dear Tennyson; may the gods be good to you."—Well, they were, after their fashion. After the poet's death the Dean of Westminster wrote to Hallam:

On my return to Oxford in October 1842 his name was on everyone's lips, his poems discussed, criticised, interpreted; portions of them repeatedly set for translation into Latin or Greek verse at schools and colleges; read and re-read so habitually that there were many of us who could repeat page after page from memory.

Canon Dixon reports the same glorification:

It is difficult to the present generation to understand the Tennysonian enthusiasm which then prevailed both in Oxford and the world. All reading men were Tennysonians: all sets of reading men talked poetry. Poetry was the thing: and it was felt with justice that this was due to Tennyson. Tennyson had invented a new poetry, a new poetic English: his use of words was new, and every piece that he wrote was a conquest of a new region. This lasted till 'Maud,' in 1855; which was his last poem that mattered. . . . There was the general conviction that Tennyson was the greatest poet of the century: some held him the greatest of all poets, or at least of all modern poets.[11]

In 1842 however, Nemesis stood ready, in anticipation of the glory to come. In this year Tennyson engaged in the one business enterprise of his career. He invested the proceeds of his little estate in Lincolnshire and the £500 left him by Arthur Hallam's aunt, and all that the resident Tennysons could scrape together, in The Patent Decorative Carving and Sculpture Company, promoted by a physician of Beech Hill, Dr. Allen. This venture, familiarly spoken of as the Woodworks, was to make machine-carved oak furniture available to the common man at cheap prices. It collapsed almost at once, with Tennyson the principal loser. "Every stick and stave is to be sold to pay A. T.," wrote Dr. Allen to Frederick, 4 March 1843. But the real savior was his brother-in-law Edmund Lushington, who the next year generously insured Dr. Allen's life for the part of the debt due to Alfred, and the doctor obligingly died in January 1845. FitzGerald's remark was: "Apollo certainly did this: shooting one of his swift arrows at the heart of the Doctor." Meanwhile Tennyson himself nearly died. "So severe a hypochondria set in upon him," says the *Memoir*, "that his friends despaired of his life." And Tennyson said: "I have drunk one of those most bitter draughts out of the cup of life, which go near to make men hate the world they move in."[12] He went to Cheltenham, where his mother and her family had been living since the autumn of 1843, for the waters, "a polka-parson-worshipping place . . . and one of the prettiest countries in Great Britain." In February 1844 he wrote to FitzGerald that he hated his water life—βίος ἄβιος—but hoped to be cured in March. In July he had had ten crises and was still hopeful but not cured, though he had "walked twice up Snowdon." After a holiday in London he returned to his hydrop athy and was still at Cheltenham in January 1845. While there he visited the Hallams at Wroxall Lodge near Bristol, but still kept away from Clevedon. In the summer of 1845 he was again in London; and here we can see him pretty plainly through the diary of Aubrey de Vere.[13] On 17 April de Vere found Tennyson "at first much out of spirits."

He cheered up soon, and read me some beautiful Elegies, complaining much of some writer in 'Fraser's Magazine' who had spoken of the 'foolish felicity' of Tennysonian poetry. . . . went back to Tennyson, who 'crooned' out his magnificent Elegies till one in the morning.
  April 18.—Sat with Alfred Tennyson, who read MS. poetry to Tom Taylor and me. Walked with him to his lawyer's: came back and listened to the 'University of Women.' . . . As I went away, he said he would willingly bargain for the reputation of Suckling or Lovelace, and alluded to 'the foolish facility of Tennysonian poetry.' Said he was dreadfully cut up by all he had gone through.
  May 4.—Brought Alfred Tennyson, murmuring sore, to Hampstead, to see Mr. Wordsworth. Mr. W. improved upon him.
  May 9.— . . . Alfred Tennyson came in and smoked his pipe. He told us with pleasure of his dinner with Wordsworth—was pleased as well as amused by Wordsworth saying to him, 'Come, brother bard, to dinner,' and taking his arm. . . . he had at last, in the dark, said something about the pleasure he had had from Mr. Wordsworth's writings, and that the old poet had taken his hand, and replied with some expressions equally kind and complimentary. Tennyson was evidently much pleased with the old man, and glad of having learned to know him.
  May 10.—I went to Alfred Tennyson, who read me part of his 'University of Women,' and discussed poetry, denouncing exotics, and saying that a poem should reflect the time and place. . .
  May 11.—Called on Tennyson. Spent three hours with him and Edward FitzGerald trying to persuade him to come to Hither Green. At last he agreed. . . .
  He is the most interesting man I ever met except [Henry Taylor], so full of the humanities, so original, and yet so rich in sympathy for all that is natural. . . .
  July 1.—Driving in from Hampstead I met Alfred Tennyson, who was little pleased to see me, and seemed living in a mysterious sort of way on the Hampstead Road, bathing and learning Persian.

July 14.— . . . Called on Alfred Tennyson, who railed against the whole system of society, and said he was miserable.

July 16.— . . . On my way in, paid a visit to Tennyson, who seemed much out of spirits, and said he could no longer bear to be knocked about the world, and that he must marry and find love and peace or die. He was very angry about a favourable review of him. Said that he could not stand the chattering and conceit of clever men, or the worry of society, or the meanness of tuft-hunters, or the trouble of poverty, or the labour of a place, or the preying of the heart on itself. . . . He complained much about growing old, and said he cared nothing for fame, and that his life was all thrown away for want of a competence and retirement. Said that no one had been so much harassed by anxiety and trouble as himself. I told him he wanted occupation, a wife, and orthodox principles, which he took well.

In August Aubrey de Vere "sat with Tennyson for an hour, during which time he read me an account of Laura Bridgman. When he came to her recognition of her mother, he threw the book over to me, and said, 'Read it for yourself, it makes me cry.' "

In September of 1845 he was cheered by receiving, through Sir Robert Peel, an unsolicited "mark of Royal Favour," namely, a pension of £200 annually, as "one who has devoted to worthy purposes great intellectual powers." This was apparently due to the influence of Monckton Milnes, urged on by Carlyle.[1] "Well, I suppose I ought in a manner to be grateful"; so he accepted the pension with the reservation that he still could "bully" the Queen, the Court, "or Peel himself," if he felt like it. "I wish the causelessly bitter against me and mine no worse punishment than that they could read the very flattering letter Peel wrote me; let us leave them in their limbo.

Non ragionam di lor, ma guarda e passa."

Who these causelessly bitter enemies were is not recorded; but one turned up presently. In December 1845 and early in the following year Bulwer-Lytton published anonymously a versified novel of London life, *The New Timon,* into which he inserted a number of satirical passages, unrelated to the story, on contemporary figures in literature and politics. One of these passages was an unprovoked and malicious attack on "schoolmiss Alfred"—

[1] Said Carlyle: "Richard Milnes, on the Day of Judgment, when the Lord asks you why you didn't get that pension for Alfred Tennyson, it will not do to lay the blame on your constituents; it is *you* that will be damned."

The jingling melody of purloin'd conceits
Outbabying Wordsworth, and outglittering Keats,

and so forth; with a note referring to the pension. Various circumstances added to the bad taste of this anonymous attack. Tennyson, when the offensive passages were drawn to his attention, and he learned, apparently from John Forster, that Bulwer-Lytton was their author, immediately composed a reply, which Forster sent to *Punch:* 'The New Timon, and the Poets,' signed "Alcibiades." In the next issue, 28 February, came a repentant 'After-Thought,' with the same signature. The first of these contains some shrewd hits and indicates Tennyson's undeveloped powers as a satirist:

I thought we knew him: What, it's you,
The padded man—that wears the stays—

Who kill'd the girls and thrill'd the boys
With dandy pathos when you wrote,
A Lion, you, that made a noise,
And shook a mane en papillotes....

What profits now to understand
The merits of a spotless shirt—
A dapper boot—a little hand—
If half the little soul is dirt? ...

But as Tennyson admitted, the verses "were too bitter. I do not think that I should ever have published them." Bulwer-Lytton charged Forster with betraying a confidence and at the same time violently denied the authorship of *The New Timon.* Thus no one shows up very well. But in the third edition Bulwer-Lytton removed all trace of the Tennyson passage; and in 1870 he omitted, on Forster's advice, a slighting reference to Tennyson in the first draft of his preface to the new edition of his *King Arthur.* In 1876 Tennyson dedicated 'Harold' to Bulwer-Lytton's son and received a warmly appreciative letter in acknowledgement.[14]

Tennyson was in London for two months of the summer of 1846, according to FitzGerald, starting for Italy or Switzerland, and ended by going to the Isle of Wight till autumn, "when Moxon promises to convoy him over; and then God knows what will become of him and whether we shall ever see his august old body over here again. He was in a ricketty state of body; brought on wholly by neglect, etc., but in fair spirits; and one has the comfort of seeing the Great Man." Actually he and Moxon left England on 2nd August for Ostende, crossed Flanders and ascended the Rhine (at Cologne he thought the cathedral was "splendid but to my mind too narrow for its length"), continued then from Basel on to Lucerne, and over (via Sarnen and Lungern, where he met a "jolly old Radical who abused Dr. Arnold") to the Interlaken section. This is what delighted him most: "the stateliest bits of landskip I ever saw," the Lauterbrunnen valley seen from the Wengern Alp and the Bernese Alps, as seen apparently from Thun. "I was so satisfied with the size of crags that . . . I *laughed* by myself. I was satisfied with the size of crags, but mountains, great mountains disappointed me. I couldn't take them in, I suppose, crags I could." —This is quite Tennysonian.—On the way home they called on Dickens at Lausanne, "who was very hospitable" and gave them biscuits and a bottle of Liebfraumilch. On his return to England he read *Festus* and found "really *very grand* things" in it.

The *Poems* of 1842 had now gone into a fourth edition, and after a five-year interval the Prince of Promise came forward with 'The Princess.' Everyone was disappointed. Sir William Hamilton may have thought it a much wiser book than his own *Quaternions,* but the critics were baffled by the triviality of the subject and the badness of the blank verse. To FitzGerald Tennyson wrote: "My book is out and I hate it, and so no doubt will you." He did. On 4 May 1848 he wrote to Frederick: "I am considered a great heretic for abusing it; it seems to me a great waste of power at a time of life when a man ought to be doing his best; and I almost feel hopeless about Alfred now. I mean about his doing what he was born to do. . . ." And in this perverse heterodoxy FitzGerald remained firm to the end, grumbling, with occasional bits of grudging praise, but unreconciled. Nearly thirty years later he told John Allen: "I think he might have stopped after 1842, leaving Princesses, Ardens, Idylls, etc., all unborn; all except The Northern Farmer, which makes me cry. . . ." He made no secret of this judgment even to Tennyson: "But he has so many worshippers who tell him otherwise." Of 'In Memoriam' when it appeared he wrote to Frederick: "it is full of finest things, but it is monotonous, and has that air of being evolved by a Poetical Machine of the highest order. So it seems to be with him now, at least to me, the Impetus, the Lyrical oestrus is gone. . . ." And a year later: "What can 'In Memoriam' do but make us all sentimental?" Others have felt like agreeing with FitzGerald, but important qualifications would be necessary. As with all half-truths, one must be sure which half is right.— Alongside this interim judgment of FitzGerald's may be set, for curiosity's sake, the similar semi-prescience of Richard Hengist Horne. Tennyson, said Horne in 1844, is "sure of his power, sure of his activity, but not sure of his objects. . . . He constantly gives us the impression of something greater than his works. And this must be his own soul. He may do greater things than he has yet done; but we do not expect it. If he do no more, he has already done enough to deserve the lasting love and admiration of pos- terity."[15]

In spite of his unsettled life, his Odyssean wanderings about England, partly out of sheer restlessness and partly in the interests of hydropathy, the forties might be called his London period, his days of contact with the active world. He knew everybody of im- portance, especially of course literary people, but others also, and was known in various London clubs. "People fête and dine me every day but I am somewhat unwell and out of spirits," he wrote to Mrs. Burton in 1846, and to FitzGerald in 1847: "I have been be-dined usque ad nauseam."[16]

The years 1848 and 1849 lead up naturally to the principal climax of Tennyson's life. 'The Princess' had failed to satisfy the hopes of his friends for a great work, and now, though there were on hand the accumulated Elegies and there were revisions to be made in 'The Princess,' his thoughts turned to the unwritten 'epic' of King Arthur, and he set out for Cornwall in search of local color and inspiration. "I hear," he said, "that there are larger waves there [at Bude] than on any other part of the British coast: and must go thither and be alone with God." This communion began with a small misfortune. "Arrived at Bude in dark," runs his diary, "askt girl way to sea, she opens the back door . . . I out and in a moment go sheer down, upward of six feet, over wall on fanged cobbles. Up again and walked to see over dark hill." But in the fall he injured his knee and required the services of a surgeon. The surgeon introduced him to various friends so that he obtained a series of introductions and thus was passed on from town to town without benefit of hotels. Through June and most of July he 'did' the western end of Cornwall, bathing, talking, reading, and sight-seeing, around to Plymouth. For the first two weeks his knee kept him near Camelford; after that there is nothing in the diary about Arthurian backgrounds. But Aubrey de Vere, whom he visited at Mortlake in January 1849, wrote then to Miss Fenwick: "He is more full than ever of King Arthur, and promises to *print* at least his exquisite Elegies, and let his friends have a few copies." [17] Arthur was to wait nearly ten years yet, 'In Memoriam' less than two. Moreover, Aubrey de Vere had written to Mrs. Villiers while Tennyson was visiting him at Curragh Chase in 1848: "He is as simple as a child, and not less interesting for his infirmities.ʲ He is all in favour of marriage, and indeed will not be right till he has some one to love him exclusively."

It was not merely fortuitous that marriage and 'In Memoriam' came together. The story is this. Moxon asked for a manuscript, Tennyson gave him 'In Memoriam' and Moxon offered him £300 in cash and a certain annual royalty.[18] On the strength of this financial arrangement the engagement with Emily Sellwood, which had been broken off in 1840, was renewed. Her family then had forbidden all correspondence, and because of "an overstrained, morbid scrupulousness," it seemed to Tennyson an article of duty to release her. They had communicated, nevertheless, through his sister Emily, but they did not see each other until now. (In all this the attitude of the Sellwood family is a matter of inference. If, as I have heard, one of their objections to Alfred was that the marriage of his brother Charles and Emily's sister Louisa had not turned out well, Charles having more of the Tennysonian black blood than Alfred, it is a compound irony that Charles was, as apparently he was, the negotiator of this second marriage and that he and Louisa were absent from the wedding.) 'In Memoriam' was published, anonymously, on 1st June 1850 in an edition of 5,000 copies; the

---

ʲ So Coventry Patmore wrote, somewhat later: "Tennyson is like a great child, very simple and very much self-absorbed. I never heard him make a remark of his own which was worth repeating, yet I have always left him with a mind and heart enlarged. In any other man, his incessant dwelling upon trifles concerning himself, generally small injuries—real or imaginary—would be very tiresome" (Basil Champneys, *Memoirs and Correspondence of Coventry Patmore*, London, 1900, I, 198).

marriage took place at Shiplake the 13th of June. The next day they set out for Clevedon; "It seemed a kind of consecration to go there," said Tennyson. And well it might. For in spite of manifold wanderings over most of England since 1834 he had never yet seen Arthur Hallam's grave in the Clevedon church.[k]

There has never been any doubt that the marriage was a very happy one.[l] Spedding at once gave Aubrey de Vere "an excellent account of Mrs. Tennyson"; and a little later, after he had met her at Coniston, Aubrey de Vere told Miss Fenwick that Mrs. Tennyson was

a very interesting woman—kindly, affectionate . . . and, above all, deeply and simply religious. Her great and constant desire is to make her husband more religious, or at least to conduce, as far as she may, to his growth in the spiritual life. In this she will doubtless succeed, for piety like hers is infectious, . . . Indeed I already observe a great improvement in Alfred. His nature is a religious one, and he is remarkably free from vanity and sciolism. Such a nature gravitates towards Christianity, especially when it is in harmony with itself. . . . and Alfred has always been, to an extraordinary degree, human. He has been surrounded, however, from his youth up, by young men, many of them with high aspirations, who believe no more in Christianity than in the Feudal System, and this no doubt has been a great hindrance to one with his strong sympathies. . . . [Tennyson] is far happier than I ever saw him before; and his "wrath against the world" is proportionately mitigated. He has an unbounded respect for his wife, as well as a strong affection, which has been growing stronger ever since his marriage. That marriage was obviously, equally creditable to his judgment and his heart, and it will, I doubt not, be attended by a blessing.

---

[k] When 'In Memoriam' was published he still supposed that Hallam was buried in the churchyard, and the text is still unaltered:

> *We may stand*
> *Where he in English earth is laid,*
> *And from his ashes may be made*
> *The violet of his native land.*

This is to be sure an easy metaphor, and "ashes" as well; but Tennyson always prided himself on accuracy of detail.

[l] At Coniston, 1850, late one evening Aubrey de Vere and Tennyson were talking. "After a time he spoke but like one thinking aloud. 'I have known many women who were excellent, one in one way, and another in another way: but this woman is the noblest woman I have ever known.' No friend who had then heard him could have felt any further anxiety as to his domestic happiness. During the following days," continues de Vere, "I had many opportunities of remarking how much better his spirits had become. He was now not seldom mirthful." And much later Tennyson: "The peace of God came into my life before the altar when I wedded her." There have always been, however, differing opinions about her influence on Tennyson's poetry.

The proportions of judgment and heart which went into the making of this marriage can only be guessed. Neither the *Memoir* nor any of the various published reminiscences throws any light on Tennyson's interest in women.[19] But it cannot be supposed that no other "dear gazelle" ever touched his imagination. He was clearly not, however, of an amorously passionate temperament. His imagination fed delicately on the airy-fairy ladies of his own creation, but he was not, in these matters, a Shelley or even a Wordsworth: he was a model Victorian. And since he was a friend of Coventry Patmore's (though we are told too little about that friendship) it may be noted in passing that his most passionate love poems, his most nearly passionate love poems, one should say, were composed after his marriage—after, that is, he had passed forty.

This year of miracles reached its climax the 19th of November. One night, earlier in the month, Tennyson dreamed that Prince Albert came and kissed him on the cheek, and he said, in his dream, "Very kind, but very German." The next morning he received a letter from Windsor offering him the office of Poet Laureate. His first appearance at Court was in the following March, and he wore the costume of Rogers (who had just declined the office on account of his age) which had been worn a few years before by Wordsworth. It was almost like a laying on of hands.

On the return from their honeymoon in the Lake District the Tennysons, after an unhappy experience in a town with the ominous name of Warninglid, settled in Twickenham, where their first son was born and died on Easter Sunday, 20 April 1851. In the summer they went to Italy, as far as Bagni di Lucca (where he should have remembered Shelley) and Florence (where he visited his brother Frederick, there domiciled); then returned through Switzerland and Paris (where they met the Brownings). Parts of this journey are affectionately chronicled in 'The Daisy,' composed in a specially invented stanza in imitation of Horace's alcaics, but not a piece which could gratify Mrs. Tennyson's eagerness for her husband to write poetry. Nor were the 'National Songs' such, written after Louis Napoleon's *coup d'état* in December and published in the *Examiner* early in 1852, though they testify to his sense of responsibility as Laureate.

In the spring of 1852 the Tennysons went to Malvern; then back

49

at Twickenham they entertained many of his London friends and
visited the Exhibition together. But in July he ran away to Whitby,
partly on account of his hay-fever and partly because of bachelor
nostalgia, and on his way home spent a week with his brother
Charles at Grasby. On 11 August Hallam was born. Tennyson now
wrote to Milnes: "I have given up dining out and am about to re-
tire into utter solitude in some country house"; and after miscel-
laneous travel—they separated at Grasby in July 1853 and he went
to Scotland for August with Palgrave—and various temporary resi-
dences, in November 1853 they settled at Farringford on the Isle
of Wight. Meanwhile the general abuse of the 'Ode on the Death
of the Duke of Wellington,' his first important Laureate poem,
must have hinted to him that he was neglecting his profession.

With the purchase of Farringford, Tennyson's biography comes
almost to an end. He was now between forty-four and forty-five
years old, and most of us suffer a kind of death at that age, however
much longer mind and body may hold together. The molds are
formed, the machine is finished; it may continue to operate with
increased smoothness but it changes little. The product may even
improve in quality, but neither machine nor product will greatly
alter in kind. Tennyson now lived according to a favorite couplet
of Goethe's 'Tasso':

> *Es bildet ein Talent sich in der Stille,*
> *Sich ein Charakter in dem Strom der Welt.*

His character being formed, he retired into the stillness of Far-
ringford to develop his talent to the uttermost. His restless wander-
ing life of the past twenty years yielded to the solace of domesticity
and the calm cultivation of Pierian fields; though he travelled a
great deal, travel became no longer a flight from himself but a
search for poetic material and impetus. His spirits improved cor-
respondingly, as success gave him confidence; and his health, under
Mrs. Tennyson's protective ministrations, became at least more
manageable. He even forgot, except during attacks of gout, that his
health had been indifferent: for years later when Hallam showed
him a published letter of old Rogers' imputing to him "many in-
firmities" because of his hydropathic treatments, he made light of
the charge and said: "What mine were I know not unless short-

sight and occasional hypochondria be infirmities." In a word, he "settled into a country life at once" (as the *Memoir* puts it) and divided his activities between composition and the mild exercise of mowing his grass, sweeping up leaves, and building "what he called 'a bower of rushes' in the kitchen garden": the life of a gentleman farmer and professional poet.[m]

In this Georgic setting the English Vergil continued to write his English eclogues and soon began in earnest his epic-idyll. But as the clouds of glory gathered about him they increased his seclusion from the world in which character is moulded and from which nourishment is drawn. He settled not only into a country life, but into himself. The clouds of glory wove themselves into a vatic robe, and while the glory continued and the prophet spoke Apollo withdrew. This is a hard and perhaps dangerous generalization. It is not meant to diminish the splendor of his later accomplishment, the great exceptions of his later years; it does not signify that the poet had ceased in him. But some such formulation is necessary to indicate the choice and the change of which the retirement to Farringford is merely an external mark. The choice was a natural one. The influence of Mrs. Tennyson, which he needed as a man unable to take care of himself, and the commercial success of his poetry, which is so often a clog for the Muses, combined to restrict his growth, if growth were likely; but the choice was none the less natural because even without her influence and the confidence of popular approval it is not clear that growth would have continued in the right direction. It is the constant human irony that what saves us from one evil exposes us to another.

One large work of originality and inspiration, however, remained in him, and in a curious way it is the product of the forces which were gradually to narrow his scope. His marriage seems to have released whatever elements of passion he possessed, as witness the songs added to 'The Princess,' which were written, of course, before the marriage. But a more important release took place in 'Maud,' begun soon after he settled at Farringford. Not only does 'Maud' contain some of his best love poetry—best in the sense of

[m] "I am inclined to think," says his grandson, "that the first ten years which Tennyson spent at Farringford were the happiest of his life" (Charles Tennyson, "Tennyson's England," *The Geographical Magazine*, XIII (1941), 121-131; p. 128).

being less artificial and conventional—but it is a specially personal poem. That Tennyson knew this subconsciously is hinted by his statement about 'Maud' and similar dramatic poems. "In a certain way, no doubt," he said, "poets and novelists, however dramatic they are, give themselves in their works. The mistake that people make is that they think the poet's poems are a kind of 'catalogue raisoné' of his very own self, and of all the facts of his life, not seeing that they often only express a poetic instinct, or judgment on character real or imagined, and on the facts of lives real or imagined." This is a wise word. It points, although not too clearly, to the distinction which seekers of autobiography in art frequently miss. The facts of a poet's life and the facts of his imaginary characters' lives may be poles apart, but the implications and interpretations of those facts are, save in the really exceptional instances, part of the poet's own character. No artist creates anything except out of himself; the necessary distinction is between "out of" in the literal and in the metaphorical or spiritual sense; and most of the critical confusion springs from failure to see or maintain this distinction. The hero of 'Maud' is a projection of Tennyson himself both in his love of Maud—a love which was (incidentally, and only incidentally) thwarted by family circumstances—and in his incipient madness. By 1854 Tennyson felt safe enough to explore this phenomenon for artistic purposes. His own inherited melancholia, which in his father had taken the form of extreme eccentricity and in his brother Charles a more distressing form, was now under control. He need no longer fear any malignant manifestation of it, for he was now settled and successful, happily married and devoted to his chosen profession. He could now turn it to poetical uses. It gave him an opportunity not only for rhetorical experiment but for 'raving' against some of the social conditions of which he disapproved, in the voice of an imaginary character (and he was properly indignant when his hero's opinions were attributed to himself, even though they were his own); it gave him an opportunity not only to dramatize himself, but also to remind himself how he had been saved from possible disaster by a pure love. The duel was crude melodrama, attributable perhaps to too much reading of sensational fiction, and the Crimean War was a topical convenience, but the psychology of his hero reflects, not factually or literally, of course, the Tennysonian black blood, the atrabiliar tendencies of his family. This was probably not conscious, certainly not deliberate; but it was a psychological release and a further mark of that change which divides the earlier and the later Tennyson. To about 1855 there was growth and development; after that largely repetition and the perfection of manual dexterity. To be sure, in the last thirty-five years he tried new methods and new ideas, particularly the drama and religious poetry, but without real success. He withdrew from the world, and by devoting himself to the inner life only betrayed the limitations of his own inner spirit. It may be said that the world came to his door, and certainly in the form of sightseers it did; but only a select world that came to worship was admitted. For this withdrawal, so reasonable because it was meant to protect him from the interruptions and distractions of quotidian life and free him for the life of communion and dedication, left him only himself, which was not enough.

And apparently he was not altogether happy. Mrs. Warre Cornish, meeting him at Farringford, reports: "He moved slowly . . . and looked sad. . . . There were hard lines, too, near the mouth, which, like his grave motion, marked him as a man of sorrows."[20] And Sir Henry Taylor wrote of him in 1860: "In the midst of all this beauty and comfort stands Alfred Tennyson, grand, but very gloomy, whom it is sadness to see; and one has to think of his works to believe that he can escape into regions of glory and light."[21] Hawthorne, seeing him in July 1857 at Manchester, set down in his journal a fuller impression.

Tennyson is the most picturesque figure, without affectation, that I ever saw; of middle size, rather slouching, dressed entirely in black, and with nothing white about him except the collar of his shirt, which methought might have been cleaner the day before. He had on a black wide-awake hat, with round crown and wide, irregular brim, beneath which came down his long black hair, looking terribly tangled; he had a long, pointed beard, too, a little browner than the hair, and not so abundant as to encumber any of the expression of his face. His frock coat was buttoned across the breast, though the afternoon was warm. His face was very dark, and not exactly a smooth face, but worn, expressing great sensitiveness, though not, at that moment the pain and sorrow which is seen in his bust. His eyes were black; . . . There was an entire absence of stiffness in his figure; no set-up in him at all; no nicety or trimness; and if there had been, it would have spoiled his whole aspect. . . . I heard his voice; a base voice, but not of resounding depth; a voice rather broken as it were, and ragged about the edges, but pleasant to the ear. . . . in his whole presence, I was indescribably sensible of a morbid painfulness in him, a something not to be meddled with. Very soon he left the saloon, shuffling along the floor with short irregular steps, a very queer gait, as if he were walking in slippers too loose for him. . . . He is exceedingly nervous, and altogether as un-English as possible; . . . Un-English as he was, and sallow and unhealthy, Tennyson had not, however, an American look. . . .[22]

For these last forty years we have (roughly) 650 pages of *Memoir* as against 350 for his earlier life: if a real biography is ever written the proportions will have to be inverted.

On 16 March 1854 Lionel was born, and while Mrs. Tennyson was ill afterwards her poet "set her right by mesmerizing—the effect was really wonderful." At the same time he was injuring his eyes with a small-print Persian grammar. In August he gave himself a holiday at Glastonbury and down along the coast as far as Bournemouth. Later, at Farringford he was visited by the Simeons and Aubrey de Vere, and discussed Roman Catholicism with them. At the end of the year came the incident of 'The Charge of the Light Brigade,' which carried over into the next (25 April 1855). By spring he had finished 'Maud' and in June went up to Oxford for his honorary D.C.L. In September he was walking in the New Forest, gathering imagery for 'Vivien,' and in February of the next year he "resumed" his Arthurian plans, that is, he really began, with 'Nimuë,' the series of episodes which grew gradually into the Idylls of the King.[23] In April 1856 he bought Farringford with the proceeds of the sale of 'Maud.' In July and August the family travelled in Wales, Tennyson continuing his work on 'Enid' and incorporating Welsh scenery in the text. For 9 July 1857 Mrs. Tennyson wrote in her diary:

A. has brought me as a birthday present the first two lines that he has made of 'Guinevere' which might be the nucleus of a great poem. Arthur is parting from Guinevere and says:
> 'But hither shall I never come again,
> Never lie by thy side; see thee no more:
> Farewell!'

This, the Parting of Arthur and Guinevere, was finished in January 1858 and the Idyll completed in March. In the summer he wrote, for variety, 'The Grandmother,' and continued his Idylls with 'The Fair Maid of Astolat';[n] and later made a trip alone to Norway gathering imagery. Soon after, he finished 'Sea Dreams,' and his friends urged him to publish, in spite of the "mosquitoes," *scil.,* the critics.

The intrusion of 'The Grandmother' and 'Sea Dreams' into this Arthurian group, that is, the interweaving of Idylls of the King and Idylls of the Hearth, indicates either a rich fecundity or else something less than complete absorption in the great subject of the Round Table. The answer is to be found both in Tennyson's subsequent hesitation, even after the popular success of the first Idylls in 1859, and in the two long letters of December 1858 from Jowett to Mrs. Tennyson. The first of these begins: "You asked me whether I could suggest any subjects for poetry"; and continues to oblige through two printed pages, with a tactless intercalary remark that "Subjects like blackbirds seem to me capable of being gathered off every hedge." Half of the second letter is devoted to the same problem.[24] The words of FitzGerald at once come to mind: "He wants a story to treat, being full of poetry with nothing to put it in."[25]

The first four Idylls were thus written almost *dans un jet.* For ten years Tennyson had been meditating the subject, and when the impulse to write came composition was easy. But after that the impulse flagged. He began reading at once for 'Pelleas and Ettarre'

[n] Woolner wrote to Mrs. Tennyson, 7 June 1858: "I most earnestly wish you could persuade him to do the Maid of Astolat, not only for the extreme beauty of the subject, but for the sake of introducing much of Sir Launcelot, he being a character of such terrible importance to the 'Guenevere' poem, and the immense suggestions arising from the poor lady's death." On 12 October Mrs. Tennyson implied that the Maid of Astolat was progressing; and 19 February 1859: "The 'Maid of Astolat' is quite finished now, all but last touches. I do not think you will find her all unworthy of your ideal. A. is better again and very cheerful." On 26 March 1859 Woolner heard the poem read at Little Holland House, and the next day wrote to Mrs. Tennyson: "I think it all that can be possibly desired and its completeness struck me equally with its versatility. I think if there is one portion more beautiful than any other, it is that which was the most difficult to do, and which you thought the only part likely to jar upon the modern mind; I mean that where the Lily Maid herself makes love to Launcelot just before he takes his final leave; nothing could have been more perfect and nothing more sublimely modest; in fact I think this particular part a consummate triumph of poetic skill; and this very boldness of the girl's evidently springs from the most absolute purity of heart; and this with shadow of doom that we feel surely to be creeping over her, create a pathos in the hapless Maiden's favour, which, together with the sense of what Launcelot loses in the loss of her love, actually are the poem." (Cf. Woolner, *Life and Letters,* pp. 149, 153, 163, 168.)

and possibly made now his prose sketch, but it was nearly ten years before he wrote the Idyll; and in the summer he considered the Tristram and Iseult story, but got no farther with it. In February 1859 he tried an experimental poem of some power, 'Boadicea,' and then, while the last proofs of the Idylls were being corrected he responded to the political turmoil on the continent, and to what some regarded as threats of invasion, by dashing off 'Riflemen, Form!' Then he went with Palgrave to Portugal and was very uncomfortable there, but returned with some pleasant memories. The next summer (1860) however he set out for Cornwall, followed by Woolner, Palgrave, Holman Hunt, and Val Prinsep at various stages, and sometimes walking ten miles a day for several consecutive days covered the same ground as in the summer of 1848. As usual he gathered his "nature-similes," but there is no mention of King Arthur either in his own or in Palgrave's account of the journey.

In February 1861 he wrote 'The Northern Farmer,' a nostalgic poem drawn not from his present life but from old memories of Lincolnshire; and read Malory without tangible result. In May he started for Cambridge to receive a degree, but before reaching London he was turned back by a palpitation of the heart and stopped at Winchester on the way home. Later in the summer the family travelled in the Auvergne and the Pyrenees (where they met Clough) and he wrote the reminiscent 'All along the Valley' at Cauteretz. In October he produced, at the request of Her Majesty's Commissioners the 'Ode Sung at the Opening of the International Exhibition'; in November his mind was working on "Woolner's fisherman's story"; and after the death of the Prince Consort in December he began the Dedication to his new edition of the 'Idylls,' which pleased the Queen and led to his first personal interview.

In January 1862 Spedding, "extremely anxious to know what was being done in the way of poetry," inquired of Woolner and Woolner related the fisherman story and received Spedding's approval, which he passed on to Tennyson. Spedding thought it was "the finest story he had ever heard and was more especially adapted for [Tennyson] than for any other poet, from its piercing sweetness and sublime greatness of soul, tho' such a story he said would make the fortune of any poet."[o] By April he was reading the finished 'Enoch Arden' to Spedding—the actual writing took only a fortnight, though in preparation he consulted FitzGerald and received two long letters together with copious extracts from *Dampier's Voyages*—and Spedding saw his prophecy justified two years later. The August holiday this year was with Palgrave in Derbyshire and Yorkshire, but no verse is reported therefrom; nor from the family tour of southern Yorkshire in 1863, nor from the tour of Brittany in 1864. During these years, after the completion of 'Enoch' in April 1862 Tennyson's muse was quiescent, but besides the distraction of his travels, his social intercourse had become considerable: a great many chosen people were entertained at Farringford (Garibaldi among them), and he was entertained a great deal in London; and in the summer of 1863 the first attack of gout is reported. In 1864 he declined to be made F.R.S. but accepted membership in the Royal Society of Edinburgh. In addition to the Laureate piece, 'A Welcome to Alexandra,' the Milton 'Alcaics' and the other experiments in classical meters, his chief poetic work was 'Aylmer's Field.' This story, like that of 'Enoch,' was a contribution of Woolner's, but the poem itself Tennyson found "incalculably difficult" to write "because the dry facts are so prosaic in themselves."[p]

[o] The history of 'Enoch' goes back much earlier. Just as Mrs. Tennyson had written to Jowett in December 1858 seeking subjects for Alfred's muse, so now she wrote to Woolner, 16 November 1859: "I wish you would give Alfred something to do. He is pretty well but for want of this." Woolner replied, 5 December: "I grieve to hear that the Poet is not well, and most sincerely hope that if a subject for a poem will make him better that he will soon succeed in pleasing himself. I wish I could persuade him to do the tale of the Sailor which I told him of years ago I should think." Apparently nothing happened; for 11 April Woolner promised to write out the Sailor story; and 7 December 1860 Mrs. Tennyson wrote to Woolner: "Beyond all price to me would be a worthy subject for Alfred, one which would fix him whether he would or no." Cf. Woolner, as above, pp. 181, 184, 189, 202; Woolner's prose version of 'The Fisherman's Story' may be found pp. 208-212.

[p] Mrs. Bradley's diary, in Materials, ii, 383. Cf. also the Reminiscences of

Sir Frederick Pollock: "'Aylmer's Field' had given him more trouble than anything he ever did. At one time he had to put it aside altogether for six months, the story was so intractable, and it was so difficult to deal with modern manners and conversation." The distractions of these years may have increased the difficulty. Woolner wrote out his sketch of 'The Sermon' and sent it to Mrs. Tennyson early in July 1862. By the end of the year Tennyson was working at it. So late as 24 October 1863 Mrs. Tennyson wrote to Woolner: "He will not give 'The Sermon' up, though I advise him, wicked creature that I am, you will say. I long for him to be at the 'sangreal,' feeling sure that this is his work and the days are going fast for him and for me." After the poem was finished Woolner wondered "whether it is not too beautiful almost—and whether something more stern and craggy would not have seemed to me more appropriate." Cf. Woolner, as above, pp. 218, 219, 230, 240, 252; Woolner's prose version of 'The Sermon' may be found pp. 219-225.

For some time now tourists had been "overwhelming Fresh-water in the summer," and in June 1867 the Tennysons found and bought Blackhorse Copse, an almost inaccessible place in Black-down, a few miles from Haslemere, and started plans with James Knowles for the new house, henceforward called Aldworth. In December, says Mrs. Tennyson's diary, "He brought down to me his psalm-like poem, 'Higher Pantheism.' Louise Simeon [daughter of Sir John Simeon], who was with us a day or two later, said: 'As I sat at breakfast, he came behind me, and in fun dropped on my plate the MS of 'Wages' which he had perfected during the night." Nothing, it must be said, in the Materials or in the *Memoir* prepares us for two poems of this sort at this time; it appeared that he was reading Lucretius, but not that he was at work on a poem about him.[26] But evidently after a period of desuetude the urge to compose had returned, or at least "a longing came for regular work."[q] Mrs. Tennyson's diary for 2 March 1868 contains this interesting fact: "A. T. read some of his own Poems from the 1830 book and made merry over them." The same entry records Tennyson's decision, after taking legal advice, to sever connections with the Moxon firm, which had published his poetry for thirty-six years. There had been rumors of the firm's impending bankruptcy, and more recently Tennyson was annoyed by its form of advertising. In January of the next year he signed with Strahan, who promised him £4000 per annum. Meanwhile, he had entertained Longfellow in July (thought him "very English") and discussed spiritualism with him; and in August, Darwin, who agreed that his "theory of Evolution does not make against Christianity." And in September he had written the 'Holy Grail' Idyll very rapidly, having "seen the subject clearly for some time" and made a prose outline of it;[r] and

q Cf. Mrs. Bradley's diary: *"Jan. 25th* [1868]. A long afternoon before dinner talking with E. T. [Mrs. Tennyson]. Two chief topics: *The Boys* [Hallam and Lionel], and her desire to get 'the Lover's Tale' added to etc. and published. A. T. told us how much better he felt spiritually, mentally, and bodily, while engaged on some long Poem, and how often in the intervals, when only throwing off small things such as 'Wages' and others for Magazines, he found time hang heavily, life became wearisome, and a longing came for regular work.

(He told us this at Winchester, . . .)." Mrs. Bradley's diary makes record also of an evening's enjoyment of waltzing, in which Tennyson "did not sit down once, he was so merry and full of fun."

r "It came like a breath of inspiration," says Mrs. Tennyson. "I was pleased to think that the Queen and the Crown Princess wished him to write it." So also did Macaulay and the Duke of Argyll. In May she wrote: "I doubt whether the 'San Graal' would have been written but for my endeavour and the Queen's wish, and that of the Crown soon he was planning to "write three or four more 'Idylls' and link them together as well as I may."[27] It was now, accordingly, that the 'Idylls of the King' in the form we know it—as a series of more or less related 'epical' episodes—was conceived. By the end of February 1869 'The Coming of Arthur' was "finished" and Leodogran's dream added in May, "giving the drift of the whole poem." At the same time 'Sir Pelleas' was commenced, but was interrupted for a rapid tour of Switzerland with Frederick Locker and moving into the newly finished house at Aldworth; and then work was resumed in the autumn with 'Gareth and Lynnette.' By December the new volume was ready, containing, besides the poems already mentioned, 'The Passing of Arthur' and 'The Golden Supper' (a kind of conclusion to the old 'Lover's Tale'). This year of 1869 he could look upon as eminently successful. In addition to the continental holiday, the completion of Aldworth, and the entertaining of many friends at Farringford, he had been made an honorary Fellow of Trinity College, Cambridge (after twice declining an honorary degree from the University) and had helped found the Metaphysical Society (which lasted till 1880); and, more than all this, he had found time and inclination to write. The profits of his publishing amounted this year to £10,000.

"I don't think I have yet finished the Arthurian legends," he wrote to Spedding 19 January 1870, "otherwise I might consider your Job theme." And in the same letter he announced that he had "taken chambers in Victoria Street for 3 years": the taste of 'the world' was still sweet. But in July he was seized with gout in town, was brought to Aldworth, and there worked on 'The Last Tournament.' November 1871 found him still writing 'Gareth.' In the same month he sent 'England and America' to the New York *Ledger* for £1,000. 'Gareth' was finished in July 1872; and in December the Epilogue to the 'Idylls.'

The year 1873 continued much as before: Farringford, Aldworth, London, and many visitors. On 10 March came a telegram inquiring if some honor were offered him by the Queen, would it be acceptable. He replied courteously that "he did not himself care

---

Princess. Thank God for it. (He had the subject on his mind for years, ever since he began to write about Arthur and his Knights.)" This Idyll was more to Mrs. Tennyson's taste than the 'Vivien' for example.

for any honour except as a symbol of the Queen's kindness." On the 29th Gladstone offered him a baronetcy. Tennyson said he and his wife preferred to "remain plain Mr. and Mrs.," but suggested: "if it were possible, the title should first be assumed by our son at any age it may be thought right to fix upon." Since this was contrary to all precedent the matter was dropped. In December 1874 the Queen renewed the offer, now through Disraeli, with the same result. But in 1883 the offer (through Gladstone again) was raised to a barony, and after some hesitation (and to the distress of many admirers) Tennyson accepted "for the sake of literature."

Towards the end of 1873 a new note is heard. On 8 November he went with Thackeray's daughter and his two sons to see Irving's *Richelieu,* and after the performance he "told Irving how he thought that *Hamlet* ought to be acted."[8] A few days later Furnivall wanted to make him president of the new Shakespeare Society he was founding. And finally the matter becomes quite plain when Mrs. Tennyson's diary for 11 March 1874 says: "A. T. thought of making a play of 'Lady Jane Grey' "; for 10 April: "Lately we have been reading Froude's *Mary,* for A. T. had been thinking about a play of 'Queen Mary,' and had sketched two or three scenes." He had considered also William the Silent, but preferred an English subject. Knowles' suggestion of the Armada was rejected as unworkable. He began now to attend the theatre in London and to read Shakespeare (always a favorite), more than before; and for the next seven years he devoted himself to dramatic composition.

In 1872 his great work, of such irregular growth and structure, the 'Idylls of the King,' was all but complete; the one additional Idyll, 'Balin and Balan,' a final effort to make the story seem continuous, was written at this time but withheld from the public until 1885. The poet was now sixty-five years old, but there was no reason why he should lay down his pen; for, as the event proved certainly, he still retained his mental vigor and the old dexterity of hand. He had written, with varying success yet without conspicuous failure, nearly all kinds of poetry, lyric and narrative, and reflective, with occasional hints of satire, and there remained but one untried, the most difficult of all, poetic drama. Not literally un-

[8] On a similar occasion, according to Miss Thackeray (later Lady Ritchie), Tennyson explained their art to some actors, "going straight to the point in his own downright fashion."

tried, however, for he had begun, or almost begun, his long career of composition with a blank verse drama at the age of sixteen. Now at the age of sixty-five he might well resume. The reasons for this remarkable extension of his poetic activity are not recorded in the *Memoir*, but some of them are not difficult to infer. The desire to enlarge his scope need not be taken seriously as a conscious or prideful motive. Yet the way was open and the difficulties were such as he could not understand. The opportunity was there and the signs of forbiddal were not obvious to him. This was probably the real reason: he saw the opportunity and seized it, without comprehending its snares. As early as 'Maud' he had experimented in a quasi-dramatic mode. There were elements of dramatic construction in 'The Last Tournament,' which were perhaps indicative of a subconscious tendency towards dramatic form, and his sense of being handicapped by narrative technique while composing 'Gareth and Lynnette'[28] suggests again the direction of his mind. And he may have known that 'Enoch Arden' had already twice been turned into acting drama by other hands.[29]

'Queen Mary' was finished and published in 1875, and a new ending added for the acting edition in 1876. 'Harold' was ready before the end of 1876 (the first edition is dated 1877), and in December 'Becket' was begun. But 'Becket,' by far the most ambitious of the historical trilogy, took longer. It was finished and privately printed in 1879, but Tennyson "considered that the time was not ripe for its publication" and withheld it for revision (and perhaps for negotiation with Irving with a view towards acting versions) until 1884. It was not performed until 6 February 1893, after the poet's death.

Meanwhile, the advancing years brought their customary changes. He continued to entertain many friends at Aldworth, though no longer with the almost perpetual motion of their coming and going which marked the pre-Aldworth days. "My father was extremely happy," says the *Memoir*, s.a. 1870, "now that he felt his great work of the Epic of Arthur was nearing its completion: and it impressed the Bradleys that, in spite of vexatious publishing matters, he was marvellously calm and genial." And a little later, as of 1875: "As years went by he became calmer and more restful in himself. To plant new trees and to watch the growth of what were already planted, continued to be unfailing sources of pleasure to him. His hours of work were somewhat changed, Sir Andrew Clark [his friend and physician] having insisted on his walking before luncheon and resting afterwards." Until 1882, with the exception of 1874, he took a house in London for part of each winter (usually from February till Easter), spent the summers at Aldworth, and other months at Farringford—a settled routine varied by holidays of decreasing frequency on the continent.

In the spring of 1879 his favorite brother Charles (Tennyson Turner) died, and soon after this he became "very unwell, suffering from a liver attack, and hearing ghostly voices." Sir Andrew in the following spring ordered him either to America or to Venice. Finding at the moment no suitable passage to Canada, Tennyson elected Venice (which anyway he had never seen); and after reaching Venice *via* Munich, Innsbruck, and the Dolomites, returned *via* Verona and the Lago di Garda, where he composed one of his prettiest occasional poems, "Row us out from Desenzano." This was in 1880. Later in the year he published *Ballads, and Other Poems,* containing 'Rizpah' and 'The Revenge.' And meanwhile his new play 'The Falcon,' having enjoyed a run of sixty-seven nights beginning in December 1879 at the St. James' Theatre, was followed by 'The Cup,' which Irving and Ellen Terry performed at the Lyceum for over a hundred and thirty nights beginning 3 January 1881. The success of these plays on the stage, however much it may have been due to the acting, the mounting, or the impetus of Tennyson's popularity as a poet, and regardless of their dramatic merits, was encouraging and gratifying,[t] and led to 'The Promise of May.' This "unlucky piece,": which was really a domestic idyll in dramatic form, was written "somewhat unwillingly, at the importunate entreaty of a friend who had urged him to try his hand on a modern village tragedy," and was advertised as an attack on Socialism; but it ran for five weeks with a sort of *succès de scandale.* This was the end, for 'The Foresters,' written in 1881, was reserved for production in New York eleven years later and just before the aged author's death. For seven years, at

[t] A pleasantly ironic by-product was Tennyson's letter to Browning about 'The Cup,' 8 February 1880: "That you, whom Professor Morley calls a born dramatist, should approve of my little play, is good news to me and mine."

the age of sixty-five to seventy-one, Tennyson was an active prac-
tising dramatist and in that time wrote seven plays.

On the publication of 'Despair' in the *Nineteenth Century* for
November 1881, came "much bitter criticism," says the *Memoir*
indignantly, "since the public did not recognize it as a 'dramatic
monologue.'" The critical attacks are known, and Swinburne's
parody, 'Disgust,' but they represent the *public* only in a limited
sense. What we should like to know is Tennyson's feeling; but we
are not told.

The year 1883 was notable for three things: the death of Fitz-
Gerald, the voyage to Norway and Denmark with Gladstone in
September, and the peerage in December. On the last "much bitter
criticism" followed again,[u] but the voyage was an unmixed pleas-
ure: the *Memoir* gives a full account of it, including Gladstone's
tribute to the poet in a speech before the magistrates of Kirkwall,
en route, the grand dinner given by the King of Denmark and the
luncheon on shipboard next day attended by an Emperor and his
Empress, two Kings and their Queens, eight Princes, six Princesses,
a Grand Duke, several Counts and Countesses, a Commodore and
three Admirals, and various Ministers of State, before whom
Tennyson read 'The Grandmother' and the 'Bugle Song.' After
his return home he "was in great spirits" and wrote to Mary Boyle
(aunt of the Audrey Boyle who in the following year became Hal-
lam's wife): "I verily believe that the better heart of me beats
stronger at 74 than ever it did at 18."[v] The death of "his old and
valued friend Fitzgerald" is recorded briefly in the *Memoir*. Old

u "Why should I be selfish," said
Tennyson, "and not suffer an honour
(as Gladstone says) to be done to litera-
ture in my name? For myself I felt,
especially in the dark days that may be
coming on, that a peerage might pos-
sibly be more of a disadvantage than an
advantage to my sons: I cannot tell. I
have been worried because, being of a
nervous, sensitive nature, I wished as
soon as possible to get over the dis-
agreeable results, and the newspaper
comments and abuse." But not without
a sense of humor (I suppose) he wrote
to Francisque Michel: "I thank you for
your kind congratulations about the
peerage; but being now in my 75th year,
and having lost almost all my youthful

contemporaries, I see myself, as it were,
in an extra page of Holbein's 'Dance of
Death,' and standing before the mouth
of an open sepulchre while the Queen
hands me a coronet, and the skeleton
takes it away, and points me downward
into the darkness. Pardon me, if this
sounds too tragic."

v Yet, as always, he was moody. Phillips
Brooks tells of a meeting about this time
(perhaps in the spring of 1882: the *Me-
moir* is vague): "Tennyson was inclined
to be misanthropic, talked about Social-
ism, Atheism, and another great catas-
trophe like the French Revolution com-
ing on the world . . . . but he let himself
be contradicted about his gloomy views,
and by and by became more cheerful."

Fitz, a trying friend sometimes because he was gruff and spoke the truth, but none more honest and faithful, fitted ill into the Far-ringford life, and even less into that of Aldworth, if he had gone there. In youth they had been kindred souls and boon companions, grumbling and laughing together; but their paths diverged, and yet FitzGerald in his blanket and his East Anglian solitude never envied Tennyson his success and his noble friends. He remained "Still your old Fitzcrotchet, you see, still!" though neglected. Tennyson's perfect little poem, 'To Edward Fitzgerald,' written after their last meeting in 1876 though not published until two years after FitzGerald's death, was ample amends, however, if amends were wanted.

The Laureate suffered more frequently now from gout and com-plained of his eyes, but he continued to compose and by the end of 1885 had a new volume out, *Tiresias, and Other Poems,* most of them however already published in the periodicals. Then in April 1886 his younger son Lionel died of jungle fever in India and as a kind of solace he worked harder than ever on the new 'Locksley Hall.' This poem, with two small pieces and 'The Prom-ise of May' (already acted but never published) made up a volume issued (as usual for the Christmas trade) in December, but dated 1887. The summer excursion this year was taken on a yacht, and when he landed at Tintagil he had to be helped up the cliff. In 'Vastness' he continued his insistence on the immortality of the soul and in 'Owd Roa' he versified a contemporary incident in his old domestic-idyll manner. Jowett (still offering subjects) wrote to Lady Tennyson: "His memory and his powers are so undiminished and his experience so increased, that I think he might even now surpass himself"; but this was dictated more by courtesy than by conviction. He continued at Aldworth to take his two-hour walk in all weathers; his recorded conversation is full of the splendid commonplaces of wisdom which often sound so impressive from the lips of very old men. In the autumn of 1888 he became danger-ously ill of rheumatic gout and was "as near death as a man could be without dying"; yet he continued to write ('By an Evolutionist' and 'The Throstle') and by April the doctor pronounced him "per-fectly recovered, quite healthy and sound.[w] The birthday tributes

[w] Another of those serio-comic inci-dents which are strewn through the *Memoir* occurred at this time. The doc-tor, Sir Andrew Clark, when about to

in August gratified him: some of the fulsome adulation made him "miserable" and "Most of most of the things said of me in the newspapers are lies, lies, lies"; but he was none the less pleased and wrote himself to thank Swinburne for his "praise or overpraise."[30] Most of the other congratulators were answered by an advertisement in the *Times*.

And still the immortal muse continued active. In December 1889 he published a collection of old and new poems—among the latter the titular 'Demeter,' 'Merlin and the Gleam,' and 'Crossing the Bar'—and was full of plans for yet more. 'Ormuzd and Ahriman' he had sketched in 1885; now he "thought of weaving into a great stage drama" the old Tristram story. But it was of course too late: he could never have managed the Tristram subject even in his best years—it has snared many another poet—and the posthumous volume underscores with pathos his

> *Still nursing the unconquerable hope,*
> *Still clutching the inviolable shade.*

One admires his indomitable intention. In the summer of 1892 his walks at Aldworth "dwindled down"; the weather was bad, and he gradually grew weaker. By the end of September Death had his hands on the Bard, the skeleton was pointing him "downward into the darkness." On Tuesday, 4 October, he cried "I want the blinds up, I want to see the sky and the light" and repeated "the sky and the light"; and in the early hours of Thursday he set forth

> *To the island-valley of Avilion.*

---

make his last visit to Tennyson (for this illness) was summoned by the Shah of Persia, then in London. Sir Andrew refused the summons, and the Shah, with a noble sense of both humor and dignity, bestowed upon Tennyson the order of The Lion and the Sun.

CHAPTER THREE

The Palace of Art

BY THE phrase Tennyson's *early poems* is usually meant those which are grouped in the collective editions as Juvenilia and The Lady of Shalott and Other Poems; more strictly the phrase should mean the contents of the volumes of 1830 and 1832, together with, of course, Alfred's share of the *Poems by Two Brothers*. In this chapter I shall review not only these, but also the new poems in the two volumes of 1842, on the ground that they represent Tennyson still largely untouched by external influences—what is sometimes called the essential Tennyson. It is not necessary to hold with FitzGerald that Tennyson produced almost nothing after 1842 that is worth reading; nor is it necessary to maintain with Professor Lounsbury that Tennyson was not much influenced by the reviews of his first two volumes. So far as any generalizations are true, however, one may confidently say that by 1842 Tennyson, at the age of thirty-three, had found himself and had reached such a stage in his development as to show what sort of poet he was by natural gifts and temperament. After 1842 the outside pressures became plainly effective: certain latent or obvious characteristics were either suppressed or enhanced and a few notes added to the scale, but while the poetical qualities remained nearly constant throughout the remaining fifty years, the tone and color of Tennyson's work changed—changed for the worse, in the opinion of many critics. Really, Tennyson became not a better or a worse poet but a different man, practising his art, exercising his gifts on alien material. Superficially it seems rather damaging to assert (or admit) that the elder Tennyson was not a better poet than the younger. There may be some truth in the familiar observation that all poets are young men and that the world does something to their original endowment which is detrimental. Certainly the number of Victorian poets who outlived their best artistic powers is notable: Arnold, Rossetti, Morris, Swinburne, Browning —and perhaps Tennyson. Nearly all of them.

If, therefore, one is to know Tennyson, I will not say at his best but at his most characteristic, one must examine closely the poems collected and rejected in 1842. Tennyson himself reprinted nothing from *Poems by Two Brothers*. His share of that little volume (which he called his "early rot") has only the curious interest of revealing the range of his reading and his earliest models. The influences of Byron, Scott, Moore, Leigh Hunt, and Keats are palpable, particularly that of Byron. The eighteenth century is apparent in

> *All hail, Sublimity! thou lofty one,*
> *For thou dost walk upon the blast, and gird*
> *Thy majesty with terrors, and thy throne*
> *Is on the whirlwind, and thy voice is heard*
> *In thunders and in shakings: thy delight*
> *Is in the secret wood, the blasted heath,*
> *The ruin'd fortress, and the dizzy height,*
> *The grave, the ghastly charnel-house of death,*
> *In vaults, in cloisters, and in gloomy piles,*
> *Long corridors and towers and solitary aisles!*

The lines on 'Midnight' might be studied as a neat composite of various influences. But apart from the great facility in imitation and in conventional prosody there is little from which to prophesy the poems published three years later. The compounds are perhaps worth noticing as anticipating a later mannerism—the "glenriver" and "tendriltwine" of 'Œnone'—

> *And though the cloud-capped mountains, still the same,*
> *Uprear'd each heaven-invading pinnacle;*
> *Yet were the charms of that lone valley fled,*
> *And the grey-winding of the stream was gone.*

And there may be a foretaste of 'In Memoriam' in

> *Almighty Love! whose nameless power*
> *This glowing heart defines too well,*
> *Whose presence cheers each fleeting hour,*

Whose silken bonds our souls compel,
Diffusing such a sainted spell,...

Before whose blaze my spirits shrink,
My senses all are wrapt in thee,
Thy force I own too much, to think
(So full, so great thine ecstasy)
That thou art less than deity!

Thy golden chains embrace the land
The starry sky, the dark blue main;
And at the voice of thy command,
(So vast, so boundless is thy reign)
All nature springs to life again!

Besides the fifty-odd juvenile poems by Alfred in the *Two Brothers* volume and a few more published in the *Memoir* we have now as samples of the pupil pen an extremely remarkable drama (three acts of it) 'The Devil and the Lady,' written at the age of fourteen, though perhaps touched up in the next year or so, and the small volume of *Unpublished Early Poems*.[1] The drama is remarkable from every point of view and justifies Jowett's remark (echoing Dr. Johnson's on Chatterton) that it was "wonderful how the whelp could have known such things." Even the precocity of Swinburne hardly matches it. An aged magician leaves his young wife in charge of a Devil, and in his absence a Lawyer, an Apothecary, a Sailor, a Mathematician-Astronomer, a Soldier, and a Monk all come to make love to her. When the Necromancer suddenly returns the Devil forces them to hide ignominiously and leave the situation in his master's hands. *Caetera desunt.* The various wooers talk each in character, and in the worst tradition of Elizabethan low-comic wit,—

STEPHANIO   *Consider, prithee,*
    How shall the airy ardent kiss make way
    Through the thick folds of that dark veil, which bars
    All access to the fortress of thy soul.
ANTONIO *Ay! Ay! unveil.*
ANGELO   *Disperse thy 'nebulæ.'*
DEVIL *Ay and the* nebulones *that surround me.*

There is a great deal of this in Acts II and III, with strangely learned words for a fourteen-year-old. There is the inevitable Elizabethan joke—

> *My horny scalp*
> *Is buried in the foldings of this veil*
> *To save thy scalp from horns.*

And there is a great deal of fine fustian—

> MAGUS   *Now doth the vollied and rebellowing thunder*
> *Rock the huge earth, and all the dizzy hills*
> *Quake at his coming, while the arrow bolt*
> *With ravaging course athwart the dark immense*
> *Comes rushing on its wings of fire—the North*
> *With hoarse congratulation and wild threats*
> *Gives answer to his brother winds.*

And occasionally something better—

> *The grey cock hath not crow'd, the glow-worm still*
> *Leads on unpal'd his train of emerald light*

and

> *Then came a band of melancholy sprites,*
> *White as their shrouds and motionlessly pale*
> *Like some young Ashwood when the argent Moon*
> *Looks in upon its many silver stems*

and

> *The summer fly*
> *That skims the surface of the deep black pool*
> *Knows not the gulf beneath its slippery path.*
> *Man sees, but plunges madly into it.*

But that the poet whose talents were anything but dramatic should have begun and ended his career with Elizabethan imitations was a mad trick of the Ironies.

In his second year at Cambridge (1829) Tennyson was urged by his father to compete for the Chancellor's medal. Instead of composing a new poem on the set subject of 'Timbuctoo,' thriftily he sent home for the manuscript of a poem called 'Armageddon' written probably when he was fifteen—with the hope of making the old verses over to fit the new topic. Yet, contrary to the usual statement, his prize poem, 'Timbuctoo,' is substantially a new work: only thirty-five of its two hundred and fifty lines are taken from the earlier 'Armageddon.'[2] Interestingly enough, one of the best passages of 'Timbuctoo' occurs in the older version—

> I look'd, but not
> Upon his face, for it was wonderful
> With its exceeding brightness, and the light
> Of the great Angel Mind which look'd from out
> The starry glowing of his restless eyes.
> I felt my soul grow godlike, and my spirit
> With supernatural excitation bound
> Within me, and my mental eye grew large
> With such a vast circumference of thought,
> That, in my vanity, I seem'd to stand
> Upon the outward verge and bound alone
> Of God's omniscience. Each failing sense,
> As with a momentary flash of light,
> Grew thrillingly distinct and keen. I saw
> The smallest grain that dappled the dark earth,
> The indistinctest atom in deep air,
> The Moon's white cities, and the opal width
> Of her small, glowing lakes, her silver heights
> Unvisited with dew of vagrant cloud,
> And the unsounded, undescended depth
> Of her black hollows. The clear galaxy
> Shorn of its hoary lustre, wonderful,
> Distinct and vivid with sharp points of light,
> Blaze within blaze, an unimagin'd depth
> And harmony of planet-girded suns
> And moon-encircled planets, wheel in wheel,
> Arch'd the wan sapphire. Nay—the hum of men,
> Or other things talking in unknown tongues,
> And notes of busy Life in distant worlds
> Beat, like a far wave, on my anxious ear.[3]

This is the first expression, moreover, of Tennyson's experience of the mystic's trance; and the lines beginning "I saw The smallest grain" seem unmistakably to echo Shelley, though they were written before Tennyson became acquainted with Shelley.[a] He as-

[a] So, at any rate, it would seem: for he says (Memoir II, 285) that 'The Lover's Tale' was written in his nineteenth year "before I had ever seen a Shelley."

serted, moreover, that 'Timbuctoo,' as well as 'The Lover's Tale,' was not "in any way imitative of any poet," [4] yet one can hardly miss the Wordsworthian tone of part of the passage just quoted and particularly of the lines closely following—

> *the level calm*
> *Is ridg'd with restless and increasing spheres*
> *Which break upon each other, each th' effect*
> *Of separate impulse, but more fleet and strong*
> *Than its precursor, till the eye in vain. . .*

Others besides the academic judges admired 'Timbuctoo.' Bishop Wordsworth (nephew of the poet) called it a wonderful production and said "if it had come out with Lord Byron's name, it would have been thought as fine as anything he ever wrote";[5] which was high praise indeed for 1829. Arthur Hallam, writing about it to Gladstone, 14 September 1829, spoke of its splendid imaginative power, and added: "I consider Tennyson as promising fair to be the greatest poet of our generation, perhaps of our century." Matthew Arnold also prophesied Tennyson's greatness when as a youth he first read 'Timbuctoo.'[6] This may now seem more like divination than prophecy. Certainly the greatness which followed was of a different cast.

Poems, Chiefly Lyrical, 1830, brings us the first real Tennyson. The little volume contains fifty-six poems, most of them short, poems by an undergraduate nineteen years old. Nearly half of them (twenty-three, to be precise) were afterwards suppressed, that is, never reprinted in any authorized edition;[7] and they may properly be left in limbo. The others, though very unequal, are enough. They include the little gallery of feminine portraits, fragile, moody, and pretty (some too-pretty), but in spite of affectations charming in their kind. They include the studies in delicate realism from which was to develop that passion for absolute accuracy which becomes a hall-mark of the later poet—

> *The seven elms, the poplars four . . .*
> *One willow over the river wept . . .*
> *. . . that sharp-headed worm*

and in the second stanza of 'Song' ("A spirit haunts the year's last hours") where the method betrays itself—

71

The air is damp, and hush'd, and close,
As a sick man's room when he taketh repose
  An hour before death;
My very heart faints and my whole soul grieves
At the moist rich smell of the rotting leaves,
  And the breath
  Of the fading edges of box beneath,
And the year's last rose.

and best of course in 'Mariana'—who was the poetic mother both
of the Lady of Shalott and of the Blessed Damozel—

The rusted nails fell from the knots
That held the pear to the gable-wall . . .

Her tears fell with the dews at even . . .
She could not look on the sweet heaven,
  Either at morn or eventide . . .

And ever when the moon was low . . .

And they include, along with these verses of more melody than
meaning, the earnest but too ambitious 'Supposed Confessions'
and his first attempt at the lyrical grand manner, almost successful—

The poet in a golden clime was born,
  With golden stars above;
Dower'd with the hate of hate, the scorn of scorn,
  The love of love.

The rest is not quite equal, but the aim is high and the long-
breathed sentences running from stanza to stanza are an achieve-
ment—

The viewless arrows of his thoughts were headed
  And wing'd with flame,

Like Indian reeds blown from his silver tongue,
  And of so fierce a flight,
From Calpe unto Caucasus they sung,
  Filling with light

And vagrant melodies the winds which bore
  Them earthward till they lit; . . .

Meaning strains at the words, and Shelley's voice is almost too clear; one is not sure how seriously to take the poet's claim; but the claim to be taken seriously is obvious.

Some of the lesser notes also sound in these poems. The hyphenless compounds which needlessly vexed the early reviewers were a passing affection. The tendency to philosophise, however, which might now be dismissed as a youthful errancy, has already begun and will prove itself a growing bane: 'Nothing will Die,' 'All Things Will Die,' 'Supposed Confessions,' 'The Deserted House': an unleavened didacticism cherished for its own pretentious sake. And, finally, the crisp and easy personal poems begin in this volume: 'To——' and 'A Character': later to become a Tennysonian staple for which he has seldom received due credit.

The next volume, less than two years after the first, confirmed both the weakness and the promise of 1830. In *Poems,* 1833,[8] the die was cast; with this volume (as FitzGerald said) "he took his ground." The female portraits continued, but no better for being less airy-fairy. The sonnets continued, but they too were no better; Tennyson never adjusted his talents to the special requirements of this form. It cannot be said that he was unable to master them; it must have been that after sundry trials he lost interest. With 'The Miller's Daughter' he approached the precipice; with 'The May Queen' he plunged; and thereafter the perils of bathos lay all about him. The success of these poems with so many of his readers betrayed not only what was false within Victorian taste but what was false in the poet's temperament. By these two poems the Devil, or whoever it is that rules the netherworld of art, made his first overtures to Alfred Tennyson, and before long, the good people of England abetting, Alfred Tennyson, soon to be their Laureate, had bartered half his artistic soul. The path of this *facilis descensus* I shall attempt to follow in a later chapter. It is enough to record here that the fall began in 1832; throughout the remaining sixty years of constant composition he never freed himself from the foul mire of Victorian sentimentality. This was his special compromise with the Age.

The good things of this volume are still, one must remember, the work of a young man of twenty-two or twenty-three. And if, as one critic says, "Tennyson never looked younger" than when he wrote

73

The yellowleavèd waterlily,
The greensheathèd daffodilly,
Tremble in the water chilly
Round about Shalott—

one may answer: why should he not look young? And did he not
write just a little below—

All in the blue unclouded weather
Thick-jewell'd shone the saddle-leather,
The helmet and the helmet feather
Burn'd like one burning flame together,
  As he rode down from Camelot;
As often thro' the purple night,
Below the starry clusters bright,
Some bearded meteor, trailing light,
  Moves over green Shalott.

("From" was wrong, so he changed it to "to"; and "green" became
"still" for plain reasons.) And as for youthful-looking, did he not
write 'What did little birdie say' when he was fifty and 'The Bee
and the Flower' when he was over eighty? Certainly there were
flaws in the first version of 'The Lady of Shalott,' but he soon re-
vised it very thoroughly, and removed all but one or two of them.
'The Lady of Shalott' of 1842 is as near perfect as the work of
mortals ever gets to be, in structure, in details, and in the evoca-
tion of sight, sound, and feeling. It is a pure distillation, with the
aid of Spenser and Keats, of Malory's soft romanticism, and is of
course more brilliant than Malory could hope to be. It is not a kind
of poetry one wants many examples of: even Tennyson did not
try to repeat his success with it. But a few years later Rossetti car-
ried the method—fantasy crossed with realism—one step farther in
'The Blessed Damozel.' For music, sheer decorative richness, and
magic these two poems are *hors concours.* Keats had first found the
tune, in the melancholy key; Tennyson added splendor; Rossetti,
with less of both these qualities in obvious form, reduced them to a
quintessence.

'The Lotos-Eaters' also deals in magic, yet of a different kind.
The introductory Spenserian stanzas, consciously archaized in
language, are deliberately unnatural. The 'Choric Song' has al-
ways been a favorite, but it is uneven—the first and fourth stanzas

being easily the best—and imperfectly sustained, and the revised final section contains a palpably false note: "Let us swear an oath."

The other two fine poems of this 1833 volume 'Œnone' and 'The Palace of Art,' remind us of an important distinction sometimes overlooked. These two poems as we read them now are the revised versions of ten years later. Much more than in the case of the two just commented upon, the revisions remade the poems. Scholars have often complained of the harshness of contemporary criticism of the first volumes, especially Christopher North's, and biographers have complained of the violence of Tennyson's sensibilities and the time lost in those ten years of silence. But the truth is quite otherwise. It would not be unfair to say that the second volume followed too soon after the first. It showed progress, but not enough progress; for Tennyson, in spite of his precocity did not mature rapidly. He needed the rebuff of the reviewers and the unsettling shock of Hallam's death. Properly described, therefore, the good things of 1833 are really the resultant of the critical attacks and his own slow development, for they are really the work not of the year 1833 but of his ten years' revising. Or, to say this more crudely, the poems of the 1833 volume which we now admire are the poems of 1842. Most of the excellences of 'The Lady of Shalott' and 'The Lotos-Eaters' are present in the earlier versions; but this is not true of 'Œnone' and 'The Palace of Art,' and for this reason the warning is necessary.

To illustrate this development it will be profitable, I believe, to examine in some detail the alterations in 'Œnone,' even at the risk of seeming pedestrian and pedantic. The 1833 text (which for convenience I shall call A) contains 256 lines; the 1842 text (B) is 8 lines longer. Slightly more than half of the two versions (144 lines) are identical, and in 27 other lines the differences are not great. Six lines of A were cancelled and 14 new lines were added in B, nearly all in the last paragraph, and 9 of them in one consecutive passage. The first line shows a typical improvement, from "There is a dale in Ida" to "There lies a vale in Ida." A few lines below B adds "at noon" partly to fill out the line (which had lost two syllables in the rewriting of the long description) and partly to make clearer the time, which is a little confused by the antecedent action of the three goddess' offers. In line 18 the "vine-entwined stone" became "fragment twined with vine": the compound is removed but not the rime. And in the next line "mountain-shadow" became "mountain-shade," as being more accurate and perhaps to avoid the feminine ending. In Here's speech (B 113)

> *Or upland glebe wealthy in oil and wine.*
> *Honour and homage, tribute, tax and toll*

was changed to

> *Or labour'd mine undrainable of ore.*
> *Honour," she said; "and homage, tax and toll.*[b]

Ore may suggest greater wealth than oil and wine, but the alteration seems unnecessary. In the other line something had to be done with the overworked alliteration, so we separate the *h*'s and throw out one *t,* though "tax and toll" is on the verge of pleonasm and it would have been better (meter permitting) to retain "tribute." Two lines farther on "beneath" is substituted for "below"; in line 135 "spirit" is substituted for "heart" to avoid the rime with "apart"; and in line 145 "Will" becomes "Would," a nice point of idiom. The last of these smaller changes to be noted is that of "oceanborn" to "beautiful"—

> *Idalian Aphrodite oceanborn*

> *Idalian Aphrodite beautiful.*

The reason for this change is clear enough, although not necessarily sound; and the new line is weaker—but Tennyson must have liked the effect, for in 'Timbuctoo' he has

> *Shorn of its hoary lustre, wonderful*

and in 'Morte d'Arthur' thrice

> *Cloth'd in white samite, mystic, wonderful.*

The line which apparently gave Tennyson the most trouble, the only one which was changed after 1842, was 27. In the final text (1884) we read

[b] It is possible to see in this revision an influence of James Beattie's 'The Judgment of Paris' (1765). Cf. Juno's speech—

Deep in yon mountain's womb. . . .
Does the rich gem its liquid radiance wave,
Or flames with steady ray th' imperial ore.

> *The lizard, with his shadow on the stone,*
> *Rests like a shadow, and the winds are dead.*

At first these lines went—

> *The lizard, with his shadow on the stone,*
> *Sleeps like a shadow, and the scarletwing'd*
> *Cicala in the noonday leapeth not.*

This was weak, since the cicala is better known for its singing than for its leaping; so in 1842 it was simplified to

> *Sleeps like a shadow, and the cicala sleeps.*

Tennyson was not satisfied, however. "In these lines describing a perfect stillness," he said, "I did not like the jump, 'Rests like a shadow—and the cicala sleeps.' Moreover, in the heat of noon the cicala is generally at its loudest, though I have read that, in extreme heat, it is silent." So the cicala had to go.[c] The first of the six cancelled lines (A 16)

> *Her neck all marblewhite and marblecold*

had to go because whiteness was not likely in a shepherdess (similarly in A 56 "white" was removed describing Paris' shoulder) and coldness unsuitable for a pursuing lover. B has simply "Her cheek had lost the rose." Then at the end of Here's speech A had two lines of weak and needless repetition

> *The changeless calm of undisputed right,*
> *The highest height and topmost strength of power.*

The omission of these lines is notable because it shows that Tennyson was aware of one of the frequent faults of his early verse, the addition of phrases for phrases' sake. All of the alterations thus far mentioned however are minor ones; all except the last are matters of detail. But when in A Pallas begins

> *Selfreverence, selfknowledge, selfcontrol*
> *Are the three hinges of the gates of Life*
> *That open into power, everyway*
> *Without horizon, bound or shadow or cloud*

[c] But in his note he adds (remembering the earliest version, which only the erudite could be expected to know): "In the Pyrenees, where part of this poem was written, I saw a very beautiful specimen of cicala, which had scarlet wings spotted with black. Probably nothing of the kind exists in Mount Ida."

and the image of the gates (which had been expanded too wide) is reduced to one line

> *These three alone lead life to sovereign power,*

then we feel that Tennyson has taken himself in hand. And this becomes even plainer when the larger revisions are examined.

> *There lies a vale in Ida, lovelier*
> *Than all the valleys of Ionian hills.*
> *The swimming vapour slopes athwart the glen,*
> *Puts forth an arm, and creeps from pine to pine,*
> *And loiters, slowly drawn. On either hand*
> *The lawns and meadow-ledges midway down*
> *Hang rich in flowers, and far below them roars*
> *The long brook falling thro' the clov'n ravine*
> *In cataract after cataract to the sea.*
> *Behind the valley topmost Gargarus*
> *Stands up and takes the morning: but in front*
> *The gorges, opening wide apart, reveal*
> *Troas and Ilion's column'd citadel,*
> *The crown of Troas.*

This is in the best manner of florid descriptive writing; the picture is clearly constructed, and Gargarus is thrown in for local color. But compare the first version, in which the compounds are vexatiously affected and the details are not composed—

> *There is a dale in Ida, lovelier*
> *Than any in old Ionia, beautiful*
> *With emerald slopes of sunny sward, that lean*
> *Above the loud glenriver, which hath worn*
> *A path thro' steepdown granite walls below*
> *Mantled with flowering tendriltwine. In front*
> *The cedarshadowy valleys open wide.*
> *Far-seen, high over all the Godbuilt wall*
> *And many a snowycolumned range divine,*
> *Mounted with awful sculptures—men and Gods,*
> *The work of Gods—bright on the darkblue sky*
> *The windy citadel of Ilion*
> *Shone like the crown of Troas.*

Just what are, for example, the "awful sculptures" distinguishable from the dale in Ida?

The thirty-five lines beginning at B 52 were similarly rewritten.
Here is the first version, with asterisks before the unaltered lines:

*O mother Ida, hearken ere I die.
 I sate alone: the goldensandalled morn
 Rosehued the scornful hills: I sate alone
 With downdropt eyes: whitebreasted like a star
 Fronting the dawn he came: a leopard skin
 From his white shoulder drooped: his sunny hair
*Clustered about his temples like a God's:
*And his cheek brighten'd, as the foambow brightens
 When the wind blows the foam; and I called out,
 'Welcome, Apollo, welcome home, Apollo,
 Apollo, my Apollo, loved Apollo.'

*Dear mother Ida, hearken ere I die.
 He, mildly smiling, in his milkwhite palm
 Close-held a golden apple, lightningbright
 With changeful flashes, dropt with dew of Heaven
 Ambrosially smelling. From his lip,
 Curved crimson, the fullflowing river of speech
*Came down upon my heart.
                          'My own Œnone,
 Beautifulbrowed Œnone, mine own soul,
*Behold this fruit, whose gleaming rind ingrav'n
 "For the most fair" in aftertime may breed
 Deep evilwilledness of heaven and sere
 Heartburning toward hallowed Ilion;
 And all the colour of my afterlife
 Will be the shadow of to-day. To-day
 Here and Pallas and the floating grace
 Of laughterloving Aphrodite meet
 In manyfolded Ida to receive
 This meed of beauty, she to whom my hand
 Award the palm. Within the green hillside,
 Under yon whispering tuft of oldest pine,
 Is an ingoing grotto, strown with spar
 And ivymatted at the mouth, wherein
 Thou unbeholden may'st behold, unheard
*Hear all, and see thy Paris judge of Gods.'

In revision the repeated "I sat alone" is removed, and the fivefold
"Apollo," and most of the compounds; and the smaller changes

are all strengthening improvements. Cancelled also is Paris' prediction of the downfall of Troy, which was not only unnecessary, but also inconsistent with the Cassandra passage at the end; and some classical color, with the early history of the apple, is inserted. The omission of "lip Curv'd crimson" is offset by the addition of the equally bad "blossom of his lips"; and there is little to choose between

> *Thou unbeholden mays't behold, unheard*

and

> *Mayst well behold them unbeheld unheard.*

A little farther on, the fine flower passage is new—

> *And at their feet the crocus brake like fire,*
> *Violet, amaracus, and asphodel,*
> *Lotos and lilies;*

replacing

> *Lustrous with lilyflower, violeteyed*
> *Both white and blue, with lotetree-fruit thickset,*
> *Shadowed with singing pine.*

The introduction of "Fulleyèd Here" in A is much altered in B, where she is identified by her peacock without being named. "Ambrosial" is omitted, having been used once already, and the lush phrase "more lovelier." The flabby line

> *How beautiful they were, too beautiful*

is removed; and, a few lines below, the jingling

> *Such boon from me Heaven's Queen to thee.*

In the second part of Pallas's speech three images are discarded: the miser, the snakes, and the "darkbody of the Sun" and replaced with lines that are simpler and more pointed. The first version went

> *Not as men value gold because it tricks*
> *And blazons outward Life with ornament,*
> *But rather as the miser, for itself.*
> *Good for selfgood doth half destroy selfgood.*

The means and end, like two coiled snakes, infect
Each other, bound in one with hateful love.
So both into the fountain and the stream
A drop of poison falls. Come, hearken to me,
And look upon me and consider me,
So shalt thou find me fairest, so endurance,
Like to an athlete's arm; shall still become
Sinew'd with motion, till thine active will
(As the darkbody of the Sun robed round
With his own ever-emanating lights)
Be flooded o'er with her own effluences,
And thereby grow to freedom.'

But in the revision we get the prudish "divinity disrobed," although he had already been so bold as to call the goddesses naked; and further along, in Œnone's final plea, the "hot lips" and "fruitful kisses" would have been branded as *fleshly* in a poem by Rossetti or Swinburne. The description of Aphrodite is partially rewritten. The goddess draws "backward" (in place of "upward") from her "brows" (in place of "brow")

> *her deep hair*
> *Ambrosial, golden round her lucid throat*
> *And shoulder: from the violets her light foot*
> *Shone rosy-white*

(in place of

> *her dark hair*
> *Fragrant and thick, and on her head upbound*
> *In a purple band: below her lucid neck*
> *Shone ivorylike, and from the ground her foot*
> *Gleamed rosywhite).*

The next line, with its odd word and peculiar rhythm stands unchanged—

> *Between the shadows of the vine-bunches.*

In the remaining eighty-odd verses of the poem the alterations are not extensive. The refrain is changed, a compound ("green-gulphèd") is removed, and for the fine premonitory cry "I will not die alone" two lines are inserted to emphasize Œnone's childlessness. The principal differences are the addition of nine lines expressing her hatred of Eris; and when Paris makes his decision a change which is certainly not an improvement: for the simple

> *I only saw my Paris raise his arm,*
> *I only saw great Here's angry eyes*

the firmer, less rhetorical, but less moving

> *But when I look'd, Paris had rais'd his arm,*
> *And I beheld great Herè's angry eyes.*

Altogether it will be manifest—if anything can be made of such a fragmentary account of the multifold alterations in this poem—that during the ten years' silence Tennyson had not only improved the various details but also made it "almost a new work."[9] When all is said, however, the second 'Œnone' is not a very fine poem. It hardly rises to the passionate pitch that one has a right to expect from the subject. It hardly portrays the intensity of feeling which one has a right to expect from a heartbroken jealous woman. It is not a study either of passion or of character. But as a youthful work of soft romanticism and decorative, in contrast to emotional, poetry it is highly remarkable. Tennyson was quite frank in using the Pyrenean landscape which had stirred his imagination during that revolutionary holiday with Hallam in 1830; he may have regretted at the moment "the impermanence of his impressions in the hurry of travel," but they served him well for this and other poems. He could add enough classical echoes and allusions (some dozen or more are duly noted by the poet himself) to give the requisite tone. He could add also the didactic note about self-reverence, etc., which is certainly off-key in the poem though it is not unclassical in itself. But the real merit of the poem is its exuberant sweetness. The theme is old, but the handling is fresh—the first of Tennyson's quasi-classical pieces. "There is more passion in *Ulysses*," says Mr. Humbert Wolfe, a little scornfully, "than in all the dove-like lamentations of *Oenone*." True; but there is no need to cry down one poem in order to praise another. If 'Œnone' depended for its artistic effects on passion it would be doomed. On the contrary, real feeling, really powerful feeling would interfere with its purpose; for its purpose (whatever Tennyson may have thought) is to be decoratively beautiful, with just enough of the rest—'thought' and 'drama'—to make a setting for the jewel. It is a large decorative panel, no more, in the Palace of Art.

In the poem of this name, however, 'The Palace of Art,' Tennyson both stated his case and gave it away. 'The Palace of Art' is therefore central in his early work and with very little forcing may be made the clue to his subsequent course. According to the story, Archbishop Trench had said, when the two were fellow students at Cambridge, "Tennyson, we cannot live in Art"; and Spedding in his review elaborated the point. The poem, he tells us, "represents allegorically the condition of a mind which, in the love of beauty, and the triumphant consciousness of knowledge, and intellectual supremacy, in the intense enjoyment of its own power and glory, has lost sight of its relation to man and God.' But Tennyson allows himself the luxury of having it both ways. He revels unashamed in the power and glory of art, and at the same time he asserts the power and glory of man and God. The poem is too long and too obviously made up, but through most of it Tennyson achieves for the first time a kind of imaginative description, which is not only superior to the merely decorative beauty exhibited in other early poems, but rivals the maturer descriptive passages which rely so largely on "absolute accuracy" and metrical sleight. It is as though in designing the Palace his interests were profoundly engaged and while he knew that the plan was bad he resolved to have the décor right.

> *I said, 'O Soul, make merry and carouse,'*

a splendid carousal: and he builds lovingly for that purpose. One of the tapestries, for example,

> *One seem'd all dark and red—a tract of sand,*
> *And some one pacing there alone,*
> *Who paced for ever in a glimmering land,*
> *Lit with a large low moon.*[d]

This is not Tennyson's visual description: it offers little to the eye and everything to the imagination. It is not like the accumulation of bright and clear detail in 'The Lady of Shalott' or like the later

[d] I quote the 1842 text, but though the 1833 version is inferior the point remains. The other stanzas quoted here are the same in both texts. A detailed comparison is left to the reader's industry.

work which relies on our recognition of the familiar, our childlike gratification in beholding 'poetry' where we had supposed was only commonplaceness. So in the last of these arrases he practises economy where it would have been easy to be lavish:

> *And one, an English home—gray twilight pour'd*
> *On dewy pastures, dewy trees,*
> *Softer than sleep—all things in order stored;*
> *A haunt of ancient Peace.*

or later:

> *A still salt pool, lock'd in with bars of sand,*
> *Left on the shore; that hears all night*
> *The plunging seas draw backward from the land*
> *Their moon-led waters white.*

Is it simply because these stanzas are in the best tradition of romantic essential poetry that one approves of them, or also because they are addressed to the mind's eye? Is there not more of the sea in those last lines and in Arnold's

> *Its melancholy slow withdrawing roar*

than in all

> *The league-long rollers thundering on the reef?*

And finally, though the Biblical echo helps and the "great perplexity" is a handicap:

> *As in strange lands a traveller walking slow,*
> *In doubt and great perplexity,*
> *A little before moon-rise hears the low*
> *Moan of an unknown sea;*

> *And knows not if it be thunder, or a sound*
> *Of rocks thrown down, or one deep cry*
> *Of great wild beasts; then thinketh, 'I have found*
> *A new land, but I die.'*

Tennyson prefixed to 'The Palace of Art' some lines 'To ———' (that is, R. C. Trench) in which he calls his poem 'a sort of allegory" of a "sinful soul" who loved Beauty alone, who loved knowledge and God only for their beauty—

> *A glorious Devil, large in heart and brain.*

84

This may mean Goethe, or no one in particular.[10] The sarcastic
stanzas beginning "O Godlike isolation" suggest, at any rate, the
supposed Goethean theory. But if the allegory is chiefly (and sim-
ply) that the Soul cannot live content with Beauty alone, the irony
is that "she" still cherishes her Palace—

> *Perchance I may return with others there*
> *When I have purged my guilt.*

The guilt is of course pride—

> *I sit as God holding no form of creed,*
> *But contemplating all,—*

and scorn of the swine who "roll a prurient skin" outside the
Palace. Yet how she will purge her guilt and who are the "others,"
deponent saith not. This was the compromise with Beauty, Tenny-
son's compromise with art. And it is written, He that saveth his own
soul shall lose it. Just as the 'Supposed Confessions' and 'The Two
Voices' show the young man arguing with himself about moral
questions, trying to find his way in a confusing world, just so 'The
Palace of Art' shows the young poet arguing with himself—some
say, preaching to himself—about a question which concerns him
particularly, the ethics of his profession. His position in 1832, re-em-
phasized in 1842, could not have been satisfying, for he had stated
the case against himself in very extreme terms and his answer was
equivocal. Inasmuch as he was still young, this uncertainty is par-
donable, but it is also symptomatic of the intellectual confusion
which pursued him through the rest of his life. The domestic in-
fluences were all on the side of man and God; and a little later the
reviews, both friendly and unfriendly, were to support these in-
fluences; whereas his instincts as a poet were of course all for art.
What is interesting and significant now is the anxiousness with
which he faces a problem which can never be met dogmatically, his
evasive answer to a question which is fundamentally insoluble, his
almost passionate desire to force a decision in a case which, so to
say, ought to be settled out of court, a case which really ought not
to arise. The ancient quarrel between the didactic and the æsthetic
functions of art is an academic, scholastic matter: the poets join
issue in it at their own risk. But Tennyson, soon to be literally a
'Victorian,' and then the representative and interpreter of his 'age,'

was bound to take sides for didacticism in his own interest, against his instincts. And although in this poem he exaggerated the opposition, made art needlessly odious and selfish and sinful, and in the last stanza took back what he had given, it is plain that the choice was made. Thereafter he was seldom didactic in the eighteenth-century sense; he assumed the not impenetrable disguise of "a sort of allegory," and so added confusion to his other disabilities. He did not openly teach, but he had to have his message.

How much responsibility the reviewers must bear for Tennyson's 'silence' between 1832 and 1842 is still a moot question. No doubt his very sensitive skin felt their palpable hits; no doubt also their strictures were salutary for one so shy and inclined to godlike isolation. But they were harmful in the encouragement they gave to his desire to be 'deep,' to say something of man and God, because they led him down the weedy path of popular appeal. Those who felt, with Carlyle, that 'The May Queen' was "tender and true" received more for their money in the next volume; while those who hoped for better work from the writer of 'Mariana' and 'The Lady of Shalott' also had their reward; and ten years of maturing was not too high a price to pay for the best of the new poems. On the other hand, Tennyson was not so much silenced by the critics as he was crushed by the death of Arthur Hallam: and the death of Hallam—though one should not perhaps say it so boldly —was one of the most beneficial events in Tennyson's experience. It stirred his emotional nature to the depths, and his emotional nature was in great need of a shock; in truth there was too little throughout his life really to unsettle his placidity, to nourish his poetic growth, to pull him out of his egocentric brooding and enlarge his communion with humanity. It freed him from what seems to have been a youthful infatuation and (if there is anything in the suggestion of Mr. Humbert Wolfe) opened the way for his marriage. It gave him the one right means of escape from the Palace of Art, the key to the true compromise between the art which in his poem seduces and imprisons the soul and the "cottage in the vale" (to wit, his domestic idylls), which is of course something to think and feel deeply about and make poetry of, in place of his graceful but insubstantial subjects of 1830 and 1833. It gave us 'In Memoriam,' and better still, 'Ulysses' and 'Break, break, break.'

These two poems, 'Ulysses' and 'Break, break, break,' together with 'Morte d'Arthur' and 'Locksley Hall,' are the best of the new poems of 1842. The domestic idylls added to his contemporary reputation, these four abide no question, for each in its way is a star in Tennyson's crown. 'Morte d'Arthur' is by definition and by the poet's conception also an idyll. Perhaps one should say an heroic idyll. It is besides a mark of progress in Tennyson's handling of the Malory material, a transition piece between 'The Lady of Shalott' and the 'Idylls of the King.' It is universally praised, and deserves its praise. It is also worth examining closely, both because it is a good illustration of Tennyson's position in 1842, and because it is also a portent of his native weaknesses. His soul is still in the Palace of Art.

The relation of "the old *Morte*," as FitzGerald fondly called it, to Malory's short chapters is familiar and needs no recapitulation. Tennyson read his Malory, remembered a few phrases, closed the book, and wrote his own poem. He begins "So all day long" as though we had just read, as he had done, the antecedent story; but he omits Modred and the serpent and most of Malory's details.[e] The description is, one notes immediately, of the nonvisual, imaginative sort, like that of the best stanzas of 'The Palace of Art': the chapel standing on a dark strait between the ocean and a "great water" in the light of the full moon, with the mountains close by. No one misses the fine effect, although as topography it will not bear scrutiny; but the effect is somewhat weakened by the three-fold repetition of "King Arthur" and "Sir Bedevere" in the first thirteen lines and the "broken chancel with a broken cross." This

[e] A manuscript survives with some introductory lines, quite inferior; cf. Wise, *Bibliography*, I, 211. After l.13 of the present text come the following lines:

Then spake King Arthur to Sir Bedivere:
'Well said old Merlin ere his time was come,
Experience never closes all in all
But there is always something to be learnt
Even in the gate of death. So clear a dream
Which I neglected with my waking mind
Came yesternight Sir Gawain as he lived,
Bareheaded, circled with a gracious light,
Seven ladies, like the seven ruling stars,
For whom he fought, and whom he saved from shame,
Beautiful tearful: and he spoke and said,
Go thou not forth tomorrow in the fight.
But I went forth and fought and lie here.
The sequel of to-day unsolders all. . . .

Tennyson's cancelling of these lines seems fully justified; but he remembered Arthur's dream and reworked it, with allegoric effects, in 'The Passing of Arthur,' ll.29 ff.

is clearly the luxurious, not the economical style. By these repetitions something of the epic fashion is intended, without the epic movement (already hinted, distantly, by the *in-medias-res* plunge of the first line), as well as by the formulized

Then spake King Arthur to Sir Bedevere.

The King's first speech is regal, except for the redundancy of "never more, at any future time" and the rather loose syntax of

I perish by this people which I made,—
Tho' Merlin sware that I should come again
To rule once more—but let what will be, be,
I am so deeply smitten thro' the helm
That without help I cannot last till morn.

The picture of Arthur and his knights walking about the gardens of Camelot talking of knightly deeds is romantically idyllic, but one is not so sure of their walking about "the halls Of Camelot." Like an old man Arthur dwells on the past and is a little boastful, but he checks himself—

But now delay not: take Excalibur,
And fling him far into the middle mere:
Watch what thou seëst, and lightly bring me word.

The middle mere must be the great water of line 12; "lightly" is lifted from Malory. Some readers have found fault with "white samite, mystic, wonderful," but Tennyson liked it enough to repeat it three times. The white samite is properly sumptuous, but what is mystic samite? or was the arm mystic? And the quasi-climactic "wonderful" is youthful indeed. Old Sir Bedevere is solicitous and sententious—

A little thing may harm a wounded man—

and also repetitious: he will perform *all* the King's hest *at full*.

So saying, from the ruin'd shrine he stept
And in the moon athwart the place of tombs,
Where lay the mighty bones of ancient men,
Old knights, and over them the sea-wind sang
Shrill, chill, with flakes of foam. He, stepping down
By zig-zag paths, and juts of pointed rock,
Came on the shining levels of the lake.

The lake is again the great water and the middle mere. But does Bedivere step athwart the place of tombs, or does the moon shine athwart it? or has "athwart" got the better of the poet? And if, one still asks, the tombs are flaked with sea foam, what is the relation of the two bodies of water? The lake must be considerably below sea-level, and well protected from the wind.

Came on the shining levels of the lake

is capital poetry, after the zigzag path and juts of rock, but the topography is "mystical." Moreover, here Sir Bedivere steps down from the shrine to the lake in one line; the second time he merely "went . . . Across the ridge"; the third time he leaped "down the ridges lightly"; but farther on, when he has King Arthur on his back, he apparently chooses a longer and more difficult route: one is the more mystified by the topography, but the poet wanted his *effect* and in spite of the repetition got his effect redoubled.

> *Dry clash'd his harness in the icy caves*
> *And barren chasms, and all to left and right*
> *The bare black cliff clang'd round him, as he based*
> *His feet on juts of slippery crag that rang*
> *Sharp-smitten with the dint of armed heels—*
> *And on a sudden, lo! the level lake,*
> *And the long glories of the winter moon.*

Even here, however, they seem to see, not reach, the level lake, for the dusky barge still lies "Beneath them," and they descend further towards it.

When Bedivere first drew Excalibur from its sheath the moon "sparkled keen with frost against the hilt." Is this really frost? Probably not.

> *He gazed so long*
> *That both his eyes were dazzled, as he stood,*
> *This way and that dividing the swift mind,*
> *In act to throw: but at the last . . .*

Tennyson himself certifies the echo of Vergil and Homer, but Bedivere's mind seems to be the opposite of swift. At length, however, he returns and being questioned replies:

> *I heard the ripple washing in the reeds,*
> *And the wild water lapping on the crag.*

89

In Malory he "saw nothing but waves and winds," and the second time "nothing but the waters wappe and waves wanne." Tennyson here fails to improve on Malory: there is a pretty distinction in sound between the water in the reeds and the water on the crag, but *wild* water can hardly be said to *lap*.[11] Then Arthur says:

> *Thou hast betray'd thy nature and thy name,*
> *Not rendering true answer.*

But the answer, as such, was true enough. Tennyson, however, is not content with this compact phrase: he dilutes it by adding

> *as beseem'd*
> *Thy fëalty, nor like a noble knight.*

The next sixty lines, in which Sir Bedivere debates foolishly and Arthur chides him angrily, are all admirable, without extravagance, and the poem touches a fine climax when Bedivere

> *clutch'd the sword,*
> *And strongly wheel'd and threw it. The great brand*
> *Made lightnings in the splendour of the moon,*
> *And flashing round and round, and whirl'd in an arch,*
> *Shot like a streamer of the northern morn—*

the metrical effect is incomparable and the picture impressive,—if only Tennyson could have stopped there. But he had to spoil it by adding

> *Seen where the moving isles of winter shock*
> *By night, with noises of the northern sea.*

Similarly, the dying Arthur looks "wistfully with wide blue eyes, *As in a picture.*" A few lines below "King Arthur panted hard, . . . So sighed the king." And when they come to the barge

> *they were ware*
> *That all the decks were dense with stately forms*
> *Black-stoled, black-hooded, like a dream—by these*
> *Three Queens with crowns of gold—and from them rose*
> *A cry that shiver'd to the tingling stars.*

Nothing could be better than "tingling," but how many decks has the barge? how is one to know that "these" does not modify "three queens"? how can the queens be *by* these stately forms which cover all the decks? and does the cry rise from the stately forms or from the queens? A little farther on, the "drops of onset" is as bad as "isles of winter"; and "the knightly growth that fringed his lips" is famous. (But Tennyson was impenitent; for many years later Earl Doorm was

> *Broad-faced with under-fringe of russet beard,*
> *Bound on a foray, rolling eyes of prey.)*

So we come to Arthur's farewell speech. Malory has: "Comfort thyself, said the king, and do as well as thou mayest, for in me is no trust for to trust in; for I will go into the vale of Avilion to heal me of my grievious wound; and if thou hear never more of me, pray for my soul." Tennyson's Arthur is elaborate and gnomic at once; he seems conscious of making a curtain speech and he requires twenty-five lines for Malory's fifty words. Yet it is all strictly in keeping with the poetical elaboration of the rest of the poem, and if we can accept the piety there is nothing to complain of.[12]

Some apology is probably expected for this kind of minute fault-finding. My purpose was to show up the flaws: the good things are accessible to the most casual reader. What we discover here, then, in looking narrowly at "the old *Morte*" is no more than what we should expect. If the miracle was not altogether successful, it remains a miracle nevertheless. Tennyson was not yet complete master—and even later, in the judgment of some, he was often the slave of his own mastery—he was still dominated by words, by language and 'effects'—

> *On one side lay the Ocean, and on one*
> *Lay a great water, and the moon was full*
>
> *And so strode back slow to the wounded King*
>
> *lo! the level lake,*
> *And the long glories of the winter moon*
>
> *And on the mere the wailing died away.*

The effects are so good he can almost afford to neglect their justification—almost. His luxuriance of language is itself a reward; and for certain kinds of poetry such untrimmed exuberance is enough. His 'Morte d'Arthur' is a triumph of poetical language, a triumph of the picturesque and the romantic over the real. But it is still the language of a young poet who does not need to fear being reckless. The lust for "absolute accuracy" has not bitten him: it is better—at times, certainly—to have mighty wings under imperfect control than to walk with dignity.

But if, on this debatable border of his maturity, Tennyson's step faltered a little, it must be admitted that about the same time he achieved in another poem a nearly perfect balance of feeling, substance, and technique. The superiority of 'Ulysses' over 'Morte d'Arthur'[13] may be attributed in part to its subject matter, and in part to its being the outcome of a genuine and profound emotion. Though it was written with the sense of Arthur Hallam's death strong upon him, it expresses not so much the poet's grief as "the feeling about the need of going forward and braving the struggle of life," and does so, Tennyson adds, "perhaps more simply than anything in *In Memoriam*." Perhaps without Tennyson's acknowledgement one would not have recognized Hallam's shadow across the poem, but that some powerful emotion was moving in the poet's breast is evident; and this may suggest a clue to the failure of certain other poems.

The classical inspiration of 'Ulysses' is slight. In the eleventh book Homer says (it is Tiresias prophesying to Odysseus): "But when thou hast slain the wooers in thy halls, whether by guile, or openly with the edge of the sword, thereafter go thy way, taking with thee a shapen oar, till thou shalt come to such men as know not the sea, . . . And from the sea shall thine own death come, the gentlest death that may be, which shall end thee foredone with smooth old age, and the folk shall dwell happily around thee. This that I say," adds Tiresias, "is sooth"; but like many other prophecies, it is not too lucid. At the close of the poem Athene puts an end to the fighting between Odysseus and the Ithacans, Zeus having declared: "let him be king all his days . . .; so may both sides love one another as of old, but let peace and wealth abundant be their portion."

But Tennyson had also been reading Dante, who found Ulysses among the evil counsellors in the eighth circle of Hell. "When I had left Circe," says Ulysses there,

Nè dolcezza di figlio, nè la pièta
Del vecchio padre, nè il debito amore

Lo qual dovea Penelope far lieta,
Vincer potêr dentro da me l'ardore
Ch' i' ebbi a divenir del mondo esperto,
E degli vizi umani e del valore.

I cannot rest from travel: I will drink
Life to the lees. . . .
How dull it is to pause, . . .
This is my son, mine own Telemachus, . . .
Well-loved of me. . . .

Dante is more orderly; Tennyson's Ulysses is more excited, says things as they come to him, repeats himself, returns to topics he has apparently finished; but the two characters have much in common.

Ma misi me per l'alto mare aperto
Sol con un legno, e con quella compagna
Picciola dalla qual non fui deserto.

There lies the port; the vessel puffs her sail:
There gloom the dark, broad seas. My mariners,
Souls who have toil'd, and wrought, and thought with
*   me,—*

Io e i compagni eravam vecchi e tardi,

You and I are old;
Old age hath yet his honour and his toil.

(So Tennyson adds the philosophic note.)

'O frati,' dissi, 'che per cento milia
Perigli siete giunti all' occidente,
A questa tanto picciola vigilia
De' vostri sensi, ch' è del rimanente,
Non vogliate negar l'esperienza,
Diretro al sol, del mondo senza gente.

Death closes all: but something ere the end,
Some work of noble note, may yet be done, . . .
Come, my friends,
'Tis not too late to seek a newer world.

Considerate la vostra semenza:
Fatti non foste a viver come bruti,
Ma per seguir virtute e conoscenza.

(Part of this is transferred to those who remain behind.)

>   *a savage race,*
> *That hoard, and sleep, and feed, and know not me. . . .*
>   *yearning in desire*
> *To follow knowledge like a sinking star.*

> *Tutte le stelle già dell' altro polo*
> *Vedea la notte, e il nostro tanto basso,*
> *Che non surgeva fuor del marin suolo.*

>   *for my purpose holds*
> *To sail beyond the sunset, and the baths*
> *Of all the western stars, until I die.*
> *It may be that the gulfs will wash us down; . . .*

Dante ends his canto:

> *Infin che il mar fu sopra noi richiuso.*

These snatches of Dante are not meant to prove that Tennyson used him as a 'crib,' but to show that he must have had Dante's text clearly in memory. "Tho' much is taken, much abides," however. Not only is the moralizing all Tennyson's, or nearly all, but the fuller characterization of Ulysses—his pride as well as his restless eagerness, and his determination

> *To strive, to seek, to find, and not to yield,*

which was denied to Dante's Ulisse because he must end in the Malebolge of Hell. The suggestion of Homer first stirred Dante's imagination, and Tennyson adopting it for his own purposes enlarged and intensified it. He adds not only such characteristically Tennysonian passages as

> *Yet all experience is an arch wherethro'*
> *Gleams that untravell'd world*

and

> *The lights begin to twinkle from the rocks:*
> *The long day wanes: the slow moon climbs: the deep*
> *Moans round with many voices*

(which are both in the nature of added ornamentation, but are better welded, less patently stuck on, than similar passages in the

'Morte'), but he added also a new idea—almost a philosophy of life. The Italian Ulisse has already experienced the "vizi umani" and still wishes to "seguir virtute e cognoscenza," and lo! he finds himself among the damned

> *Dove per lui perduto a morir gissi.*

The English Ulysses will not only drink life to the lees, he will follow knowledge

> *Beyond the utmost bound of human thought;*

he still hopes to perform some work of noble note

> *Not unbecoming men that strove with Gods,*

still heroic in heart and strong in will. And Tennyson was still a young man, in his twenties. Overcome with the first grief at the death of his friend, living in the "cruel fellowship" of sorrow, with all his "widow'd race" still to be run, he asked himself the usual question—was it worth while—and found the answer in terms of the aged Ulysses who had seen and known so much, enjoyed and suffered greatly, yet asked for more experience, "life piled on life." It was the same answer that he borrowed from Goethe and St. Augustine—

> *That men may rise on stepping-stones*
> *Of their dead selves to higher things,*

but it was expressed not in a metaphor but in a fully imagined picture.

Moreover, 'Ulysses' is (as has been frequently observed) the natural palinode to 'The Lotos-Eaters.' Not only is section VI of the latter poem, added in 1842, reminiscent of 'Ulysses'—

> *Dear is the memory of our wedded lives,*
> >   *. . . but all hath suffer'd change; . . .*
> *Our sons inherit us: our looks are strange: . . .*
> *Or else the island princes over-bold*
> *Have eat our substance,—*

but the whole idea of 'The Lotos-Eaters' is the antithesis of Ulysses' passion, movement, and enlarged experience:

> *Hateful is the dark-blue sky,*
> *Vaulted o'er the dark-blue sea.*

Death is the end of life; ah, why
Should life all labour be? . . .
          Is there any peace
In ever climbing up the climbing wave?

The two poems were written within a few years of each other. They show the young man's eager questioning of the purposes of life and in extreme form the two opposed answers of complete negation and earnest acceptance, the one wrought purely from the imagination, the other born of personal though youthful experience. And they point an artistic moral also. For these two poems in their way are a supplement to 'The Palace of Art' and in their way serve better the cause of poetry-cum-philosophy than the miscellany which is 'In Memoriam' and the argument which is contained in 'The Two Voices.'

Much more definitely than either 'Ulysses' or even 'In Memoriam,' 'The Two Voices' exposes Tennyson's questionings that arose from the emotional disturbance of Hallam's death. Argumentative verse has its place in our varied world, but it has a style of its own, highly cultivated in the eighteenth century, which cannot with impunity be mixed with the lyric style which is Tennyson's forte.

To which the voice did urge reply:
'To-day I saw the dragon-fly
Come from the wells where he did lie

is one thing and betrays its ancestry;

Who, rowing hard against the stream,
Saw distant gates of Eden gleam,
And did not dream it was a dream

is quite a different thing—just as

'Tis life, whereof our nerves are scant,
Oh life, not death, for which we pant;
More life, and fuller, that I want.

is pale and sickly beside the language of 'Ulysses.' To say

I cannot make this matter plain,
But I would shoot, howe'er in vain,
A random arrow from the brain

is barren, and such a style cannot be saved by adding

> *I wonder'd at the beauteous hours,*
> *The slow result of winter showers:*
> *You scarce could see the grass for flowers.*

One may accept the borrowing from 'Faust' as a sign of prentice work, and one may read with a forgiving smile the ultra-Victorian family vignette

> *One walk'd between his wife and child,*
> *With measured footfall firm and mild,*

one may commend the introduction of scientific terms and find interest in the parallels with 'In Memoriam,' but 'The Two Voices' remains a poem of the type uncongenial to Tennyson's muse. With two separate poems, 'The Lotos-Eaters' and 'Ulysses' he could do more for poetry, approaching it directly, and more for the interpretation of life, approaching it obliquely, than by any set-piece of argumentation.

And so, saving the idylls for a later chapter, we have seen Tennyson through his first climacteric, the *Poems* of 1842, seen him find his way out of the Palace of Art and ready to enter the Victorian Age.

CHAPTER FOUR

The Princess

A GOOD WORD must be said for 'The Princess'—or rather, for the first half of it. The poem fell on harsh soil when it was published, and latterly it has been handed over to children, except when, from time to time, the feminists notice it. In 1848 Tennyson wrote to FitzGerald: "My book is out and I hate it, and so no doubt will you." He said much the same to others. Nearly thirty years later Old Fitz told Hallam: "like Carlyle, I gave up all hopes of him after 'The Princess.' "

Others than Carlyle and FitzGerald have perceived, then and since, that 'The Princess' was by way of being a turning point in Tennyson's poetical career. To his admirers looking for fulfilment of the prophecy of 1842 the poem was a disappointment, quite reasonably.[a] Most of them had, like Spedding, asked and looked for a great poem and on a grand scale, and he gave them a Medley, in some three thousand lines, written in two quite disparate styles. Instead of "the predestined masterpiece, he published 'The Princess,' " said the *Quarterly* in reviewing Tennyson's work after his death. "A brilliant extravaganza on women's rights appeared to be a poor substitute for the poetry which Tennyson's latest work had promised. . . . he had frittered his powers on a glittering castle in the air, brilliant in colour, graceful in workmanship, and splendid in detail, but unequal in execution, incongruous in its parts, and incoherent in its design."[1] The subject, it is true, was novel, but in the 1840's there were more absorbing questions than the education

---

[a] Aubrey de Vere was an apparent exception. "It is frequently asked," said he in 1849, "whether Mr. Tennyson is capable of producing a great and national work"; and he replied by commending Tennyson for not trying to anticipate the requisite maturity, and adding that he "has already exhibited the faculties necessary for his success" (*Edinburgh Review* xc (1849), 432).

of women, and Tennyson suffered—though his position was less bold than it might have been—from being somewhat in advance of his audience. (Mill's Essay did not come till 1869, though *Jane Eyre* and *Wuthering Heights* were published in the same year as 'The Princess'; Mrs. Browning and Mrs. Gaskell followed almost immediately; and Harriet Martineau and Mary Somerville were well established—all visible tokens of female education and intelligence and of the new trend: to say nothing of the Queen herself.) But this new Medley, with its air of persiflage and mock-heroic in the early part, was an ironic contribution to the feminist movement, and with its florid style it seemed to add nothing to the romantic glories of 'Morte d'Arthur' and 'Ulysses,' nothing to the studied beauty of 'The Palace of Art' and 'A Dream of Fair Women,' nothing to the sweet pathos of 'The May Queen' and 'The Day-Dream,' nothing to the *thought* of 'The Two Voices' and 'The Vision of Sin,' nothing to the splendid rhetoric of 'Locksley Hall.' It was veritably a medley, not alone in having (theoretically, at least) seven narrators, and in the mixture of mediæval and modern settings in an ultra-modern framework, but in its mixture of tones. And here Tennyson was for once a sure critic of his own work.

> *What style could suit?*
> *The men required . . .*
> *The sort of mock-heroic gigantesque, . . .*
> *The women . . .*
> *They hated banter . . .*
> *—why*
> *Not make her true-heroic—true-sublime?*
> *Or all, they said, as earnest as the close? . . .*
> *And I, betwixt them both, to please them both, . . .*
> *I moved as in a strange diagonal,*
> *And maybe neither pleased myself nor them.*

Quite so. But even here one gets the satiric stroke on women's fear of banter.

He could not make up his mind and thus, with his strange diagonal, seems to have failed in both directions. But more than that, he lost an opportunity which never came again. About midway, before the end of Part Four, he lost confidence in

> *The raillery, or grotesque, or false sublime,*

shifted the blame to Little Lilia (in the Interlude), and proceeded to his "solemn close" regardless. It is as though he quite suddenly perceived that his mock-heroics were incompatible with a serious settlement of his problem. The comedy ends with Part Four. After that there are good things: The King's speech—

Man is the hunter; woman is his game . . .

parts of the Princess' surrender, and of course the "small Sweet idyl"; but it is nearly all serious; the long reconciliation of Psyche and Ida is not up to the level of good drama, it turns to second-rate heroics reaching after the grand manner; and the conclusion is a love story on stilts.

Much the same change takes place in the argument. Throughout the first half of the poem Tennyson keeps

The jest and earnest working side by side.

He lets the effeminacy of the Prince be seen (particularly after the weird seizures were introduced, in the fourth edition) and the mannishness of Ida; he treats the Female College "in a spirit rather of friendly raillery than of satire"; he reveals the jealousy and dissention within the Academy; he lets us feel that there is absurdity on both sides. But in the latter half he relies on the external means of a tournament to settle the question; he overplays the child Aglaia; and with all his solemn moralizing on "distinctive womanhood"—

The woman's cause is man's; . . .
For woman is not undevelopt man,
But diverse,

and so on (moderately advanced for 1847 but tame for posterity)— he has to admit that Ida is "a queen of farce," sternly weak, who succumbs at last to

something wild within her breast,
A greater than all knowledge,

in prose, the maternal instinct.[b]

[b] A more sympathetic view is possible (but note the caustic question which accompanies it): "It is part of the chivalry of Tennyson's nature that he represents the conversion of the Princess Ida as due not to any sense of physical or mental inferiority but to the claim set up first by gratitude, secondly by com-

But the stage was set for comedy, if Tennyson had but ventured to go on.[2] It may be a little perverse to praise the first half at the expense of the second. Yet where since Pope had (or has) the English language been used with such exquisite comic delicacy as in the earlier Parts of 'The Princess'? Who had written with such delicious wit? the

Laborious orient ivory sphere in sphere

of language, the carving of phrase, the jewels more than five words long, gleaming there appropriately and to perfection. The qualities which Tennyson too often diminished into prettiness, the millinery, the "trinketry and perfumery," of which his contemporary critics complained, the false ornament which still irks his later admirers and which seems out of place in King Arthur's hall or in Enoch's village, are just the thing in Princess Ida's candid courts. The Latinisms and affectation amount almost to wit; the play on proper names—

The foundress of the Babylonian wall,
The Carian Artemisia strong in war,

---

passion, and lastly by love in her own heart. . . . But as we close the poem with the music of its final lines ringing in our ears, we cannot but ask ourselves: What of those six hundred maidens? Did they all find satisfactory partners among the Prince's followers, or elsewhere?" (*The Princess*, ed. by Elizabeth Wordsworth, London, 1899, p. xviii). Thus it is hard to satisfy everyone. On 1st October 1847 Mrs. Browning wrote to Miss Mitford: "Do tell me your full thought of the commonwealth of women. I begin by agreeing with you as to his implied under-estimate of women; his women are too voluptuous; however, of the most refined voluptuousness." And in the following May she resumed: "At last we have caught sight of Tennyson's 'Princess,' and I may or must profess to be a good deal disappointed. What woman will tell the great poet that Mary Wollstonecraft herself never dreamed of setting up collegiate states, proctordoms, and the rest, which is a worn-out plaything in the hands of one sex already, and need not be *transferred* in order to be proved ridiculous? As for the poetry, beautiful in some parts, he

never seems to me to come up to his own highest mark, in rhythm especially. . . . Still the man is Tennyson, take him for all and all, and I shall never forgive whatever princesses of my sex may have ill treated him" (*Letters*, ed. F. C. Kenyon, New York, 1898, I, 345, 367). Mrs. Browning's last remark was apropos of her misconception that 'Locksley Hall' was autobiographical, and that the poet had been jilted by Cousin Amy for the horsey gentleman. In 1881 Swinburne commented: "I cannot say that Tennyson's lifelong tone about women and their shortcomings has ever commended itself to my poor mind as the note of a very pure or high one" (*Miscellanies*, p. 251). Against this may be put the more orotund dictum of Gladstone in 1859: "we may confidently assert it as one of Mr. Tennyson's brightest distinctions that he is now what from the very first he strove to be . . . —the poet of woman. . . . that he has studied, sounded, and painted woman in form, in motion, in character, in office, in capability, with rare devotion, power, and skill; . . ." (*Gleanings of Past Years*, New York, 1886, II, 136).

> *The Rhodope, that built the pyramid,*
> *Clelia, Cornelia, with the Palmyrene*
> *That fought Aurelian, and the Roman brows*
> *Of Agrippina—*

the playful repetition of "Are you that Psyche?"—the echo of Dante,

> *Morn in the white wake of the morning star*
> *Came furrowing all the orient into gold—*

the Latinisms—

> *Not in this frequence can I lend full tongue,*
> *O noble Ida, to those thoughts that wait*
> *On you, their centre: let me say but this,*
> *That many a famous man and woman, town*
> *And landskip, have I heard of, after seen*
> *The dwarfs of presage;*

or

> *High above them stood*
> *The placid marble Muses, looking peace.*

So the fanciful images—

> *The hard-grain'd Muses of the cube and square ...*
> *Tore the King's letter, snow'd it down ...*
> *I grate on rusty hinges here ...*
> *the porch that sang*
> *All round with laurel ...*
> *There sat along the forms, like morning doves*
> *That sun their milky bosoms on the thatch,*
> *A patient range of pupils ...*
> *At last*
> *She rose upon a wind of prophecy ...*
> *Many a little hand*
> *Glanced like a touch of sunshine on the rocks ...*
> *Cyril, with whom the bell-mouth'd glass had wrought ...*

Was partial inebriation ever more delicately put than this? or flamboyant architecture better described than as "Gothic lighter than a fire"? Is it not part of the parable that "the flower of woman-kind" should stumble into the water?

> *she miss'd the plank, and roll'd*
> *In the river.*

And with what metrical dexterity is she rescued:

> *a glance I gave,*
> *No more; but woman-vested as I was*
> *Plunged; and the flood drew; yet I caught her; then*
> *Oaring one arm, and bearing in my left*
> *The weight of all the hopes of half the world,*
> *Strove to buffet to land in vain.*

Tennyson even has the good humor to parody his own tricks; compare

> *and overhead*
> *The broad ambrosial aisles of lofty lime*
> *Made noise with bees and breeze from end to end*

in the Prologue with the famous ending of the 'Small Sweet Idyl':

> *The moan of doves in immemorial elms,*
> *And murmuring of innumerable bees.*

These gems without their setting lose much of their sparkle, but the setting is there, with touches of light comedy, a feeling for humorous character, and a sense of comic situation. Here was a field which with care and cultivation Tennyson could have made something of, had he not been bitten with the seriousness of his profession and his mission. It was a new venture for him. It was partly predictable from 'The Miller's Daughter,' 'Audley Court,' and 'Edwin Morris.' Nor is it merely in this poetic wit that 'The Princess' excels, but also in a delicate sense of human comedy, a recognition of our common weaknesses and their ineluctable absurdity. Tennyson has rarely received adequate praise for his latent humor—most of the tributes have been to his overt jocularity, as in the 'Northern Farmer'—and perhaps one might guess that the critics' failure then, as even now, to appreciate this quality discouraged and deterred him from further development. He had been marked for greater things; and instead of becoming a wit in verse, with the deftest turns of phrase and meter, with bright and light satire on our human foibles, with a capacity for satiric indignation—as in Part Four the Head, "Rob'd in the long night of her deep hair," inveighed against the brawlers and "these male thunderbolts"—instead of following this golden line for which he had genuine gifts and in which the competition has always been slight, he chose the Laureate path.

FitzGerald was right; yet it is strange that he, "with his affection for the 'champagne flavour' of the early lyrics, should have missed the sparkle and bouquet of 'The Princess.' " So Waugh; but Tennyson may well have been writing for another Victorian critic, who could say: "Its true interest lies in the power with which it presents the ideal of wedded love in opposition to a mistaken theory of woman's life in the world." Carlyle, when 'The Princess' appeared, said that it "had everything but common-sense"—which is saying a very great deal. Professor Lounsbury was more cautious and at the same time more extravagant, but he was bothered by its "limitations":

In certain ways 'The Princess' is one of the most perfect of Tennyson's works. This is not to say that it is the highest in aim or noblest in subject, though both aim and subject are high and noble. But in variety of interest, in the due proportion of means to ends, in the marvellous adaptation of treatment of the varying conditions of the subject-matter, never degenerating into the purely burlesque, never straining beyond the legitimate expression of high-wrought feeling— and both these temptations beset the poet constantly—he has succeeded in producing within its limitations what might in justice be called a nearly perfect work of art.[3]

This, however, gives a Roland by taking an Oliver away, and misses the contrast between the bright comedy of the first half and the "high and noble" subject matter of the latter end. For somewhere midway of 'The Princess' England lost a fine and promising successor to Pope; and a Victorian Pope would have been worth saving.[c]

[c] The *Quarterly*, looking back in 1893, said something like this but with a different sense: "He was destined to be the nineteenth-century Pope, to teach by example the significance of art, to create a new standard which should render slovenly work impossible, to rescue English poetry from the chaotic tendencies which Byron's haste, or Southey's amorphous masses, or Wordsworth's deliberate formlessness, had encouraged" (CLXXVI, 10). Ker was nearer the truth when he said: "Tennyson's *Princess* is full of things that make it a modern counterpart to the *Rape of the Lock*" (*Collected Essays*, I, 268).

CHAPTER FIVE

In Memoriam

It is better than any monument which could be raised to the memory of my beloved son, it is a more lively and enduring testimony to his great virtues and talents that the world should know the friendship which existed between you, that posterity should associate his name with that of Alfred Tennyson.

Henry Hallam to Tennyson, 1850

THE UNINTENDED irony in those words from Arthur Hallam's father to the poet is submerged in their sincerity. For it is true that young Hallam's immortality for this world rests on Tennyson's poem. The *Remains,* due to parental piety, would but have underlined his forgetting and the other effulgent tributes would hardly have been heard or written, but to support the poem. Yet as all earthly things fade and Arthur Hallam is remembered only as the subject of an elegy, now even the halo is becoming dim. After its enormous popular favor, which endured for nearly half a century, 'In Memoriam' as a poem has become almost like an opera which has lost everything but its overture and a few good tunes suitable for a potpourri.[a]

[a] 'In Memoriam' was certainly popular. It sold very well. It brought comfort and consolation to thousands of bereaved readers. For more than fifty years it rivalled Holy Writ in use and usefulness to Anglican and Evangelical clergymen. Nor is this popularity difficult to account for. Besides its sense of intimacy with the Laureate himself and its little domestic incidents, there was an easy appeal in its quotable beauties, its apparent simplicity (the language is almost always simple even when the meaning is obscure, and its elaborate passages are elaborate in a conventional style), its division into short sections to be read like chapters of the Bible and demanding little sustained attention, its vague religious ideas without the intrusion of dogma, its temptation to self-flattery in the familiar handling of high thoughts, or the illusion thereof, its falling in with later theological doubts and its hints of current scientific discussion, and above all its frank sentimental strain. At a somewhat higher level we have the testimony of the Bishop of Durham, writing to Hallam Tennyson soon after the poet's death: "What impressed me most was your father's splendid faith (in the

Tennyson's marriage, after the broken engagement of ten years, and the publication of 'In Memoriam' took place in the same month, June 1850. The wedding journey included Clevedon—"it seemed a kind of consecration to go there"—for it was on the prospects of the volume and Moxon's £300 advance, that marriage was risked. In the following November the elegist-benedict received the Victorian Laurel "owing chiefly to Prince Albert's admiration for 'In Memoriam.' " Thus Tennyson had reason to be grateful to Arthur Hallam and Hallam to Tennyson.

A criticism of 'In Memoriam' must face several questions, which, though interesting in themselves, are nevertheless of minor importance. Perhaps the best beginning will be a synopsis of the whole series of a hundred and thirty-one sections. Bad as any résumé of a poem is bound to be, especially a poem which is hardly intended to be read through continuously, it is necessary in this case, not only because few people will have in memory more than a general notion of its content, but also because only a rapid summary will exhibit its miscellaneousness and discontinuity. I shall omit now, however, the Prologue.

The poet, that is Tennyson, begins with a general observation: that Love and Grief must cling together in self-defence lest the "good that grows out of grief"[1] be lost (I). This is not only a capital introduction to the series, it is also the poet's self-justification for expressing his personal sorrow in verse; and it is a theme which recurs with varying modulations until past midway of the poem. In v he says that the "sad mechanic exercise" of composition is soothing to him; in VIII he compares his "poor flower of poesy" to a flower taken by a lover from his absent beloved's garden; in XII (in a kind of summary of the first large group of sections) he anticipates the criticism of effeminancy, of parading his own pain, and of indifference to the world about him: and answers that his songs are sad because his heart is sad. In XXXVII and XXXVIII he interrupts his questioning about survival after death by contrasting the Heavenly and Earthly Muses and explaining that Hallam also had

---

face of the frankest acknowledgement of every difficulty) in the growing purpose of the sum of life, and in the noble destiny of the individual man as he offers himself for the fulfilment of his little part (LIV, LXXXI, LXXXII)." See also Henry Sidgwick's testimony in the *Memoir*.

"darkened sanctities with song" and hoping that his own song will be grateful to Hallam's ear. Only a little later, in XLVIII, he disclaims the intention of handling high themes exhaustively in his "Short swallow-flights of song." And again, only a little later, in LVII, LVIII, LIX, he pauses to say: "I have built a rich shrine for my friend, but it will not last" (Tennyson in Gatty's *Key*): the high muse exhorts him however to patience and worthier efforts. There is a hint of the same note in LXIX: the scoffing of those who call him "The fool that wears a crown of thorns." Finally, in the group of five sections on Fame (LXXIII-LXXVII), after contrasting the triviality of earthly renown with the "divine inward force" (Miss Chapman) which Hallam possessed and which would have won him earthly fame but has now instead made the darkness of death beautiful, and after claiming that his own verses are at once the measure of his grief and of Hallam's greatness, he says they will last but "half the lifetime of an oak,"—and then continues, in a lower key, and with a shade of sarcasm, that there is no hope for modern rimes—yet he will go on singing "all the same" for his own solace. (Tennyson's preoccupation with this theme, running to sixty-odd quatrains, is a little unfortunate in spite of its various uses. Though it is in one way an echo of the ancient convention of the lover's unworthiness, it betrays a self-consciousness which, though natural, might well have been treated with more reticence if not altogether suppressed.)

The first large group, ending with section XXI and comprising 105 stanzas (including those of apology) is devoted to the expression of the poet's personal sorrow and mourning. Sorrow haunts his sleep and perplexes his waking hours; he hesitates between cherishing and stifling it; he fluctuates between wild unrest and the calmness of despair; and he longs for the passionate quiet of the old yew tree. He visits the house of Hallam; and then through eleven sections (56 stanzas) his mind dwells on the ship which is bringing Hallam's body home. He is sometimes fanciful (as in XII) and sometimes almost incoherent (as in XIII). His sorrows are like the tides at Clevedon, silent when fullest (XIX), and also like the garrulous servants in the house of their dead master (XX); yet he cannot refrain from giving them expression.

Then follow six short miscellaneous sections (XXII-XXVII; 26

stanzas) in which he remembers the "four sweet years" of companionship with Hallam, but life is dreary for him now; he wonders if he idealizes the past too much—anyway it was life, its burdens shared through love. If love will with time turn to indifference he prefers to die. He does not envy the tame captive or the conscienceless beast of "the heart that never suffered bcause it never loved." (The poem does not advance here, and the poetry is mediocre, except the final gnomic couplet

> *'Tis better to have loved and lost*
> *Than never to have loved at all,*

which is not quite so good as Congreve's " 'Tis better to have been left than never to have been loved.")

The first Christmas group (XXVIII-XXX; 17 stanzas) introduces a new note: "sorrow touched with joy." The traditionary celebration is a mockery now. A song once sung by Hallam brings tears, "till one strikes a note of faith and courage, persuaded of the eternal being and changeless sympathy of the dead" (Miss Chapman). This is the first ray of hope, the first groping statement of immortality. It is developed through six sections (XXXI-XXXVI; 26 stanzas) with meditations on the death of Lazarus. Mary perhaps asked no questions of the dead: for him as for her it is enough to love and worship; and her simple faith may be preferable to the superior reasoning of scorners. Without a future life this life would be "dust and ashes"; even love would not make this life worth living, for without the "instinct of immortality" (Miss Chapman) love would be mere casual companionship or brutish passion. Finally, he seeks comfort in the revelation of Christ, which has made truth accessible to limited minds. (All this is tentative, sometimes cryptically expressed, and perhaps intentionally confused.)

After two apologetic sections and the first spring lyric (XXXIX, written in 1868)—"the tender green [of the yew] will pass to gloom again, and dawning hope into regret" (Miss Chapman)—he falls into wondering about the state of the soul after death: whether the parting of death is not like a bride's leaving her father's home; whether Hallam may not now outstrip him in spiritual progress (yet as Hallam taught him wisdom on earth, may he now teach him wisdom in the future life); whether, on the double analogy of death as sleep and of the flower which closes at night, "the memory of our love would last as true, and would live pure and whole within the spirit of my friend" until dawn or resurrection (XLIII). Or, he continues in XLIV, if the dead do not sleep, but somehow remember their life on earth as the living have sometimes a faint memory of prenatal existence, then, he prays, may Hallam bring him a message and resolve his doubts. (This, XLIV, is one of the obscurest. Tennyson offers some help; Bradley has eleven pages.) This idea is given a new direction in XLV; as the child gradually becomes conscious of its self, so perhaps one use of life "may be the gradual growth . . . of the sense of personal identity" (Miss Chapman) "to realize personal consciousness" (Hallam Tennyson)— which will remain unchanged by death. (This is the first assertion in the poem of that emphasis on the survival of personal identity after death, which is one of Tennyson's main concerns and from which he derives his main logical support for immortality. The apparent futility of individual effort if it must come to nothing is so clear to him that he refuses to accept life without hope of its continuing onwards from where it leaves off at death.) Now, after interrupting himself to ask that all his life may be colored, dominated, by his love for Hallam (XLVI), he returns to the question of immortality, saying that love requires at least some "landing-place" after death before the individual soul is totally absorbed into the divine (XLVII).

Next, as a kind of revulsion to the preceding sections, after the apology in XLVIII, follow ten short sections (44 stanzas) in which he seems to abandon argument or reasoning and to give way to despair. From art, nature, and "the schools," he says, come glimpses of help, but underneath all is his great sorrow. "Be near me," he cries, in one of the best lyric sections (L). He is not afraid to reveal his weaknesses, for the dead, who see all, will understand and forgive all (LI). To his admission of humility and unworthiness Love replies with comforting words. Then he intrudes parenthetically a warning against the "doctrine" of youthful wild-oats; and seems to come back to his subject with the pathetic "we trust that somehow good Will be the final goal of ill" and the recognition that he is but an infant crying in the night.

Then, in his search for analogies to support his hopes of indi-

vidual immortality, the discouraging lesson of nature occurs to
him, that she cherishes only the type (LV) and is often careless even
of that (LVI) and in deeper despair he turns again to Hallam for
help, only to be answered, "Behind the veil." So he falls back on
his songs in a kind of temporary epilogue; till the Muse counsels
"a nobler leave" (LVII, LVIII).

Now come eight sections (LIX-LXVI; 31 stanzas) which can only
be called a collection of loose jottings, all inferior. Sorrow is to be
henceforward his wife, not a "casual mistress." (This, LIX, was in-
serted in the fourth edition, 1851, "as a pendant to Section III" says
Hallam Tennyson—an odd place for it.) He is like a girl who loves
a man above her station. He pleads to be remembered by Hallam
and adds that even Shakespeare cannot love him more; unless
perhaps to remember would trouble Hallam's present joy; and
adds, again, let him be as one who had loved a girl beneath him,
but outgrew his infatuation and married his social equal. Or Hal-
lam may look on him sympathetically, just as his own love of the
lower animals does not interfere with his higher aspirations. He
compares Hallam to a country boy of gifts who achieves success yet
feels a pensive fondness for his childhood companions. He hopes
that perhaps his songs may aid Hallam onwards. His loss has made
him kindly, like a blind man, handicapped but cheerful.

(We are here about one-third through the whole poem and a
sense of monotony in spite of the variety of styles and of detail can
hardly be denied. There has been very little movement and almost
no progress. After the record of sorrow, followed by reminiscences
of Hallam, came the first Christmas, with a first ray of hopefulness
and meditations on the existence of the soul after death, which
were in turn followed by despair and miscellaneous observations
about his relations with Hallam, leading to an uncertain conclu-
sion.)

The poet continues, however, with a group of five sections (LXVII-
LXXI; 21 stanzas) concerned mainly with his dreams; then, after an
occasional poem, quite unrelated to what precedes or follows, cele-
brating the first anniversary of Hallam's death, continues with an-
other group of five (LXXIII-LXXVII) on fame. The moonlight reminds
him of the churchyard where Hallam is buried, but he cannot
dream of Hallam as dead. He has a strange dream of martyrdom,

but is comforted by an angelic voice. He cannot recall Hallam's features except when his own will is passive. But at length sleep brings back to him their holiday together in southern France. —Fame, he says, is a small thing in this vast universe; it may be left with God. A man's true glory is the "divine inward force" which Hallam possessed and which would have brought him fame if he had lived. Then unexpectedly the subject becomes not Hallam's but the poet's fame; and again he apologizes for writing.

The Second Christmas (LXXVIII) is outwardly calm and the poet's tears are dry "with long use" (however that may be), but the mood does not greatly change until LXXXVI—rather there is a gradual amelioration of sorrow. He first tells of his brother Charles, some- what hesitantly. The reflection that if Hallam had died first *he* would have suffered nobly is a lesson helpful to the poet. In three very compact quatrains (LXXXI) he recognizes that though time would have increased his love for Hallam, death has ripened it at a touch. He complains that they are separated, though Hallam is full of good works elsewhere. Delaying spring is a symbol of his prolonged sorrow. His imagined picture of their happy life if Hal- lam had lived (and had married his sister) only reopens the wound. Then comes the long section (LXXXV) addressed to Edmund Lush- ington, who is going to marry another sister, which contains what the critics call the turning point of the whole poem. It might be called The Old Love and the New. The poet finds now that sor- row has brought new strength and feels that Hallam would have him solace himself with a new "friendship for the years to come." In a word, he has mourned long enough and must now live his own life. The next section (LXXXVI) characteristically mannered (written at Bournemouth in 1839) registers this achievement of peace. He now revisits Cambridge with cheerful memories of Hallam and after an intercalary section in which he takes pleasure in the joy and grief of the nightingale's song (the nightingale stanzas sepa- rate two contrasting styles) he recalls the calm and delight of their earlier associations at Somersby.

Yet he is still haunted by the question of communion with the dead and he returns to it in a group of six sections (XC-XCV). First he repudiates the notion that the dead would not be welcome if they should revisit us; he urges Hallam to return to him visibly;—but

111

no, he says, such earthly visions would be but illusions; he wishes rather than Hallam come as spirit to his spirit, with such communion as is possible only to those who are at peace with God and man. And so, finally, after reading Hallam's letters one quiet summer evening at Somersby he falls into a trance and enjoys for an instant complete spiritual reunion with his friend—or perhaps with the divine spirit ("Maybe the Deity").

Three miscellaneous sections follow this climax: how some one (perhaps Hallam?) fought through honest doubt to fearless faith (xcvi); how a mortal who loves one who is dead "resembles the wife of a great man of science. She looks up to him—but what he knows is a mystery to her"; and how a friend departs for Vienna, but the poet is satisfied with what Hallam had written him about that city (xcviii). Then comes the second anniversary of Hallam's death (1835): it is a calm morning and the poet feels in sympathy with all who mourn for their dead (xcix).

In 1837 the Tennyson family moved away from Somersby and held its Christmas celebration on the "unhallowed ground" of Waltham Abbey. This is the extreme limit of the poet's including us in his private affairs. Leaving Somersby, he tells us, is like losing Hallam over again, for he hardly knows whether its associations with his family or its associations with Hallam are the stronger in his heart. But on his last night there (ciii; 14 stanzas) he has a symbolic dream which envisages "the great progress of the age, as well as the opening of another world" and all "the great hopes of humanity and science." At the end, by his own interpretation of the vision, we learn that "Everything that made Life beautiful here we may hope to pass on with us beyond the grave." The new note of the *larger* hope is now first sounded, faintly and allegorically, to be made clearer at the close of the poem. Meanwhile, Christmas in the new home is strange and without *élan*, but when the wild bells of the Abbey church ring in the new year it is the new era of all-embracing hope, of "progressive Christianity," and quite literally a new golden age (cvi). And in this spirit Hallam's birthday is now celebrated, "with festal cheer," although the weather is bad (cvii).

These exuberant outbursts however cannot of course be maintained. He will not grieve alone: "it is useless trying to find [Hal-

lam] in the other worlds," so he will try to learn the lessons of
sorrow in human fellowship (cviii). And now his thoughts slip
back to the grave where lies his ideal man: he pays formal tribute
to Hallam in six sections (cix-cxiv), culminating in the wish that
the whole world might grow—as Hallam did—in wisdom as well as
in knowledge. Spring returns

> *and my regret*
> *Becomes an April violet* (cxv)

and he feels

> *Less yearning for the friendship fled,*
> *Than some strong bond which is to be.* (cxvi)

(Both Gatty and Miss Chapman understand this as "a future tie of
lasting blessedness with Arthur"; can it possibly be, since we are
already introduced to the family fireside, his long deferred mar-
riage with Emily Sellwood?) Their separation here will but double
the sweetness of their embrace to come.

The next section (cxviii; 7 stanzas) is the celebrated anticipation
of Chambers' *Vestiges*, 1844 (and Darwin's *Origin* fifteen years
later). Some of the language is obscure, but the drift is sufficiently
plain. "They say" that earth developed from "fluent heat" through
"seeming random forms" to man,—to man who similarly has de-
veloped through his own fires of fear and storms of suffering to his
present "shape and use," and who is now exhorted to

> *Move upward, working out the beast.*

This idea is introduced by the statement that "human love and
truth" cannot turn to "earth and lime," but rather do the dead
continue in "an ampler day" " For ever nobler ends." This sec-
tion, if its chief theme is evolution, stands isolated in the poem, a
kind of parenthesis; nothing leads up to it, and the following sec-
tion is a lyric interlude in which the poet cheerfully revisits Hal-
lam's house in London, measuring the distance he has come since
the earlier visit in vii. Next (cxx) he says he would not care to live
if physical life were all; or in other words, materialistic science is
not enough. And in the next, written in 1849 at Shiplake (where he
was married in June 1850) he reflects that as the Morning and
Evening star are one, so Hallam remains the same in his past and

present life. And finally, in a very cryptic section (CXXII) he craves the renewal of Hallam's inspiring presence.

The closing nine sections (CXXIII-CXXXI; 37 stanzas) contain his doctrinal climax, interrupted only by the apology for mingling bitterness with songs of love and sorrow (CXXV) and the two dithyrambic addresses to Hallam (CXXIX, CXXX). (Note that the method of interruption or interweaving continues to the end.) The things of earth may change and fade, but the spirit abides, and he clings to his dream of reunion after death. Knowledge of God comes not by reason but by intuitive feeling. Love was and is his "Lord and King"; the sentinel whispers assurance that all is well,— in spite of the blindness and madness of the world to-day. Then, lest he seem to have exceeded his commission, he insists that the faith and love which have overcome his personal despair at the death of one he loved are akin to, are really identical with, the faith and love which overcome despair in human progress; he has risen from the depths of private grief to the great height where he can confidently assert the future triumph of the race. His own sorrow and love are now sublimated; he soars from this ecstasy to a hymn to the living will of man, a prayer for faith and the "truths that never can be proved" until we are all ultimately united "soul in soul"—

> *Until we close with all we loved,*
> *And all we flow from, soul in soul.*

This is a splendid ambiguity, like that of an oracle. "All we loved" must mean Hallam in particular and in general all who are separated by death from their loved ones; "all we flow from" must mean the divine soul, God. Thus the reconciliation of all human sorrow and the consummation of all earthly existence in a future life are blended for the grand climax.

According to the poet himself, 'In Memoriam' "begins with a funeral and ends with a marriage"; the Epilogue is therefore integral. And Miss Chapman, with Tennyson's approval, says: "such a marriage is the very type and hope of all things fair and bright and good, seeming to bring us nearer to . . . that crowning race, that Christ that is to be." Tennyson's favorite solvent of all hard

questions, the little child, very plain at the end of 'The Two
Voices'—

> *And in their double love secure,*
> *The little maiden walk'd demure,*
> *Pacing with downward eyelids pure,*

and still plainer through the latter half of 'The Princess,' here
functions in more delicately allusive form as the soul which is to
"draw from out the vast" and so as a symbol of our racial progress
towards the divine event of which Hallam has now become an
anticipatory "noble type." Thus the elegy ends on the cheerful
note of reproduction and our racial hopes remain in the Tenny-
son family.

These poems or 'sections' were composed, as is well known, over
a period of sixteen or seventeen years, the earliest probably soon
after Hallam's death in September 1833 and the latest (CXXI) not
long before publication in June 1850. Some twenty more may be
approximately dated from various kinds of external and internal
evidence; the others cannot now be assigned to a particular time.[2]
It is not even possible to say certainly that most of them were com-
posed in the thirties or in the forties. Moreover, the poet himself
makes record that "The sections were written at many different
places [as well as times], and as the phases of our intercourse came
to memory and suggested them."[3] And since he added: "I did not
write them with any view of weaving them into a whole, or for
publication, until I found I had written so many," we are not justi-
fied in looking for unity of tone or plan. In truth, it is greatly to be
regretted that, whenever it was that he decided to publish, he ever
made the effort to superinduce an appearance of arrangement upon
the various sections; for the two anniversary and the three Christ-
mas poems produce only an illusion of order and have led in-
cautious readers to assume (and somehow find) more method than
actually exists. It would have been better to leave them as a mis-
cellany, like the Psalms or the sonnet-sequences of Shakespeare and
others, with only the most general order of emotional development.
But Tennyson made the initial error, and no doubt the anxious
commentators may be forgiven their exceeding zeal; though both
they and he may have prejudiced their case by undertaking too
much.

At the moment when Tennyson perceived that he had on hand
a collection of elegies or, as he called them, "memorial poems,"
which might be worked up for publication as parts of a single long
poem, just what (one may ask) was the state of his artistic con-
science, if he submitted it to a rigid examen? The earliest-written
sections were certainly the spontaneous overflow of real and im-
mediate feeling and the later-written sections a somewhat idealized
projection of the first experience, in which Hallam became less the
deceased friend and more and more the symbol of personal loss. In
this way, which would be entirely natural and in no sense impugn
the poet's sincerity, the original loss would become depersonalized,
a generalized loss used for artistic purpose as the basis for reflection
on death and the future life. Somewhere in this gradual extension
of a personal feeling into an impersonal situation, however, there
may well arise the danger of—not so much insincerity as—artificial-
ity. Remembering Tennyson's habitual search for poetic material,
we may be permitted to wonder if sometimes in the passage of
seventeen years the composition of these elegies did not become a
kind of habit and the death of Hallam a kind of convenience to
the muse.[b]

In different ways and in different degrees this is one of the dangers
of all artistic work. There is the impulse, the motion of the spirit
disciplined by craftsmanship, and when the impulse flags, as it al-
ways must, the craftsman takes over. Only the most skilful and
most gifted can surmount the danger; the others resort to artificial
stimuli to re-beat the flame. Tennyson was exposed to this danger
from two directions. What began as an intense private experience,
recorded in some of the opening sections of the poem, became con-
fessedly a mere starting-point for the expression of feelings and
ideas which were intended to be of 'universal' significance ("the

[b] This is not exactly the "sad me-
chanic exercise" of v. There is a sug-
gestion of it, however, in one of the
grumbling letters of FitzGerald, 28 Feb-
ruary 1845, who had seen part of the
manuscript: "If one could have good
lyrics, I think the World wants them
as much as ever. Tennyson's are good:
but not of the *kind* wanted. We have
surely had enough of men reporting
their sorrows: especially when one is
aware all the time that the poet wil-
fully protracts what he complains of . . .
and yet we are to condole with him,
and be taught to ruminate our losses &
sorrows in the same way. I felt that if
Tennyson had got on a horse and ridden
20 miles, instead of moaning over his
pipe, he would have been cured of his
sorrows in half the time" (*A FitzGerald
Friendship being Hitherto Unpublished
Letters from Edward FitzGerald to Wil-
liam Bodham Donne*, ed. N. C. Hannay,
New York, 1932, p. 10).

way of the soul"); and 'In Memoriam' in its final arrangement of parts does not seem to be or pretend to be a continuous development from the personal to the general, but rather an intermingling of the two kinds. The question would not present itself if the whole poem were dramatic, if the personal loss of the poet were from the outset submerged or sublimated into a general grief whence spring the reflections on death and immortality. And secondly, this danger is the more acute and obvious when the poet is trying to add from without a structure which is admittedly inorganic to a number of lyrics which have accumulated in his notebooks.

Another result of the irregular composition of 'In Memoriam' is its variations in style—not the inequalities of poetic merit or the unevenness which is inevitable in any long poem, but the mixture of incompatible styles. This is in part a concomitant of the different sorts of subject matter, but it is more. It might be amusing to classify the sections from this point of view. About 70 per cent of them are 'simple' in the sense that they are readily understood and not markedly ornate; and these could be subdivided into three nearly equal groups, according to degree, as fairly simple, simple, and too simple. In contrast some twenty-five sections are either cryptic or obscure, and the rest elaborate or rhetorical in style (sometimes in the good sense, sometimes in the bad sense). The so-called Epilogue contains illustrations of all these manners, but some other examples will serve better. Put the third stanza of LIX beside the last stanza of CXXII or the third of CV:

> *My centred passion cannot move,*
> *Nor will it lessen from to-day;*
> *But I'll have leave at times to play*
> *As with the creature of my love....*

> *And all the breeze of Fancy blows,*
> *And every dew-drop paints a bow,*
> *The wizard lightnings deeply glow,*
> *And every thought breaks out a rose....*

> *No more shall wayward grief abuse*
> *The genial hour with mask and mime;*
> *For change of place, like growth of time,*
> *Has broke the bond of dying use.*

Or read consecutively the soaring ecstatic LXXXVI (which has been called the climax of the poem)—

> *Sweet after showers, ambrosial air,*
> *That rollest from the gorgeous gloom*
> *Of evening over brake and bloom*
> *And meadow, slowly breathing bare*
>
> *The round of space*

and the following section (of whose ten stanzas I quote only the first and fifth)—

> *I past beside the reverend walls*
> *In which of old I wóre the gown;*
> *I roved at random thro' the town,*
> *And saw the tumult of the halls; ...*
>
> *Another name was on the door:*
> *I linger'd; all within was noise*
> *Of songs, and clapping hands, and boys*
> *That crash'd the glass and beat the floor.*

"That crash'd the glass" is one thing; the "gorgeous gloom of evening" is quite another. Or take the last stanza (plain) of XC with the first (colored) of the next section—

> *Ah dear, but come thou back to me:*
> *Whatever change the years have wrought,*
> *I find not yet one lonely thought*
> *That cries against my wish for thee....*
>
> *When rosy plumelets tuft the larch,*
> *And rarely pipes the mounted thrush;*
> *Or underneath the barren bush*
> *Flits by the sea-blue bird of March.*

And finally read XLIV, to which Bradley devotes eleven pages of inconclusive exegesis, alongside the too easy transparency of LX. Sometimes, of course, the style is aspiring and difficult because the matter is difficult and cannot be communicated in simple language; and sometimes it seems just needlessly cryptic (as in I). The opening and closing stanzas of XCV illustrate the old-fashioned descriptive technique of the best eighteenth-century; XV the newer romantic style which became Tennyson's staple. And so on. It is only natural that during seventeen years a poet's style should vary, and should vary with the different kinds of subject, but at a sacrifice of unity; in this poem, however, the variations are not so much due to Tennyson's maturing as to his choice of manners. In 'In Memoriam' which predominates, uniformity or variety?

But these are secondary questions. Even if faults of artistic insincerity and of unevenness are fully admitted, they would damage but not seriously undermine 'In Memoriam.' The primary question is: is it a true poem, a poetical treatment of its chosen subject?

The subject of 'In Memoriam' is twofold: Alfred Tennyson's grief for the death of Arthur Hallam (or the poet's grief for the loss of his friend) and Tennyson's battle with doubt, ending with victory (or the poet's reflections on death and immortality, the "way of the soul"). 'In Memoriam' is therefore both an elegy and a philosophical poem; and each aspect, sorrow and consolation, has a double meaning, the personal and the impersonal, which cannot be evaded in spite of Tennyson's warning. "It must be remembered," said he,

that this is a poem, *not* an actual biography. It is founded on our friendship, on the engagement of Arthur Hallam to my sister, on his sudden death at Vienna, just before the time fixed for their marriage, and on the burial at Clevedon Church. The poem concludes with the marriage of my youngest sister Cecilia. It was meant to be a kind of *Divina Commedia,* ending with happiness. . . . The different moods of sorrow as in a drama are dramatically given, and my conviction that fear, doubts, and suffering will find answer and relief only through Faith in a God of Love. 'I' is not always the author speaking of himself, but the voice of the human race speaking thro' him. . . .

A few points here demand annotation. Cecilia is of course not the sister who was to marry Arthur Hallam. The meaning of "It" in "It was meant to be a kind of *Divina Commedia*" is not entirely perspicuous. The reference might be vaguely to the epithalamic epilogue. But Tennyson seems to have meant that his whole poem was like the *Divine Comedy* in that both works end happily. Surely he did not wish to imply comparison with Dante's poem in any other respect. Further, "was meant to" must refer to a time after he decided to arrange the elegies for publication. The dramatic ef-

119

fect of the different moods is not obvious. The cardinal 'teaching' of the poem, a belief in personal immortality, is not hinted as part of his "conviction." And finally, the "always" should be underscored.[c] In a word, the poem is, on the poet's own testimony, partly personal and partly impersonal—"the voice of the human race"; but it is left for our own tact to distinguish the two voices.

The form of the poem *as elegy* is well fitted both to the subject and to Tennyson's genius. For a record of sorrowing moments and personal memories the method—short lyrics without noticeable connection—is well chosen. But for a long philosophic poem it cannot be maintained that this method is a happy one. Moreover, the mixture of personal elements and universalizing elements is an 'inconvenience' (as Bacon would say) troublesome both to the poet and to the reader. There is a good deal in 'In Memoriam' about the private and domestic relations of Arthur Hallam and Alfred Tennyson, some of which is poetically unmanageable. Although there is never any doubt, biographically, of Tennyson's sincerity, there is a question whether he has made his personal suffering interesting, sufficiently real to the reader and therefore worthy of such protracted mourning. It is a question if parts of the poem are not too personal and intimate, and therefore if our attention is not drawn so specifically to Arthur Hallam and Alfred Tennyson (to say nothing of the poet's sisters and their marriages) that we cannot easily accept the data as a basis for generalizing the "way of the soul." The autobiographic and the speculative are side by side: they may "cleave" but do they "incorporate"?

Though the direct celebration of Hallam occupies relatively small space in the whole poem, and that chiefly towards the end, his presence is felt in many sections where he is not even mentioned.[4] We receive, nevertheless, no clear conception of him as an individual; and in LXXV the poet says expressly: "by the measure of my grief I leave thy greatness to be guess'd." This grief is itself rather implied than portrayed, except in a few early sections, and is accordingly less powerful dramatically, that is, less likely to move our sympathy and secure our understanding of the poet's argument

---

[c] The whole paragraph is so filled with confusion that one hesitates to confront the poet with it; but it is set forth without qualification in the *Memoir* (I, 304-305). Tennyson was often unfortunate in commenting on his own work.

which is founded upon his grief.[d] Yet, paradoxically, his grief is rendered poetically effective by virtue of the skill and beauty of the language. The number of sections in which this is true is not large, but it is large enough. The distinction is quite simple and fairly significant. His private sorrow, which was the starting point of his poem, has failed to stir us deeply, although he exhibited it freely, with realistic details. His accomplishment is due to his art, and not at all to the personal impulse towards composition; and the personal impulse becomes therefore irrelevant, intrusive, wrong. To put the paradox in another way: 'In Memoriam' would have been just as impressive as a lament if the sorrow had been 'dramatic' rather than 'real,' and such an imagined sorrow would have been equally powerful as a basis for the philosophical or religious 'teaching' which Tennyson develops from his private emotion.[e]

'In Memoriam' is not only a monument to Arthur Hallam and a record of Tennyson's personal suffering at Hallam's early death, it is also the "way of the soul"—a somewhat pretentious phrase, but Tennyson's own—his representation of everyman's pain when confronted with death, the struggle with doubt, and the triumphant assertion of God's love. The poet is at first overcome with his own loss, questions the ways of God to man, seeks consolation for himself, and in fighting his own fight reveals the grounds of consolation and hope for all mankind.

What, now, is Tennyson's answer? Put in the briefest form, Tennyson's answer to the problem of human existence is the belief in personal immortality. "His belief in personal immortality," said Knowles, "was passionate—I think almost the strongest passion he had"; and outside of 'In Memoriam,' in the *Memoir* and in other records of conversations with the poet, there is abundant substan-

[d] Possibly the dispersion of expressions of grief through a long poem has something to do with this. If they were all brought together and read consecutively the effect might be greater. But note Andrew Lang's comment: "in *In Memoriam* sympathy and relief have been found, and will be found, by many. Another, we feel, has trodden our dark and stony path," and so on (p. 71).

[e] This view is interestingly supported by the English elegiac parallels. Although each one is very different from the other, the personal element has been remarkably slight in our great elegies. In Gray's it is almost nil, so far as we are aware; in Milton's nearly nil, and so also in Swinburne's; in Shelley's certainly not strong; and in Arnold's it was a distraction. One cannot quite say that the poetry varies in inverse ratio to the personal concern of the poet, yet there is a hint of this. Sentimental readers may well have been affected by Tennyson's baring of his own heart to their view; but while he won readers at the outset he has lost them in the sequel.

tiation of this statement.ᶠ "The chief consideration which induced Tennyson to cling to faith in immortality," says Masterman, "and the argument which he asserts almost defiantly throughout the remainder of his poetical career, is the impossibility of the deliberate acceptance of the negative belief." For to Tennyson as to many others "life, regarded simply as life terminating in death, yields no meaning whatever."⁵ As a corollary to this, he clings to a belief in the possibility of communion with the dead. Thence he proceeds, relying on the then undeveloped theories of evolution, to a belief in the gradual improvement of the human race. Accepting the doctrine of development from the inanimate to animate life, or at least of the development of brute into man and man into superior man, he found it repugnant to think that this development should stop abruptly with death. And further, in order that this view should yield its fullest meaning and satisfaction, there must be the concomitant development of the spiritual element, already latent in man, into the highest and ultimate realization, its absorption into the divine—though in consistency with his belief that "individuality endures" he was obliged sometimes (as in XLVII) to deny absolute absorption or to speak with oracular ambiguity.

Such, crudely stated, is Tennyson's position in 'In Memoriam.' It is certainly incomplete and not inexpugnable. But *that* is not our concern. We do not now read *Paradise Lost* and the *Divine Comedy* for their doctrinal content; we do not read the Oedipus plays or *Hamlet* with anxious concern over the ethical principles underlying them; we do read Chaucer's *Troilus* and Byron's *Don Juan* without distress at their 'immorality.' And so we are now able to read 'In Memoriam,' as our fathers and grandfathers were unable to read it, without being swayed by the religious value of its central 'argument.' It has been said, with some exaggeration perhaps, that to-day the belief in personal immortality is a matter of taste. It is at any rate not a burning question.ᵍ

ᶠ Tennyson is reported once as saying: "I'll shake my fist in God Almighty's face and say it isn't fair, if I find there is no immortality" (D. A. Wilson, *Carlyle on Cromwell and Others*, p. 325). The vehemence betrays a want of confidence. Said Tennyson to Carlyle: "Your traveller comes to an inn and lies down in his bed almost with the certainty that he will go on his journey rejoicing the next morning." Carlyle only grunted in reply. Afterwards FitzGerald remarked to Tennyson: "You had him there"; but Tennyson admitted later to Miss Thackeray (Lady Ritchie) that it only proved "how dangerous an illustration is."

ᵍ There used to be debate whether this position had anything novel or ori-

It would be tempting, but profitless, to pursue some of the awkward puzzles which spring to most modern readers' minds when they seriously consider the 'theology and philosophy' of the poem—Tennyson's infirmity in the face of doubt; his failure as Seer and Prophet to speak forth with the confidence of Faith; his admission (privately to Knowles) that the conclusion reached in the poem is "too hopeful";[h] his seeming helplessness before simple logical processes (not that one expects a poem to be a syllogism), and his reliance upon "Short swallow-flights of song" in preference to a reasoned progress of ideas when he is working in the domain of reason; his rejection of the standard ontological and teleological arguments as well as Christian revelation; the only half-hidden spiritual pride of his exaltation of personality and his insistence on self; his apparent surprise at finding that certain points cannot be "proved"; his unwillingness to admit, with Pascal, that "Le cœur a ses raisons, que la raison ne connaît pas" and proceed accordingly, or with St. Augustine that faith depends upon the will as much as upon the reason, and advance from there; and beyond all, the illogical conclusion, the happy ending wherein the immortality of mankind through evolution is substituted for the immortality of the individual soul, and, Hallam having died without issue, the future of the race is entrusted to the poet's sister. But of course a poem may be "somehow good" in spite of such handicaps.

ginal in it. The case for the negative was cogently put by Frederic Harrison, who might be expected to take issue with a branch of the evangelical creed. Cf. *Tennyson, Ruskin, Mill*, 1900, pp. 10-11. For the other side, see Andrew Lang's *Tennyson*, pp. 63 ff. Professor H. V. Routh (*Towards the Twentieth Century*, 1937, pp. 86-88), without mentioning either Harrison or Lang has answered them both. "The influence of *In Memoriam* has steadily declined. By the end of the century it was valued only as a phrase-book, a metrical triumph, a masterpiece of poetic expressiveness, and as such, generally relegated to schools and colleges.

"In one sense the poems deserved this fate because their author (through no fault of his own) did not face the spiritual problem of the nineteenth century; he only appeared to do so." In 1902 Churton Collins had said much the same

thing. "As a contribution to theological thought and philosophy—and on its first appearance it was hailed as a momentous contribution to both—*In Memoriam* has a very wasting hold on life. . . . We may perhaps think that its power is not equal to its charm, that it practically leaves us where it found us, that it furnishes faith with no new supports and truth with no new documents" (ed. *In Memoriam, The Princess, and Maud*, p. 20).

[h] "More than I am myself," said Tennyson (*Nineteenth Century*, XXXIII (1893), 182). And then he continued: "I am thinking of adding another to it, a speculative one, . . . showing that all the arguments are about as good on one side as the other, and thus throw man back more on the primitive impulses and feelings." Luckily he abandoned the purpose.

The real charge, however, against 'In Memoriam' is of course not that it is Victorian in theology and social ideas or that its answers to the doubts which spring from intense sorrow are not the answers which we of another generation desire—not, in a word, in the *thought* of the poem at all (though largely in the *thinking*), but rather that it does not satisfy what Arnold called "the laws of poetic truth and poetic beauty." Arnold never quite explained what these laws are, nor has anyone else, but we have a general idea. 'In Memoriam' is certainly a criticism of life and it has plenty of high seriousness—though many of the sections are seriously deficient in this quality—but it lacks form and coherence (what Arnold called, after Goethe, architectonics) and it lacks that clearness and sureness of treatment which its subject emphatically demands.

The form, a series of short lyrics, is not suited to a sustained philosophical poem. The plan, a discontinuous record of incidents, moods, and meditations, is fatally improper to a serious presentation of one of the most difficult and profound subjects which interest the human mind and spirit; and Tennyson's own confession (or boast) of the casual way in which the poem grew would be sufficient, if internal evidence were not abundant, to condemn his method. For such a subject only a carefully plotted and clearly articulated plan could hope to succeed; yet Tennyson's plan was, having let his little memorial poems accumulate until they were numerous enough to publish, to give them the appearance of order by indicating a few dates and grouping them as best he could on a theoretical thread of grief, doubt, hope, and faith. The series of lyrics shows a kind of progress, to be sure, but it is so frequently interrupted and diverted that the reader is constantly left in uncertainty. Tennyson might better have claimed less than he did in this respect; but he was tempted beyond his strength when he saw his poem's popular success.

'In Memoriam' has moreover too much variety, both of style and of content. In style it ranges from the plainest possible language to passages which are exceedingly obscure, not only because the subject matter is difficult but because the expression is over-elaborate, even to loose grammar and faulty syntax. In style it ranges also from a fine simplicity to false rhetoric and pseudo-poetic diction; from pure lyric strains to displays of over-strained virtuosity. It shifts without warning from the communication of high thoughts and powerful emotions to the cheap and easy sentimental appeals of the domestic idyll.

And this excess of variety is not only in style, but likewise in content. The poem includes more kinds of subject than can be successfully moulded into a real unity. There are splendid descriptions of nature, in which Tennyson almost always excels; lyric cries of the suffering heart; moving analyses of both doubt and despair; confused and almost inarticulate outpourings of grief; expositions, both straightforward and indirect, of reasoned questioning;—and all these blend together into one great elegiac tone. But there are also many *excursus*, digressions, footnotes, irrelevancies— for example, about his brothers and sisters and their personal affairs, details about Arthur Hallam which he fails to make interesting to us though they interest him closely, details about the family's moving from Somersby and the Christmas celebrations—all of which he has reported faithfully but has not transmuted into poetry. Besides these foreign elements which he has not integrated with his elegy there are the uncomfortably frank personal apologies about his own indulgence in grief, the sad mechanic exercise of composition, and the futility of fame; and still less amenable to incorporation with his main theme, the little indignant observations about contemporary conditions. But the poem's greatest handicap of disunity springs from Tennyson's deliberate extension of his professed subject, the consolation which came to him from his hardwon belief in personal immortality, to include an assured prophecy of a golden age upon earth. Not only do we mortals pass (under conditions never even examined) to a state of both human and spiritual perfection in a life beyond this life, but the race itself is promised a similar perfection in a future life terrestrial. This, if it is an argument at all, is an argument by analogy merely, and a very imperfect analogy, but it is an argument extraneous to his chief concern which was the reconciliation to death. It suggests a confusion between two kinds of immortality which is patent in the Epilogue.

These faults of unity, both of subject and of treatment, may seem secondary. They are readily recognized, but they inhere in Tennyson's conception of his artistic problem. They must have been as obvious to him as they are to us. More fundamental even, and much more difficult to exposit, because they involve us in doctrinal disputes, are the inner faults, those which come from the poet's insecure grasp of the subject itself.

Probably the root of the main difficulty is Tennyson's immaturity; for it must always be remembered that Tennyson was only twenty-four when Hallam died and 'In Memoriam' was begun, and a great philosophic poem on death and immortality is not to be expected from a poet of that age. Most of the sections, at any rate, were probably composed by the time he was thirty-five; and the same remark obtains: a great elegy, yes—witness Milton (who was twenty-nine when he wrote 'Lycidas') and Shelley (who was twenty-nine when he wrote 'Adonais'). And during the sixteen-year interval in which the memorial poems accumulated not only was Tennyson's spirit disturbed by the doubts and questionings which sprang from this one personal loss, but his whole life was unsettled by a series of other distractions which prevented that quiet meditation which alone could have helped him to a clear understanding of his artistic task of making the elegies into a philosophical poem:—the death of his father and the almost-poverty of his family, the pyroglyphic calamity of his one financial speculation, the broken engagement to Emily Sellwood, his persistent ill-health, part cause and part result of his morbid mental states, the attacks of reviewers on his first two volumes, his highly varied but intermittent studies, and his restless wanderings which were also both cause and result of his emotional unbalance. During this sixteen-year interval, moreover, there are few signs of mental development. His one fresh creative impulse came from the death of Hallam, and this took the form of fragmentary elegies. The rest of his artistic energy went into the rewriting of his published poems for the volume of 1842 and after that to the completion of his half-whimsical and half-solemn medley of 'The Princess,' begun when he was still at Cambridge or soon after. Some even of the 'new' poems of 1842 were by-products of the death of Hallam—'The Two Voices,' 'Ulysses,' and of course 'Break, break, break' (which missed getting into 'In Memoriam' only by the chance that it came in a different meter). The rest of the 'new' poems of 1842 are nearly all examples of those genre pieces, English idylls, which throughout his long life provided him with the opportunity to *write something* more than they released the pressure of creative feeling or thinking: interstitial, avocational work of a man who was in the habit of composing verse. 'Locksley Hall' is the one significant exception. 'In Memoriam' may therefore be regarded as the great product of Tennyson's maturing period, between the ages of twenty-five and forty, when the youthful promise was either to prove itself or betray its emptiness. Its enormous success with Victorian readers, so far as their judgment was to be trusted, must have given Tennyson great confidence in his powers; and if he felt the position it gave him to be a false eminence, there was no sign. Nevertheless it was unfortunate that he should have begun—unintentionally, as it were —at the age of twenty-five the poem which was to be the testing-ground of his maturing genius.

From Tennyson's statement that the sections were composed somewhat at haphazard, together with the fact that he did not succeed in arranging them, either by mere transposition or by filling out with fresh sections the wanting parts, into a formal unity and orderly coherence, we are warranted in reading them as a note-book or journal of mourning and of the loss and recovery of faith. The logical steps by which Tennyson's mind and heart ascended from despair to consolation, from doubt to an assertion (even if not a conviction) of faith are not all present in the poem: they do not need to be, since it is a poem. We have only the steps which the poet chose to record and publish. We do however witness his suffering in many intimate details; he confides to us the shadows and gleams of light as they came to him, the moments which to him seemed important then though to us they may appear inconsequent because they are not ours and because he has not fused them into a true whole. We are thus permitted to observe Tennyson's mind through many of the stages of his experience, even when his thoughts are unworthy and the tone confessional; we are permitted to hear him talking to himself, now about Arthur in the other world, now about his brothers in this; we are permitted to see him now yearning for comfort, now distracted by trivial incidents, now seeking ecstatic communion with the dead, now agreeably at home with the living. Read in this sense 'In Memoriam' is a remarkably frank and disarming revelation. If we find some of Tennyson's meditations uninteresting, some of his observations commonplace, some of his experiences without salt or liveliness for us, this is (to put it paradoxically) a judgment on the poet not on the poem, on the material, not on the treatment—though such a distinction may be critically improper—for he has put before us a narrative of his experience, realistic at the risk, which all realism runs, of being dull, but impressive in its honest unreserve, even if unimpressive at all points in what it portrays. In so far as our minds are in sympathy with the kind of experience Tennyson has to display we shall be moved by his sincerity, touched by his sorrow, and gratified by the comfort which he finally wrings from his suffering. Read in this sense 'In Memoriam' becomes a long lyrical domestic idyll, autobiographical in the first instance, with the immediate appeal of all autobiography, but also a story-situation like that of 'The May Queen' or 'Enoch Arden' and the other Idylls of the Hearth, though different in technical presentation just as 'Maud' is different, and like 'Maud' somewhat rambling and unfocussed in outline but brightened by fine passages of varying tone and color. This, I submit, is a sympathetic way of reading 'In Memoriam' and was that of many of the poet's contemporaries; but it is uncritical.

For if, on the other hand, our minds are not naturally sympathetic to a story of this sort, if we do not readily share the kind of personal suffering which was Tennyson's, if the kind of religious doubt which he felt is foreign to us, if our hearts do not passionately yearn for direct communion with those who are separated from us by death, and if our minds can be satisfied without a belief in the everlasting survival of the individual self; then, in spite of the biographic interest in 'In Memoriam' the poem will not awaken a quick response in us (as it did at first), and we will look for that literary art, that dramatic power by which all great poetry enlists our affections and stirs our emotions and creates a sense of our common human experience even when the immediate grounds for it are not there. We will demand in the poem that dramatic art by which we are made to share those emotions and experiences which are not naturally within our range, that intense illusion of reality which makes the characters and incidents of great drama and fiction, and the emotions of great lyric poetry, more real than our own little lives. And this quality we shall not always find, for 'In

Memoriam' as a whole does not possess it. Tennyson seems at first glance to have been fortunate in producing a poem with a direct and universal appeal, on a subject of universal interest. Yet like many popular writers he was betrayed by the contemporary elements of his appeal, and lacking the power which fortifies the temporary with the universal, which emphasizes our common humanity above its momentary and local concerns, he has left us a poem which as a whole is of considerable biographic and documentary interest, but without permanent attractiveness.

"It must be remembered," however, said Tennyson, "that this is a poem, *not* an actual biography. . . . 'I' is not always the author speaking of himself, but the voice of the human race speaking thro' him." *Not always;* but how is the reader to know when Tennyson is speaking in his own voice and when through the mask? The "way of the soul" seems very like an afterthought and "not always" an evasion. Yet this would not greatly matter if the poem would support the interpretation which Tennyson has asked us to read into it. One could not only forgive, one could even justify, the poet in claiming a deeper significance than he was at first aware of, if that meaning can be fairly found in it. If it can, we shall abandon the position which regarded 'In Memoriam' as a large-scale domestic idyll and reread the poem as—though not always—the way of the soul. That is, we shall project the incidents of the poem beyond Tennyson's own personal experience and regard them as typical of the experience of the race. Tennyson is to be identified with mankind and the domestic details of his story are to be understood as but illustrations of what we all have suffered and learned—not all of them, to be sure, but we are to use our tact and discretion in deciding which to generalize and which to accept literally. Such is Tennyson's claim. It means that we, all men, share not only his passionate sense of bereavement (as at times we all have done), but also his anxiety to know and see after death the friend he has lost in his life; not only his questionings of divine justice, but also his acceptance of honest doubt as the ground of religious faith; not only his gradual acknowledgement of faith without the necessity of proof, but his special reasons, never made entirely perspicuous, for intuitive faith; not only his belief in the evolution of man from the brute animals (now a commonplace), but also his hopes of a millenial perfection of the race as a source of comfort in our daily discomfitures. Again Tennyson seems to have mistaken some of the ideas prevalent in his time and cogent for many of his generation (but not questions of importance at all times) for the simple universal beliefs which in one language or another all civilized mankind accept. Just as the intimate details about Arthur Hallam and Tennyson's family were too specific to be acceptable for the purposes of poetic truth, so the religious and social tenets, vague as some of them are, are too specifically local and topical for the appeals of universal truth. This does not mean that they are all wrong; only that they are Victorian and cannot be ackowledged without the discount to which all local and temporary versions of truth are subject. Some of the emotions, some of the experiences, some of the findings of 'In Memoriam' *are* of universal application, and by them parts of the poem will live; but as a single poem it has had its day and ceased to be. —To most of us this was already obvious, but the reasons for its failure had to be examined.

The facts, moreover, of the poem's irregular origin, its growth by accumulation rather than by design, must be held to militate against its success as a philosophical delineation of the soul's education by love and sorrow. In this sense, Tennyson's soul was self-educated. Without a carefully conceived plan no poet could hope to execute such a grandiose design,—the chief theme fully thought through and its many implications and contributory elements plotted and placed. Instead, Tennyson seems to have improvised, to have felt his way along—the poem itself is evidence of this, without his own statement—and the most he could expect or claim is that we should recognize with sympathy the drawbacks of such a method. Nor is it to be denied that there is a certain piquancy or immediacy in this friendly appeal. But it was a small gain for a great loss.

Indeed, the subject, if firmly grasped and clearly developed, has immense advantages. To record the suffering of a personal loss and make that the basis of a declaration of faith fought for against the heavy odds of philosophic and religious doubt was a new opportunity, apparently never seized by any poet before him. It was an opportunity for a great original modern work, the great Christian poem of the nineteenth century (as Kingsley actually called it);

but Tennyson was unfitted for it by his youth, his training, and his theology. His mind had not been disciplined with a severe application to logical thought and speculation. He was not deeply read in the best that philosophy and religion had discovered on his special subject, though he read widely. He was not really a Christian, though Stopford Brooke tried valiantly to prove that he was. (Emily Sellwood knew better, and this was one of the reasons which postponed their marriage.) He felt no profound faith which was wrested from him by Hallam's death—at least I find no evidence of it either in the biography or in the poem. He was still searching for the grounds of faith when Hallam died; he had not reached the stage which genuinely religious minds achieve early or never at all, though they may lose it again and again, the recognition that faith is either a gift or an act of will, and not a matter for argument and logical demonstration. In spite of going through the motions, or rather, going through the emotions, Tennyson never quite reached that stage. He tried logic and it failed him (as of course it must); or if not logic, the method and appearance of logic. And he fell back upon assertion in lieu of conviction, upon trust and hope because he found nothing else. What he really sought, like so many of his contemporaries, was not faith, religious faith, but confidence and assurance of his own religious inclinations. His culminating achievement is the great hymn to Divine Love which is the Prologue to 'In Memoriam.' It is a humble confession of human weakness and his own impotence, and clutching after comfort—"believing where we cannot prove"—with full admission of its elusiveness. There is all the sadness of defeat and none of the triumph of victory in the crucial stanza—

> *We have but faith: we cannot know; ....*
> *And yet we trust it comes from thee,*
> *A beam in darkness: let it grow.*

This is still the language of doubt, for beneath its humility is uncertainty. True faith is acceptance, whole and unqualified. Read for example, Gerard Manly Hopkins, Tennyson's later contemporary. Yet against this stand the assertions of triumph in the latter part of the poem (CXXIV-CXXXI), a fine poetic climax (barring the overfeminine language of CXXIX); and this contrast, together with

Tennyson's remark to Knowles that it was all too hopeful, makes the question of insincerity difficult to escape, or what is equally damaging, mental confusion. To have staked his whole theological position on the survival of personality after death marks a limitation in Tennyson's grasp of religion; and the brave summing up by his son in the *Memoir* (i, 311) shows that while Tennyson regarded himself in his later life as thoroughly religious the terms of his thinking were vague, indecisive, and not a little confused.

Lest some readers, however, may be disappointed with these conclusions I refer them to chapter XIV of the *Memoir* and append a few selected appreciations.

These touching lines evidently come from the full heart of the widow of a military man. (From an early review, quoted *Memoir* i, 298)

. . . in our eyes the noblest christian poem which England has produced for two centuries. (Charles Kingsley, *Fraser's Magazine*, September 1850)

Though I have been familiar with the poem from boyhood, it is only in the last few years that the full import of that problem and of the noble solution offered by the poet has become clear to me. The work, as I now understand it, seems to me . . . one of the great world-poems, worthy to be placed on the same list as the *Oresteia*, the *Divina Comedia* [*sic*], and *Faust*. (Thomas Davidson, *Prolegomena to In Memoriam*, 1889, Preface)

It is a song of victory and life arising out of defeat and death; of peace which has forgotten doubt; of joy whose mother was sorrow but who has turned his mother's heart into delight. The conquest of love—the moral triumph of the soul over the worst blows of fate, over the outward forces of Nature, even over its own ill—that is the motive of the poems which endure, which, like the great lighthouses, stand and shine through the storms of time to save and lead into a haven of peace the navies of humanity. (Stopford Brooke, *Tennyson*, 1894, p. 189)

Surely it is not a little that we, a world of mourners, should be taught how to grieve; that a great and noble man should have laid bare to us his spiritual life through years of much tribulation; should have allowed us to watch the conflict waged within his soul between the powers of doubt and darkness and weakness and selfishness on the one side, and on the other, faith, light, strength, and love; that he should have gained the victory—our victory no less than his; for who can read 'In Memoriam' without being wiser, and happier, and better? (Morton Luce, *Handbook*, 1895, p. 292)

The range and scope of *In Memoriam* is practically boundless. It takes all human knowledge and all spiritual development for its province. Every feature of our complex modern life . . . all are lucidly mirrored, all blend in the perfect harmony. (Henry E. Shepherd, *A Commentary upon Tennyson's In Memoriam*, New York, 1908, p. 17)

CHAPTER SIX

Maud

BESIDES BEING a child of the Crimean War, 'Maud' had several godfathers. In 1837 Lord Northampton, getting up a volume, called *The Tribute,* for a sick clergyman, solicited a contribution from Tennyson; who after some grumbling sent in a poem (it was headed 'Stanzas') of a hundred and ten lines beginning "O that 'twere possible." This poem was neglected for seventeen years, until in 1854, according to the usual account, Sir John Simeon suggested that to make it fully intelligible it should have an introductory poem; and after this was written a further introduction was seen to be necessary: and so it grew into 'Maud.'[1] According to another account, it was Mrs. Drummond Rawnsley who proposed to the poet, when he was "casting about" for a subject, that he work up the "O that 'twere possible" verses in *The Tribute.* But 'Maud' traces its ancestry also to the Russo-Turkish War, which England had entered in March 1854. On September 20 the battle of the Alma was fought (for which Tennyson began a little song; on 25 October, the charge of the Heavy Brigade at Balaclava (which he later turned into verse); and early in December occurred the horrible blunder which he promptly celebrated in 'The Charge of the Light Brigade,' dashed off in a few minutes and sent immediately to the *Examiner.*[a] England was full of war excitement,

[a] This pretty piece of martial rhetoric became at once very popular. In the first text occurred the familiar phrase, lifted from the *Times,* "some one had blundered," and Capt. Nolan, who had issued the blundering order, was called by name. When the poem was reprinted in the 'Maud' volume the following summer, this phrase (together with the Captain's name) was removed; whereupon arose a noisy protest. Then a chaplain in the Crimea wrote home asking for copies of "Mr. A. T.'s 'Charge at Balaclava'" and Tennyson excitedly had a thousand copies printed off at his own expense, with a revised text, which he called "the soldiers' version of my ballad," restoring the *Times* phrase. —Part of the story of this amusing contretemps may be read in the *Memoir* 1, 385 ff.

the newspapers were full of sanguinary details; one of Tennyson's neighbors, Col. Hand, was killed in the trenches, and men-of-war were seen and heard in the Solent, near Farringford. Tennyson felt strongly the martial atmosphere.

Thus from the Crimean War and from a long lyric slightly reminiscent of Coleridge and Poe 'Maud' was born; and to this ancestry must be added some reading in the popular fiction of the early nineteenth century. Very little is told us of Tennyson's light reading. The *Memoir* piously records his perusal of Homer and Vergil and Dante and similar classics, but there is a blanket statement towards the end that "he had a very catholic taste" in contemporary novels, and along with Stevenson, Meredith, Hardy, and Henry James are mentioned Walter Besant, Conan Doyle, Hall Caine, and Ouida, Edna Lyall, Miss Braddon, and Miss Broughton. Catholic enough. Scott and Jane Austen were among his earlier favorites. He liked *Clarissa Harlowe,* which he called one of "those great *still* books."; and then follows a remark (the italics are mine) which might serve as an anti-epigraph for 'Maud': "*I hate* some of your modern novels with numberless characters thrust into the first chapter and nothing but modern society talk, and also *those morbid, and introspective tales, with their oceans of sham philosophy.*" Recall now the plot of 'Maud.'

A young man of twenty-five, with a taint of inherited madness, is rendered frantic by the memory of his father's suicide following the loss of his fortune in a speculation which has apparently enriched his neighbor, and by seeing his mother die of a broken heart. The neighboring family, after some time travelling abroad, returns: the coldly beautiful Maud and her pompous effeminate brother. Our hero (he is never named) and Maud had played together as children, and at her birth there had been a kind of pre-contract that the two should marry. He falls in love with her now—she is "not seventeen"—and she returns his affection, without enthusiasm or passion, however. During an absence of her brother he obtains her consent to marry him, actually telling her that thereby he hopes to save himself from his incipient madness (I, XVI, i). But when her brother returns, his madness returns also. There is a "grand political dinner" at the Hall, at which her engagement to some "fool lord" is perhaps to be announced, but to which the hero is not invited. After the dinner he is to meet her, however, in the garden. They are there interrupted by Maud's brother, who is of course properly angry. A duel follows, in which the hero kills the brother and then flees to France. There he goes quite mad, but finally pulls himself together through his enthusiasm for the Crimean War, and goes off, mentally and morally restored, to fight for his country.—All this is presented not in the usual manner of fiction, but in the words and from the point of view of the morbid and introspective hero.

A general similarity between this tale and the plot of *The Bride of Lammermoor* was noticed by Andrew Lang, but Scott had advantages as a writer of full-length fiction which Tennyson as a lyric poet denied himself. It almost looks as though he was aiming at the readers of popular fiction from Mudie's, aiming to give them their favorite kind of melodrama plus poetical graces and an immediate topical appeal. But he missed; for the critics fell foul of him for the war-mongering of his final section and the general readers of verse were baffled by his dot-and-dash method of narration. No accumulation of poetical beauties could possibly render attractive the tale of a morbid youth of twenty-five making clandestine love to a girl of sixteen and killing her brother when he interferes; and the inconveniencies of method which the poet voluntarily assumed left the case nearly desperate.

Controversy arose, Dr. Robert James Mann, F.R.A.S., etc., came to the rescue with his *Maud Vindicated,* and Tennyson thanked him saying: "No one with this essay before him can in future pretend to misunderstand my dramatic poem, 'Maud': your commentary is as true as it is full." And he desired that a long quotation from Dr. Mann's Vindication should be added to his Notes on the poem. In later editions he affixed "A Monodrama" to the title and divided the sections (which had at first been numbered consecutively) into three Parts. Still later he provided captions for the several sections, which are printed in the *Memoir* and in the Notes to the *Works,* but not with the text of the poem. Further, for the Eversley Edition he wrote out the following statement:

This poem is a little *Hamlet,* the history of a morbid, poetic soul, under the blighting influence of a recklessly speculative age. He is the heir of madness, an egoist with the makings of a cynic, raised to a pure and holy love which elevates his whole nature, passing from the height of triumph to the lowest depth of misery, driven into madness by the loss of her whom he has loved, and, when he has at length passed through the fiery furnace, and has recovered his reason, giving himself up to work for the good of mankind through the unselfishness born of a great passion.[2]

The picture is completed by Hallam Tennyson's note: "My father liked reading this poem, a 'Drama of the Soul,' set in a landscape glorified by Love, and, according to Lowell, 'The antiphonal voice to *In Memoriam*,' which is the 'Way of the Soul.' "

Apart from these pretentious claims, Tennyson is chargeable with misinterpreting his own poem. Where has he shown that a pure and holy love elevated the whole nature of his hero? Through four sections of Part I, beginning with XIII (which Tennyson calls "morbidly prophetic") the hero has worked himself from the depths of bathos about "Maud's own little oak-room," to a climax of selfishness:

> *But if I be dear to some one else,*
>   *Then I should be to myself more dear.*
> *Shall I not take care of all that I think,*
> *Yea, even of wretched meat and drink,*
> *If I be dear,*
> *If I be dear to some one else?* (xv)

Is the man sane who talks like that? But he resolves to declare his love—

> *I know it is the one bright thing to save*
> *My yet young life in the wilds of Time,*
> *Perhaps from madness, perhaps from crime,*
> *Perhaps from a selfish grave.*

Maud accepts him: he becomes lyrical (XVII), exultant (XVIII), ecstatic (XVIII, viii), but in the next section (XIX)—which was not in the first edition, but was added to help clarify the story—his morbidity returns.

> *Her brother is coming back to-night,*
> *Breaking up my dream of delight. . . .*
> *So now I have sworn to bury*
> *All this dead body of hate,*
> *I feel so free and so clear*
> *By the loss of that dead weight,*
> *That I should grow light-headed, I fear,*
> *Fantastically merry;*

> *But that her brother comes, like a blight*
> *On my fresh hope, to the Hall to-night.*

He continues in the next section:

> *Strange, that I felt so gay,*
> *Strange, that I tried to-day*
> *To beguile her melancholy;*

calls himself "a little lazy lover," complains that she has chilled his caresses

> *By the coldness of her manners,*
> *Nay, the plainness of her dresses.*

Nay, the truth seems to be that the hero has had a brief lucid in-terval of selfish exaltation, but the relapse is too rapid to certify a real cure. His whole nature is elevated for only a moment. Nor is he actually "driven into madness by the loss of her whom he has loved," for the madness seizes him before he has lost her; he chose the worst possible method of winning her, shooting her brother in a duel. And finally his enlistment for the Crimean War is oddly described as "giving himself up to work for the good of mankind." If Tennyson could be so muddled about his own poem he should not have complained that others misunderstood it.

Not much can be said for the characters in this monodrama. Maud's brother is seen only through the eyes of the jealous lover: the poet may have wanted to sentimentalize him (one of his rings has his mother's hair in it) but he remains in our memory as a mere boor. Maud herself has no chance, really no character; she is beautiful and cold, inactive and uninteresting. The hero is all-in-all: selfish, morbid, with a tendency to madness and a tendency to rave even when he is not mad; then completely insane; finally, "sane but shattered" (as Tennyson puts it) he takes up the "blood-red blossom of war" and embraces "the purpose of God." The proper uses of morbidity and incipient madness in poetry are diffi-cult to determine, but few would look for them in the hero-solilo-quist of a love tale. Such a hero, however, was a convenience to Tennyson when he chose to inveigh against Mid-Victorian ills, for he could thus have it both ways: he could let himself go with all the elocutionary bitterness of 'Locksley Hall' and he could pass

off the outburst as dramatic, the raving of a "morbid poetic soul."
(But this is confusing to the reader.) He could write gnomically,
at the end,

> *It is better to fight for the good than to rail at the ill;*

his hero had done both, and learned resignation—

> *I have felt with my native land, I am one with my kind,*
> *I embrace the purpose of God, and the doom assign'd.*

As was said long ago, 'Maud' is Tennyson's worst poem and con-
tains some of his best poetry. The indictment of social conditions
in I, I, iv is brilliant in its kind; it is violent and strident, and, as
Lyall said, 'Locksley Hall' pitched an octave higher, but none the
less clever (though *Blackwood's* called it a "screed of bombast").
If Tennyson has a single *worst* line it is in 'Maud' (I, x, i)—

> *Whose old grandfather has lately died;*

but there are whole passages nearly as bad, which it would be as
painful as it is unnecessary to quote. He certainly betrayed his
youth, though he was now forty-five, when he wrote—and left un-
altered, for he never quite outgrew this kind of youthfulness—

> *I kiss'd her slender hand,*
> *She took the kiss sedately;*
> *Maud is not seventeen,*
> *But she is tall and stately.*

But there is subtle music in the stanza beginning

> *There is none like her, none,*
> *Nor will be when our summers have deceased;*

the early lyric "O that 'twere possible" has admirable quasi-ballad
qualities, slightly old-fashioned and derivative; and "See what a
lovely shell" (II, II, i) exhibits Tennyson's workmanship at its best.
(The shell is obviously symbolic. It might be the hero's frail hold
on sanity, or as Tennyson suggested, with a "perhaps," "his own
first and highest nature." Tennyson *ought* to have known.) Every
reader will have his favorites. And there is of course the famous
"Come into the garden, Maud," which besides being a metrical
masterpiece, a *tour de force* of virtuosity of all sorts, is also cur-

iously suited to the mentally unbalanced speaker. His queer state of mind betrays itself in the second line, where he calls the night a "black bat," and in the second stanza with its perverted idea of Love dying with her beloved. When he cries, "I said to the lily," and "I said to the rose," it is still plainer that his mind is slightly unhinged.[b] The last four stanzas are almost delirium itself, and in the very last he is completely off balance. Such skill is beyond all comparison, and of course greatly superior to the Bedlam scene of which Tennyson boasted. To write a lyric which can pass for sheer beauty—perhaps even deceive the incautious—and at the same time be dramatically so perfect, with sense, delicate and lovely, balanced on the fine edge of nonsense or mere music, is given to very few poets indeed. Out of its context this song is *in posse* if not *in esse* almost too frail and pretty-pretty; in its context, at the emotional climax of the poem, just before the speaker goes utterly insane, it is a miracle of finesse. One may say this confidently, whether Tennyson was or was not aware of what he had done.[3]

The controversy over Tennyson's war-mongering in Part III, taken so seriously at the time, is now somewhat stale. There is no doubt that he was misinterpreted in good faith; there is also no doubt that he was himself confused and invited misinterpretation. The *Westminster Review's* charge that I, x, iii was an attack upon John Bright, Tennyson rebutted by saying: "I did not even know at the time that he was a Quaker" (which is an interesting fact in itself); but Hallam adds, a little more helpfully: "It was not against Quakers, but against peace-at-all-price men that the hero fulminates."[4] So be it. The real issue, however, was the poet's advocacy of war on the wrong grounds. His hero turns to the Crimea for a cure of his "old hysterical mock-disease" (love having failed him)—

> *Let it go or stay, so I wake to the higher aims*
> *Of a land that has lost for a little her lust of gold,*
> *And love of a peace that was full of wrongs and shames, . . .*
> *And hail once more to the banner of battle unroll'd.*

You might think he was still not cured, but Tennyson did not make this defence, he insisted that a righteous war was better than

---

[b] The echoes of 'Annabel Lee' in the fifth stanza, and perhaps in the seventh and eighth, should not pass unnoticed. "As the pimpernel dozed on the lea" is dangerously close to jabberwocky.

a bad peace. He had expressly written, a war "in defence of the right" against "an iron tyranny"; England was wreaking "God's just wrath" on "a giant liar," Nicholas I. But he, or his hero, confused the issue by implying that a righteous foreign war was not only a happy recourse for the mentally ill but also a fine remedy for domestic evils; or, as the *Blackwood's* reviewer put it, a little unfairly, "war upon a large scale is the only proper remedy for adulteration of comestibles, house-breaking, and child-murder." Certainly there was nothing dreadfully wrong or unusual in proposing a strong outside interest as a cure for selfish morbidity; and *du reste,* as a professed interpreter of his age Tennyson took what lay at hand for a concrete example.

Well, Gladstone recanted handsomely in 1878, pleading that the war spirit of 1855 (when he wrote his attack in the *Quarterly*) "dislocated my frame of mind"; and the question may be called closed. Nevertheless Tennyson was never a pacifist. The *Poems* of 1830 contained a rousing 'English War-Song' (not reprinted by the poet); in January 1852 the *Examiner* printed, anonymously, his 'Britons, Guard your Own,' which ends with a prophecy of 1941—

> *Although we fought the banded world alone,*
> *We swear to guard our own;*

and in the following number his poem on Napoleon's *coup d'état,* 'The Third of February, 1852' and the patriotic 'Hands All Round,' admired by Landor. There was a marked martial note in his 'Ode on the Death of the Duke of Wellington.' The Balaclava poems have already been mentioned. In the *Times* (1859) appeared his stanzas, 'The War,' reprinted in the posthumous volume as 'Riflemen, Form.' In 1882 he published in *Macmillan's Magazine,* for March, a 'Prologue. To General Hamley,' celebrating the Egyptian war of that year. In 1885 he sent a jingoist poem, 'The Fleet,' to the *Times.* When he was working on 'Maud,' in 1854 his frame of mind was also no doubt dislocated; but he was never a war-monger. In his later years as the idea of racial perfection grew on him and general hopes of a millenium (in lieu of more immediate reform) became a kind of obsession, he made it plain that wars, even just wars, were to be no more. The same volume which reprinted 'The Fleet' contained in its titular poem, 'Locksley Hall Sixty Years After,' the lines:

Earth at last a warless world, a single race, a single tongue—
I have seen her far away—for is not Earth as yet so young?— . . .

Robed in universal harvest up to either pole she smiles,
Universal ocean softly washing all her warless isles.

This last line Tennyson admired, characteristically with the qualifying uncertainty: "who can fancy warless men?"

Warless? war will die out late then. Will it ever? late or soon?
Can it, till this outworn earth be dead as yon dead world the moon?

and with this he changes the subject back to Amy.

The little tumult over 'Maud' is now dead and the offensive words of the first critics buried in the bound periodicals of our larger libraries. We can all now, with the accumulated helps, follow the story and grasp Tennyson's intention. He undertook a bold experiment, both in subject and in method. It proved then to be too bold, but there are some later critics who hail it as an anticipation of things now called modern and akin to the stream-of-consciousness writing. Whether one calls it an amusing irony or the slow workings of justice or merely the vagaries of taste, 'Maud' again finds defenders; but still—as always with Tennyson—the parts are greater than the whole. "The winding up is magnificent," wrote Mrs. Browning to Mrs. Jameson,

full of power, and there are beautiful thrilling bits before you get so far. Still, there is an appearance of labour in the early part; the language is rather encrusted by skill than spontaneously blossoming, and the rhyme is not always happy. The poet seems to aim more at breadth and freedom, which he attains, but at the expense of his characteristic delicious music. People in general appear very unfavourably impressed by this poem, *very unjustly,* Robert and I think. On some points it is even an advance. The sale is great, *nearly five thousand copies already.*[c]

[c] *Letters of Elizabeth Barrett Browning,* ed. F. G. Kenyon, New York, 1898, ii, 209. A few months later Mrs. Browning added a further comment to Mrs. Martin: ". . . the Laureate, who, being in London for three or four days from the Isle of Wight, spent two of them with us, dined with us, smoked with us, opened his heart to us (and the second bottle of port), and ended by reading 'Maud' through from end to end, and going away at half past two in the morning. If I had had a heart to spare, certainly he would have won mine. He is captivating with his frankness, confidingness and unexampled *naïveté!* Think of his stopping in 'Maud' every now and then—'There's a wonderful touch! That's very tender. How beautiful that is!' Yes, and it *was* wonderful, tender, beautiful, and he read exquisitely in a voice like an organ, rather music than speech" (*ibid.,* p. 213).

CHAPTER SEVEN

Idylls—of the Hearth and Others

T HE CONTENTS of the second volume of *Poems, 1842,* are described by Hallam Tennyson as "English Idyls and Eclogues, pictures of English home and country life"; and in the Collected Poems of 1884 and in subsequent editions (except the Eversley) the heading "English Idyls and Other Poems" is given to the group equivalent to the contents of this volume. Tennyson himself first used the word *idyl* in 1859, to the perplexity of critics, for his first instalment of the Arthurian epic, 'Idylls of the King,' now with two *l*'s. For his next volume, 1864, he chose the title 'Idylls of the Hearth,' but changed it at the last minute to 'Enoch Arden and Other Poems.' In 1885 he described 'Tiresias' as "this small idyll."

When the historical dramas and 'In Memoriam' and the numerous lyrical and occasional pieces are set aside, nearly all of what remains falls into the class which Tennyson thought of somehow as idyllic. These idyls, or idylls, not only comprise a very large portion of his poetic work, they contain most of his contribution to the history of Victorian England. As the self-chosen portrayer of his age Tennyson was an idyllist. This was probably not deliberate, but it turned out so.

The type is foreshadowed in the first poem of his first volume: 'Claribel: a Melody.' Among the fifty-three lyrics of this volume there were five more of a similar kind, the gallery of female portraits, 'Lilian,' 'Isabel,' 'Mariana,' 'Madeline,' and 'Adeline'; and in the volume of 1833 five more, 'Margaret,' 'Rosalind,' 'Eleänore,' 'Kate,' and 'Mariana in the South.'[a] "All these ladies," said Tenny-

---

[a] In *Unpublished Early Poems* there are three more, 'Marion,' 'Lizette,' and 'Amy.' Of these only 'Lizette' is finished, and she is brighter than the rest— "grave and shrewd, And half a prude, And half coquette."

son, "were evolved, like the camel, from my own consciousness"; but 'Isabel' was "more or less" done from his mother. They are all studies in mood and meter, though they may seem like character studies. But with four poems from the volume of 1833, 'The Lady of Shalott,' 'Œnone,' 'The Miller's Daughter,' and 'The May Queen,' the type is established which will continue, with modulations of course, for the next sixty years, through the posthumous volume of 1892. This became and remained Tennyson's *line*.

The type, like the name, descends from Theocritus, gathering small changes along the way, as the lyrical, or narrative, or other component elements tend to predominate. But all the examples are little pictures or studies, now chiefly lyrical, now largely narrative, now presenting a static situation and now a character. With Tennyson they frequently became genre pictures and in his later career lyricized narratives. Sometimes there were symbolic overtones for additional dignity or 'weight.' In different poems the elements were compounded in varying proportions, according to the subject, the aim, or the special effect desired.

It will be noticed that thus far all of Tennyson's idyllic studies are concerned with women. At first the handling is mainly lyrical and static, but in 'Mariana in the South,' artificial as it is with its piling up of motionless detail—like a sort of *pointillisme*—there is a sense of climax and a hint of wider meanings. The later and larger examples contain a little more narrative; they also establish the three great divisions of Tennyson's subject matter, the classical, the mediæval, and the contemporary. 'Œnone,' though written in blank verse, is more lyrical than narrative; most of the action is reported action; and as a study of a lovelorn maiden or jealous woman it has little interest. 'The Lady of Shalott' is likewise mainly lyrical, yet with notable structure—a Mariana of the Middle Ages, an accumulation of the most brilliant and lavish descriptive details to create a mood, a little precious, perhaps, but precious in the other sense also; mediæval magic distilled from Scott and Keats and Coleridge (with something of *Aucassin et Nicolette,* if Tennyson knew it).[b]

b The connections with Scott are less familiar and may be illustrated by extracts from Lyulph's Tale in 'The Bridal of Triermain.' Their common ground is of course imitation of the ballad-romance.

Above the moated entrance slung,
The balanced drawbridge trembling hung,

With 'The May Queen' we plunge into a very different world—and it is no small marvel that Tennyson moved easily in both—with 'The Miller's Daughter' for transition. 'The Miller's Daughter' is not a bad poem for a young man of twenty-three to have written, and in its revised form of 1842 it was much better. So late as 1895 a critic could write: "This poem, as now perfected, needs no praise; it is one of Tennyson's many masterpieces, and, again, it is strikingly original." It added "a new wonder and delight . . . to our common life."[1] Young Rossetti might have written twenty years later:

> At last you rose and moved the light,
> And the long shadow of the chair
> Flitted across into the night,
> And all the casement darken'd there.

The particular kind of sentimentality exhibited in 'The Miller's Daughter' is now utterly out of fashion, but the poem is relieved by a pleasant humor, and with a little historical allowance it can be enjoyed to-day. 'The May Queen,' however, which in 1833 was a portent, has now long since become a sign.[c] Against the modern judgment that it is pathos of the least pardonable variety may be set Carlyle's "Ah, but that's tender and true." The critic of 1895 (Luce again) could write of its "richness and novelty both of material and method disguised beneath an impression of the most perfect simplicity." But it need not be thought that Tennyson deliberately wrote down to a middle-class audience for the mere sake of popular appeal. The temptation to do so may have existed later, yet there was something genuine in Tennyson as in his contemporary readers which made this kind of thing attractive. Both he and they liked it. It was part of the sentimenal *strain*, beginning

---

As jealous of a foe;
Wicket of oak, as iron hard,
With iron studded, clenched, and bar-
    red,
And pronged portcullis, joined to
    guard
    The gloomy pass below. . . .
The lists with painted plumes were
    strown,
Upon the wind at random thrown,
But helm and breastplate bloodless
    shone,
It seemed their feathered crests alone

Should this encounter rue.
And ever, as the combat grows,
The trumpet's cheery voice arose,
Like lark's shrill song the flourish
    flows,
Heard while the gale of April blows
    The merry greenwood through.

[c] The 'Conclusion,' which contains the famous line—
    And that good man, the clergyman,
        has told me words of peace,
was added in the 1842 volume, and is even worse.

before the accession of Victoria, which made Victorian hearts bleed easily and which Tennyson came to rely upon hereafter to satisfy his numerous following. A sincere insincerity made him falsely true.

Thus was the mould set. But there were in 1833 other types with a deeper tone and greater promise. The new poems of 1842, however, were all—apart from the six short lyrics and 'The Vision of Sin'—idylls and are so denominated in the Collected editions. They are not all English, for the classical subjects reappear in 'Ulysses' and the mediæval in 'Morte d'Arthur,' 'Godiva,' and 'St. Simeon Stylites' (and the two Arthurian lyrics); but of the sixteen remaining titles in this volume, twelve are idylls of the English hearth: 'Dora,' 'The Gardener's Daughter,' 'Audley Court,' 'Walking to the Mail,' 'The Epic,' 'The Talking Oak,' 'Love and Duty,' 'Locksley Hall,' 'The Day-Dream,' 'Edward Gray,' 'Lady Clare,' 'The Lord of Burleigh,' with which should be reckoned 'The Golden Year' (added in the fourth edition, 1846), 'Edwin Morris' (added in the seventh edition, 1851), 'Lady Clara Vere de Vere' (a new poem but printed in vol. I), and perhaps 'Will Waterproof's Lyrical Monologue'—fifteen or sixteen in all.

With the Classical subjects[d] might be included 'Tithonus,' most of which was written in the thirties, thought it was not finished and published until 1860—a quiet poem on the theme

> *Why should a man desire in any way*
> *To vary from the kindly race of men,*
> *Or pass beyond the goal of ordinance*
> *Where all should pause, as is most meet for all?*

'Tiresias' also was partly composed at the same time as 'Ulysses,' though not published until 1885, and then with a riming accompaniment to FitzGerald (written in 1876), not only describing the poem as a "brief idyll" but half-apologizing for its "diffuse and opulent end." When Tiresias relates to Menœceus the vision of Pallas Athene which caused his blindness, there is something of 'Œnone' in the description. The preceding lines might have been written on the same day—

---

d 'Amphion' is ambiguously classical or modern, and inconsiderable from either point of view.

> *the winds were dead for heat;*
> *The noonday crag made the hand burn; and sick*
> *For shadow—not one bush was near—I rose*
> *Following a torrent till its myriad falls*
> *Found silence in the hollows underneath.*

This is good imitation-Tennyson at least, and the rest of it justifies Tennyson's withholding publication for some fifty years. The conclusion, which has something of the glory of 'Ulysses' about it and which was one of the poet's favorite passages, is a magnificent example of the climax of ascending spirals:

> *But for me,*
> *I would that I were gather'd to my rest,*
> *And mingled with the famous kings of old,*
> *On whom about their ocean-islets flash*
> *The faces of the Gods—the wise man's word,*
> *Here trampled by the populace underfoot,*
> *There crown'd with worship—and these eyes will find*
> *The men I knew, and watch the chariot whirl*
> *About the goal again, and hunters race*
> *The shadowy lion, and the warrior-kings,*
> *In height and prowess more than human, strive*
> *Again for glory, while the golden lyre*
> *Is ever sounding in heroic ears*
> *Heroic hymns, and every way the vales*
> *Wind, clouded with the grateful incense-fume*
> *Of those who mix all odour to the Gods*
> *On one far height in one far-shining fire.*

There was a wide gap of years between these three 'Greek' poems of his "poetic prime" and the two composed at the end of his long life, with a corresponding change of attitude and a natural loss of youthful fervor. But between the early and the late classical pieces stands 'Lucretius,' Tennyson's one essay with a Roman subject and in certain respects the weightiest of them all.

'Lucretius' was welcomed and acclaimed when it first appeared in *Macmillan's Magazine* for May 1868: as one critic said (in *Tinsley's,* for July of that year), "The Tennysonian world was hungry and stood agape for Tennysonian food, . . . and on four several occasions he threw them out a stone." But this was notable and nourishing food, not merely for its execution "but because the thought worked out is a beautiful and noble thought." His only regret was for the final paragraph, which showed great condensation but was prose—"almost pure prose." His indignation mastering his grammar he says: "Having passed from the first idyllic paragraph into the dramatic method, the mere return to narrative constitutes an anticlimax."

In the very next number of *Macmillan's* (June) Professor Jebb honored Tennyson's poem with a special article, laying emphasis on the historical truth of the portrait and praising Tennyson's adaptation of the genuine Lucretian tone to the morbid agony of a mind baffled by its own predicament. These echoes and translations have been carefully canvassed, and Tennyson himself was plainly gratified by Monro's comment (than which none could have then carried more weight) that "everything was Lucretian."[2] A more recent scholar is equally emphatic: "to the lover of Lucretius' own poem, every jot of characterization, of atmosphere, every tenet of the message, nay, every phrase and figure, almost every word recalls the master himself." This is perhaps an exaggeration; it is certainly misleading. In so far as it is true it testifies to Tennyson's care and accuracy, but it leaves his poem hardly more than a masterly condensation. Such skill we are prepared to expect in Tennyson and he should have the tribute he deserves for it. But it cannot have been his chief purpose to summarize the *De Rerum Natura* and portray the character and message of the Roman poet. If it had been he would not have chosen the dramatic moment when Lucilia's "wicked broth" had

Confused the chemic labour of the blood

and "Made havock" of his mental powers. Jebb saw a little deeper when he wrote:

It seems to us one of the finest touches in Mr. Tennyson's poem, that it represents these doubts as starting up just when the laws of the man's inner life have been unsettled, the old balance of his faculties disturbed. . . . But, for Lucretius, the loss of this part of his faith was only a sentimental loss; it could not add to the reality of his anguish, or furnish a distinct motive for desiring death. He dies because he has lost the tranquil mind which alone, in his belief, can make life tolerable:

But now it seems some unseen monster lays
His vast and filthy hands upon my will,
Wrenching it backward into his; and spoils
My bliss in being.

This is a nice point. At the beginning of Book v Lucretius describes the abodes of the gods as unlike our own, being "tenues de corpore eorum,"—

quae tibi posterius largo sermone probabo. (v, 155)

A little later (v, 1161-1240) he inserts a long parenthesis on the spread of popular religion and man's need of the gods, but then continues with his explanations of natural phenomena, reminding Memmius from time to time that the world is not indestructible, but never fulfilling the promise of his *largus sermo*. It is Tennyson therefore and not Lucretius who introduces the question of the immortality of the gods. How Lucretius would have explained it in terms of his atomic theory we do not know; making Lucretius doubt when his mind has been unsettled by the wicked broth is Tennyson's extension. But if Tennyson's poem is a portrait, is it not unfair for him to press Lucretius on a point which Lucretius had perhaps never faced and on which he had certainly not expressed an opinion? This alone, if there were not abundant clues elsewhere in the English poem, would show that Tennyson was not concerned with a rifacimento of the *De Rerum Natura* so much as with a study of Lucretius' mind after the havoc had been wrought in "those tender cells" of his brain. In other words, Tennyson's poem is a study in abnormal psychology, a revelation of the philosophical spirit of Lucretius when it had been subjected to the distorting influences of the aphrodisiac philtre. The poem is thus not a portrayal of Lucretius at all, not properly a philosophical poem, but a study in morbid degeneration. All the Lucretian reminiscences are 'local color,' a point of departure, whose value lies not so much in their accuracy as in their dramatic usefulness for contrast between the lucidity and the madness of the soliloquy. Tennyson would perhaps have liked to have it both ways, but he chose his emphasis and his success should be estimated thereby.

Since its welcome in 1868 'Lucretius' has met with criticism either favorable or neutral: it appears in most selections, but it has never been a favorite. Only a few critics, like Mr. Nicolson, have been positively hostile. It is different from the staple "Tennysonian food." Not that the Laureate had not already occupied himself with morbid subjects: witness 'St. Simeon' and 'Maud'—'Balin and Balan' was to come later—and the maudlin pathos of certain idylls of the hearth. But here was a subject more weighty, both tragic and noble: the great mind of a poet and a seer despoiled through poison administered by a loving wife. The style was, to all appearance lofty, without the decorative affixed beauties which sometimes mar his work; it was a plain style, but not bare. Besides, there was the piquancy of a few erotic touches, the better appreciated for lacking the true Swinburnian flavor. (*Poems and Ballads* preceded 'Lucretius' by only two years.) And for full measure there was the modern note of science-and-religion and the problem of immortality, both left shrewdly in their antique setting to be their own commentary.[e]

Yet all this is from the point. For the poem remains not a representation of the Lucretian philosophy, but a revelation of mental decay. Tennyson himself said that Lucretius "is now tortured by unrest. The unrest drives him to frenzy and he kills himself"; and this is so obtuse and inadequate that one hesitates to look for more than the poet intended. But Tennyson's comments on his own poetry are so often disappointing that one must not be critically bound by them.

The intervals of lucidity in Tennyson's Lucretius have been noticed by nearly all readers. There is however no real line to be drawn between his lucidity and his madness, for throughout the poem he hovers on the border line, neither quite sane nor quite delirious. His mind swings from conscious grasp of its old power to a painful consciousness of its loss, yet is never wholly clear and never wholly confused. There is a constant weaving and unweaving of the philtre's influence and his resistance to it, of music and discord, with his one passion, the divine calmness of the gods, sounding throughout like an organ-point.

A kind of threefold theme is announced at the beginning of the soliloquy, his dreams, to which he continually recurs. The first

---

[e] As Professor Bush sagely observes: "the nature of the treatment forbids any Christian answer to the despair of the materialist."

dream is an echo of an actual introductory storm (which he describes in excited terms—

> *the flash of a thunderbolt. . .*
> *Struck out the streaming mountain-side);*

and is drawn by Tennyson from Lucretius' version of the world's destruction: "that was mine, my dream," he cries, speaking with two voices. The second dream is an erotic confusion of contemporary events ("the blood by Scylla shed," "the mulberry-faced Dictator's orgies") and a crowd of hetairai which presses on him, nearly suffocating him. The third is wholly the effect of the philtre (though Tennyson borrows it from Euripides): the sword which threatened Helen's breasts and the flame from them which consumed Troy. He thinks at once of the Venus to whom he had dedicated his poem: is this her vengeance for his denial of her as the goddess of love? He boasts that his prooemium will outlive her deity—(a too modern note, it would seem)—but immediately is aware that he has said more than he intended; and then adds, from his own conviction, that she cannot feel anger if she is one of the immortals who "live the great life . . . centr'd in eternal calm"; or, if she *can* share human feeling, let her kiss Mars and win him from

> *the lust of blood*
> *That makes a steaming slaughter-house of Rome.*

Thus his mind shifts from one side to the other of this erotic theme, and in a lucid moment he declares that his true concern with Venus was only as the goddess of procreation among the lower animals: he seems afraid to recognize the human act. Now the thought of suicide presents itself, already hinted after his second dream; "if I go *my* work is left Unfinished—*if* I go." For only by taking his own life can he achieve the divine calm of the immortal gods. Or *are* the gods immortal, not subject to the great law of atomic change? He meant to explain that in his poem. Meant? How can he explain, now that his "faculties are lamed" by the philtre? (It is never clear in the poem that Lucretius is aware of the cause of his confusion; one mentions the philtre, therefore, only as an expository convenience.) He looks at the sun, another of the gods, Apollo, and becomes incoherent, lyrical, and bitter by turns. The idea of suicide is natural, an easy short-cut, and he repels it only because

151

of his pride. He recalls Plato, and answers him with a quibble:* if the gods are careless of mankind, why should man care how he escapes from life—from disease and especially from this torment of obscene desire. His mind slips back to the hetairai and confuses them with his *simulacra,* the "idols" of Epicurus. He would slough off "this horror" as Nature smiles after storm. He remembers Numa's attempt to exploit the rustic gods, laughs—and is beset by the vision of a satyr pursuing an oread, who seems about to throw herself upon him. Under the philtre's influence the oread becomes too too fleshly, the satyr too too beastly, and in an agony of self-contempt he cries—

> *Catch her, goat-foot: nay,*
> *Hide, hide them, million myrtled wilderness,*
> *And cavern-shadowing laurels, hide! do I wish—*
> *What?—that the bush were leafless? or to whelm*
> *All of them in one massacre?*

Then his mind suddenly jumps back: the gods are careless, yet he once thought he lived in as calm and secure a happiness as they; but again the "unseen monster" lays "filthy hands" upon him and he reflects that his former joy was slight, merely the refuge of composing his poem. Now he argues: since life is such a poor thing, why should he not show his superiority to the beasts by ending it? why should he subject himself to the humiliation of a Roman triumph, he who has the blood of Lucrece in his veins? (And with this, Tennyson deftly mingles three motifs; for from her suicide

> *sprang the Commonwealth, which breaks*
> *As I am breaking now!)*

Therefore, he reasons, let the inevitable dissolution of nature come, destroy both him and his work (a summary of the introductory storm, his first dream, and his resolution to take his own life), so that he may win at once the

> *Passionless bride, divine Tranquillity,*

which he confuses with death—

> *thus*
> *I woo thee roughly, for thou carest not*
> *How roughly men may woo thee so they win.*

Thus the sequence of ideas through the poem, both logical and illogical, as incipient madness affects the mind of Lucretius, Tennyson has handled consummately; he has adroitly represented the uncertain balance of reason and unreason, the fumbling grasp of Lucretius towards his true nature as it constantly eludes his will. This recognized, it remains however to inquire how far Tennyson's treatment of the abnormal psychology is deliberate and conscious or perhaps intuitive, if we remember his own "black blood"; and also whether he made a great poem out of such a subject. To the first question there is no positive answer, but in critical honesty he should have the benefit of every doubt. He has followed the course of Lucretius' thoughts with great skill, mingling the various elements of his poem (the philosophy of the historical Lucretius, the influence of the philtre, and the problem of self-immolation) with just the right confusion to reveal the disorder of a noble mind. Tennyson's other attempts in this field of the morbid are trivial beside his 'Lucretius,' and few other poets have done better. The 'evidence' is all in his favor.

Our answer to the second question must rest of course on the uncertainty of all literary opinion. There can be no doubt of the felicity of many passages, both in themselves as language and in their appropriateness to the theme. The 'fine lines,' the *purpurei panni*, catch every reader's attention and most of them can be justified in their context. Even the description of the oread may be accounted for as the kind of erotic outbreak which is to be expected from a man like Lucretius, rather than the crude thing which it seems to be in Tennyson's poem. (Perhaps Lucretius and Tennyson should divide the honors.) But there are infelicities which cannot be so explained. The dog which in sleep "plies His function of the woodland" is pure Tennyson on the debit side. The allusion to Paris as a "beardless apple-arbiter"; the prosaic phrase "dire insanity"; the figure "cloudy slough" (though the picture in which it occurs is probably borrowed from Lucretius); the colloquialisms "half an hour" and "Cracks all to pieces" (even if *all* is not an adverb); the image of Lucrece's blood "flushing the guiltless air" and "the maiden fountain of her heart"; and the labored sound effects of—

> *But he, his hopes and hates, his homes and fanes,*
> *And even his bones long laid within the grave—*

these are evidences of either unskilful writing or a characteristic Tennysonian weakness. The occasional irregularity of the versification and the extraordinarily long and loose sentences may be taken as appropriately reflecting the state of Lucretius' mind; but Tennyson alone must be charged with the stagey exclamations: "what dreams, ye holy gods, what dreams!" "terrible!" "The Gods, the Gods!" "For look! what is it? there?" "a satyr, see, Follows." These suggest that Tennyson was not sufficiently master of the dramatic style. They suggest something more than this.

For though so much seems in order, so much carefully arranged and calculated for a powerful projection of character and psychology, something is absent, the fundamental emotional power which would melt down all crudities and tell us as no display of technique could do, that Tennyson had himself been moved by the dominant feeling of his splendid subject. These flaws, not numerous though they are, betray the fact that Tennyson was not *inspired* in the Socratic sense, not divinely possessed. "Passion and not thought makes tragedy." In truth, if there were no other signs, the prosaic introduction and the bathetic conclusion are enough to give Tennyson away; and the soliloquy itself stands as a fine studio-piece rather than a masterpiece. The Tennysonian world is vindicated, both in its acceptance of 'Lucretius' as a *tour de force,* and also in its refusal to include it in the canon of favorites.

Tennyson was eighty years old when 'Demeter and Persephone' was published. The lines 'To Professor Webb' which accompany it begin

> *Fair things are slow to fade away—*

meaning the old legend which he had caused to

> *Blossom again on a colder isle;*

but one feels also a looking backward to warmer days on the same cold island. His son asked him to write it "because I knew that he considered Demeter one of the most beautiful types of womanhood." But the old poet called it an antique, said nothing about beautiful motherhood, and insisted on "a frame—something modern about it." What we get accordingly is Demeter's welcome to her daughter on her first return from Hades, a reminiscent account of the long search, and the "frame," Demeter's recognition of "the younger kindlier Gods" who will displace the old

> *Till thy dark lord accept and love the Sun*
> *And all the Shadow die into the Light*

and—though the language is far from lucid—there shall be no more hell, but all one heaven.

The other, last and posthumously published, classical piece is a return (from what a distance and with what a difference!) to the 'Œnone' with which he began. There are but faint echoes of the old melodies, pale memories of the old tricks of skill. The very first line betrays the weakened hand—

> *Œnone sat within the cave from out*
> *Whose . . .*

The situation is unfelt. But one wishes King Arthur could have lived to read it; one wonders if Tennyson, in indicating, though not portraying, Œnone's remorse could have recalled, with regret, the King's treatment of Guinevere.

In Tennyson's six essays on Greek subjects there is very little of the Greek spirit. They make no pretence to topographical accuracy—Tennyson had not been to Greece—and the first was done frankly from a Pyrenean background. They are hardly Greek in modern dress. They are subjects taken from Greek story and translated into pure Tennyson. Yet he knew the Greek classics well, read them constantly, and admired them genuinely. It is just that his own feeling was too completely his own to let him adopt theirs even for a moment. Yet in his last seven years he choose three of the six as title-poems for his volumes: *Tiresias, and Other Poems,* 1885, *Demeter, and Other Poems,* 1889, *The Death of Œnone, . . . and Other Poems,* 1892. Perhaps he fancied the poems themselves, perhaps he imagined they gave distinction to a title-page; they were in no case (unless possibly the last) typical of the contents of their volumes.

The mediæval subjects, begun so auspiciously with the 'Morte' and crossed with the Claribels and Kates, blossomed presently into Idylls of a larger growth. Translate

> *Faintly smiling Adeline,*
> *Scarce of earth nor all divine,*

155

Nor unhappy, nor at rest,
But beyond expression fair

and the Kate known

by her angry air
Her bright black eyes, her bright black hair,

with a dash of real malevolence added,—translate the early female portraits, insubstantial and melodious, into the mediæval world of Malory, with a story to tell about them in place of the immobile descriptions, and you have the first two 'Idylls of the King' (Enid and Nimuë: The True and the False) of 1857. These plus the quasi-allegorical scheme hatched in the thirties and later variously modified, grew and grew until the serio-jocose prophecy of 'The Epic' prefixed in 1842 to the 'Morte d'Arthur' was finally fulfilled.

The only other poems which might be called mediæval are 'Godiva,' which Tennyson composed ("shaped" is his word) while waiting for a train at Coventry in 1840, and 'Saint Simeon Stylites,' which really belongs with the psychopathic studies, and to which he added a posthumous pendant in 'St. Telemachus.' The Idylls with Arthurian subject were, in a way, his hostage to epic fortune; the idylls with contemporary subjects his interpretation of Victorian life. The list of these latter is long and their artistic interest usually small, but at the risk of seeming tedious it will be necessary to fill up the catalogue.

'The Epic' is a little *jeu d'esprit* framing the 'Morte d'Arthur'; in style an anticipation of the Prologue to 'The Princess.' The light conversational blank verse is marred by one or two formalisms—

How all the old honour had from Christmas gone . . .
With cutting eights that day upon the pond—

but parts of it are Tennyson's best—

and half-awake I heard
The parson taking wide and wider sweeps,
Now harping on the church-commissioners,
Now hawking at Geology and schism;
Until I woke, and found him settled down
Upon the general decay of faith
Right thro' the world.

And at the end occurs a line, often forgotten in the interpretation of the 'Idylls of the King'—

> *King Arthur, like a modern gentleman*
> *Of stateliest port.*

The next few poems represent the pure type of English idyll. 'The Gardener's Daughter; or, The Pictures,' written at Cambridge (that is, before February 1831) and retouched just before publication, is the lushest of them all: "full and rich," said Tennyson, "to a fault, especially the descriptions of nature, for the lover is an artist." It is nearly all description of nature, for the 'story' is only that an artist from the city finds in a suburban garden

> *Love at first sight, first-born, an heir to all,*

"a Rose in roses," hears her faltering "I am thine," declines to tell us

> *How passion rose thro' circumstantial grades*
> *Beyond all grades develop'd,*

and at the end points to a veiled picture—

> *the idol of my youth,*
> *The darling of my manhood, and alas!*
> *Now the most blessed memory of mine age.*

There is perhaps a palpable reminiscence of Keats:

> *My heart was like a prophet to my heart,*

and (with a fine metrical exhibit) a too ambiguous trope—

> *as once we met*
> *Unheedful, tho' beneath the whispering rain*
> *Night slid down one long stream of sighing wind,*
> *And in her bosom bore the baby, Sleep.*

But there are also the favorite lines

> *that hair*
> *More black than ashbuds in the front of March*

and

> *The mellow ouzel fluted in the elm*

and the Whistler-like picture of the garden—

> *sitting muffled in dark leaves, you hear*
> *The windy clanging of the minster clock;*
> *Although between it and the garden lies*
> *A league of grass, wash'd by a slow broad stream,*
> *That, stirr'd with languid pulses of the oar,*
> *Waves all its lazy lilies, and creeps on,*
> *Barge-laden, to three arches of a bridge*
> *Crown'd with the minster towers.*
> > *The fields between*
> *Are dewy-fresh, browsed by deep-udder'd kine,*
> *And all about the large lime feathers low,*
> *The lime a summer home of murmurous wings.*

'Dora' is a foil to this, a study in spareness: "the poem which Wordsworth always intended to have written," said Spedding, an almost perfect imitation. The subject is from Miss Mitford's story of Dora Cresswell in *Our Village*; the landscape is the same, Miss Mitford's in sunshine, Tennyson's in shadow. There is only one heightening of the deliberately level style (used twice, and borrowed from Homer, as the poet carefully tells us)—

> *and the reapers reap'd,*
> *And the sun fell, and all the land was dark.*

Tennyson's admiration for Wordsworth, a little surprising all things considered, continued throughout his life. "He seems to me at his best on the whole the greatest English poet since Milton. He is often too diffuse and didactic for me"; and as an instance he offered the "ridiculous" repetition of "that blessed mood . . . that serene and blessed mood" in the Tintern Abbey 'Lines,' but he thought

> *Whose dwelling is the light of setting suns*

"almost the grandest in the English language, giving the sense of the abiding in the transient." In contrast to Byron, whose merits are on the surface, he told Locker-Lampson: "You must love Wordsworth ere he will seem worthy of your love." Butler, the Master of Trinity, records that "he never spoke of Wordsworth without marked reverence." These are not in any way remarkable judgments, but they indicate a kind of sympathy which is shown in such poems as 'Dora' and 'The Talking Oak.' His diffuseness takes very different form from Wordsworth's and his didacticism wears quite different disguises. Both poets however concerned themselves with humble English life—'Michael' is a better English idyll than any of Tennyson's—and both like to intermingle the severely simple and the strongly imaginative styles.

More in the manner of 'The Epic,' including the Arthurian episode, is 'Audley Court'; that is, an imaginary setting "partially suggested by the Abbey Park at Torquay" in conversational blank verse, enclosing two contrasted 'songs' (also in blank verse), that by the farmer's son with the refrain "but let me lead my life," the other a plain love song. It is more than any other idyll like Theocritus transposed to nineteenth-century England. The same technique is used in 'The Golden Year,' except that there is but one song and this has a more 'modern' political cast. The idea is that of general progress

> And human things returning on themselves
> Move onward, leading up the golden year;

wealth and power will be evenly distributed, the British mercantile marine will carry education, Christianity, and free trade throughout the world,

> and universal Peace
> Lie like a shaft of light across the land,—

one of the great and proud early Victorian dreams and one that colored Tennyson's verse to the end of his career. Now he makes fun of it—"What stuff is this!" cries the interlocutor, what this country needs is work—and cleverly ends:

> He spoke; and, high above, I heard them blast
> The steep slate-quarry, and the great echo flap
> And buffet round the hills, from bluff to bluff.

This method is slightly varied in 'Walking to the Mail.' Here Tennyson uses a dramatic form, labelling the speeches of James and John. These two make casual conversation about the neighbors and James tells an unimproving anecdote; there is a hint of domestic tragedy and an oblique reference to the Chartists. If it were all better done it would be a bright little sketch—better perhaps done in prose—but it will pass as a technical experiment.

There is but one more blank verse idyll in this volume of 1842. 'Love and Duty,' an argument rather than a story: to love or not to love, slightly Wordsworthian, with the Tennysonian trick of ending on a high note—

> *Should it cross thy dreams,*
> *O might it come like one that looks content,*
> *With quiet eyes unfaithful to the truth,*
> *And point thee forward to a distant light,*
> *Or seem to lift a burthen from thy heart*
> *And leave thee freer, till thou wake refresh'd*
> *Then when the first low matin-chirp hath grown*
> *Full quire, and morning driv'n her plow of pearl*
> *Far furrowing into light the mounded rack,*
> *Beyond the fair green field and eastern sea.*

Another was added however in the seventh edition, 1851, 'Edwin Morris; or, The Lake,' a serio-comic sentimental tale in a style "elaborately good," resembling the situation in 'Locksley Hall.' Edwin Morris and "the fat-faced curate Edward Bull" (who keeps saying, "God made the woman for the man") are lay figures for background; it is the innominate 'I' who has the pathetic love affair. He gets a note from her, "Your Letty, only yours," boats across the lake, whistles for her,

> *and she,*
> *She turn'd, we closed, we kiss'd, swore faith, I breathed*
> *In some new planet: a silent cousin stole*
> *Upon us and departed: 'Leave,' she cried, . . .*

The lovers are separated and in a month's time she is married to wealthy Sir Robert with his watery smile and the lover—who to your surprise turns out to be none other than Edwin Morris himself—is arrested for trespassing.

The other English idylls of 1842 are in various meters. 'The Talking Oak' is in ballad quatrains in a style something between Wordsworth and Praed. The oak recalls its early days "garrulously," tells Walter that his Olivia is still faithful, and receives Walter's blessing. Tennyson called it "an experiment meant to test the degree in which it is within the power of poetry to humanize external nature." The experiment failed because the power of poetry was not really applied. 'Locksley Hall,' in eight-stress trochaic couplets, has Tennyson's favorite triangle with the cousin lover, but as an epitome of early Tennysonian motifs it is more than the usual idyll. 'The Day-Dream,' built up from a short piece in the 1830 volume, is a moralization, addressed to Lady Flora, of the Sleeping Beauty and the Fairy Prince tale, with the moral left hanging

> *Like long-tail'd birds of Paradise*
> *That float thro' heaven, and cannot light,*

but we are expected to see in it the urgency of contemporary problems. It is not in the strict sense an idyll; nor is 'Amphion,' a tasteless cynical contrast (the crabbedness of which is supposed to be softened by humor) of the happy days of antiquity and the "brassy age" of to-day. 'Edward Gray' is a plain ballad of the proud lover and his simple Ellen; or, as a recent critic puts it, "the educated romantic, expecting too much and gaining so little." 'Lady Clare' is another ballad, "partly suggested" by Susan Ferrier's novel *The Inheritance* (1824), about the noble Lord Ronald who persists in wishing to marry his betrothed lady Clare even though she may be "a beggar born." And still another is 'The Lord of Burleigh,' a very English version of love in a palace, based on the story of the ninth Earl of Exeter's marriage to Sarah Hoggins in 1791. "Is there a greater favorite where English is spoken?" inquires FitzGerald enthusiastically—proving that the appeal of such poems was not altogether to the uneducated.

The general point hardly needs laboring. Here are some dozen or more "pictures of English home and country life" comprising the greater portion and forming the principal emphasis of the new poems of 1842 which won popular favor and laid the foundation of Tennyson's reputation. To be sure, the volume contains four poems, 'Morte d'Arthur,' 'Ulysses,' 'Locksley Hall,' and the lyric 'Break, break, break,' covering thirty of the whole two hundred and thirty pages, which are something more than English genre pictures and on three of which a good part of Tennyson's reputation still firmly rests.[f] But these dozen idylls, soon increased to four-

[f] In this same volume is also that little lyric, 'The Skipping Rope' (omited from the seventh and subsequent editions) which should be glanced at by those who still wish to be reminded that the gold and ivory image may have feet of aluminium silicate.

teen, on very commonplace variations of faithful love and domestic tragedy, themes within the easy reach of simple readers and handled for the most part without the difficult style of sophisticated poetry—a few of them with just that element of fine language and ornamental beauty which would satisfy the higher taste—these idylls, together with similar pieces from the earlier volumes, exhibiting the homely virtues of domestic love, the tender pathos of humble suffering, the distressing misfortunes of thwarted devotion and ill-mated tempers, with touches of delicate humor to soften the harshness and sweeten the pain,—these sketches of the sturdy native Englishman, in high places a lesson to the lower, in the common man a token of sympathy and understanding, these poetic idylls, idyllic poems, are now Tennyson's established staple, from which he will vary to his peril and to which he will return for comfort throughout the succeeding half-century. He may distrust the hand that guides the plow, but his heart is where it should be. He may flatter Queen Victoria too succulently, he may offend this or that group of his growing band of admirers, but he will always come back with a moving example of wholesome sentiment or noble (even though vague) religious feeling, graced with an almost unfailing, almost inexhaustible gift of language.

Now, at the risk of becoming even more tiresome, it is necessary to call the long roll of the later idylls of hearth and home. Tennyson's first answer to the demand of friends and critics for a great work to fulfill the promise of 1842 was 'The Princess.' It was a disappointment. But it was a kind of idyll on a large scale: it had the outlines of a love story, it had abundance of brightly colored setting, it had a moral; yet it was a medley, in two styles, in two places, in two periods. The framework of Prologue and Epilogue is real genre, but the rest was a mediæval-modern mixture tending to prove by the *argumentum ex filia,* that women are in some ways very like men, or vice versa; and it was disappointing. The next publication, however, was a great success, though only in part idyllic. For 'In Memoriam' contains many little vignettes with the idyllic appeal: vi, the tremolo examples of this our common lot of sorrow; xx, the servants in the house of mourning; xl, the bride leaving home; lx, the girl who loves a man above her station; lxi, the man who marries beneath him; lxiv, the country boy who makes good; LXXXIX *et passim,* recollections of Somersby; including of course the family gatherings at Christmas, and the epithalamic epilogue. And 'Maud,' the next, is very obviously an enlarged idyll, with lyrical treatment and monodramatic adjuncts.

In the same volume with 'Maud' came 'The Brook; an Idyl,' still remembered for the rippling inset lyric while the sentimental tale is well forgotten. This is our first example, 1855, of the narrative idyll of the later manner. In form it is a monologue by Lawrence Aylmer, "in middle age forlorn," followed by a little incident. Lawrence, who has returned from India, laments the death of his brother Edmund in Florence, and also that of the talkative Philip Willows, his neighbor. Philip has left a daughter, Katie—

> *A daughter of our meadows, yet not coarse—*

and Lawrence now recalls for us how he had suffered the garrulity of old Philip while Katie made up a quarrel with her cousin James, to whom she was engaged—thus an idyll within an idyll. Katie and James married and went off to Australia. But in the closing scene Lawrence meets their daughter Katie (who has now a brother James) returned from Australia with her mother. In short, a simple sentimental story in a super-simple Wordsworthian style. You would say that badness could no further go; but besides the lyric, 'I come from haunts of coot and hern,' 'The Brook' has at least one good line, beloved of prosodists—

> *In copse and fern*
> *Twinkled the innumerable ear and tail.*

In the same volume was to be read also 'The Letters,' telling of a lover's quarrel (in a double ballad stanza) and its quick reconciliation—

> *I spoke with heart, and heat and force,*
> *I shook her breast with vague alarms—*
> *Like torrents from a mountain source*
> *We rushed into each other's arms.*

Next came the first four 'Idylls of the King'—Enid, Vivien, Elaine, Guinevere—and then 'The Grandmother,'[3] twenty-seven stanzas, of which here is the first—

And Willy, my eldest-born, is gone, you say, little Anne?
Ruddy and white, and strong on his legs, he looks like a man.
And Willy's wife has written: she never was over-wise,
Never the wife for Willy: he wouldn't take my advice.

After this, 'Sea Dreams; an Idyll,' published in *Macmillan's Magazine* for January 1860, beginning—

A city clerk, but gently born and bred;
His wife, an unknown artist's orphan child—
One babe was theirs, a Margaret, three years old.[g]

The poet himself has expounded this idyll: "The glorification of honest labour, whether of head or hand, no hasting to be rich, no bowing down to any idol." Actually the clerk has been swindled of his small savings, but for little Margaret's sake they take a holiday at the seashore. There the clerk has violent dreams (in one of which he breaks the child's medicine glass); his wife comforts him with a pleasanter dream of her own (in which she learns apparently that the swindler has died of heart-disease)—"Ah, dearest," she says:

Ah, dearest, if there be
A devil in man, there is an angel too,
And if he did the wrong you charge him with,
His angel broke his heart.

She then reaches for Margaret's cradle and sings the well-known song:

What does little birdie say
In her nest at peep of day?

In 1864 appeared the volume first called Idylls of the Hearth but published as *Enoch Arden, and Other Poems.* Besides the titular poem these lar-and-penate idylls were 'Aylmer's Field' and the reprinted 'Sea Dreams' and 'The Grandmother.' They represent therefore Tennyson's own understanding of his later idyll and suggest that *hearth* is not to be taken quite literally, but rather, as we have assumed, meaning the domestic life of the ordinary Englishman, with a generous latitude of outlying experiences. Of these

g The *Saturday Review* (14 January 1860) thought that a story "about a clerk and his wife in bed" was not what an idyll should be.

later idylls 'Enoch' is in all ways the most considerable. It is over nine hundred lines long and it moves partly on a high level of poetic description while Enoch is on his lonely tropic isle: a somewhat exalted idyll and still a Tennysonian seamark. It will therefore warrant closer inspection.

The subject came to Tennyson from Woolner and it was only after writing it up that he learned of its general currency and heard in particular of Miss Procter's poem.[4] Spedding told Woolner, after reading 'Enoch Arden' "with delight," that it was "the finest story he had ever heard, and was more especially adapted for Alfred than for any other poet." "He was especially happy," says the *Memoir,* "when writing of his 'Old Fisherman,' " and finished it off in about two weeks. In February 1862, when he was discouraged with the progress of his royal Idylls he wrote to the Duke of Argyll: "I am now about my 'Fisherman,' which is heroic too in its way." And when the poem was published he was gratified to hear from Professor J. S. Blackie, of Edinburgh:

I am not a flatterer and have no object in flattering you, but allow me to say out of plain gratitude, that in my opinion, the thing ['Enoch Arden'] is perfect. In conception, in creation, in tone—not a flaw. Thoroughly English and inly Christian, all the strength, the truth, the gentleness of true English manhood, all the quiet endurance of a thoroughly Christianized temper. If this work should in the long run be preferred to your longer scheme in the "Idylls of the King"—don't be surprised. It is such a thorough piece of reality in all its parts— whereas these old Arthurian knights, if you give them as they were, you are apt to become coarse, if you give them as you love to fancy them, they are not quite true.

This is how it struck one contemporary. Bagehot, on the other hand, reviewing the 'Enoch Arden' volume along with Browning's *Dramatis Personae,* was struck rather differently: he accused the poem of unreality.

Whatever be made of Enoch's 'Ocean-spoil in ocean-smelling osier,' of the 'portal-guarding lion-whelp, and the peacock yew-tree,' everyone knows that in himself Enoch could not have been charming. People who sell fish about the country (and that is what he did, though Mr. Tennyson won't speak out, and wraps it up) never are beautiful. As Enoch was and must be coarse, in itself the poem must depend for a charm on a 'gay confusion'—on a splendid accumulation of impossible accessories.

The story, says Bagehot, again, as Tennyson

has enhanced and presented it, is a rich and splendid composite of imagery and illustration. Yet how simple that story is in itself. A sailor who sells fish, breaks his leg, gets dismal, gives up selling fish, goes to sea, is wrecked on a desert island, stays there some years, on his return finds his wife married to a miller, speaks to a landlady on the subject, and dies. Told in the pure and simple, the unadorned and classical style, this story would not have taken three pages, but Mr. Tennyson has been able to make it the principal—the largest tale in his new volume. He has done so only by giving to every event and incident in the volume an accompanying commentary. He tells a great deal about the torrid zone which a rough sailor like Enoch Arden certainly would not have perceived; and he gives to the fishing village, to which all the characters belong, a softness and a fascination which such villages scarcely possess in reality.

Bagehot found not only an unjustifiable accumulation of commentary, but also a want of simplicity—"Nothing is described as it is, everything has about it an atmosphere of *something else*"—and the addition of false detail. He quotes

> *While Enoch was abroad on wrathful seas,*
> *Or often journeying landward; for in truth*
> *Enoch's white horse, and Enoch's ocean-spoil*
> *In ocean-smelling osier, and his face,*
> *Rough-redden'd with a thousand winter gales,*
> *Not only to the market-cross were known,*
> *But in the leafy lanes behind the down,*
> *Far as the portal-warding lion-whelp*
> *And peacock-yew tree of the lonely Hall,*
> *Whose Friday fare was Enoch's ministering.*

and says sarcastically: "So much has not often been made of selling fish." He charges that the descriptions of tropical nature are irrelevant because Enoch would not have been interested in them: "He would have known little of the scarlet shafts of sunrise and nothing of the long convolvuluses"; whereas he would have been preoccupied with his physical ailments, which Tennyson tells us nothing about. Obviously this is a little unfair, and goes farther than Bagehot needed to go to make his point. It is unnecessary, and possibly inaccurate, to call Enoch a "dirty sailor who did not go home to his wife"; yet, exaggeration aside, it is true that the poem is over-

dressed, that the intended fine simplicity of language is constantly
violated by bathos and pretence, by ornaments and affectations.
Tennyson claimed that his similes were all such as might have been
used by simple fisher-folk; but it is not the similes, it is not even
the great *pannus purpureus* with the convolvuluses and

> *The league-long roller thundering on the reef,*

it is such passages as

> *Then first since Enoch's golden ring had girt*
> *Her finger, Annie fought against his will:*
> *Yet not with brawling opposition she,*
> *But manifold entreaties, many a tear,*
> *Many a sad kiss by day by night renew'd*
> *(Sure that all evil would come out of it)*
> *Besought him, supplicating,...*

which might do in *Paradise Regained,* beside

> *Annie, this voyage by the grace of God*
> *Will bring fair weather yet to all of us.*
> *Keep a clean hearth and a clear fire for me,*
> *For I'll be back, my girl, before you know it.*

Bagehot objected to "romantic art" because it will not bear sun-
light; the moon is its goddess. But the fundamental flaw in 'Enoch
Arden' is not that stylistically it tries to live beyond its means; it is
that the story is conceived in sentiment and brought forth in com-
placency. The pathetic appeal is overt, the hero is posed as heroic,
the commonplace is invested with an air of grandeur. The em-
phasis on the sickly child and the lock of its hair, the plea for sym-
pathy for Annie who lets her children run wild because she is
incompetent as well as indigent, the elaboration of delicacy in
Philip's wooing, the natural but overplayed contrasting of Enoch's
misfortunes with the business prosperity of the unassuming Philip,

> *(For cups and silver on the burnish'd board*
> *Sparkled and shone; so genial was the hearth;—*

culminating in poor Enoch's costly funeral), and the climactic
build-up of Enoch as the strong and silent, rugged and long-suffer-
ing hero,—these too simple devices are of the essence of sentimen-
tality. Our heartstrings, clutched too violently, resound too hollow-

ly, as always happens when simplicity overreaches itself. And these effects are but underlined by the applied beauties. This is especially evident in the metrical subtleties—

> *This pretty, puny, weakly little one, . . .*
> >   *but now hastily caught*
> *His bundle, waved his hand, and went his way . . .*
> *Take your own time, Annie, take your own time. . . .*
> *Merrily rang the bells and they were wed,*
> *But never merrily beat Annie's heart, . . .*

which only set off the flatness of

> *Seem'd kinder unto Philip than to him; . . .*
> *Since Enoch left he had not look'd upon her, . . .*
> *I came to speak to you of what he wish'd, . . .*
> *It chanced one evening Annie's children long'd*
> *To go with others, nutting to the wood, . . .*

It all sums up in favor of Bagehot as against Blackie. Not content with the simple emotions which would allow the natural pathos of the subject to work its proper effect, or the simple language which would sustain without forcing the natural emotions, Tennyson thought it necessary to varnish his picture, to glorify it with artificial lighting. And his fellow countrymen, for the most part, approved.

Almost as though to prove something, Tennyson followed 'Enoch Arden' with 'Aylmer's Field.' If the former exhibits the domestic idyll gone sentimentally soft, the latter shows it satirically hard. And stylistically they are poles apart. It is as though he wished to demonstrate that he could write 853 lines of blank verse with hardly a single flourish. The gift of clear, brittle phrase-making which he lavished in the earlier half of 'The Princess' here turned sour—

> *Sir Aylmer Aylmer, that almighty man,*
> *The county God, . . .*
> *His wife a faded beauty of the Baths,*
> *Insipid as the Queen upon a card; . . .*
> >   *so that Rectory and Hall,*
> *Bound in an immemorial intimacy, . . .*
> >   *Dull and self-involved,*

Tall and erect, but bending from his height
With half-allowing smiles for all the world,
And mighty courteous in the main—his pride
Lay deeper than to wear it as his ring—
He, like an Aylmer in his Aylmerism,·...

The story of 'Aylmer's Field' was called improbable by the critics —the same word that Mrs. Barbauld applied to the story of 'The Ancient Mariner'— and the critics were told that it was a true story. It is a favorite situation of childhood affection balked by proud parents: the father kills his daughter by cruelty, the lover commits suicide, and his brother preaches a violent, almost incoherent funeral sermon which drives the parents mad. This is not poetic material, in the Tennysonian sense, and Tennyson, be it said in his favor, did not try to make it 'poetic.' He tried rather to make it a vehicle for his "prophet's righteous wrath against this form of selfishness; and no one," continues the *Memoir,* significantly, "can read his terrible denunciations of such pride trampling on a holy human love, without being aware that the poet's heart burnt within him while at work on this tale of wrong." Perhaps so; but a burning heart and strong language are not enough.

To those who remember Tennyson as the Palace of Art poet, the 'Northern Farmer: Old Style' (in the 'Enoch Arden' volume) and 'New Style' (in the 'Holy Grail' volume four years later) have always seemed a strange sport. It was all very well to be told that he had a rich robustious humor in private life, but why should the author of 'Sir Galahad' and 'The Lady of Shalott' write and publish comic poems in a barbarous dialect? It was unfitting, almost indelicate. One may among friends roar at a coarse joke; but the sweet-voiced Poet fluting in his garden and the long-robed Prophet speaking from his pulpit should remain in character. Here, instead, the Poet of the People walks among his lowliest followers and speaks their language. He who had heard Juno, Pallas, and Aphrodite addressing Priam's son in Phrygia and had communed with King Arthur, now fraternizes with the peasant of Lincolnshire. A Lincolnshire farmer's daughter exclaimed when she heard the two poems read: "I thought Mr. Tennyson was a gentleman." Stopford Brooke, without a smile, called the earlier of the two "a vivid piece . . . of that elemental humorousness of things which belongs to the lives of the brutes as well as to ourselves." Certainly they are roughhewn (the queer spelling makes them look rougher than they are) and earthy, these two pieces, and shrewdly clever. One would perhaps not want more of them, because dialect verse is generally to be deplored, but one welcomes these as little monuments to a real part of Tennyson's character. He himself liked them and was fond of reading them aloud, and he resented Roden Noel's description of them as photographs. "They are imaginative," he protested.

In the next year, 1865, appeared *A Selection from the Works of Alfred Tennyson, D.C.L., Poet Laureate.* "I have been assured," said the Laureate, "that a selection from my poems would not be unacceptable to the people." (There had been five volumes published since 1842.) "I have inserted . . . such as I have been led to believe would be most popular." The choice is a little odd. One expects 'The Palace of Art' and 'A Dream of Fair Women' to be omitted, but one is not prepared for the exclusion of 'Enoch Arden,' which added more to the Laureate's popularity than any other one poem. (Two other poems from the 'Enoch Arden' volume *were* included.) One looks in vain for selections from 'In Memoriam.' One is surprised to find only "Come into the Garden" and "Go not, happy day" from 'Maud.' The choice seems to be a compromise between what the Laureate thought was popular and what he thought was good. The Preface continues: "not without hope that my choice may be sanctioned by their approval I dedicate this volume to 'The Working Men of England.' " This is the appeal direct. One hopes the Working Men enjoyed 'Œnone' and 'Guinevere' and the 'Small Sweet Idyl' and the Wellington 'Ode.'

Since there is no good chronological place for 'The Lover's Tale' I place it here, after the recapitulatory *Selections* and before the group of later idylls. It is one of the most *idyllic* of all Tennyson's poems and yet quite unlike the idylls of the hearth. It consists now of four Parts, the first two of which, over a thousand lines long, were written in 1828, in Tennyson's nineteenth year, and were printed for, but withdrawn from, the *Poems* of 1833. Proof copies were somehow circulated, however, and the two parts were "mercilessly pirated"; and in his own defence (and apologetically: "boy's work," he called it, and added: "seeing . . . that what I had deemed scarce worthy to live is not allowed to die") Tennyson finished and published it in 1879. He then equipped it with an "Argument"—

Julian, whose cousin and foster-sister, Camilla, has been wedded to his friend and rival, Lionel, endeavours to narrate the story of his own love for her, and the strange sequel. He speaks (in Parts II. and III.) of having been haunted by visions and the sound of bells, tolling for a funeral, and at last ringing for a marriage; but he breaks away, overcome, as he approaches the Event, and a witness to it completes the tale.

The first two Parts are extremely fluent, not to say voluble, blank verse, in style a middling Wordsworth plus a sweetened Byron: ultraromantic, with a vague remote setting. Part III, written in 1868, is short and stylistically transitional. Part IV is a poem which was published under the title of 'The Golden Supper' in the 'Holy Grail' volume, 1870. The story of Part IV is taken from Boccaccio's *Decameron*:[5] Camilla dies and is buried, is resuscitated by Julian, gives birth to a young Lionel, and is restored to her husband after a gorgeous banquet. All of which is indubitably "sad, sweet, and strange together"—a Tennysonian curio with a history somewhat parallel to that of the heroine. Almost its only interest (except historical) is that Tennyson did not allow it to die after he won his suit in Chancery against the piratical Herne Shepherd in 1876.

'The Window; or, Song of the Wrens' might perversely be called an idyll, but really it is "a little song-cycle, German fashion" composed by request for Sir Arthur Sullivan "to exercise his art upon." 'The Victim,' though also doggerel, is a sort of idyll, written *en passant* at Marlborough, from a story in Charlotte Yonge's *Golden Deeds*. They are both oddments. Meantime, having completed his 'Idylls of the King' Tennyson turned to the special form of poetic drama and, having completed his historical trilogy to supply Shakespeare's omissions, he produced 'The Falcon,' which is an idyll in dramatic form, and then published his *Ballads and Other Poems*, 1880, which contains five true idylls of the hearth and six other pieces of similar kind.

'The First Quarrel' is sufficiently described by Carlyle's remark: "Ah, but that's a dreary tragic tale. Poor fellow, he was just an honest plain man, and she was a curious production of the century, and I am sorry for that poor girl too." The story was founded on facts. 'The Northern Cobbler' was also so founded and is also in dialect: the anecdote of a reformed drunkard. So also for the most part was 'The Sisters,' but on a slightly higher level and not in dialect: the story of "a girl who consented to be the bridesmaid of her sister, although she secretly loved the bridegroom." She ran away after the marriage and was found insane at the door of the church, in the rain. 'The Village Wife; or, the Entail' is another Lincolnshire dialect piece, a "portrait drawn from life." Similarly 'In the Children's Hospital' is based on a story related to the poet by Mary Gladstone; "the two children . . . are taken from life." The poem was said to be "marred a little by the needlessly harsh attack on the practice of modern surgery"; Tennyson replied that the nurse, not he, was the speaker.

With the same kind of story as these Tennyson made an entirely different kind of poem in 'Rizpah.' He transposed the low notes into a higher key, made almost a lyric cry from them, and admixed, for weight, a sort of Locksley Hall-Maud indignation at social conditions. The contrast is enlightening. Equally successful is 'The Revenge'; but as though to show us how good it was Tennyson immediately followed it with 'The Defence of Lucknow'—not quite so good a subject, to be sure, but with much the same appeal and without any of the same effect. The meter has a similar base but is almost stodgily regular. 'The Revenge' touches our imagination; this is directed at the sense of fact. Even the ornamentation fails—

Heat like the mouth of a hell, or a deluge of cataract skies,
Stench of old offal decaying, and infinite torment of flies,
Thoughts of the breezes of May blowing over an English field,
Cholera, scurvy, and fever, the wound that would *not be heal'd,* . . .

Still further descending one reads 'Sir John Oldcastle,' in curiously bad blank verse, a little suggestive of Browning, but with the old attempted pathos. Sir John was "a fine historical figure," said Tennyson. Descending further: 'Columbus,' based on a passage in Irving's *Life* and written to satisfy "repeated entreaties from certain prominent Americans."[6] Finally, 'The Voyage of Maeldune,' written again in the regularized six-beat line of 'Lucknow'—which William Morris had already supplied in sufficient quantity in 'Sigurd the Volsung' (1876). Tennyson begins:

I was the chief of the race—he had stricken my father dead—
But I gather'd my fellows together, I swore I would strike off his
   head.

The rest is not so bald; rather, it is like a study in conventional epithets, remarkable for a poet of Tennyson's ability when he chose to write brilliant description. But it is predictable of a poet of his tastes writing for his audience that he should exchange (and almost boast of it) the Celtic bizarreries of his source for easy and commonplace incidents of his own.[7]

Here then are eleven pieces grouped under the heading of Ballads and other poems, three of them in blank verse, the rest in ballad meter or a closely related form. All are recognizable variants of the idyll and five are clear and crude examples of the domestic idyll—'Rizpah' is a clear example but not crude. They comprise the bulk of the 1880 volume and they represent its poetic value; they all share a direct appeal to the simple tastes of the common reader. Yet there was only one edition, for the tens and more of the earlier volumes.

Tennyson might seem to be losing on his own ground, but he persevered in the same path. Six long poems in *Tiresias and Other Poems,* 1885, are idylls, and the rest of the volume, with the exception of 'The Ancient Sage' and 'To Virgil,' is made up of small things. 'Tiresias' is of course 'classical' in subject matter, the other six idylls are idylls of the hearth: 'The Wreck,' a quasi-ballad with a Marie Corelli plot founded on fact; 'Despair,' in the same, now favorite, meter, about a man and his wife who decide to drown themselves because they have lost their faith in God; 'The Flight,' same meter, Irish dialect (the one example of this), about an old woman and the body of her lover who had been lost when young in a peat-bog; and 'The Spinster's Sweet-Arts,' same meter, Lincolnshire dialect.

Locksley Hall Sixty Years After, Etc. (1886) contains, besides the titular poem (in which the incumbent of the Hall has aged sixty years in forty-two and shows it), a Laureate ode, a topical rime ('The Fleet'), and a domestic idyll, dialect and all, in three acts— 'The Promise of May.' Three years later, *Demeter and Other Poems* adds three more idylls to the list: 'Owd Roä,' 'Happy: the Leper's Bride,' and 'Romney's Remorse' (the last showing some influence of Browning); and two semi-idylls, 'The Ring,' and 'Forlorn.' Finally, the posthumous volume, 1892, closes the list with another three—besides 'The Death of Œnone' and 'St. Telemachus' already mentioned—all in the six- or seven-beat quasi-ballad meter and one of them in dialect: 'The Church-Warden and the Curate,' 'The Bandit's Death,' and 'Charity.'

Enfin, it has been a long list and for the most part a dull one, concluding with a sigh. And when the whole column is added up it yields but a few conclusions, already obvious. Although the idyll as a type must be viewed liberally because it covers a variety of closely related forms throughout the poet's sixty productive years, it embraces a very large proportion of his work. It embraces nearly all of his verse which was composed with an eye on the object, namely, that of pleasing the common reader. To hint that Tennyson wrote popular poetry merely for the market would be malicious and unjust. To suppose, on the other hand, that he devoted himself to idylls of hearth and country because he believed he could do his best in that *line* would be inaccurate. When he wrote to please himself he wrote some of his finest and some of his worst —hardly a paradox, this. What is necessary to recognize is that in Tennyson's artistic conscience there was a divided allegiance: part of him reached for the heights and part of him walked contentedly along the dusty road. Having caught the popular ear, he believed he should pipe to it, and he seems honestly confused about the result. He must have known, if he had any æsthetic instinct, that 'Ulysses' and 'The Queen of the May' were separated by a gulf, but he appears to have thought that both kinds were good and both were worth doing. And if this is incomprehensible to us of a farther day, we must try to understand his confusion. Condemn it we must, yet not without an effort to see his reasons. One of those reasons was certainly a natural defect. It seems never to have occurred to him to inquire into æsthetic principles. With all his extraordinary gift as a craftsman and his practical devotion to his art, he worked without any clear ideas of *art.* His comments on his own poetry, so revealing and so unashamed, yield no evidence of a poetic *theory;* and his criticism of other poets is limited to unanalytical approval or to points of craftsmanship. He played with ethical problems and with moral philosophy, but the philosophy

174

of art was almost unknown to him. Another reason for his con-
fusion was, to repeat, his naïve belief in popular poetry—not pop-
ular as Yeats understood the word but as Charlotte Yonge under-
stood it. Like Dickens and Trollope and many a lessor purveyor of
entertaining literature he believed in giving his followers what
they expected. The third reason was his embroilment with a mis-
sion: he was the portrayer of his age.

All these many idylls, from the small and sweet to the most pre-
tentious, suggest that Tennyson knew the skill of his hand and
turned in all directions for opportunities of its exercise. This is a
low view to take, but it is not without justice; for the impelling
demand for expression was always less with him than the impulse
to write, and after 1850 the impulse to write was too often fostered
by Mrs. Tennyson and the Jowetts. On the higher view these idylls
might be taken as the poet's revelations of human nature under
many various conditions, men and women—but that was Brown-
ing's phrase—facing their environment, struggling to understand
or to realize themselves, finding the best answers they could. (One
recalls George Eliot's admirable expression: "In these frail vessels
is borne onward through the ages the treasure of human affec-
tion.") From this point of view the great variety of subject and
setting, from 'Ulysses' to the 'Northern Farmer,' from 'Demeter'
and 'Œnone' to 'Mariana' and the 'Village Wife,' is an advantage
because it enables the poet to study and illustrate and 'interpret'
so much of life. But no; one asks then how profound was the read-
ing, how illuminating the interpretation, how great the revelation.
And one answers, with or without reluctance, that the idylls are no
more than the name he gave them—little pictures, glimpses, guesses,
incidents or angles of this our common experience, with emphasis
on the simple, the easy, the familiar; a miscellany; the work of an
enquiring, eager, sensitive mind without a penetrating vision or
profound convictions or a philosophical understanding. They are
directed to our softer readier emotions; they do not stir us or flash
light into our depths. From this judgment a few poems do of course
make certain appeal; they are noble and notable exceptions, but I
speak now of the idylls as a whole.

CHAPTER EIGHT

Idylls of the King—and Allegory

IN AUGUST 1859, when the Laureate was fifty years of age, he
had to his credit in the public esteem a moderate success with
the two volumes of *Poems,* 1842, and a very considerable suc-
cess with 'In Memoriam,' which however was more admired—or at
least more purchased—than understood. On the debit side stood
'The Princess,' which seemed trivial, a midsummer day's dream,
and 'Maud.' But in the preceding month, July, had just appeared
'Idylls of the King'; some ten thousand copies were sold in six
weeks; and the Laureate stock was up again. In these first 'Idylls'
three of which are among the best of the whole series, Tennyson
amalgamated the best of his various blank verse styles—the plain-
ness of 'Dora,' the luxuriance of 'The Gardener's Daughter,' and
the energy of 'Ulysses'—and reached a level of poetic narrative
which he later sometimes equalled but hardly exceeded.

These 'Idylls' have a long and complex history which began
nearly thirty years earlier and was to continue twenty-five years
into the future.[1] In 1830 Tennyson wrote part, if not all, of his
first experiment with the Matter of Arthur: 'Sir Lancelot and
Queen Guinevere. A Fragment.' This is a merely descriptive-deco-
rative piece, in a stanza resembling that of 'The Lady of Shalott,'
with nothing of the story except the closing lines:

> *A man had given all other bliss,*
> *And all his worldly worth for this,*
> *To waste his whole heart in one kiss*
> *Upon her perfect lips.*

FitzGerald remembered also some verses on Lancelot's courtship
"handed about among us in 1832 (I think) at Cambridge"—

Light of the Life within my Blood,
Light of the Light within mine Eyes . . .

And in the 1833 volume was published 'The Lady of Shalott,' which not only deserves the trite comment of being the finest thing of its kind in our language, but is an example of what is probably the best way for moderns to handle the Malory material. At any rate, it marked Tennyson's way very plainly; it added virtuosity and brilliance to Malory's colored lights on the chivalry of the Middle Ages. The next step was then to transpose the ballad-romance form into narrative; which Tennyson took in 'Morte d'Arthur,' begun only a little later. Meanwhile, "about 1833" he began a prose sketch, wrote out a set of allegorical equivalents, and (soon after) drafted a sort of pseudo-classical drama, or as the *Memoir* calls it a musical masque, in five acts. In the first of these tentatives allegory was implicit—"But all underneath it was hollow, and the mountain trembled . . ."—and elaboration obvious:

It was night. The King sat in his Hall. Beside him sat the sumptuous Guinevere and all about him were all his lords and knights of the Table Round. There they feasted, and when the feast was over the Bards sang to the King's glory.

But if this suggests Milton, the allegorical plan was too Spenserian. Arthur was to stand for religious faith, Modred for the sceptical understanding, Merlin for science, the Round Table for liberal institutions; the Saxons were to be the seapeople; and to make it all quite baffling Arthur was to have three Guineveres: the first, Primitive Christianity, whom he would "put away," the second, Roman Catholicism, who "flies. Arthur takes to the first again but finds her changed by lapse of Time"; the third was apparently to be the Guinevere of the flesh, whom Modred (as sceptical understanding) pulls from the throne. For a poet of (say) twenty-four this was rather ambitious, and it is hard to see what Tennyson would have done with it at the age of twenty-four, even with the active collaboration of Milton and Spenser. The five-act masque also he put away; it might have rivalled Dryden, but one does not think of Dryden the playwright as a model for Tennyson.

Another fragment of the subject appeared, in 1842, in the spirited, but also sugared, 'Sir Galahad,' the maiden knight who "never felt the kiss of love, Nor maiden's hand" in his. Already one of the dangers of the subject betrays itself. "After this," says the *Memoir,* without precise reference to time, Tennyson "began to study the epical King Arthur in earnest. . . . He thought, read, talked about King Arthur." He even composed in his head a very good poem on Lancelot's quest of the Grail, but soon forgot it. The enthusiasm for this "the greatest of all poetical subjects" did not last, however. It may well have bogged down in its allegorical impedimenta. But other poetical subjects occupied him, until 1855 when he "determined upon the final shape" of his epic. What relation this final shape of 1855 had to the jocularly described work in the introduction to the 'Morte d'Arthur' of 1842—

> *His epic, his King Arthur, some twelve books,*

of which Arthur's death was the eleventh, and in which

> *Were faint Homeric echoes, nothing-worth,*

it is impossible to say; nor what relation it bore to the completed 'epic' of 1888, but on a guess one would say, not much.

In 1856 the Merlin and the Enid Idylls were written, and privately printed the next year with the title: "Enid and Nimuë: The True and the False";[2] in 1859—the Elaine and Guinevere Idylls having been written meanwhile—"The True and the False: Four Idylls of the King" was privately printed; and in July of the same year was published 'Idylls of the King.' The labels *true* and *false* were happily removed. These Idylls were, to give them their present titles, with the division of the original 'Enid' into two parts: 'The Marriage of Geraint,' 'Geraint and Enid,' 'Merlin and Vivien,' 'Lancelot and Elaine,' and 'Guinevere.'

It is important, thus, to note that the Merlin Idyll was the first written. Jowett liked it best and called it "the naughty one"; and there can be little doubt that Tennyson's poetical handling of the seduction scene gave satisfaction to many other readers. Victorian reticence had here successfully, for a moment, raised the veil. Compared with this, Matthew Arnold's

> *They sate them down together, and a sleep*
> *Fell upon Merlin, more like death, so deep*

is the very acme of restraint. Yet the picture of a seductive woman making love to an aged seer is altogether repulsive in itself, if not a little ridiculous:

> *There while she sat, half-falling from his knees,*
> *Half-nestled at his heart, and since he saw*
> *The slow tear creep from her closed eyelid yet,*
> *About her, more in kindness than in love,*
> *The gentle wizard cast a shielding arm.*
> *But she dislink'd herself at once and rose;*

and just a few lines before she had (an unlucky Latinism)

> *Leapt from her session on his lap . . .*

Here is the first sign of the maladjustment of Malory to modern literary uses which has always disturbed the critics. Part of it is due to the differences in atmosphere between Malory's work and for example Tennyson's and also the differences in tempo; for in Malory, where so much happens so rapidly the reader has little opportunity or desire to examine details, and most modern renderings are slow-motion in comparison. Part is due, in Tennyson's case, moreover, to his allegorical intention.

Readers of the 'Idylls' of 1859 were little bothered by allegory. They had not been told to look for it and they probably did not perceive it. Nor do we who have inherited so much authorized and unauthorized exegesis know quite what to think. How are we profited by supposing that Merlin stands for Intellect and Vivien for Sin?[a] There may be single passages along the way which are underlined by the double meanings, as when Vivien says;

> *Have I not sworn? I am not trusted. Good!*
> *Well, hide it, hide it; I shall find it out,*
> *And being found take heed of Vivien.*

This is also what the sins of the flesh might say to the power of Intellect; and if we hear both meanings simultaneously we may enjoy something like the exhilaration of a pun. Or when Vivien says of Arthur:

[a] It has been wisely said that "Merlin is the type of the sceptical intellect which can discern the true spiritual king and enlist in his service, and therein perform mighty works, but which is not spiritual itself, and is thus exposed to the snares of Sense" (Frederick S. Boas, "Tennyson and the Arthurian Legend," in *From Richardson to Pinero*, New York, 1937, p. 218). But this is not an *allegorical* interpretation.

Man! is he man at all, who knows and winks?

we recognize perhaps that Tennyson means this as a malicious judgment, obvious enough however without alleged allegory. And since many other judgments of Vivien are both shrewd and sound from the realistic point of view we may infer that Sin has no place in a romantic tale. But when we hear Merlin say that

> *... men at most differ as Heaven and earth,*
> *But women, worst and best, as Heaven and hell,*

is it Intellect or Sin speaking? Or in the larger view is the main drift of the Idyll enhanced by our thinking of the destruction of Intelligence by Sin? This notion that man's gift of intelligence can be and often is subdued by the wiles of the flesh is a simple and familiar idea. It is within the grasp of most adult readers. Is it made more effective as a criticism of life or more powerful as a moral warning by Tennyson's Idyll? The criticism of life and the moral warning of this Idyll do not lie in the allegory and what little the allegory can be said to add to them is so obvious and so trivial as to have no artistic value or human interest.

Or, to put the matter a little differently, the point of the Merlin and Vivien story, for Malory and for most readers, is the pity that Merlin could become so assotted, not the shockingness that Vivien could be so wicked. And for the purposes of allegory this is exactly what we want: the damaging picture of intelligence a prey to sensuality. But instead, in the Idyll we are regaled with the seductive wiles of a *femme fatale*—Tennyson's small contribution to the large literature of this subheroine—and the emphasis seems to have gone wrong. For if we are supposed to feel—and certainly from the point of view of the whole 'Idylls' we are supposed to feel—that here is an example of sensuality destroying the moral virtue of Camelot society, then we must feel that Merlin is ill chosen as victim. For it is not through the senile weakness of its wise men that society is corrupted, but through the unrestraint of its passionate youth. Perhaps Tennyson had a glimpse of this when he made Merlin say:

> *She cloaks the scar of some repulse with lies;*
> *I well believe she tempted them, and fail'd,*

"them" being Merlin's friends of the Table Round. Or, but un-thinkable, if Vivien had seduced Galahad or had seriously tempted Arthur, the effect would have been powerful and the allegory pointed; but of course such a twist of the story would have been "inutterable unkindliness."

Moreover, Merlin "overtalk'd and overworn" (as Tennyson deli-cately puts it) falls victim not to the snares of the flesh but plainly to Vivien's flattery, with the aid of a violent storm wonderfully described. This throws light on the human intelligence but is not what the allegory demands. In a word, however one fix the allegori-cal equation in this Idyll the reader is puzzled and the answer is wrong.

But if an uncomfortable sense of ill-fitting allegory perplexes the reader to-day, it was not so for the reader of 1859. That reader could enjoy the descriptions, could make the best of an unpleasant story, could understand Vivien as the personification of misan-thropic sensualism which finds its satisfaction in scorn and hate and recognize Merlin as weak perhaps in the face of flattery but strong in good sense when the rumor of scandal is breathed—

> 'Yea, I know it.
> ...let them be....
> I know the Table Round, my friends of old;
> All brave, and many generous, and some chaste.-

A little more of this plain speaking and simple appreciation of the shortcomings of life would have saved the moral-immoral tone of the 'Idylls' and possibly have helped Arthur, the "selfless man and stainless gentleman," from the inevitable failure of those who ex-pect too much.

Only a fortnight after finishing 'Merlin and Vivien' Tennyson began his long story of Enid the True, taken not from Malory but from the Mabinogion. It is an unfortunate descent in tone, not a part of his 'epic,' but one of his genre pieces in a mediæval setting, a variant of the poor girl ("one so bright in dark estate") and the prince combined with the Griselda theme of patient wife and de-manding husband. The story itself is uninteresting in Tennyson's version, and the repeated incidents of Enid's riding ahead into am-bushes without permission to speak are too crude for modern taste. There are even times when Tennyson seems to approve of Geraint's masterful treatment of his wife; and through most of the Idyll Geraint, though he is meant to be noble, is a disagreeable picture of the jealous husband. In this rôle, to be sure, his suspiciousness makes a good offset, if Tennyson could have seen it so, to Arthur's blindness. But what Tennyson does try to make of him is a type of the good days when Arthur's court was comparatively pure—at the price of showing one of these good knights as a thoroughly unpleasant character who believes that if there is suspicion of the Queen no woman can be trusted. Then at the end Geraint recovers his senses, Edryn, the Victorian cousin-lover, reforms, Enid nurses her husband back to strength, Arthur sets out to purge the neighboring districts, and the whole reveals itself as an improving anecdote overelaborated,—to say nothing of the "little Enids and Geraints Of times to be." [b]

And the language of these two Enid Idylls is no better than the story. It hesitates between the bareness of

> *and there fell*
> *A horror on him, lest his gentle wife,*
> *Thro' that great tenderness for Guinevere,*
> *Had suffer'd, or should suffer any taint*
> *In nature*

and the *faux bon* of

> *Who, moving, cast the coverlet aside,*
> *And bared the knotted column of his throat,*
> *The massive square of his heroic breast,*
> *And arms on which the standing muscle sloped,*
> *As slopes a wild brook o'er a little stone,*
> *Running too vehemently to break upon it.*

Only a few good things afford relief: the fresh metaphor of Geraint's followers in battle hearing his voice

> *as one*
> *That listens near a torrent mountain-brook,*

[b] For a contrary opinion see W. P. Ker, *Collected Essays*, London, 1925, I, 274, 275: "It may be observed that some of the best and most elaborate [of Tennyson's similes come in the Idyll of *Enid* . . . and that the story of Enid will stand any fair test of criticism with regard to its plot, its characters, its unity of narrative. It is a poem which atones for a great neglect in English poetry. . . . Tennyson perhaps never wrote any story with better success."

> *All thro' the crash of the near cataract hears*
> *The drumming thunder of the huger fall*
> *At distance,*

the glimpse of

> *A little town with towers, upon a rock,*
> *And close beneath, a meadow gemlike chased*
> *In the brown wild, and mowers mowing in it,*

and Darwin's worm (a little ahead of time)

> *whose souls the old serpent long had drawn*
> *Down, as the worm draws in the wither'd leaf*
> *And makes it earth.*

In the latter half of the year 1857 the Laureate Tennyson was composing his idyll of 'Guinevere' and the obscure William Morris was composing his 'Defence of Guenevere' and 'King Arthur's Tomb.' Two more diverse *rifacimenti* of Malory or more antithetic masterpieces, written at the same time, the world has seldom seen; and the god of Irony may well have allowed himself an Homeric laugh. Morris's poems are crude enough in their way, ungrammatical, unpunctuated, unconstructed, but they are vivid and alive and passionate to the very verge of delirium. Tennyson's 'Guinevere' is grand and lofty and solemn to the last degree, in the judgment of those who admire it; and it is one of the most severely criticized of the Idylls by those who are not in sympathy with the Laureate. Meredith's stricture that King Arthur talks in it like a curate is famous. On the other hand, it is reported that George Eliot wept when she read it (perhaps a little over its personal poignancy) and Gladstone praised as the climax of Arthur's nobility—"the great pillar of the moral order, and the resplendent top of human excellence"—those "two really wonderful speeches" at the end. It seems to be a matter of taste.

The Idyll opens with an incident explaining Modred's hatred of Lancelot, continues with a statement (hardly more, since it is not developed emotionally) of Guinevere's remorse, and her farewell to her lover, and then moves into the long scene of Guinevere and the garrulous Little Novice. This scene would have been still more affecting if the irony were not so overworked; but it contains one very important passage. The Little Novice says of the King that

> *no man knew from whence he came; ...*
> *They found a naked child upon the sands*
> *Of dark Tintagel by the Cornish sea,*
> *And that was Arthur; and they foster'd him*
> *Till he by miracle was approven King;*
> *And that his grave should be a mystery*
> *From all men, like his birth; and could he find*
> *A woman in her womanhood as great*
> *As he was in his manhood, ...*
> *The twain together well might change the world.*

From the point of view of the finished 'Idylls' this restates, just before the tragic conclusion, the principal motif of the whole poem. From the point of view of 1857 (or 1859, when it was published) this is even more significant, since it suggests that then Tennyson really had in mind "a more or less perfected scheme" of the Idylls, "the final shape of the poem." It involves also the elementary allegory which the poet asserted when he said "By Arthur I always mean the soul"; and it leads to the more elaborate allegory of 'The Coming of Arthur.' As story this passage has no point and little meaning, but it gains both point and meaning when Arthur is viewed as representing the soul and perhaps (though there is no authority for saying so) Guinevere as this our mortality. Symbolically: when the soul takes on flesh it becomes an uplifting influence, unless the flesh proves too strong and betrays it. This must be the "allegory in the distance" which Jowett saw darkly, but which once seen is both clear and simple. It is this, also, which explains and justifies the extravagant claims or assertions of Arthur's purity and perfection, and even his likeness to the Christ, as when he cries (in 'The Passing of Arthur'):

> *My God, thou hast forgotten me in my death!*

It explains also Arthur's general passionlessness and want of humanity, his abstractness. It focuses, moreover, very sharply Arthur's failure as a human being, his failure as a leader, and most clearly of all his failure as the hero of a story: he is overthrown by his allegorical attributes. But chiefly it explains Tennyson's failure in the two hundred lines in which Arthur denounces judgment on Guinevere in a "changed" voice. If those "two really wonderful speeches" are read as the words of a self-righteous husband condemning the infidelity of his wife, or of a 'mediæval' King charging his Queen with responsibility for the loss of his kingdom—"And all thro' thee!"—they are intolerable. Yet it is plain that Tennyson expects us to read them so and that many of his readers enjoyed them for the moral indignation they abound in.[c] But if they are read as the divine voice condemning the evil in this poor world, as the suffering Soul crying out against the flesh it inhabits, then the arrogance and self-satisfaction of King Arthur disappear and the grovelling of the Queen becomes but a symbol. Perhaps it was greatly daring for a poet to mix the moulds in this fashion, for if he had succeeded it would have been a triumph indeed: but it remains a masterpiece of artistic blundering, because Arthur's real voice and his "changed" allegorical tones together produce a sort

[c] For contemporary admiration we have both Gladstone's and Dickens' testimony. Said Gladstone: "Then follow two most noble speeches of the King. They are hard to describe. They are of a lofty, almost an awful severity; and yet a severity justified by the transcendent elevation, which the poet has given to the character of Arthur. . . . We know not where to look in history or in letters for a nobler and more overpowering conception of man as he might be, than in the Arthur of this volume" (*Gleanings from Past Years*, II, "Personal and Literary," New York, 1886, p. 166; reprinted from *The Quarterly Review*, October 1859). Said Dickens, in a letter of August 1859: "How fine the *Idylls* are! Lord! what a blessed thing it is to read a man who really can write. I thought nothing could be finer than the first poem, till I came to the third; but when I had read the last, it seemed to me absolutely unapproachable" (Forster's *Life*, ed. J. W. T. Ley, London, 1928, p. 730.) The most ecstatic approval of all comes from J. M. Ludlow (the "modern critic" who drew Matthew Arnold's fire in the 1853 Preface): "And then comes at last that passage, as noble of its kind, I believe, as any ever penned by poet or dramatist since the world was —more touching, I think, than any in our language, except King Lear's lament over Cordelia, beginning (p. 253) with—

'*But now to take last leave of all I loved,*'—

and concluding with Arthur's farewell and blessing. We see there, risen to its fullest height, the true, noble purpose of the writer. We see that which Christianity alone has made possible or intelligible—a representation of the absolutely unselfish love, the love of the worthy for the unworthy,—the saving love, which overcomes sin by excess of loving" ("Moral Aspects of Mr. Tennyson's 'Idylls of the King,'" in *Macmillan's Magazine* L (November 1859), 63-72; pp. 64-69). On the other hand, the *Quarterly*, in 1870, saw in the 'Idylls' "a purity for the most part living and sincere, but sometimes (as in the last speech of Arthur) showing too much of that ostentatious cleanliness of the hands which indicates a desire to stand well with the respectabilities of the world" (*Quarterly Review*, CXXVIII (January 1870), 1-17; p. 4). Edward Lear, Mrs. Tennyson's friend, records (18 July 1859): "Of course prudes are shocked" at the Guinevere idyll. And Dean Alford, a little later, had difficulty in finding terms polite enough to mention her.

of inarticulate double-talk: each blurs the other, confuses the reason and undermines the poetry.[d]

As Guinevere was *false* Elaine was *true*. To be sure, Guinevere was true to Lancelot and Elaine was saved from a *faux pas* only by the superior honor of Lancelot; but these are moral casuistries beneath the attention of a Victorian Laureate. One cannot think of everything. If on sober judgment Lancelot cuts a better figure than the Lily Maid we swathe reason in pathos, for of such illusions is romantic poetry made. Certainly the idyll of 'Lancelot and Elaine' is one of the best. The subject was congenial to Tennyson and the matter not beyond his range. It is not quite an epic fragment; it is in fact the better for not having the epical pretence with which he tried to elevate some of the other Idylls; but it is a fine piece of narrative poetry in its own tradition. The mere story is something like that of a humbler genre idyll, but the chivalric setting and the decorative language suit it perfectly and work harmoniously to educe Tennyson's best qualities. The little incident of love in Astolat, moreover, is easily attached to the larger story of adulterous love in Camelot which seemed so important to Tennyson and therefore fits well with the "perfected scheme" of the whole poem. And what is still more, there is no involvement with allegorical meanings. And what is more important still, the two principal characters become almost human beings: Guinevere and Lancelot more nearly come alive in this Idyll than anywhere in the series.

The Idyll exhibits all the variety of Tennyson's blank-verse style, from the trickery of

> *I know not if I know what true love is,*
> *But if I know, then, if I know not him,*
> *I know there is none other I can love*

[d] The miscegenation of a symbolic Arthur and Guinevere a pure woman (as Hardy denominated Tess) is painfully evident here. "A keener sense of the incongruous would have saved him from exposing his ideal King in a situation round which cluster a thousand disturbing associations from the novel and the stage" (F. S. Boas, cited above, p. 226). Boas' essay is a professed attempt to justify Tennyson's interpretation of the 'legend' and also to note "some of the difficulties to which it inevitably gave rise"—such as the allegory more or less throughout, the inconsistency of the two Viviens (in the Merlin Idyll and in 'Balin and Balan'), the "gingerly handling of the passion of Lancelot and Guinevere" for "moral edification," and the "twisted" symbolism of the Grail quest.

(which Tennyson calls "simple") and the famous oxymoron:

> *His honour rooted in dishonour stood,*
> *And faith unfaithful kept him falsely true,*

to the splendid simile

> *They couch'd their spears and prick'd their steeds, and thus,*
> *Their plumes driv'n backward by the wind they made*
> *In moving, all together down upon him*
> *Bare, as a wild wave in the wide North-sea,*
> *Green-glimmering toward the summit, bears, with all*
> *Its stormy crests that smoke against the skies,*
> *Down on a bark, and overbears the bark,*
> *And him that helms it; so they overbore*
> *Sir Lancelot and his charger,*

and the Sophoclean irony of Arthur's

> *Lancelot, my Lancelot, thou in whom I have*
> *Most joy and most affiance . . .*
> *. . . a man*
> *Made to be loved; but now I would to God,*
> *Seeing the homeless trouble in thine eyes,*
> *Thou couldst have loved this maiden;*

from the stilted

> *How came the lily maid by that good shield*
> *Of Lancelot, she that knew not ev'n his name?*

and the Wordsworthian

> *The grace and versatility of the man!*

to Elaine's

> *I have gone mad. I love you: let me die,*

and the metrical exhibitionism of

> *But ten slow mornings past, and on the eleventh*

or

> *she stole*
> *Down the long tower-stairs, hesitating.*

There is equal variety in the subject matter. Nothing could be better than the simple dignity of Elaine's letter (nothing but Malory, of course) and Lancelot's speech that follows and the Queen's outburst—

> *Sea was her wrath, yet working after storm—*

on to the end of the Idyll, except for Arthur's ambivalent moralizing about free love. Best of all, I think, is the conflict in Lancelot's heart between pride and love, between 'sin' and duty,[e] between devotion to Guinevere and remorse for his failure to the King—with the contrasting glimpse of Gawaine, whose old courtesy has fallen upon its attendant vices, as now the elegant philanderer. For only here, with the poignant opposition of the Queen and the Lily Maid, could this conflict be made clear and powerful. Elaine makes a better foil to Guinevere and brings out her 'character' better than the prattling novice. And

> *The flower of all the west and all the world,*

whose mood was often like a fiend,

> *Marr'd as he was . . .*
> *And bruised and bronzed,*

becomes almost a real dramatic figure. For only here, I repeat, and for a moment, could Tennyson get far enough away from his Victorian program to show the nobility of both kinds of love.

The 'Idylls' of 1859 was a success: the critics praised it and it sold very well. Yet Tennyson delayed ten years before publishing the next instalment. Then in 1869 appeared *The Holy Grail and Other Poems* (dated 1870) containing 'The Coming of Arthur,' the title poem, 'Pelleas and Ettarre,' and 'The Passing of Arthur.' In the December 1871 issue of the *Contemporary Review* 'The Last Tournament' was published; in the next year came 'Gareth and Lynette'; and finally in the 'Tiresias' volume, 1885, 'Balin and Balan.'[3] Thus, said the American critic Stedman, apparently without sarcasm, grew the *Idylls of the King,* "nave and transept, aisle after aisle . . . a cloister here and a chapel yonder."

In the meantime, between 1859 and 1870 Tennyson had published a half dozen poems and some metrical experiments in peri-

---

odicals, then the 'Enoch Arden' volume, 1864, a volume of *Selections*, 1865, and five more poems in periodicals. The principal work of these years was thus 'Tithonus,' 'Enoch Arden,' 'Aylmer's Field,' 'Northern Farmer, Old Style,' 'Lucretius,' and a few lyrics. Why the ten-year hesitation? Why did Tennyson not take advantage of the success of the first *Idylls* and proceed at once with the completion of his great plan?

The official explanation why "In spite of the public applause he did not rush headlong into the other *Idylls of the King*" is twofold. "For one thing, he did not consider that the time was ripe. In addition to this, he did not find himself in the proper mood to write them, and he could never work except at what his heart impelled him to do." The first of these might mean so many things that it means substantially nothing; the second still requires explanation. One of the first signs that everything was not going well comes from Jowett's letter to Mrs. Tennyson in December 1858, suggesting to the Laureate some "subjects for poetry" and encouraging him to go on with the Idylls; but a few years later (and after the first volume was out) Jowett wrote to another tune.

He sometimes talks of going on with 'King Arthur.' For my own part I hope he won't; he has made as much of it as the subject admits. Twenty years ago he formed a scheme for an epic poem on 'King Arthur' in ten books; it is perhaps fortunate for himself that circumstances have prevented the completion of it.[4]

Whether this is entirely just or not, it represents one view of Tennyson's friends, and sensitive as he was he may have reckoned with it. But the plainest statement of the case comes from the poet's letter to the Duke of Argyll in February 1862: "I have thought about it and arranged all the intervening Idylls, but I dare not set to work for fear of a failure, and time lost. I am now about my 'Fisherman,' which is heroic too in its way." This is certainly no proper mood in which to prosecute the "greatest of all poetical subjects." The humility is admirable, but the timidity argues perhaps not so much a want of self-confidence as a loss of interest; and the resort to Enoch Arden's kind of heroism is pathetic. The spirit failed and "the highth of this great argument" no longer moved him.[f]

[f] A writer in the *London Quarterly Review* ("The Laureate and his 'Ar- thuriad,'" xxxiv (April 1870), 154-186) suggests a reason for Tennyson's resump-

There might even be a sound reason for this loss of hope. While it is profoundly true that Tennyson chose wisely as best suited to his own gifts the episodic plan of a series of 'idylls,' still at the back of his mind was the idea of an epic of "twelve books" with which he introduced the 'Morte d'Arthur' in 1842. An epic, even one composed of twelve episodes, must have some sort of unity. The general scheme was now already formed and four (five with the division of 'Enid') were already executed. And with the earlier fragment of the 'Morte' he had used up nearly all the best parts of his material in the first instalment of 1859: the Lancelot and Elaine story, the Merlin and Vivien incident, and the tragic culmination of 'Guinevere.' What now remained but episodes which might have some interest in themselves but could contribute little to the main drift of his epic? There was an embarrassment of little stories in Malory, but how much would they *add?*

Well, an introductory poem was necessary: 'The Coming of Arthur'; and of course a conclusion. " 'The Coming and the Passing of Arthur,' " he said afterwards, "are simpler and more severe in style, as dealing with the awfulness of Birth and Death." This is reasonably true of the 'Coming,' not so obviously of the 'Passing.' In 1862 he wrote to the Duke of Argyll: "As to joining these [first idylls] with the 'Morte d'Arthur,' there are two objections,—one that I could scarcely light upon a finer close than the ghostlike passing away of the King, and other than the 'Morte' is older in style." Older, certainly, in the sense of earlier, and the very antithesis of simple and severe. Yet he inserted it without change, hoping we would overlook the contrast. There was nothing else for him to do, and it is praise enough to say that the blank verse of the introductory portion is about as fine as any of Tennyson's and better than that of the old 'Morte' because less florid. For the rest

---

tion of his "early project," namely, the "issue and approval of several recent works, on a large scale, by other poets." "If this be so, it was perhaps a pardonable weakness in a man whose judgment is so endangered by public adulation, and peradventure by private too, to turn to the vastly popular *Idylls of the King*, patch them together with a few new ones, crown them with the vigorous, youthful *Morte d'Arthur*, and present them as his *magnum opus*" (pp. 162-163). For example, the *Saturday Review* (30 November 1867), apropos of the Doré edition of the Vivien and Guinevere Idylls, had expressed the hope "that the Laureate himself may yet be induced or inspired to weave these noble fragments into a nobler whole. Or is it that the complete Arthuriad is destined for ever to elude the final grasp of the Epic Muse?"

he makes the most of the 'mystery' of death, but he cannot save his poem from a pessimistic ending which neither moves us emotionally nor satisfies us intellectually. The confusion, doubt, and uncertainty are too patent: they trouble even the faithful. It will not do to call it, as he does, "the temporary triumph of evil" because no ground has been laid which is convincing or even persuasive that the "new year" without Arthur and his knights, with Lancelot in a monastery and the throne vacant, will be better, will restore the moral order. Tennyson's problem was to save his hero for our admiration in spite of his defeat. He seems hardly to have tried. When Arthur cries

> *I know not what I am,*
> *Nor whence I am, nor whether I be King,*

and the bold Sir Bedevere says

> *After the healing of his grievous wound*
> *He comes again; but—if he come no more—*

the effect is disastrous, especially when we remember that "by Arthur I always mean the soul." Tennyson's comment on 'In Memoriam,' "It's too hopeful, . . . more than I am myself," is fully supported by the despair at the end of his 'Idylls of the King.'

A similar shadow lies across the opening Idyll. Arthur's supernatural origin may be taken for granted, in view of the poet's allegorical intention, but this is confused by the doubts of his legitimacy. Tennyson was concerned, of course, to suppress some of the 'grossness' of Malory's version. When the case is argued for Leodogran's benefit it is unfortunately not clear which side Leodogran believes or Tennyson accepts—though Tennyson had, by the terms of his allegory, no choice—for Leodogran's acceptance turns on a vision. It is all very poetical, but at some sacrifice of reason.

When the Duke of Argyll passed on to Tennyson Macaulay's suggestion that the High History of the Holy Grail should form a part of the Idylls the poet replied, 3 October 1859; "I doubt whether such a subject could be handled in these days without incurring a charge of irreverence. It would be too much like playing with sacred things. The old writers *believed* in the Sangreal." Just who these old writers were may have been vague in Tennyson's mind, and of course he knew nothing of the early tabu concerning the grail itself—

> *S'en puet avoir et paine et mal*
> *Cil qui s'entremet a conter*
> *Fors ensi com il doit aler—*

nor of the intricate theories of origin and interpretation developed by modern scholarship, which date from the eighteen thirties and forties but came mostly too late for his use. He was probably vague also about the precise kind of irreverence which might entangle a poet who did not *believe* in the Holy Grail. Having no sympathy with mystical religion, he made an ingenious choice for his own treatment of the story: he chose to represent the quest as a symbol of social disintegration.[5] "Faith declines," he said, "religion in many turns from practical goodness to the quest after the supernatural and marvellous and selfish religious excitement." True, of course. Or again: "The King thought that most men ought to do the duty that lies closest to them, and that to few only is given the spiritual enthusiasm. Those who have it not ought not to affect it." Thus he overcame his scruples against playing with sacred things and wove this attractive piece of mediæval color into his Arthurian tapestry. It enabled him to illustrate another kind of corruption in Camelot society than the immorality supposed to spread from the loves of Guinevere and Lancelot, and it enabled him to emphasize the practical ideal of "warriors, perfect men," men

> *With strength and will to right the wrong'd, of power*
> *To lay the sudden heads of violence flat,*
> *Knights that in twelve great battles . . .*

This is a limited ideal, but very important to Arthur. When, moreover, Arthur says sarcastically: "one hath seen, and all the blind will see," he recognizes, what he apparently recognized nowhere else, a danger from within; though he does not recognize its cause, his own failure to offer his knights a better plan for the spiritual regeneration which they need. Guinevere's dictated line—

> *This madness has come on us for our sins—*

is not enough.

But the triumphant descriptive passages almost redeem the Idyll.

Once Tennyson had mastered his special application of the story it all "came like a breath of inspiration"—as Mrs. Tennyson put it. In spite of the awkwardness of having Percivale narrate the whole account to Ambrosius (who is surely the most tiresome of question-askers), and in spite of the mid-Victorian lapse of Percivale's encounter with his "wealthy bride," the successive visions of the Grail are beautifully adjusted and magnificently vivid—from the first faint one of Percivale's sister,[g] to the vague tempting glimpse vouchsafed to all the knights when Galahad sat in the Siege Perilous, to the long approach and great climax of Percivale's own vision, to the simple appearance to Sir Bors, a "square-set man and honest," to the dynamic, almost apocalyptic description of Lancelot's

> But such a blast, my King, began to blow
> ...I had sworn I saw
> That which I saw; but what I saw was veil'd...

where even the master exceeds himself; for Lancelot's failure is, as some critics have complained, more splendid than the success of the others.

The 'idyll' of Pelleas and Ettarre, when the last veil of poetical adornment has been twitched off, is one of the poorest of them all. It is the story of a boy (whom Arthur has just created knight to fill up the ranks depleted by the Quest) who falls in love with a wicked lady-knight-errant, callowly follows her and allows himself to be insulted by her. But Gawaine coming along has pity on him and takes possession of the lady; and so Pelleas finds them together

> The naked sword athwart their naked throats,
> There left it, and them sleeping—

and himself runs amok. He suddenly decides he had not really loved this lady, has a bad dream and wakes up hearing Sir Percivale (who should have been above peddling scandal) dropping a hint of Guinevere's adultery, rides down a poor beggar, blindly attacks Lancelot—and somehow precipitates the end.

> The Queen
> Look'd hard upon her lover, he on her;
> And each foresaw the dolorous day to be.

[g] The poet forgot perhaps for the moment his earlier assertion that "woman is not undevelopt man." St. Teresa's comment on this treatment of Percivale's sister might be worth having.

And this ridiculous story Tennyson relates with a grave face, lavishing on it his rich ornaments of language and meter. It is almost as though he meant to caricature himself.[h]

Before these last four Idylls were published in 1869 'The Last Tournament' had been written and the Gareth idyll begun. But the former of these was held back for revision and not published until December 1871; and the second, which gave Tennyson more trouble than the others, was not finished until July 1872,—by which time he had begun the last of the series, 'Balin and Balan.' In December 1868 he told Palgrave: "I shall write three or four more of the 'Idylls' and link them together as well as I may." And now apparently he began to face the difficulty of getting some sort of unity into the whole poem. The published letters and diaries throw very little light on this belated process—the experience of 'In Memoriam' had taught him nothing—but we have some help in Sir Charles Tennyson's account of the manuscripts.[6] For the Holy Grail idyll the poet had written a draft partly in prose, partly in verse, and this method he now adopted for the 'Gareth' and the 'Balin'; and from these cartoons we can trace some of the efforts to "link them together." The one thread of story which runs through all the Idylls, discontinuous enough and often all but lost in the episodic narratives, is of course the gradual development and influence of Guinevere's liaison with Lancelot. This is the apparent "story." It is at once the cause and the symbol of Arthur's failure—as symbol it does well enough, as cause it is certainly an unfortunate choice, but we must accept it as one of the *data*. To enforce this idea at the outset Tennyson now invented an incident for the opening of the Gareth idyll, that is, immediately after the 'Coming of Arthur,' representing Bellicent, queen of Orkney, as yielding to an illicit passion for Sir Lamorac because she has heard that Guinevere has been false with Lancelot.

[h] Pelleas as the type of foolish boy who believes too easily and who when he learns the commonplaces of human imperfection leaps to the extreme of "wrath and shame, and hate" and (yes, Tennyson himself adds it) "evil fame," is developed and magnified out of all proportion. Such youths must exist in the world, but they do not make interesting poetry. On the other hand, Gawaine, as the example of a courteous knight turned degenerate might well have claimed larger place in the whole history of chivalric *Entartung*, but Tennyson wisely gave us only glimpses. Why then bring forward and exploit poor little Pelleas—unless perhaps Tennyson meant to imply that Arthur was driven to recruit the Round Table from such ineffectuals.

But now she said to herself "Lo if Guinevere have not sinned and this rumour is untrue, I shall be the first woman to have broken the fair order of the Table Round and made a knight forego his vows and so my name shall go down thro' the world for ever; but if Guinevere have sinned, then the sin will be hers, and my shame covered by her shame."

Along with this is another incident, also discarded:

Sir Dagonet, the King's fool, stood before the hall of Arthur and the wind was blowing and the leaves flying in the woods below. . . .
And about an hour after there rode into the wood Sir Lamorack [sic] and his head was down and his heart darkened for his old love Bellicent was dead.
And the dwarf skipped upon the steps of the hall and out of the hall came Tristram and cried to him:
"O fool, why skippest thou?"
and the dwarf pointed to the wood and said:
"They are gone to keep the vows of the King"
and Tristram said: "Who are gone?" and he answered, "The sons of the Queen: for Lancelot has kept the vows of the King and thou also: for ye have all lain by Queens so that no King knoweth his own son."

This was suppressed no doubt as a too barefaced avowal of the Queen's guilt so early in the poem, but part of it was used for the opening lines of 'The Last Tournament'; and these two Idylls (the second and tenth in the final arrangement) are also "linked" through the introduction of Mark's messenger in the 'Gareth' (which is not in the first sketch) and the extensive use of the Isolt story in 'The Last Tournament.'[7] It seems therefore that Tennyson meant to use the Tristram and Isolt parallel to his principal adultery as a secondary thread of continuity and with it the maleficent figure of Mark and the villainess Vivien. Accordingly Mark,

A name of evil savour in the land,

is brought into the second Idyll, indirectly through his messenger, as a foe of King Arthur; he is mentioned in the fifth Idyll (but last written), 'Balin and Balan,' in connection with Vivien; he appears in the long *added* passage at the beginning of the next Idyll, 'Merlin and Vivien,' where he comments sarcastically on the rumors about Lancelot and the Queen; and finally he makes his melodramatic entrance after the last Tournament, when Tristram gives Isolt the jewels—

195

Behind him rose a shadow and a shriek—
'Mark's way,' said Mark, and clove him thro' the brain.

Whereas Malory had subordinated the Tristram story lest it over-shadow the similar Lancelot triangle, Tennyson turned it to his own ends by blackening Mark as the companion-in-wickedness of Vivien, and by making Tristram ironically the victor in the Tournament of the Dead Innocence, the last pageant of Arthur's demoralized knighthood.

For 'Gareth and Lynette,' which was begun in November 1871 and sent to the printer as soon as it was completed, Tennyson took the Beaumains story from Malory's Book VII and adapted it to the special purpose of picturing "the golden time of Arthur's Court" (Lady Tennyson); and accordingly it stands second in the series. Though Browning described it as "so beautifully noble and deli-cate," it is certainly one of the inferior Idylls, being too long for one thing and for another overridden with overt allegory. The first two-fifths is devoted to the domestic scene of Gareth and his mother, which drops to the low level of the 'hearth' idylls, and to the illus-trative examples of Arthur's meting out justice to the widows and kinsmen of one of them, to King Mark's messenger, and "many another suppliant." Meanwhile, the allegorical intention is sig-nalled by the comments of Gareth's two companions as they ap-proach Camelot, by the symbolic description of the city gate, by the speech of the "old Seer" (who was at first plainly called Merlin but later left innominate, probably because of Merlin's disgraceful ad-venture with the harlot), and presently by the shields of stone, blank, carven, and blazoned. The Seer's account of the city as en-chanted is a good case of Tennyson's device of poetical summary.

> *For there is nothing in it as it seems*
> *Saving the King; tho' some there be that hold*
> *The King a shadow, and the city real.*
> *. . . for the King*
> *Will bind thee by such vows, as is a shame*
> *A man should not be bound by, yet the which*
> *No man can keep; but, so thou dread to swear,*
> *Pass not beneath the gateway, but abide*
> *Without, among the cattle of the field.*
> *. . . seeing the city is built*

To music, therefore never built at all,
And therefore built for ever.

And this 'mystery' is anon made 'real'—

And ever and anon a knight would pass
Outward, or inward to the hall; . . .
And out of bower and casement shyly glanced
Eyes of pure women, wholesome stars of love;
And all about a healthful people stept
As in the presence of a gracious king.

When the story itself begins (line 573) with the entrance of Lynette, it turns at once to manifest allegory in Gareth's successive encounters along the stream of life with Sir Morning-Star, Sir Noon-Sun, Sir Evening-Star, and Night (or death).[1] Lest we have eyes to see and see not, however, Lynette explains the business and adds the label:

'Sir Knave, my knight, a hermit once was here,
Whose holy hand hath fashion'd on the rock
The war of Time against the soul of man.
And yon four fools have suck'd their allegory
From these damp walls, . . .'

(The inconvenience here of letting Gareth temporarily usurp Arthur's place as representing the soul need not be noticed.) But when the cloven helm of Death reveals

> *the bright face of a blooming boy*
> *Fresh as a flower new-born*

we rebel at the poet's frankness and reach for Malory.

Not only has Tennyson daubed the Beaumains story with allegory, he has made the incidents difficult to accept. In Malory's "fashion of that old knight-errantry," confused and erratic as it often is, King Arthur's reply to Lynette, giving her a kitchen-knave when she asks for Lancelot, is pleasantly irrational; but from Arthur as the perfect gentleman and ideal king we are led to ex-

[1] The meaning of all this, not too subtle or arcane at best, has been enthusiastically exposited by Elsdale. He makes Gareth the arm of the flesh, Lynette the rational soul, and Lyonors immortal spirit. There is no record of Tennyson's judgment on this, but it serves well enough to show how unlimited are the possibilities of allegorical interpretation.

pect more wisdom and less foolery. We are inclined to sympathize with Lynette, petulant though she is. Even good Tennysonians have complained that she is too realistic, a bit of a shrew, in spite of her pretty songs.

One more Idyll remained to write, for Tennyson was still set on having twelve, and he immediately began the composition of 'Balin and Balan'; but he refrained from publishing until 1885. Then his readers, less interested in the conventional number of twelve and long since accustomed to regard the *Idylls* as complete, felt it to be an unnecessary supplement, a posthumous child. Tennyson's excuse however was the need for some kind of introduction for Vivien—(which is more proof that the whole plan was not formed in advance)—and to add indirect confirmation of the growing suspicions of scandal. In reality it might in the eyes of the judicious tend to disprove the evil rumors since Vivien would not be a reliable source; and moreover, as the critics at once observed, Vivien is not here the symbol of the flesh—else why should she flee from Mark—as they had been accustomed to regard her.[j] The moral purpose of the new Idyll was to show that "Loyal natures are wrought to anger and madness against the world" (Tennyson); which may be true enough but is not easily illustrated in a pathological character like Balin's.[k]

For the story Tennyson chose one episode from the involved series of incidents in Malory's Book II, but though from one point of view he simplifies Malory, from another he only substitutes another form of incoherence,—with King Pellam, Garlon and his uncertain relations with Vivien, the woodman and the mysterious demon, and the unreclaimed savagery of Balin himself. It was not easy, at best; and from the disconnected verse and prose fragments which are scattered through three different notebooks it appears that Tennyson first "tried several arrangements of certain incidents of the story" before he wrote out the prose cartoon called 'The Dolorous Stroke,' printed in the *Memoir*. But still he succeeded, because of his zeal for developing the scandal motif, in missing the

[j] Of course she stood already for paganism and the spirit of malice in the Idyll of 1859, though the critics had not perceived it. But this only adds to the confusion.

[k] Perhaps a secondary allegory of sense at war with soul is to be perceived in the conflict of Balin's savage temper and his blind loyalty to the Queen; but if so Tennyson left it unannounced.

two chief elements of his material, the character study of the two brothers and the tragedy of fratricide. Swinburne's 'Tale of Balen' is a very good answer.

So now the whole Round Table series was finished as Tennyson saw fit to leave it: the gay promise of 1842—

His epic, his King Arthur, some twelve books,

—now somehow fulfilled, the magic number twelve, however, slightly disguised by the final arrangement—

> *The Coming of Arthur*
> *The Round Table*
> > *Gareth and Lynette*
> > *The Marriage of Geraint*
> > *Geraint and Enid*
> > *Balin and Balan*
> > *Merlin and Vivien*
> > *Lancelot and Elaine*
> > *The Holy Grail*
> > *Pelleas and Ettarre*
> > *The Last Tournament*
> > *Guinevere*
> *The Passing of Arthur*

It had been a long journey from the first allegorical scheme, the 'Morte,' the contrasting female portraits of the true and the false, the accretion of episodes, the attempts at joinery, the final stroke of 1885—more than fifty years, a sort of life work. The critics worried about its morality (to which I shall return) and whether to call it really an epic. But Tennyson would have been gratified, though I hope not deceived, by Waugh's judgment, which appeared just after the poet's death, that "the gradual fusion of the different divisions into a whole has given it its essential epic character, and welded the isolated stories into a connected and progressive narrative, moving from a definite starting-point to a clear and distinct goal." There were of course other similar pronunciamentos, flattering rather than critical. But the storm-center of criticism has always been the conception and character of the King, with its concomitant of allegory.

It seems clear beyond a doubt that from the first Tennyson dallied with the idea of an allegorical treatment of the Arthurian story. The strongest testimony of this is the early 'memorandum' which he showed Knowles in October 1869. But the Idylls of 1857 and 1859 are not unmistakably allegorical in intention, beyond the simple symbolism of "true" and "false," unless 'allegory' is read into 'Merlin and Vivien' where it is, as I have tried to show, intrusive and inept, and in 'Guinevere' where I find it by implication but not organically. It is therefore not quite accurate to say, as some have said, that Tennyson first turned to allegory in the 1869 Idylls, for in those four, 'The Coming of Arthur,' 'The Holy Grail,' 'Pelleas and Ettarre,' and 'The Passing of Arthur,' allegory is still latent or incidental rather than explicit and functional. Tennyson may have been influenced by Jowett's remark apropos of the first volume, that "the allegory in the distance *greatly strengthens, also elevates the meaning of the poem"*; he was almost certainly affected by Dean Alford's review of the second volume, which contained all but the last three Idylls.[8]

Alford was a friend of the poet's and seemed to speak in some sense with authority; but Tennyson never publicly accepted the Alfordian position and we are left to wonder how much of it was inspired and how much tolerated, and how much deplored. The Dean was predisposed to the discovery of deep mysteries: he felt that the Arthurian 'legends' are themselves "illustrations of the presence of Christian virtues, or of their defect,—and of their victory in temptation, or their defeat,—in various members of a community bound together for a glorious purpose." He quotes thirty lines from 'The Coming of Arthur' beginning

A doubtful throne is ice on summer seas

and says:

This passage, if there were no other of the same kind, would be decisive as to more being meant than is shewn on the mere outward surface of the narrative. The divine influence of the King over his knights . . . the three heavenly colours coming through the Crucified One, and falling on the three Queens, representing we suppose the three heavenly virtues, Faith, Hope, Charity . . .—all these would be simply superfluous in a mere secular narrative, and get their full meaning only as supplying the true key of the parable.

Then he quotes, still from Bellicent's speech, fifteen lines beginning

There likewise I beheld Excalibur

and adds triumphantly: "And thus we have the King, supported by the three great Christian virtues, counselled by Wisdom, and armed by Holy Justice, setting forth on his great career." Nothing could be plainer, moreover, in the Alfordian sense, than this:

Now this higher soul of man, in its purity, in its justice, in its nobleness, in its self-denial, we understand Mr. Tennyson to figure forth by "the King." In his coming—his foundation of the Round Table—his struggles, and disappointments, and departure,—we see the conflict continually maintained between the spirit and the flesh; and in the pragmatical sense, we recognise the bearing down in history, and in individual man, of pure and lofty Christian purpose by the lusts of the flesh, by corruptions of superstition, by human passions and selfishness. . . .

This is the theme which we trace through the "Idylls of the King," . . . One noble design rules, and warms, and unites them all.[1]

Tennyson's own utterances on the question of allegory are confusing: a hostile witness might call them shifty. At one time he said: "The whole is the dream of man coming into practical life and ruined by one sin. Birth is a mystery and death is a mystery, and in the midst lies the tableland of life, and its struggles and performances. It is not the history of one man or of one generation but of a whole cycle of generations." This is perhaps merely vague and suggests parabolic rather than allegoric intention. Hallam Tennyson's testimony in the *Memoir* seems to be more positive. After his father's death he wrote to Watts-Dunton (then, of course, only Watts): "My whole chapter on the Idylls was to state that my Father at all events in later life, took the view you proposed, of the *allegorical* interpretation." Yet if the chapter is examined closely it yields nothing more concrete than:

the author has carefully shadowed forth the spiritual progress and advance of the world. . . . Most explanations and analyses, although

[1] And by way of conclusion Dean Alford writes: "Thus we have seen the arising and crowning of man's higher soul, and the brightness of its opening reign: then gather round it the storms of passion, of lust, of vain superstition, ever thickening and blasting all fair prospect; until, baffled and discomfited in its earthly hopes, it sinks in the mist of death, but at eventide there is light, and the end is glory." Even so?

eagerly asked for by some readers, appeared to my father somewhat to dwarf and limit the life and scope of the great Arthurian tragedy; and therefore I will add no more, except what Jowett wrote in 1893: 'Tennyson has made the Arthur legend a great revelation of human experience, and of the thoughts of many hearts.'[m]

On the other hand, Hallam Tennyson quotes Knowles' testimony: "He [the poet] often said, however, that an allegory should never be pressed too far"; and he reports his father as often saying "in later years": "They have taken my hobby, and ridden it too hard, and have explained some things too allegorically, although there is an allegorical or perhaps rather a parabolic drift in the poem." Moreover, there is another deliverance from the poet himself, the first part of which is peculiarly baffling and the second ambiguous: "Of course Camelot for instance, a city of shadowy palaces, is everywhere symbolic of the gradual growth of human beliefs and institutions, and of the spiritual development of man. Yet there is no single fact or incident in the 'Idylls,' however seemingly mystical, which cannot be explained as without any mystery or allegory whatever." Most helpful is Tennyson's reply to Boyd Carpenter when he asked the elementary question whether the commentators had correctly interpreted the three queens as Faith, Hope, and Charity. Said Tennyson, with not unjustifiable impatience and not without suspicion of a quibble: "They are right and they are not right. They mean that and they do not. They are three of the noblest of women. They are also those three Graces, but they are much more. I hate to be tied down to say, 'This means that,' because the thought within the image is much more than any one interpretation." One may take this as a full admission of allegorical intention ("They are right") and as a formal denial of allegorical intention ("they are not right"). Well, it is and it is not. Perhaps all one needs to say is that Tennyson's mind worked in that fashion: he could not reject the proffered emolument of allegorical interpretation and he would not deny the impeachment. And this

m Still more indefinite is the statement (*Memoir* II, 130): "To sum up: if Epic unity is looked for in the 'Idylls,' we find it . . . in the unending war of humanity in all the ages,—the worldwide war of Sense and Soul, typified in individuals, with the subtle interaction of character upon character, the central dominant figure being the pure, generous, tender, brave, human-hearted Arthur,—so that the links (with here and there symbolic accessories) which bind the 'Idylls' into an artistic whole, are perhaps somewhat intricate."

cherished ambivalence would probably be unimportant if it were not symptomatic of the larger confusion. For it was Tennyson's willingness to have any truck with allegory at all, for the sake of enriching his poem and unifying his twelve books, that undermined his whole treatment of the materials; and it is necessary to emphasize this ambiguity if one is to understand why, with all its merits, the 'Idylls of the King' is the kind of poem it is.[9]

One last word about this question of allegory. Tennyson and the critics—the earlier ones at any rate, some friendly and some perhaps too officious—have done themselves wrong because of a careless or imprecise use of the term, and it might have been better, in the preceding discussion, to have enclosed the word in quotation marks. For allegory in the sense in which the *Roman de la Rose* and *Pilgrim's Progress* or even *The Faerie Queene* are allegories the 'Idylls of the King' certainly is not. The people in Tennyson's poems are not abstractions or qualities dressed up like human beings, except a few like the Lady of the Lake and probably the Three Queens (though Tennyson refused to commit himself here) and the little company of Phosphorus, Meridies, Hesperus, Nox, and Mors. But there is the grave possibility that Tennyson sometimes thought of some of his characters as allegorical figures, with combined human attributes and abstract qualities, people who might live and move as our fellowmen, but who at the same time acted consistently with a certain dominant characteristic and were in a sense representatives of that characteristic in human form. Arthur is the clearest example; he is a man, who marries a wife; he is a king, who leads an army; he is the ideal man or perfect gentleman; but he is also, on the poet's direct testimony, the Soul, and sometimes Conscience. It is no wonder that with these various rôles to perform Arthur has puzzled both his critics and his creator. "Let not my readers press too hardly on details," says Tennyson defensively, "whether for history or for allegory. Some think that King Arthur may be taken to typify conscience. He is anyhow meant to be a man who spent himself in the cause of honour, duty and self-sacrifice, who felt and aspired with his nobler knights, though with a stronger and clearer conscience than any of them, 'reverencing his conscience as his king.'" The "anyhow" is pregnant. Simpler is Enid, who acts more or less like a woman in a

story, but is also Female Fidelity or the True Wife. Like Enid, yet
unlike, is Vivien, a harlot interested in King Mark and capable of
seducing old Merlin, but also representative of the False in woman-
kind,—unlike because Vivien exceeds her commission and becomes
both more and less than her type. In this way danger lies, for an
allegorical figure which cannot be readily recognized is a menace.
If the reader is allowed to feel that Vivien stands for something
else, but has no way of making sure *what* else, he has grounds for
complaint; for if he makes a wrong guess he is lost in dubiety. This
was Henry Van Dyke's case: he assumed that Arthur was the Con-
science and Guinevere the Flesh, and asked "What business has
the Conscience to fall in love with the Flesh?" He assumed that
Merlin represented Intellect, and asked "What attraction has
Vivien for the Intellect without any passions?" Troublesome ques-
tions, because they betray the uncertainty which Tennyson's
method both permitted and encouraged. Like a faint-hearted al-
legorist, he would not bother to be consistent; desiring the ad-
vantages, he was unwilling to pay the fair price.[n]

No doubt certain of the Idylls are enriched by their allegorical
coloring, the 'Coming' and the 'Passing' for example, and in a con-
fused way the 'Merlin.' But on the other side, 'Lancelot and Elaine'
is, or seems to me, quite without these overtones. Somewhere be-
tween might be 'The Last Tournament.' And this intermittence,

[n] Or to say it somewhat differently:
The 'Idylls' is not an allegory at all,
though it has some allegorical elements,
but a distended parable—i.e., the story
may be given an inner or secondary
meaning which is supposed to dignify
and enhance the superficial meaning.
For example, Arthur's unfortunate mar-
riage with Guinevere is like the unhappy
union of the immortal soul with this our
mortal flesh, and his defeat in the great
battle is like the apparent defeat of the
soul at the dissolution of the body it in-
habits. This seems quite elementary, but
there are certain minds which revel in
such parallels and enjoy working out the
details even unto seventy times seven.
(Cf. Henry Van Dyke, *Studies in Tenny-
son*, 1920, pp. 151-160.) There are others
to whom it seems a little barren and
trivial. But there can be no doubt that
Tennyson was tempted by it and liked
to think, especially after some enthusi-
astic adept had revealed an unguessed

depth, that the mysteries were thereby
illuminated somehow and his poems in-
creased in profundity. Moreover, he had
started with a plan of full-dress allegory,
almost to rival *The Faerie Queene*, and
when that was abandoned the parabolic
method was its natural heir. Besides, he
still had not fulfilled the promise of
1842, he still felt the need of self-justifi-
cation; and a loose collection of mediæ-
val charades (as Hopkins called them,
later) would seriously disappoint his
followers. But the price was heavy, and
the poet himself was sometimes vexed
by the devotion of his interpreters. Yet
he never issued a clear statement with
his own voice; he sometimes spoke in
amphibologies, he sometimes allowed it
to be known that so-and-so had been
vouchsafed a whisper from the cloud. Of
course, as a poet he was not required to
explain his poem; but he should either
have remained silent altogether or ex-
pressed himself clearly.

this irregularity of treatment, gives rise to three difficulties for the common reader. He must pass without warning from one Idyll in which allegorical intention is apparent to another in which it is optional or non-existent. He must try to distinguish the general unifying principle of the gradual disintegration of Arthur's kingdom under the influence of Guinevere's 'sin,' which is the *story*, from the general allegorical or parabolic significance of this story as illustrating the conflict of Soul with its material environment. And he must constantly pause to ask whether this or that incident should be read for its merely narrative interest or adjusted to some second, inner value which is not clearly revealed, whether optional or imperative. In a word, he must wage for himself, artistically, the war of soul and sense.

Yet without 'allegory,' without this parabolic support, what would these twelve epical books be? Was this the great work clamored for by friendly critics to justify the promise of 1842? something largely conceived, greatly planned, and weightily fulfilled? Not really. It was a long dream which obsessed Tennyson's imagination but never became a reality; a hope rather than a plan, never carefully thought through, no matter what he pretended to himself; fitfully undertaken, laid aside and timidly resumed, it drifted into completion—a collection of fragments united by threads. Not that he should have begun with line 1 and continued to the last line with persistent protracted fury, without intermission. Not that he could not have turned, in a interim, from Arthur to Enoch. But the first four Idylls, written almost continuously, were in different conflicting manners, a domestic encounter, a dramatic dialogue, a poetic narrative, the end of a tragedy. 'The Holy Grail,' which more than the others was written *dans un jet,* was done under a kind of duress, and is moreover an irrelevance to his theme because it has nothing to do with the corrupting influence of Guinevere—"and all through thee!" But there is no need to labor the argument.

It was natural that Tennyson should turn for fresh material from contemporary domestic scenes to the mediæval world of chivalry. Malory had twice served him well. But there is a deceptive lustre in Malory's style which conceals the bold bawdry and open manslaughter of his tales and the reckless inconsistency of his telling.

The mediæval romances have tempted more poets than Tennyson to their undoing. The best of them have great qualities of crude energy and subtle understanding, yet it would be hard to name a single one which has been successfully modernized: the translations have a vacancy, like all translations, and the *rifacimenti,* whether plain or colored fail each for its special reason. The stories are mediæval, they wither when transplanted. For that part of his work Tennyson was properly unambitious; he makes no pretence of reinterpreting the Middle Ages; he does not try to recover the spirit of the sixth century or of Malory's fifteenth; he cannot be said to have aimed at revivifying the old stories. He was content to borrow the outlines and give them frankly, for what it was worth, his own Victorian valuation. So there can be no question of anachronism, for there was no pretence of being historical. The incidents are mostly from Malory or like Malory—for though Tennyson 'invented' more than is often recognized, and knew Geoffrey and other 'sources,' most of the inventions were in Malory's trend,—the costuming is off-hand Victorian Gothic, and the ideas are unconcealedly modern, that is, Victorian. If the 'Idylls' are to bear inquiry as an interpretation of life, Tennyson would be the first to say that the life and the interpretation are nineteenth-century. The attempt at a reconstruction of the mediæval world would have been preposterous. If, however, discords came in when the old tunes were reset to modern harmony, Tennyson must be held responsible.

It was also by a valid instinct that, led by the attractions of Malory, he turned to the Middle Ages—valid for him, though it led to unfortunate conflicts—because hardly anywhere else was there such opportunity for his natural gifts of applied beauty and extrinsic decoration, hardly anywhere else than in this unreal world of romance could the hardness of life be so easily disguised or evaded. He had not, like Morris, absorbed Froissart and learned the cruelty and bitterness of mediæval men. It would never have occurred to him that there might be a Locksley Hall in the domain of King Arthur. When he looked at the world beside him he saw little heroism, little but meanness or sentimentality, out of which he could make poetry; but when he looked away, into the uncertain past, life became simpler and more malleable and more readily glorified. The kind of ornamentation in which his muse specialized was natural and welcome there; he could take or leave whatever elements of human nature suited his purpose.

Under the spell of Malory it seemed to him that plausibility could be neglected; the story, with only such human attributes as he cared to select, would be enough. In the rapid encyclopedic narrative of Malory, where so much is left out and the imagination is so busy with the constant change of scene and incident, our disbelief is very willingly suspended; our belief indeed is hardly ever consulted because we regard the many characters first as painted figures in a moving panorama and only secondly as human beings. But when single episodes are enlarged and brought close before us, those figures have to be made very real and human or they lose their power. The details, if magnified, become grotesque; what before was vaguely beautiful and picturesque becomes distorted and ugly. We see too much. Tennyson's failure to face this difficulty is one of the principal causes of the failure of his 'mediæval charades.'

Tennyson rests his case, in the 'Idylls of the King,' on the representation of a semibarbaric, semi-ideal state of civilization corrupted by domestic sin. His Calvinistic point of view may be accepted—or call it Pauline. But his choice of the semibarbaric setting presents many an awkwardness which cannot be disguised by the glamor of chivalry. To interpret the modern world by scenes from the Middle Ages would be asking too much: to disengage the universal from the quasi-mediæval was his self-set task, and there is no sign that he approached it with sufficient preparation or caution. He drifted down to many-towered Camelot with the Lady of Shalott, bringing in one pocket his Malory and in another a small parcel of allegory.

His choice of adultery as the subversive force—he might better have made it purely symbolic, but he chose to take it very realistically—in Arthur's kingdom had certain advantages. It was prominent enough in Malory, therefore one of the *data,* and Malory had used it in his fashion successfully to give a kind of coherence to his miscellany. For his own immediate readers Tennyson could rely on a problem of domestic morality as very attractive. But there were also disadvantages. The first was over-emphasis. His reliance on Guinevere's infidelity as the chief cause—one might almost say, excuse—of Arthur's failure to build the kingdom of his dreams was a serious error. This enlarged hint from Malory would have done well enough as poetic fancy, but does not commend itself to reason in a real world. It would have done well enough as a symbol of social disintegration. But Tennyson makes it bitterly, poignantly actual. Arthur brutally blames her for wrecking his plans, in his most solemn tones. When at long last he perceived her sin[o] and Lancelot's betrayal of him, Arthur, when he had to face his crisis, was not great enough to defeat and exile Lancelot, to reclaim or repudiate Guinevere, but (as I shall try to show) was betrayed by what was false within.

A second inconvenience of the adultery motif is the conflict of conventional moral standards and the code of *amour courtois*.[p] Malory at least preserves some of the forms of Courtly Love, though he hardly understands them. He says of Guinevere that she was a good lover and met a good end,[10] and he makes Lancelot deny the Queen's guilt, even when he brings her back to Arthur. And Morris, for quite different reasons, managed better in having his Guenevere deny her own guilt because she could not accept Arthur's claim on her. Morris shrewdly avoids the impasse by showing her driven frantic by her tragic situation, but this way, admirable for fragmentary treatment, was closed to Tennyson, who was involved in universal truths and was obliged to assert the divine wisdom. For Tennyson, therefore, the central story of his poems could be only a tale of adultery gradually revealed, a modern triangle, with Arthur as the wronged Victorian husband. The attempt to combine the two codes was a fundamental tactical error. Such a story cannot be reduced to the forms of modern Christian ethics without excessive loss and without sacrificing the dignity of the husband. The real values of the story are falsified and the added values distorted.[q] Perhaps only at one period and among a few

[o] It is surely no great tribute to Soul to be so long in finding out that it was at war with Sense.

[p] This is a matter which caused Chaucer, himself a mediæval, some embarrassment. Humor, his main reliance to bridge the gulf, was denied to Tennyson. But when his heroine violated her own code he was more humane than Tennyson, or Tennyson's Arthur, and could not bring himself to scold her.

[q] For example, Miss Julia Magruder ("Lancelot, Guinevere and Arthur," in *The North American Review*, CLXXX (March 1905), 375-380) was "forced to the admission that our most Christian poet, Tennyson, accepted the definition of marriage" as merely a legal ceremony. In the Elaine and Guinevere Idylls he "has drawn a picture which, if it means anything in the way of ethical teaching, means that, in marriage, the letter is everything—the spirit nothing." He has regarded Arthur as a holy man because he was chaste, and Lancelot as unholy "because he had not the chastity which consists in fidelity to the legal bond."

people (not Anglo-Saxons) where there was an easy equilibrium between the two sets of values, could a poet feel comfortable with such a story as this of Arthur and Guinevere and Lancelot. Elsewhere it becomes at best artificial tragedy, because the suffering falls where there is but a technical guilt, and at worst mere sensationalism. In modern times the French dramatists have especially exploited the triangle of adultery, but they have missed the note of genuine tragedy; for in spite of the real tragic conflict, either between the loyalties of the protagonists or between the claims of self-realization and duty to society, there is no good solution. The possibilities are suicide, which is good theatre but a moral evasion, or mutual forgiveness, which is tame and usually unconvincing, or plain cynicism, which is not a solution at all and certainly not in the proper sense moral. Perhaps Tennyson felt this awkwardness without fully analyzing it when he turned to 'allegory' and profound parabolic mysteries, superimposing the higher morality on the realistic situation. But the strictures on Arthur's treatment of Guinevere are not all due to post-Victorian a-morality, for in 1878 there was at least one critic so bold as to protest earnestly not only against Arthur's "unwarrantable assumption" that the whole blame for his failure rested upon the Queen—"It is no fault of hers now that, in his absorbing schemes for his knights and people, he neglects his own household and the wife of his bosom"—but against his tone of irreproachable morality: instead of dismissing her with lofty reproaches Arthur should "have knelt down in the dust beside her, and confessed that he himself was partly to blame . . . —in fact, that he had neglected his wife, . . ."[11] So much for realistic common sense, and from a contemporary; and the same critic continues in the same strain: if Arthur's character was to be saved, it would have been necessary to blacken Guinevere as a woman capable of the long subtle deceptions of an adulterous intrigue, and so to render implausible Lancelot's continued devotion. To this Tennyson made of course no reply. This position and his position were simply incompatible. Truth must be kept above reason. But Tennyson would have recognized that in undertaking such a story he exposed himself to such criticism.

Lancelot is the great neglected character of the poem and should have been the hero if Tennyson's allegorical 'scheme' had not prevented him from doing Lancelot justice. "We think," said Maga (when the poet had been "just laid in Westminster by the side of Browning, at the feet of Chaucer"), "that the conception of this Lancelot will be Tennyson's great crown in poetry to after-ages."[r] Alas, no; but the elements of greatness were there. He was peerless in courtesy and in valor, and not without understanding—

> *In me there dwells*
> *No greatness, save it be some far-off touch*
> *Of greatness to know well I am not great.*

And so, alas, entirely human, with the one tragic flaw, his passionate love of the Queen. He enjoyed deeply and suffered deeply. Yet the flaw was not in his character, but a trick of destiny, which gave Guinevere to the man who did not deserve her. But Tennyson's preoccupation with the faultless king and his chill allegory of Arthur's failure came between him and this artistic opportunity. Lancelot's greatness limited by circumstance: this is the true tragedy of Tennyson's subject: man destroyed by passion. Let Arthur have enough humanity to make Guinevere love him, even a little, let Lancelot's conflict of love and honor represent the struggle of Arthur's knights to achieve perfection (or, if need be, Arthur's to establish his ideal kingdom), and you have an 'allegory' whose terms are plausible and whose outcome is tragic without being pessimistic. But it could not be. Tennyson had chosen otherwise, and left this for some other poet.[s]

[r] "Tennyson was no creator in the Shakespearian sense of the word. . . . and yet to ourselves Lancelot gives place in the world, if to Hamlet, yet to him alone. There are some points in which he is more near and touches us more deeply than even that prince of all our thoughts. . . . we know no such embodiment of high and fatal passion, of that extraordinary capacity of human nature, which sometimes can combine the sublime of noble character with deadly and degrading sin, . . . as in the character of Lancelot of the Lake. . . . But Tennyson has dared to take up this blot and work it into the most noble, the most sad, the most wonderful of sinning men" (*Blackwood's Edinburgh Magazine*, CLII (1892), 764, 761-762).

[s] This had already been said by the *Quarterly* in 1870. "Lancelot ought to have been much more seriously and fully drawn than he is: in his person is the centre of the tragedy; in his heart is the key of the failure of the ideal plan; we must needs sympathise with him, we must needs condemn him. Through him it is that, as far as the society around him is concerned, the evil is victorious, and chaos returns where there had for a moment been a spark of light. Yet in himself, at the worst, he is never actually bad; at the end, we are told (and it is not impossible, however rare) he becomes even saintly. The event, then, has the essence of tragedy; Fate, that is something terrible and unknown, is the agent of the calamity; . . . It would have been well worth the while of a poet to draw out the terribleness of such a contrast, such a law as this; to show the rigour of necessity as opposed to the softness of our hearts. But this is beyond Mr. Tennyson's power: in the delineation of such things a firm adherence to fact and circumstance is wanted, not symbolism

For Guinevere Tennyson has done less than for Lancelot. She has moments of real feeling, especially her jealousy of Elaine and her 'remorse' when she grovels before her husband; but as a character she is flat, without the excuse alleged for Arthur, that of being a symbol. (She might represent Feminine Weakness, but there is no place for this in the allegorical 'scheme.' She might stand for Primitive Christianity or for the Roman Church, as in the Knowles 'memorandum,' but one would never know it without being told, or grasp it having been told.) She was never wooed and won by Arthur, she was given to him by her father. We are shown no reason why she should love Arthur, but by implication reason enough why she loved Lancelot. In spite of the fact that she is, on the poet's testimony, the prime cause of the King's downfall, she is left in the bankground and seldom allowed a part in the dramatic action; she is a lay figure, not an actor, in her own tragedy.

But Tennyson, in the 'Idylls,' was not interested in character—not, at least, in the dramatic sense of the term—nor much interested in a hero. There is in fact no internal evidence that he conceived of Arthur as a hero, tragic or even pathetic. His Arthur is a brave ruler, or rather, a conqueror. He has a divine mission which at first inspires confidence and loyalty in his followers. But the only activity we hear about is his efforts to overcome the surrounding tribes without the law, peoples who have not accepted his suzerainty; and at two most crucial moments he is abroad on such expeditions, when his knights swear the Grail vow and when the last tournament is fought. He is thus chargeable with neglect of his own subjects. There is no indication that he possesses the ordinary abilities of statecraft or leadership among his knights, or practical interest in social organization within the state. He has not even the intelligence to recognize defection and corruption when they threaten his throne: he therefore cannot take steps to combat them. He is at best a passive character; but he is really not a character at all: only a name, an abstraction, a symbolic figure, without human reality. For this reason it is critically improper to judge him as a human being although he lives and moves among human beings; and therefore improper to suggest that this abstract-

and imagery" (*Quarterly Review*, CXXVIII (January 1870), 1-17; p. 8). Therefore   Tennyson called his critics "insects."

ness accounts for the failure of Lancelot's loyalty and Guinevere's affection. Yet we are nevertheless expected to think of him as human. The one time when he takes on human parts and passions is when he pretends to forgive the convicted Queen, and then he shows himself least human and therefore true to his allegorical nature. We are accordingly not moved by his downfall:[t] it cannot have been Tennyson's intention that we should be moved, for he is only the Soul incarnate in a wicked world returning to his true place outside this all too human world. Under his other symbolic aspect Arthur is a ruler only temporarily defeated, and in this light he is unconvincing because Tennyson has done nothing to make his return probable and because he has shown the Round Table completely disrupted beyond hope or promise of recovery.[12]

One hardly knows where to take a stand. Fallacies crowd one from all sides. In the war of Soul with Sense, Soul has lost; and yet by the poet's assertion Soul will *perhaps*—"if he come no more"— somehow rise triumphant. It is not a satisfying conclusion. One feels that the issue was never joined. By an inexplicable blunder the tragedy has been inverted. It is not that evil, or Sense, prevails, but that good has not been represented by a strong protagonist. The conflict was not between the good and evil principles of life, but between weakness (which we are asked to respect) and certain forces of evil which are not adequately opposed. Thus the tragic impression is dissipated, or rather, it was never rightly focussed, and we are presented either with a concealed pessimism or with a disingenuous answer. As Mr. Tattle says at the end of the play: "This is all very confusing." But one thing is clear: the justice of Tennyson's plea, "Let not my readers press too hardly on details whether for history or for allegory." If he had only added "coherence" he would have given his case away completely.

This interpretation differs, I am aware, in many respects from the accepted views, while it makes use naturally of many elements which are familiar. No one would wish to belittle the beauties of the poem, its extraordinary richness of imagery, its wealth of similes, its occasional moving passages, and its frequent skill in narration—the purely poetic qualities which Tennyson had so abundant-

[t] Nor are we permitted, moreover, to feel deeply for the genuine tragedy of Lancelot and Guinevere, since this would distract our interest from Arthur. By engaging our sympathy for these two sufferers Tennyson would have exposed too nakedly the negative abstractness of his chief figure.

ly at command, along with many things which the older critics called millinery and which we are all agreed to condemn. But in view of certain kinds of praise which have been lavished on it and certain kinds of censure, it has seemed necessary, without attempting to review all the arguments pro and con, to restate the critical problem as fairly as possible and cast up the accounts. The poem seems to me utterly wanting in unity and coherence of structure—and for this fault I would blame the irregular fashion of its inception and growth and perhaps also some of the friendly critics who encouraged the poet too far—and utterly wanting also in unity and coherence of meaning—and for this I blame Tennyson's weak and unfortunate shift of claiming, or half claiming and half denying, a deep, inner, 'allegorical' significance. As clearly as anywhere he made this claim in his appended 'To the Queen' in 1872. This "old imperfect Tale, New-old," he said there, is not about the shadowy semi-historical Arthur, or Geoffrey's Arthur, or Malory's Arthur (as it indeed is not), but a tale "shadowing Sense at war with Soul." Then with a bow to the throne he added in 1891,

Ideal manhood closed in real man.

Apart from the question of Prince Albert, most of us deny the reality of Tennyson's Arthur and are dubious about his ideal. It is not as though Tennyson were conscious of the shortcomings of his poem as a story or a collection of stories and felt that they must be supported by alleging that they were something more. But if as a whole the *Idylls* will not bear scrutiny as story, and if as allegory it shows signs of incoherence and confusion, what remains? The answer must be: many brilliant passages, many splendid descriptions, many fine fragments of narrative.[u]

---

[u] Or as Swinburne put it (in spite of his cheap witticism, "the Morte d'Albert, or Idylls of the Prince Consort"): "The most mealy-mouthed critic or the most honey-tongued flatterer of Lord Tennyson cannot pretend or profess a more cordial and thankful admiration than I have always felt for the exquisite magnificence of style, the splendid flashes of episodical illumination, with which these poems are vivified or adorned. But when they are presented to us as a great moral and poetic whole, . . . ("Tennyson and Musset," (1881), *Miscellanies*, London, 1886, p. 246). Or as the *Quarterly* put it: "The Idylls are but one long example of his skill in artistic grouping of details, of his tact in losing no opportunity for graceful ornament, of his gift of elaborating rough sketches into finished pictures, of expanding mere hints into detail, of transmuting bare statements into the gold of effective contrasts. From no other single poem can be gleaned a richer treasure of pictorial language, graphic similes, fine strokes of realistic detail, felicities of expression and of symbolism, epithets that reveal the very nature of the nouns to which they are linked" (*Quarterly Review*, CLXXVI (January 1893), 1-39; p. 37).

CHAPTER NINE

Poet as Playwright

IT IS SO much easier to attack than to defend Tennyson's dramatic poems that one must be careful to do them justice. His desire to strike out a new path for himself, still employing "that one talent which is death to hide," was of course commendable. But the choice of drama was doubly unfortunate. He knew very well that the writing of stage plays requires a special training which he did not possess, however much (not a great deal anyway) and however critically he had attended the London theatres: and this handicap he took seriously, for he expected to have his plays 'edited' for stage production by those who had the special training. Collaboration in the usual manner seems however not to have occurred to him. He simply wrote his dramatic poems according to literary tradition as he understood it and left the rest to whatever 'editor' fortune might provide. This was the second unhappy element in his choice: the English stage in the eighteen seventies offered no sound literary tradition for drama, no proper models. Had he possessed a genuine dramatic instinct, cultivated by an acquaintance with theatrical procedures, he might have created for himself a new mould. Instead he fell in with the nineteenth-century tradition of closet drama as written by Wordsworth, Coleridge, Shelley, and Byron, that is, the Elizabethan tradition modified by literary rather than theatrical considerations. In fact he passed over whatever help might have accrued from an examination of the work of Sheridan Knowles and Bulwer-Lytton, and even of his friend Browning, who had written experimental drama (of a sort) since 1837, and went direct to Shakespeare's chronicle plays for his model. If, as seems likely, it was Irving's performance

of 'Richelieu' and 'Hamlet' towards the end of 1873 which pro-
vided the 'inciting moment' for Tennyson's dramatic career, his
return to the far past is somewhat explained, for we are told that
"he did not like *Richelieu*"; and he certainly did not like Bulwer-
Lytton. His choice of a form which Shakespeare himself abandoned
in the course of his development and which had been extinct on
the stage for two hundred and fifty years had a corollary inconven-
ience; it induced Tennyson to write in a no-language, a synthetic
Elizabethan compounded of the sixteenth century and standard
poetic diction with modern touches. Take for example Howard's
speech in Act IV, scene iii of 'Queen Mary'—

> *Have I not seen the gamekeeper, the groom,*
> *Gardener, and huntsman, in the parson's place,*
> *The parson from his own spire swung out dead,*
> *And ignorance crying in the streets, and all men*
> *Regarding her? I say they have drawn the fire*
> *On their own heads: yet, Paget, I do hold*
> *The Catholic, if he have the greater right,*
> *Hath been the crueller.*
>
> PAGET   *Action and re-action,*
> *The miserable see-saw of our child-world,*
> *Make us despise it at odd hours, my Lord.*
> *Heaven help that this re-action not re-act*
> *Yet fiercelier under Queen Elizabeth,*
> *So that she come to rule us.*
>
> HOWARD   *The world's mad.*

Or take the country dialect of Joan and Tib in the same scene; or
the stagey humor of First and Second Citizen in the opening scene
of the play.

The chronicle play is itself a bastard literary form, but the
closet-historical-drama is twice removed from legitimacy. 'Queen
Mary' could not help therefore being a brave step in the wrong
direction. Tennyson was very careful about the history; he read
assiduously for the facts, and in consequence the piece is over-
loaded with history and overcrowded with details and miscellane-
ous information, to the detriment of whatever plot a chronicle
play is expected to have. There are forty-five speaking parts be-
sides the Marshalmen, Citizens, Pages, Lords, Officers, and the

usual "others."[a] He prided himself on the character-painting and
was correspondingly vexed when he found he had done an injus-
tice to Sir Thomas White and when the living descendant of Sir
Henry Bedingfield wrote to him in complaint about his ancestor.
Some of the characters are really well-drawn, or rather described,
for Tennyson's gift lay in description. Thus Gardiner describes
Cardinal Pole (Act III, scene iv):

> *Pole has the Plantagenet face,*
> *But not the force made them our mightiest kings.*
> *Fine eyes—but melancholy, irresolute—*
> *A fine beard, Bonner, a very full fine beard.*
> *But a weak mouth, and indeterminate—ha?*

He is less successful in the dramatic method of letting the character
portray himself.

"The real difficulty of the drama, as my father was aware," says
the *Memoir,* "is to give sufficient relief to its intense sadness." A
less partial judge might think that the real difficulty was to reduce
the multifarious material to coherence. The first act opens with
a Procession (commented on by Citizens) of Mary and Elizabeth
entering Aldgate. Then in Lambeth Palace Peter Martyr urges
Cranmer to flee. Then Father Bourne, while preaching at St. Paul's
Cross, is attacked by the mob, who turn also upon some passing
Spaniards, and the French Ambassador tempts the Earl of Devon.
Then, in a "Room in the Palace" the Earl finds Elizabeth—

> *The Princess there?*
> *If I tried her, and la—she's amorous—*

and tries to interest her also in the conspiracy to prevent "this
Spanish marriage"; they are interrupted by Mary; the Earl leaves,
Mary leaves, Lord William Howard enters and warns Elizabeth,
and to them enters Gardiner with a message from Mary. After

---

[a] Tennyson "always hoped," says his
son, "that the State, or the Municipali-
ties, as well as the public schools, would
produce our great English historical
plays, so that they might form part of
the Englishman's ordinary educational
curriculum." One recalls Heywood's
boast (1612): "Plays have made the ig-
norant more apprehensive, taught the
unlearned the knowledge of many fa-
mous histories, instructed such as can-
not read in the discovery of all our Eng-
lish chronicles; and what man have you
now of that weak capacity that cannot
discourse of any notable thing recorded
even from William the Conqueror, nay
from the landing of Brute, until this
day?"

these four scenes, the fifth and last is longer; and now that these
historical preliminaries have been put before us the action begins.
Mary is in love with Philip and is determined to marry him. Gar-
diner, her Lord Chancellor, warns her; Nailles, the French ambas-
sador,. warns her; Simon Renard, the Spanish ambassador, flatters
her; and her Council (off stage) approves of the marriage. The sec-
ond act is given to the suppression of Wyatt's conspiracy: it ends
with a grand climax (threatening the ludicrous) in which Mary
consigns Howard, Devon, Courtenay, and Elizabeth seriatim to the
Tower, and condemns Dudley, Suffolk, and Jane Grey to death—
all in thirty lines. Act III (nearly 1200 lines long: almost a third
of the whole drama) reports the marriage, introduces Philip and
Cardinal Pole, shows the English lords accepting Papal dominion
with various reservations, and ends (after an interlude with Eliza-
beth at Woodstock) with the parting of Mary and Philip. The act
has one emotional moment, Mary's soliloquy (in an interesting
variation of the blank verse staple) when she thinks she is preg-
nant:

> He hath awakened! he hath awakened!
> He stirs within the darkness!
> Oh, Philip, husband! now thy love to mine
> Will cling more close, and those bleak manners thaw,
> That make me shamed and tongue-tied in my love.
> The second Prince of Peace—
> The great unborn defender of the Faith,
> Who will avenge me of mine enemies—
> He comes, and my star rises.
> The stormy Wyatts and Northumberlands,
> The proud ambitions of Elizabeth,
> And all her fieriest partisans—are pale
> Before my star. . . .

It contains much historical talk, talk which is good perhaps but
not good enough, and even when very good too much. Act IV is
occupied wholly with the martyrdom of Cranmer. Act V opens
with the last parting of Mary and Philip, Philip's directions to
Feria to make overtures to Elizabeth, and Renard's announcement
of the war with France. Then Pole tells of his recall to Rome on a
charge of heresy, Sir Nicholas Heath reports the capture of Calais,
and Mary picks up a "paper dropt by Pole":

MARY (reads) *'Your people hate you as your husband hates you.'*
Clarence, Clarence, what have I done? what sin
Beyond all grace, all pardon? Mother of God,
Thou knowest never woman meant so well,
And fared so ill in this disastrous world.
My people hate me and desire my death.

The final scene is almost moving. The Queen is pacing up and down, trying to write a last letter to Philip; suddenly she cries to one of her Ladies:

What is the strange thing happiness? Sit down here.
Tell me thine happiest hour,—

and then interrupts the Lady's narrative—

O God! I have been too slack, too slack;

reviewing with mingled anger, pride, and weakness her own situation. It is not only good dramatic writing, or rather a splendid imitation of good dramatic writing, but also a remarkable achievement for a novice. It is a long way from the kind of writing Tennyson had practised in the 'Idylls,' kingly or domestic. It testifies to the extraordinary skill of Tennyson's hand. But as drama the whole play fails because the aim is divided and the central character weak. Perhaps it was a shrewd stroke for a beginner to choose the chronicle play for his first model, since the structural demands of the form were less exigent; and Tennyson might have forestalled criticism by naming his play, after the early Elizabethan examples, 'The Troublesome Reign of Mary, Queen of England.' But he seems to have looked for tragedy where he found only pathos. Mary hardly exists as a character: her only acts are to condemn rebels to the tower or the axe, her only motive is to win the love of Philip. Alice, her Lady in Waiting, gives the case away when she exclaims:

Ay, this Philip;
I used to love the Queen with all my heart—
God help me, but methinks I love her less
For such a dotage upon such a man. (v, ii)

Tennyson may make a fine patriotic appeal by exhibiting the troubles of Mary's reign, and for a moment may touch us with the pathos of her weakness; he may astonish us by his manual dexterity as an imitator; he may crowd the stage with carefully accurate portraitures and even present an historically sound comprehensive view of those five confused years (though he doesn't quite do that either, because of his anti-Catholic bias), but this is all. It is of course not drama.

With Irving as Philip 'Queen Mary' had a moderate stage success. Tennyson's next play, 'Harold,' only a year later, ought to have been a better one, yet it has never been publicly performed. The new subject had several attractions. On the historical side it presents "the great conflict between Danes, Saxons and Normans for supremacy, the awakening of the English people and clergy from the slumber into which they had for the most part fallen, and the forecast of the greatness of our composite race" (so the *Memoir*). Most of the dramatis personae are merely names and there was the greater opportunity for the creation of character: the facts of history could not tyrannize over the poet's imagination. And at the same time the two best known and most important figures were sufficiently complex: Harold another Lancelot whom faith unfaithful kept falsely true, and William a man at once both cruel and masterful, with justice as well as strength on his side. And with these dramatic opportunities Tennyson had also the Greek element of Fate as a powerful adjunct. He called it his "tragedy of doom" and emphasized that motif throughout the play. Yet these advantages were either dissipated or disregarded. With Bulwer-Lytton's full-length novel at hand and Freeman's three-volume history, besides all the 'source material,' Tennyson became absorbed in the historical rather than the dramatic situation: he again took the chronicle play as his model for a "tragedy" without the power of making that ambiguous form dramatic, as Marlowe and Shakespeare had done, through selection and characterization.

In spite of some confusion caused by unfamiliar names in the first act, Tennyson's play does give us not only a sense of the complex hostilities, family feuds, and conflicting interests, but also a pretty clear picture of the details: the rivalries among the sons of Godwin, the feud between the Godwinsons and the children of Alfgar, and the conflict between the native British and the invading Normans, as well as the opposing religious allegiances. The piety and incompetence of Edward are honestly reported. The inconsistencies of Harold's character are not concealed and everything possible is done to make him a hero, yet this very fidelity to historic truth weakens the dramatic effect because our sympathies are uncomfortably divided; and the revelation in the last act of his bigamous marriage, though a fine melodramatic *surprise,* seriously endangers whatever feeling we have for him as a man. The twist of circumstance which involves him in his false oath makes a nice point of morals, which we can enjoy; but his secret marriage with Edith and his political marriage with the widow Aldwyth are rather more than we can honestly accept from a hero, and the bigamy weakens the moral effect of the oath. (Even Lancelot did not secretly marry Elaine.) Aldwyth is likewise a distracting figure. In the early part of the play she appears as a stock character out of Restoration drama, one of those masterful females of heroic temper,[b] but later she seems to have been motivated more by human passion than by political intrigue. Something less than justice is done to William of Normandy: his cruelty and cunning are dwelt upon, but not the qualities of one who is to mould "the greatness of our composite race."

The whole drama is thus a resultant of four forces. It is a tragedy of doom, the national destiny of England in a crucial hour, when apparent defeat leads (ironically, though Tennyson of course concealed the irony) to success; it is also a tragedy of the fatal feuds of two ruling houses, somewhat after the Greek manner, in which Nemesis has her way; it is also a tragedy of character, in which the protagonist meaning to do right is worsted at each turn; and on a lower level it is a drama of intrigue, in the Aldwyth plot and the deceits of William. And all this richness is an embarrassment to the play, because it produces a confusion of interests none of which is sufficiently strong to dominate. And as if not content with all these motifs Tennyson has almost wilfully added not only the rawly Victorian touch in Edith's cry:

[b] Cf. her soliloquy in Act I, scene ii:
I love him, or I think I love him.
If he were King of England, I his Queen,
I might be sure of it. Nay, I do love him.
. . . Should not England
Love Aldwyth, if she stay the feuds that
part

The sons of Godwin from the sons of Alfgar
By such a marrying? Courage, noble Aldwyth!
Let all thy people bless thee.

O Thou that knowest, let not my strong prayer
Be weaken'd in thy sight because I love
The husband of another! (v, i)

but his own anticlericalism. In Act III, scene ii Harold says:

But a little light!—
And on it falls the shadow of the priest;
Heaven yield us more! for better, Woden, all
Our cancell'd warrior-gods, our grim Walhalla,
Eternal war, than that the Saints at peace,
The Holiest of our Holiest one, should be
This William's fellow-tricksters;—better die
Than credit this, for death is death, or else
Lifts us beyond the lie.

And Harold's contempt for the Norman saints because they have tricked him and for Rome because Rome is on William's side is also a reflection of Tennyson's religious attitudes, more Tennyson than Harold—

This memory to thee! [Edith]—and this to England,
My legacy of war against the Pope
From child to child, from Pope to Pope, from age to age,
Till the sea wash her level with her shores,
Or till the Pope be Christ's. (v, i)

And at the end of Act III Harold says:

The Lord was God and came as man—the Pope
Is man and comes as God.

It is almost unkind to mention Tennyson's imitation of Shakespeare's low-life humor (as in Act II, scene i) or that favorite Elizabethan fault of wordplay—

Perchance against
Their saver, save thou save him from himself.

More kinglike he than like to prove a king.

PAGE *My Lord! thou art as white as death.*
HAROLD *With looking on the dead. Am I so white?*
Thy duke will seem the darker.

These three examples are from Act II, scene ii; in Act III the dying Edward calls on Tostig, who is absent:

> *Tostig, raise my head!*
> HAROLD (raising him) *Let Harold serve for Tostig!*
> QUEEN   *Harold served*
> *Tostig so ill, he cannot serve for Tostig!*

These false adjuncts of the dramatic style were not obvious in 'Queen Mary'; their introduction into 'Harold' betrays Tennyson's ambition to be Shakespearean *coûte que coûte* and therefore challenges comparison in Shakespeare's higher reaches and therefore exposes Tennyson to more serious charges. The suggestions of 'Richard III' and of 'Julius Caesar' in Act v are thus more unfortunate, and even the slight reminiscence of 'Hamlet' in

> *Edith, Edith,*
> *Get thou into a cloister . . .*

becomes disturbing.

There is however something on the credit side. The emphasis upon Harold's wilfulness and self-confidence in Act i is well handled; the scene of the oath in Act ii, the climax of the play, is (or would be when performed) dramatically effective, using Wolfnoth and Malet to point up the different influences on Harold's decision —the appeal of country, of ambition, of love, both for Edith and for his brother, and of truth—and revealing Harold's conscious casuistry, with a bit of pageantry when the Bishops are shown, and with William's ranting lines:

> *Ay, thou hast sworn an oath*
> *Which, if not kept, would make the hard earth rive*
> *To the very Devil's horns, the bright sky cleave*
> *To the very feet of God, . . .*

In 'Harold,' moreover, Tennyson indulged himself in the kind of splendid blank verse which is one of the excellences (here and there) of the 'Idylls of the King' and which he had used with great sparing in 'Queen Mary.' Edward's vision in Act iii is a good example:

> *Then a great Angel passed along the highest*
> *Crying, 'the doom of England' and at once*
> *He stood beside me, in his grasp a sword*
> *Of lightnings, wherewithal he cleft the tree*
> *From off the bearing trunk, and hurl'd it from him*

Three fields away, and then he dash'd and drench'd,
He dyed, he soak'd the trunk with human blood,
And brought the sunder'd tree again, and set it
Straight on the trunk, that, thus baptized in blood,
Grew ever high and higher, beyond my seeing,
And shot out sidelong boughs across the deep
That dropt themselves, and rooted in her isles
Beyond my seeing; . . .

But when all is said for the parts, the whole is still wanting; and even more fatal than the failure of the characterization is the uncertainty of the moral effect. For although Harold's shortcomings are not concealed—his promise to marry William's daughter, however, is never mentioned—and it is made clear that his perjury must be avenged, we are nevertheless expected to feel that might has prevailed over right, that there was no justice in William's claim to the throne, that Harold is the real hero. The issue between right and might is never clearly drawn: for we are permitted to see that right is not all on Harold's side and yet we are supposed to believe in the rightness of Harold's cause. We are shown a hero who is wilful (in leaving England on a pleasure trip when political conditions required him at home) and self-indulgent (in marrying one woman for love and at the same time another woman for reasons of state) and treacherous (in swearing an oath he does not intend to keep), and yet we are asked to sympathize with his downfall. These flaws of character, as Tennyson has managed them, go rather beyond the *hamartia* which brings tragedy; and to pose a man of this character as the victim of circumstance and of the superior might of another is moral confusion. Finally, Tennyson's nationalistic enthusiasm tends to minimize the chaos into which Edward's piety and the feuds of the native rulers had thrown the country, and he is rather embarrassed at the end to assert the future greatness of England under a foreign conqueror. It was a logical difficulty requiring drastic sacrifice and Tennyson sacrificed the logic of tragedy to the facts of history.

Reviewing 'Becket' in the London *Times,* Jebb observed shrewdly that "the poet of *In Memoriam,* of *Maud,* and of the *Idylls* has no rival to fear in the author of *Queen Mary,* of *Harold,* and now of *Becket.*"[1] While the phrasing is somewhat left-handed, the sub-

stance is sound; and yet if Tennyson is to be credited with a good
Elizabethan imitation, 'Becket' is the play. For it is a laboriously
prepared, carefully planned, and skilfully written tragedy. Jebb, in
1884, obviously wishing to pitch his praise as high as the circum-
stances allowed, said nearly the same thing: "a drama of great
power, finely conceived and finely executed, as well as a poem of
great and varied beauty." And George Henry Lewes opined, apro-
pos of 'Becket': "I have no hesitation in saying that whatever the
critics of to-day may think or say, the critics of to-morrow will
unanimously declare Alfred Tennyson to be a great dramatic gen-
ius." Lewes was manifestly wrong—if the lapse of seventy years will
pass as "to-morrow"—and yet Jebb's cautious statement is correct.
The distinction is an interesting one. Compared with the best that
nineteenth-century closet drama can show—Wordsworth, Cole-
ridge, Byron, Shelley, and later Browning, Swinburne, and some
lesser names—'Becket' is a genuine masterpiece. It has almost every-
thing that a great tragedy should have, except the power of "great
dramatic genius" behind it. It is really a closet drama, and was so
designed, unless Tennyson was disingenuous in his dedication to
the Lord Chancellor ("not intended in its present form to meet the
exigencies of our modern theatre"), and nevertheless it had such
elements as Irving by judicious cutting and rearranging, and his
own gifts as actor and producer, could make into a successful act-
ing play.[2] It would be easy and perhaps enough to say that the
popularity of Irving and Ellen Terry accounts for its success, for
no one has tried to revive it. It was written, moreover, not only on
the Shakespearean model, but in the grand manner suited to the
heavy histronics which went out with Henry Irving and Barrett
and their imitators. In fact, one can almost say that it was written
with Irving in mind, though it was apparently offered to Barrett
when Irving first refused it. 'Becket' was therefore distinctly of its
own day and its temporary success may be thus accounted for.[c]
Still, this does not account for its failure as a great tragedy to be
enjoyed in the reading. It has a capital subject, with both personal
and political interests, it has a good love story, it is full of marked
contrasts carefully pointed, it has plenty of dramatic action, a gen-

[c] Among thoughtful auditors and read-
ers of the time its deliberate exploitation
of the Roman Catholic question gave it
additional interest.

uine conflict both of men and of outside forces, and also many
fine passages; in a word, it seems to have all the elements. Yet it
lacks the inner vitality which must come from true theatrical in-
stinct and experience, and the depth of feeling which must come
from true dramatic conception. It has the movement without the
energy which produces movement; it has the trappings without the
heart and spirit within. Perhaps this is too obvious to need saying,
but the contrast of superficial virtues and fundamental weaknesses
is rarely so clear as in 'Becket' and the play is therefore instructive
as a specimen.

Tennyson commenced 'Becket' in December 1876, immediately
after the publication of 'Harold,' and in 1879 had the first version
privately printed; but he was not ready to publish, for, as he said
darkly, the time was not ripe. Nevertheless he offered it to Irving
at once, who declined it and wrote to Hallam Tennyson in May
1879 making no objection to publication.[3] He had already taken
great pains to prepare himself for the task, and in his own notes to
the Eversley Edition makes almost a display of the historical ac-
curacy of many details. Green's *Short History*, 1874, was probably
his starting point for information; and in October 1877 Green
himself visited Aldworth and gave the poet advice on the authori-
ties. (After the play was published Green declared handsomely that
"all his researches into the Annals of the 12th Century had not
given him so vivid a conception of the character of Henry II. and
his court as was embodied in Tennyson's 'Becket.' " Certainly he
read up very thoroughly, especially in the contemporary chronic-
lers.[4] John of Salisbury, for example, gave him the cue for the chess
game in the Prologue, which is a good piece of stage business.) The
Prologue is in two scenes, Henry and Becket, and Eleanor and
Fitzurse: Irving transposed them in order to strike the romantic
note—Rosamund *vs.* Eleanor—at once. But the chess game is ren-
dered almost too patently symbolic forthwith by Becket's

my bishop
Hath brought your king to a standstill. You are beaten.

And just a little later, when Henry shows Becket the chart of Rosa-
mund's bower, it is a "blood-red line" which marks the clue. So the
poet underscores his points and eschews dramatic subtlety. All the

motifs throughout the play are similarly underlined and over-written: the temperamental contrasts of Henry and Becket and of Eleanor and Rosamund; the development of Becket from the priest and courtier to the overweening archbishop, the commensurable hardening and weakening of his character (Irving of course did all he could to glorify Becket); the development of Henry from stubborn strength to stubborn defeat—his last words are to the four conspirators:

Will no man free me from this pestilent priest?—

besides the heavy documentation; the very visibly approaching martyrdom; the opposing forces; and so on. Treated less obviously, these are the materials of dramatic irony and the Greek sense of ineluctable Fate gathering its resistless forces; but exhibited with pedagogic pointer, they not only lose their power, they nullify much of the intended effect. The documentation passages, however, were the weakness to which Tennyson clung most dearly. Even the Walter Map scenes, in Act II, scene ii and Act III, scene iii, he begged Irving to retain, and only reluctantly consented to their omission. These then were the things which the old poet had not learned. It is still fair to say, with Jebb, that 'Becket' was "finely conceived and finely executed" and with Archer that it broke all the rules and violated all the formulas. For it is so carefully planned as to be too obviously planned; and it is so faithfully accurate (in the purely historical parts) as to leave history standing in its own light. (Green might well say the opposite, speaking as historian solely.) The spirit of dramatic composition had not descended upon him; the tragic muse had not touched him even lightly. From 'Queen Mary' to 'Harold' to 'Becket' there is real progress; each play is a step forward; but he still was not inside the precinct. 'Becket' at least one can read with some pleasure, skipping the historical prolixity and the coarseness of the comedy; one can watch Henry give way and watch Becket lose his soul in saving it; one can feel the poetic intention in the character of Eleanor and the portrayal of Rosamund—at least a few of us can. But we cannot call the play a good tragedy.

From 'Becket' to the other dramas is a swift easy descent. Even the *Memoir* is decently reticent about them. In November 1879

Tennyson finished 'The Falcon' and in December it was produced by the Kendals at the St. James', where it ran sixty-seven nights. It is a one-act play in prose and verse, based on the *Decameron* (the ninth tale of the fifth day); it was published in 1884. After reading it from manuscript to one of his friends Tennyson "said softly, 'Stately and tender, isn't it?' " In the following year he wrote 'The Cup,' in two acts, based on a story from Plutarch which he first read in Lecky's *History of European Morals.* (Synorix, an ex-Tetrarch of Galatia, being repulsed by a noble lady, Camma, causes her husband to be murdered; Camma then seems willing to accept her lover, gives him a cup of poisoned wine and shares it with him.) Irving mounted it sumptuously in January 1881, with Ellen Terry as Camma, and it ran for a hundred and thirty nights. The next venture was 'The Promise of May,' an extension of the English idyll, and an honest albeit somewhat forced effort towards a local-color domestic tragedy, with a Lincolnshire background.[d] It was written first in prose and so printed (privately) and acted in 1882 (11 November–15 December), and rewritten in verse, except the dialect speeches, "for the reading public" in 1886. Unluckily the stage production was advertized as an attack on Socialism (which it certainly is not) and mistaken for an attack on Free Thinking (which it also is not); and it rather seems that the joke was on the Marquess of Queensbury when he interrupted one of the early performances with a vigorous protest and followed this with a statement in the press. No doubt the Marquess and the subsequent newspaper controversy added to the material success of the piece, but the blame is altogether Tennyson's, for apart from its rustic scenes, the play is a very bad example of the then current cheap and wooden melodrama. The story is this: a city slicker seduces and abandons a country lass; she leaves a suicide note and disappears; but he suffers a pang of remorse, returns under a false name five years later and makes love to the victim's sister; then the victim herself returns and in the final recognition scene forgives him and "Falls dead." A contemporary playwright is quoted as saying that in twenty minutes he could have made this "one of the successes of the season." The most interesting part of this unhappy

d ". . . my father had written it," says the *Memoir,* "somewhat unwillingly, at the importunate entreaty of a friend who had urged him to try his hand on a modern village tragedy."

episode is a letter of Tennyson's, a grumbling letter and a revealing one.

My dear Sir,

I am grateful for your letter. I had received others to the same purport. The English drama is at its lowest ebb, and the dramatic criticism (as far as I have seen it) follows the ebb instead of bearing that light which should lead it back to the flow.

I had a feeling that I would at least strive (in my plays) to bring the true Drama of character and life back again. I gave them one leaf out of the great book of truth and nature. In Germany it would have been answered, and perhaps it will be here, who knows?

That old sonnet of Milton came into my head when I heard of the ruffians in the gallery, who were, I dare say, set on. . . .

> *"I did but prompt the age to quit their clogs*
> *Their melodrams, their sensationalism, their burlesque—"*

Burlesque, the true enemy of humour, the thin bastard sister of poetical caricature, who I verily believe from her utter want of human feeling would in a revolution be the first to dabble her hands in blood—

> *"When straight a barbarous noise environs me*
> *Of owls and asses, cuckoos, apes and dogs,*
> *But this is got by casting pearls to hogs."*

On the whole I think I am rather glad of the row, for it shows that I have not drawn a bow at a venture.

Yours very truly
A. Tennyson

And to another correspondent he wrote:

. . . I meant Edgar to be a shallow enough theorist, of *course* not one of the "ordinary Freethinkers."

The British drama must be in a low state indeed, if, as certain dramatic critics have lately hinted, none of the great moral and social questions of the time ought to be touched upon in a modern play.

Here he was both right and wrong, of *course*—and many years ahead of his time. His intentions were good and honorable, if the admission of such as are implied in the first letter are not wholly disingenuous, but his technique was faulty to a degree and the effort was almost quixotic: not pearls but husks to the swine. Lord Tennyson in his seventies was not the man to reform English drama.

The pathetic close of this dramatic sequence is a four-act play in prose and verse on Robin Hood and Maid Marian, 'The Foresters,' written in 1881, but first published (in England) and performed (in New York) in 1892 shortly before the Laureate's death. It was a moderate success in New York and on tour in the States, but a failure in London the next year. 'The Foresters' is a kind of after-piece to Tennyson's trilogy on "the making of England"—in 'Harold' the conflict of races and awakening of the English people; in 'Becket' the early struggle of Church and Crown; in 'Queen Mary' the defeat of Rome; and in 'The Foresters' said Tennyson, "I have sketched the state of the people in another great transition period of the making of England, when the barons sided with the people and eventually won for them the Magna Charta." One might have hoped that with the popular ballads for inspiration and with his long practice, from the Idylls, in making over old romantic love stories he could have done something with Robin Hood and Maid Marian, but the spirit was evidently lacking and what is worse, the taint of conventional drama as he understood it was in his blood. 'The Foresters' is, on the most charitable view, disappointing.[e]

There is no need to recapitulate. Tennyson's recourse to dramatic composition in his old age was a fine gesture, and possibly it is enough to say that the composition of drama served its purpose in that it gave him something to do. It was almost wholly a waste; but a waste of what? He had little or nothing to say which required dramatic form, but in any case he had little or nothing more to say. For the time, he certainly fell upon evil days, since the conditions of theatrical production were, as he recognized rather grumpily, at a very low ebb indeed. It was neither the moment, nor was he the man. The false conceit, frequent enough among literary men, of regarding drama as a branch of letters, was natural; and so long as he kept to Shakespearean imitation one can at least respect his endeavor. But for the rest, all one can offer is regret. Strained admiration is a poor tribute.[5]

e William Winter was enthusiastic: "For once the public is favoured with a serious poetical play, which aims simply to diffuse happiness by arousing sympathy with pleasurable scenes and picturesque persons, with virtue that is piquant and humour that is refined, with the cheerful fortitude that takes adversity with a smile, and with that final fortunate triumph of good over evil which is neither ensanguined with gore nor saddened with tears, nor acrid with bitterness" (Shadows of the Stage, Boston, [1892], p. 273).

CHAPTER TEN

The Interpreter of His Age

I

ALMOST FROM the beginning of his career and down to the present a special point has been made of Tennyson's being an interpreter, the interpreter of his age. But if the assertion be examined closely it will raise some curious questions. Mr. Alfred Noyes in defending Tennyson a few years ago gave it as his judgment that "the chief indictment that has been brought against Tennyson will, in fact, be the chief ground upon which he will be praised by posterity—the fact that he did so completely sum up and express the great Victorian era in which he lived." Yet on the same page Mr. Noyes spoke with impatience of a certain *myth*, "as if the great men of that extraordinarily various period —Carlyle, Tennyson, Dickens, Thackeray, Darwin, Newman, Browning, Swinburne, Matthew Arnold—all wrote exactly alike and from the same point of view." Apparently these nine men together could not express such a various period as the Victorian, to say nothing of summing it up; and even if we add a few more—say, Ruskin and Mill, Disraeli and Gladstone, Bulwer-Lytton and Macaulay, George Eliot and the Bronte's, Wilkie Collins and Trollope—the picture would hardly be complete. That there was a Victorian age seems to be generally accepted. The Victorians rather prided themselves on their difference from the past and were self-conscious about their scientific and social progress and their battle with religious doubt and their moral lapses in the face of this progress. Their own historians and others of our century have generalized about them and provided us with convenient summaries, not omitting their contrasts, complexities, and contradictions. But in spite of these simplifications the Victorian age still seems to us so "extraordinarily various" and multiform that we hesitate to believe that any one of its own men could adequately represent it. "It was an age," says a contemporary, in 1892, "marked by a struggle between doubt and faith, from which faith rose conqueror. Every effort of the contest was recorded in Tennyson's verse."[1] But without inquiring how secure was the victory of faith, even in Tennyson, one may still ask if Tennyson recorded the doubt of Arnold and Clough or the faith of the Tractarians. Whitman remarked in 1887 that Tennyson's "very faults, doubts, swervings, doublings upon himself, have been typical of our age."[2] Says a later commentator:

His imagination and his feelings are in love with the teachings of tradition, but his intellect was curious of the thoughts and criticisms of his day, and thus fed his imagination with food that, left unprompted, it would have rejected. In this way he became a spokesman of his age, and being the poet who expressed the age most variously, it was natural that his works should be examined for the support that they might give to the beliefs most debated in his time. The traditional party found in him feelings sympathetic, and from these feelings endeavoured to decipher a philosophy that should justify their own feelings to themselves.

But this was said about *Robert Browning,* not about Lord Tennyson.[3]

One may go further and ask how anyone represents his age. Certainly, in so far as each of us is a part of his time he is in a small and special way representative of it. Its ways have become his, they have either helped to form his own or else have provoked him to opposing views. So Tennyson personally fell into agreement with certain general tendencies of his contemporaries; he accepted many of their attributes, as was natural. When he instinctively turned them into verse he gave his fellows considerable satisfaction. They praised him for it. Or else he disagreed with them, expressed his disagreement, and won the admiration of another group of his fellows. In this sense every writer is the representative of his age; but Tennyson's admirers evidently mean much more than this.

The first man publicly to call upon Tennyson to become the portrayer of his age was a reviewer in the *New Monthly Magazine* for January 1833.[4]

.. it is time for a POET once more to arise; . . . How magnificent the objects which surround him! The elements of the old world shaken— the mine latent beneath the thrones of kings, and the worm busy at their purple—the two antagonist principles of earth, Rest and Change, mightily at war!—Every moment has its history; and every incident in the common streets of men is full of the vaticination of things to come. A poet, rapt in the spirit of this age will command the next! What themes and what fame may be reserved for one whose mind can be thus slowly nurtured to great thoughts by great events; steeped in the colours of a dread, yet bright time; elevated with the august hopes that dawn upon his species; and standing on the eminence of one of those great eras in the records of the world, in which—
"WE SEE, AS FROM A TOWER, THE END OF ALL!"

Here was indeed a challenge and a temptation. And at the same moment, Fox in the *Monthly Repository*[5] said more bluntly: "Let him ascertain his mission, and work his work."[a] Together these exhortations make up the Tennysonian program. For fifty-nine years, while the busy worm waited, Tennyson, attentive to the principles of Rest and Change, rapt in the spirit of his age, worked his work and delivered his message. With a few dissenting votes, the Victorians accepted him, but now when the long result is examined can one fairly say that this star has added brightness to Tennyson's crown?

The Victorians, acutely conscious of their historical position, recognized themselves as a new and distinct development, separable from what had gone before and a culmination: a plateau, yes, but only far far ahead the prospect of higher things. Progress had almost deceived them into believing that theirs was an end rather than a way-station. They had swallowed Progress and were puffed up thereby. *Zeitgeist* was a divinity which they worshipped along with Science and Mammon and God; it was therefore a high and honorable ambition to observe the worship and report the ritual. That Tennyson, a shy man and a recluse, who spent his

---

[a] A belated offer and welcome, suggesting that the first had not been heard, came in 1853 from the *North British Review* (IX, 112, American edition). "Poetry is scarce. Our age, famous as it is in many ways—abounding in great deeds, and far from being destitute of great men—seems unfavorable to the growth of the ever welcome flower. Many volumes of verses are published annually, evincing taste, feeling, and sometimes an artistic carefulness and finish. There is no indifference on the part of the public; on the contrary, we feel convinced that the '*Vates sacer*,' were he to come among us, could easily command an audience."

most impressionable years in an isolated village, the years of his development wandering from place to place in an effort to escape from himself, and his mature years in the seclusion of Farringford and Aldworth (open only to the select few), should aspire to this honor would seem, on second thought, rather ironic. But Tennyson was offered the opportunity and he seized it, without his or his friends' asking how or why. They did not even ask seriously whether it should be done, whether it is part of the poetic office to interpret the age. "My opinion," said Thomas Hardy, too late for Tennyson's help, "is that a poet should express the emotion of all the ages and the thought of his own." Shelley, whom Tennyson might have read, thought that a poet "would do ill to embody his own conceptions of right and wrong, which are usually those of place and time, in his poetical creations, which participate in neither." And Shelley, having not quite illustrated his own principle, adds cryptically: "By this assumption of the inferior office of interpreting the effect, in which perhaps after all he might acquit himself imperfectly, he would resign the glory of a participator in the cause." Yet to Tennyson, in the judgment of his followers, it was given to achieve the glory and enjoy the participation as well. Another observer, Yeats, saw while the Laureate was still living "that Swinburne in one way, Browning in another, Tennyson in a third, had filled their work with what I called 'impurities,' curiosities about politics, about science, about history, about religion." Here are four highly reputed poets: one of them charging the other three with alloying their poetry with an admixture of— shall one say? though Yeats does not use the phrase—social criticism. Is not poetry then a criticism of life, and can politics, science, history, and religion be excluded from the life which poetry represents?

The answer is not difficult, but it is "rapt" in a confusion for which certain sociological critics are responsible. The extreme wing of these critics appears to hold that no literature is important which does not deal with the class struggles of the nineteenth century; of them I have nothing to say. But even the more moderate brethren have mixed the moulds by a substitution of functions, for they have set up as literary critics when they are really social historians, and assumed a duty for which they are often ill equipped.

It is one thing to study Tennyson's poetry as a document; it is quite another to measure the merits of his poetry by the accuracy and completeness of his portrayal of the Victorians; and it is of course quite another to read Tennyson as poetry. Such critical folly should not bother the student of literature (unless he is deceived by the claims of the historian), but it is a pertinent concern of the student of Tennyson because Tennyson himself became involved in the fallacy; and (though this is another story) it does concern the student of literature when his own friends are found fraternizing with the enemy.

Certainly we learn something of Tennyson the man when we are told that he was greatly interested in the social and intellectual life of his time, but of Tennyson the poet, who really matters, we care only to know whether he made poetry out of the subjects which interested him. Of Tennyson the man we are glad to hear that he was eager to touch the hearts of his contemporaries and imbue them with ideals and ideas which both he and they regarded as noble. That he was moved with a desire to improve his countrymen is very commendable; that he provided them with consolation and offered them uplifting thoughts in verse is a fine thing and greatly to his credit, and even a literary critic would not wish to imply any derogation from his character on this account—quite the contrary. Yet the literary critic is bound to observe and assert that his real concern is not with Tennyson's private or public character, but with Tennyson's poetry. And in this view Tennyson would surely agree. From his youth onwards, for half a century, he devoted himself, a Nazarite, to poetry. He had no other life, having chosen no other; and therefore the poetry for which he lived is the proper basis for our judgment of him. If his desire to exhort and improve his fellow man came between him and his one great objective, that fact must be recorded—without censure perhaps (since we are all mortal) yet not without sadness. If for whatever reasons he failed of his purpose to 'make something' it may be instructive from the critical point of view to find out what those reasons were: it may be instructive, but it is of secondary importance. What is of the first importance is to recognize and appreciate the genuine poetic work which he gave us and to separate it from the inferior work which (since he also was mortal) he also gave. This is so obviously truistic that one would not venture to repeat it were it not necessary to save him from unjust praise. Had it not been imputed to him for a merit that he was or tried to be an historian and a social critic—he has at least never, I believe, been called a reformer—it would not have been necessary to reaffirm the commonplace that the functions of the poet and those of the historian and social critic are diverse. And had not Tennyson been deceived in this it would not be necessary to elaborate the point. For it is unfortunately true that Tennyson was misled, either by false counsellors or by what was false within, into regarding himself as an interpreter of his age. He accepted the titles of seer and prophet. He allowed the desire to interpret to interfere with the desire to make. And the real question is not whether he portrayed his age aright, but whether he was able to make poetry out of his age.

By way of extenuation it may be set down that he shared a weakness of his own day. The temptation was thrust upon him in the form of an opportunity to serve both himself and his readers. There was not only the excited reviewer in 1833 and the public exhortations after the *Poems* of 1842, when the critics were sorely disappointed by 'The Princess' and barely satisfied by 'In Memoriam,' but also the private encouragements by eager friends like Jowett. In 1864 Jowett wrote to Mrs. Tennyson:

I am always anxious that Alfred should be employed about some great poetical work which should express what this age is longing to have expressed. When old things are beginning to pass away and new things to appear, I think the poet's function is very plain and clear. He fancies that his thoughts have been killed by the *Quarterly*. My impression is that he could do the work now, but could hardly have done it five-and-twenty years ago. I know that I bore him about this. But I shall hardly rest until he makes the attempt.[6]

No doubt Tennyson was bored, but perhaps Jowett was satisfied in the end, for he wrote to Lady Tennyson on 5 October 1892, when the aged Laureate was dying, that he had just bought the one volume edition and reread the old poems: "They opened our minds in the best manner to the new ideas of the nineteenth century."[7] A dubious benediction, yet welcome.

The early poems had seemed insubstantial to their first readers.

They were beautiful, but beauty was not enough. These readers were earnest and hard pressed by many uncertainties, and they asked for a deliverance. And bit by bit Tennyson gave them what they wanted. True, they complained at every successive attempt— they disliked 'The Princess', they attacked 'Locksley Hall,' they misunderstood 'Maud'—but they welcomed 'In Memoriam' after a little and parts of the 'Idylls' and they rejoiced in 'Enoch Arden'; while deprecating the satirical passages they accepted the domestic idylls as a whole as portraying for them the very form and pressure of their own lives. They were not critics, of course, they were the middle-class readers of poetry.

One other reason for Tennyson's yielding to this temptation is already implied in Jowett's letter of 1864. The formal evidence is not abundant, but one gets the impression that Tennyson was not only constantly on the alert for good subjects to write about, but that his friends were equally solicitous. Not only did they urge him to fix upon some 'great' subject, they volunteered smaller ones. Two friends vie for the honor of having suggested 'Maud,' Woolner gave him the Enoch story and that of Sir Aylmer Aylmer, several proposed the Holy Grail, and Jowett was always at hand, now with one idea now with another. This was not so in the early years, yet when one reflects upon it the two small volumes of 1842, even allowing for the rejected poems, were not a large garner for twelve years of writing. Comparison with other young poets would be pointless, but it is impossible not to recognize that Tennyson's muse was hardly prolific. Tennyson's was no teeming brain. Even including 'The Princess,' which was begun in the thirties, and 'In Memoriam,' much of which was written by 1842, one finds the total amount less than impressive: about two hundred pages for the twenty years ending in 1850, when he was forty-one years old. Yet this little was mostly his own. It sprang from whatever impulses there were within him to express what had to be expressed. It contains comparatively little that can be called an interpretation of the age. It is more Tennysonian than Victorian. But after 1850 the inner impulse flags, the quest for subjects begins, the urge to compose comes from without. He must get on with the 'Idylls,' he drops Arthur for Enoch, he writes stories in verse when the stories are put before him, he writes with great skill various 'command'

and laureate poems, and starting at the age of sixty-five he devotes ten years to the composition of plays, which are not his métier. In a word, Tennyson had not very much to say, not very much that demanded utterance, not very much that overflowed from passionate feelings or profound convictions or burning enthusiasms. He therefore accepted gallantly the invitation to interpret the Victorian age to itself: it gave him something to write about and it flattered his public to know that they shared though humbly in the Laureate's high office, by sitting to him for their portrait.

Perhaps I exaggerate. But there is something more. If one concede that the Victorian age was such a unity as its incumbents believed and that it is the honorable duty of a poet to reflect and interpret his age, and that Tennyson for whatever reasons took on himself this duty conscientiously, one may still ask if Tennyson succeeded. His patriotism found frequent expression and he commented from time to time on current events in verse which was hardly intended as an offering to Apollo; he spoke of progress and its evils, as well as its ultimate goal; he took notice of science and its influence on certain kinds of contemporary problems; above all he drew poignant pictures of the domestic life of the middle classes—and gradually the conviction grew in his readers that he was the spokesman of the age, that he was κατ' ἐξοχήν the great representative Englishman of this time, the quintessence of Victorianism, an ideal figure yet one of the people, one of themselves, even when symbolically accepting a peerage. But this also is an exaggeration. How true or false is the claim for Tennyson may be left for the historian to determine. It is his business.

The literary critic, however, already has his answer. Tennyson, says Mr. Leavis, "might wrestle solemnly with 'the problems of the age,' but the habits, conventions and techniques that he found congenial are not those of a poet who could have exposed himself freely to the rigours of the contemporary climate. And in this he is representative. But Victorian poetry admits implicitly that the actual world is alien, recalcitrant and unpoetical, and that no protest is worth making except the protest of withdrawal."[8] This is true, yet not without the suspicion of fallacy. The Victorians need not be blamed for being Victorians, and their poets—if they are to be representative—must not be blamed for finding poetry where all other Victorians found it, not in the actual world but in the romantic image of the actual world. It would have disappointed the Victorians to realize that in poetry they did not make the same progress as in science, in commerce, and in social reform, to realize that they were conservative even to a fault, that they kept to the romantic conception of poetry and when they wished to make poetry out of the actual world, out of science, commerce, and social reform, they felt the necessity of making these things look poetical with the language of Wordsworth, Keats, and the other elders. In this way Tennyson was representative, that he saw his age as it saw itself, and so portrayed it. What else would Mr. Leavis have? Apparently that Tennyson and his fellow poets should embrace the actual world in all sympathy and make poetry of it. But that they simply could not do, simply because they were Victorians.

Arnold was the one great exception: he fought for his soul against the world, and so long as he remained a poet his soul was victor. But the world soon prevailed and he made his compromise as he could. In youth he exposed himself to the rigors of the contemporary climate, and then as a poet he succumbed. Tennyson's however was not a protest of withdrawal, since he was never exposed. As a poet he interpreted the romantic dream as his contemporaries preferred to dream it—from the Claribels and Lilians and Marianas to the Enids and Elaines and Guineveres and the Galahads and Arthurs and Enochs. The historian may find that these were Victorians in disguise—in pleasing disguises—but for Mr. Leavis and the new century they were never real people and Tennyson's poetry was therefore unreal. Perhaps we had better leave it as an unprofitable paradox.

Certainly the problem is not likely to be solved by any set of phrases: the best one can hope to do is to restate it more clearly. The matter of intention is important but, I think, secondary. As each of us is the resultant of the forces of temperament and surroundings, we are all somehow representative of our times; but in so far as Tennyson chose deliberately to write as historian or critic rather than as poet he debased his metal with such impurities as religion, politics, and so on. Nevertheless, result is more than intention, and since nearly all poets have included some of these impurities in their ware, the question appears to be one not of impropriety but of effect. All subjects are (theoretically at least) available to art provided they be wrought into such a form as will satisfy the artistic sense. Mr. Leavis' complaint really is that Tennyson and his fellow poets chose only those subjects which they could easily work into the accepted moulds and, like all romantics, avoided the hard actualities of life as not suitable or manageable; a truer complaint would be that they did not make poetry out of whatsoever subject they chose, but rather left the impurities un-amalgamated with the finer metal. Tennyson is censurable for having chosen only the easy subjects whose poetical effects were ready to hand, and though he treated them with consummate skill he cannot be said to have portrayed his age because the age embraced so many other subjects which he left untouched. This is the historical analyst's view. The truer view, at least the view of the student of poetry, is that he did not always transmute many of the subjects which he did touch. Mr. Leavis would approve the Miller sitting

Beneath those gummy chestnut buds
That glistened in the April blue;

but Tennyson on second thought preferred

Below the chestnuts, when their buds
Were glistening to the breezy blue.

He must call a bottle of burgundy

The foaming grape of eastern France,

making simple things poetical by fancy names. He must make pathos lachrymose and nobility stilted and decency prudish, and so on. Not always, but when he was being Victorian.

II

But now to descend from these generalities to the mere text. I assume that the first two volumes and most of the new poems of 1842 were not written with a conscious desire to portray or interpret the age. This desire really began with the laureate accolade of 1850. But the first shadows stretch back to 1842 and even earlier; they lie across every poem with topical subject matter. The 1830 volume contained an English Warsong and a National Song; the 1833 volume three political sonnets and the two earliest domestic idylls, 'The Miller's Daughter' and 'The May Queen.' By 1842, in the second volume of *Poems,* the domestic idylls became a leit-motif and some of these are genuine genre sketches, with "Flemish detail," of contemporary life, but it is with 'Locksley Hall' that the curtain rises.

'Locksley Hall' is a product of Tennyson's youth—it was written some time in his twenties and was hailed by contemporary youth as a charter of their own romantic freedom.[b] It is both ficti-tious and autobiographic. The Hall, he said, "is an imaginary place (tho' the coast is Lincolnshire) and the hero is imaginary. The whole poem presents young life, its good side, its deficiencies, its yearnings"; and he added, betraying an intention: "Mr. Hallam said to me that the English people liked verse in Trochaics, so I wrote the poem in this metre." And his own son Hallam remem-bered his saying that "the idea of the poem" came from Sir Wil-liam Jones' prose translation of the Moallakát.[9] But early readers took it more literally. A Cambridge undergraduate claimed to be the unhappy hero: "It is the story of my cousin's love and mine, known to all Cambridge when Mr. Tennyson was there, and he put it into verse." And Miss Mitford told Mrs. Browning she knew a man who knew the heroine; Mrs. Browning replied: "Well I don't agree with Mr. Harness in admiring the Lady of 'Locksley Hall.' I *must* either pity or despise a woman who could have mar-ried Tennyson and chose a common man. If happy in her choice, I despise her."[10] One hardly knows whether to censure the naïveté of such readers or to praise Tennyson for the air of verisimilitude he gave the poem. Later critics have censured the poet, particularly in 'Maud,' for not making a plainer distinction between his own views and those of his characters; but this is one of the penalties a

---

[b] "Never shall I forget the thrill, the ecstasy, with which I read and re-read the passionate lines until they seemed to burn themselves into my memory. New feelings of ardour were aroused in me, my mind seemed to open to splendid revelations, . . . in ringing lines it proclaims the aspirations and voices the desires of all youthful natures yearn-ing for action. It is 'the passionate chant in which are so vividly uttered all the undisciplined thoughts, the wayward fancies, the lofty but vague aspirations. that effervesce in the spirit of the culti-vated youth of the nineteenth century,' says Professor Ingram, and as such it is not only an inspiration and incentive, but it is a revealing to the young of the thoughts that surge in their expanding minds. The hero of *Locksley Hall* was fiery, impulsive, and unrestrained, but his nature was none the less noble and his ideal none the less worthy and true." This tribute is from J. Cuming Walters, *Tennyson: Poet, Philosopher, Idealist,* London, 1893, pp. 49-50.

poetic annotator of his times must pay—another, more serious, will have to be mentioned presently. It is really too bad, however, that readers of poetry will never learn that the first personal pronoun does not signify a personal confession. In point of fact—and it was a fact as plain in 1842 as to-day—the incumbent of Locksley Hall was the old Byronic hero in modern dress, "born into a democratic world, uncongenial to his ideals and ruinous to his hereditary fortune."[11] He was also the perennial spirit of youthful yearning and revolt in Tennyson himself. If he was painting a wholly dramatic picture Tennyson might have enhanced it with a sense of humor; both the satire and the melancholy might have been a little less rhetorical. If the poem had been less personal it would have been not only more critical but artistically more sincere. In a word, Tennyson was not quite able to dramatize himself disinterestedly, for the sake of art. But, by a natural irony, he made a more powerful appeal to contemporary youth than a detached documentary representation would have done. In letting himself go he gave other young men of his generation a voice: as Kingsley said, "he, living amid the same hopes, the same temptations, the same sphere of observation as they, gives utterance and outward form to the very questions which, vague and wordless, have been exercising their hearts."

The poem is in the form of a dramatic monologue or soliloquy. The style like the content is a motley. To the Gothic setting of a dreary Hall by the sea, and ivy casements, and an unhappy lover, there is added rich romantic description—"hollow ocean-ridges roaring into cataracts"—"great Orion sloping slowly to the west"—

> *Many a night I saw the Pleiads, rising thro' the mellow shade,*
> *Glitter like a swarm of fireflies tangled in a silver braid*

—and also the modern "Fairy tales of science" and the evolutionary doctrine of "the long result of time"; and also the note of social criticism. Immediately following the Byronic

> *Better thou and I were lying, hidden from the heart's disgrace,*
> *Roll'd in one another's arms, and silent in a last embrace*

comes the contemporary

> *Cursed be the social wants that sin against the strength of youth!*
> *Cursed be the social lies that warp us from the living truth!*

and a few couplets later the middle-class Chartist appeal

Men, my brothers, men the workers, ever reaping something new;
That which they have done but earnest of the things that they shall
  do.

And with these varied tones is mingled the typical Victorian motif
of the lover rejected by his shallow-hearted and weak cousin, and
the ill-bred rival, and the romantic escape to the "savage" Orient.
Everything is here that might be expected to make an appealing
potpourri of the old Wertherian tunes, yet as Kingsley insisted
the final note is not Werther but anti-Werther; it is pure Early
Victorian, with its cry of "Forward, forward" and its vision of a
"crescent promise" of the spirit rising above the old-fashioned
storm which envelopes the Hall and the departing soliloquist.
Then, as if these were not enough, Tennyson added to them the
poetic adornments of the "sorrow's crown of sorrows" from Dante,
the gnomic "knowledge comes, but wisdom lingers," the two
spring stanzas, and the simile which he in later life came to regard
as one of his finest:

Love took up the glass of Time, and turned it in his glowing hands;
Every moment, lightly shaken, ran itself in golden sands—

these and other flourishes.

Forty-four years later Tennyson revived this rhetorical hero in
a poem which gave its title to the whole volume of 1886, 'Locksley
Hall Sixty Years After.' This hero, now very advanced in age, has
become garrulous as well as disillusioned; his monologue now
(which Tennyson explicitly labels *dramatic* though it is not) is
nearly a third again as long as in his youth, and his style has lost
its spring as his spirit has lost its *élan*. In the first fourth of his
speech he recalls the past—"Amy was a timid child"; she now lies
"All in white Italian marble" in the Locksley chapel—in language
which recalls that of 'The May Queen,' and dwells particularly
on his son's death (speaking for the poet on the death of *his* son
Lionel); through the remainder of the poem he decries the pre-
sent age for disappointing his early hopes—

Gone the cry of 'Forward, Forward,' lost within a growing
  gloom; . . .

Half the marvels of my morning, triumphs over time and space,
Staled by frequence, shrunk by usage, into commonest common-
place!

and shouts—

Chaos, Cosmos! Cosmos, Chaos! who can tell how all will end? . . .
When was age so cramm'd with menace? madness? written, spoken
lies?

Men are equal as the lion and the cat are equal. When Russia
threatens the Empire we pause to hear "the voices from the field"
and "take the suffrage of the plow." Not that some plowmen and
shepherds are not noble, but that

Here and there my lord is lower than his oxen or his swine.

The old man's voice rises to a falsetto—

Authors—essayist, atheist, novelist, realist, rhymester, play your
part,
Paint the mortal shame of nature with the living hues of Art.
Rip your brothers' vices open, strip your own foul passions bare;
Down with Reticence, down with Reverence—forward—naked—
let them stare.
Feed the budding rose of boyhood with the drainage of your sewer;
Send the drain into the fountain, lest the stream should issue pure.
Set the maiden fancies wallowing in the troughs of Zolaism,—
Forward, forward, ay, and backward, downward too into the abysm!

He describes a re-made world—

Every tiger madness muzzled, every serpent passion kill'd,
Every grim ravine a garden every blazing desert till'd,
Robed in universal harvest up to either pole she smiles,
Universal ocean softly washing all her warless isles.

and then asks—warless? with the menace of overpopulation? and
with

Evolution ever climbing after some ideal good,
And Reversion ever dragging Evolution in the mud.

Thus he tries to have it both ways.

Follow Light, and do the Right—for man can half-control his
doom—

243

and "Love will conquer at the last." It is the same ambivalent attitude of despair and hope which marked 'In Memoriam'; the same battle was still to be fought and to end in a stalemate: "Chaos, Cosmos! Cosmos, Chaos!"

Tennyson was seventy-seven years old when this poem was published; no wonder a contemporary reviewer should lament that the Laureate had not yet won the "Passionless bride, divine tranquillity." Waiving the precise question, how much Tennyson believed all this rant, how far the two Locksley Halls portray the changes in his own judgment and follow his own maturing criticism of life, we may still echo the lament that Tennyson had not achieved "a due superiority to and detachment from" the influences of his own age. A true poet "will absorb, but not be absorbed by them. . . .He will register the hopes and disillusions of his time, but he will not be the dupe of the first or the victim of the second. . . .Others may be catechumens. He is initiated." [12] For in spite of his insistence that this was a "dramatic poem, and Dramatis Personae are imaginary," in spite of all denial vain and coy excuse, Tennyson's defence of his hero, in his Notes, is a tacit admission of his own *parti pris*. Gladstone maintained that the method in both poems was "strictly 'impersonal.' " Which is true, in the sense that it is not Tennyson speaking with his own voice, but with the voice of his dramatis persona. It is true, also, on the dramatic side, that "the old lover of 'Locksley Hall' is exactly what the young man must have become, without any changes of character by force of time and experience, if he had grown with the growth of his age"; though this is not extravagant praise. But it is gross exaggeration to add that "the poem in its entirety has a peculiar historical importance as the impersonation of a whole generation," [13] for surely not all young men of 1840 abandoned hope, in old age, with such stridency as this hero, nor was Locksley Hall the whole of England.

The second 'Locksley Hall' was at once attacked as a defeatist repudiation of the old Liberalism: the Poet had lost his faith in progress, the Laureate had betrayed his people by emphasizing their failures and belittling their achievement, the Seer had heatedly reminded them that the millenium was still a million years away and left them with the cold consolation that Love would somehow conquer in the end. A dramatic and objective repre-sentation of certain disappointments is not enough; from Tenny-son more was expected. The critic of *The National Review* put it thus: "Essentially the creature, and, as far as opinions go, the sport of his Age, the author of the two Locksley Halls has reflected its intellectual oscillations with absolute fidelity. He has taught it nothing, and has learnt nothing from it, except to echo in verse its unstable and contradictory conclusions." On the other hand, the best defence of the poem came from R. H. Hutton, and it was the better because for once Hutton took the poems as poems rather than as documents. In contrasting the first and second Locksley Halls he pointed out that

in the former, all the melancholy is attributed to personal grief, while all the sanguine visionariness which really springs out of overflowing vitality, justifies itself by dwelling on the cumulative resources of sci-ence and the arts;—in the latter, the melancholy in the man, a result of ebbing vitality, justifies itself by the failure of knowledge and sci-ence to cope with the moral horrors which experience has brought to light, while the set-off against that melancholy is to be found in a real personal experience of true nobility in man and woman.[14]

This does not altogether meet the case, but it shows the importance of seeking a literary judgment instead of criticizing the poet's personal views, as the whole issue illustrates the dangers of a poet's rushing across the social battlegrounds of his own day inadequately armed.

In happy contrast to the poetic raptures and noisy indignations of the Locksley Halls is 'The Golden Year,' which was added to the *Poems* in their fourth edition, 1846. This little poem puts forward, with some of the best Tennysonian tricks of blank verse and not without a humorous touch, both views of progress, the immediate and the distant. It lacks the popular elements of 'Lock-sley Hall,' the bright rhetoric, the love interest, the excited ap-peals, and the trochaic movement, but it covers the same ground and keeps within the reasonable limits of poetic treatment. It says nearly all that both 'Locksley Hall' poems say, and says it in small compass with proper detachment.

'The Princess,' possibly regarded by its author as a hortatory comment on the position of Early Victorian woman, was certainly not accepted in that sense by the first critics: it satisfied neither the hopes of those who wanted a long serious poem from him nor the expectations of those who wished him to be "rapt in the spirit of this age." Nor was 'In Memoriam,' though it went far towards meeting the demands of the former; and if it was greeted later as holding a mirror up to the *Zeitgeist*, this was accidental or derivative from a certain parallel between Tennyson's struggle with doubt and that of many other men and women his contemporaries. It was an echo, not a picture; more like the first than the second 'Locksley Hall.' It gratified many readers who saw Tennyson wrestling with questions of religion and science and atheism and who liked the language in which he wrote out his answers, just as it comforted many readers who were suffering a similar bereavement; but it was not written to clarify the doubters any more than to console the bereaved. Neither do the war poems of 1852 deserve more than mention here: they were deliberate 'interpretation,' to be sure, but they were not children of the muse, they were political verses.

Now, however, Tennyson wore the official bay and his voice was the poetic voice of England. When therefore the Duke of Wellington died, 14 September 1852, Tennyson knew that a poem would be expected of him, his first large utterance as Laureate; and when two months later the Duke was buried in St. Paul's he had ready an 'Ode,' for sale on the day of the funeral, 18 November. This Ode was greeted, as he acknowledged, with "all but universal depreciation." In extenuation it is commonly said that Tennyson was obliged to write in haste; but his subsequent alterations though numerous are not very striking, and opinion has now swung to the favorable side. For one thing, the 'Ode' has none of those 'beauties' which his readers were accustomed to expect: the style is almost severe. For another, his idealization and overpraise of the Duke was bound to produce murmurs of disapproval which even the strong patriotic note would not drown. He invoked the civic muse and blew loud the trumpet of England's greatness; he thanked God for the protecting seas, and even for the abundant rain; he dared to sound Pharisaical—

> *We are a people yet,*
> *Tho' all men else their nobler dreams forget;*

he prayed

> *O Statesmen, guard us, guard the eye, the soul*
> *Of Europe;*

and to increase the volume of patriotic fervor he represented Nelson, "The greatest sailor since our world began," as welcoming the Iron Duke into the crypt of St. Paul's. But in truth the 'Ode' leaves modern readers cold, even those whose imagination is readily touched by the fame of Wellington. It is an occasional piece, Laureate work, and adequate as such; but as a poem, lacking in the Tennysonian richness of language, it depends for its effect on an elocutionary fluency, some of it very fine—especially when the poet read it aloud[15]—as in the fifth stanza where the guns boom and the bell is tolled (unless one is reminded of the tintinabulation of Poe) and in the slowly majestic opening lines. On the whole, however, its dignity is marred by its fluency and by its patriotic over-emphasis.

Then came 'Maud,' in which also the contemporary accent was felt to intrude upon the ostensible subject. There was the same confusion of the poet and his dramatis persona, not only in the apparent advocacy of war (which in a lesser poet would have been taken for crude popular appeal) but in the rhetorical condemnation of social conditions.—But it would be otiose to follow through the successive domestic idylls, most of which have an implication or a direct expression of social criticism—the "glorification of honest labour," as Tennyson said, in 'Sea Dreams' (1860), with the sad story of the little city clerk who was duped into buying "strange shares in some Peruvian mine"; the "terrible denunciations" of Sir Aylmer's pride and its painful consequences (1864);[c] and the rest. Nor is it necessary to run through the various Laureate pieces, most of them adequate enough as such but not poetry in any true sense. These and the genre idylls are parts of a picture and may be useful to the historian of manners; they are interesting as the products of a poet who was fulfilling an obligation or who had nothing better to write about; they are in truth the earthy part of Tennyson and have already gone to their native dust, whence only for the purposes of a general review may they be for a moment removed.

c The date of the story is 1793, but the treatment is obviously Victorian.

III

It will be apparent that in this chapter I have had two related and not altogether distinct points of view: Tennyson as representative in that he resembles the typical 'Victorian,' representative also in the sense that every man represents that of which he is a part (and the larger the part, the more popular Tennyson was, the more representative); but besides this, Tennyson as representative, as one who consciously aimed at portraying and interpreting the Victorians to themselves. On the one hand an unconscious and on the other a deliberate representativeness: there is no doubt that Tennyson partook of both. And I have suggested that he suffered on both counts. The more emphatically he was of his own age, rather than for all time, the more his work will go down with that which was but temporary and will have inevitably but an historical or curious interest for posterity. This is to be sure the lot of all poets; but that portion which retains a permanent interest is what we judge them by. It is true, moreover, and must be remembered in Tennyson's behalf, that as a poet's period becomes remote we pay less attention to the merely contemporary elements, partly because we are less aware of them and partly because being unfamiliar with them we lightly pass them by. There must have been a great deal in Homer, there certainly was in Dante and Chaucer and Shakespeare, which his immediate readers recognized and which we do not recognize, in spite of elaborate commentaries, as contemporary detail. Dante has lost much by being intensely mediæval, but we are reconciled to his contemporary emphasis because there is so much else. A large part of what Milton had to say is now uninteresting because it was addressed to his fellowmen of the seventeenth century, and he would perhaps not be pleased to know that the "few" who now read him care little or nothing for his method of justifying the ways of God to man. But Tennyson and his advisers believed that the more attention he gave to the life of his own day the more important his work would be. They may have thought it was a paradox; it was in fact a fallacy. They might have read with advantage Matthew Arnold's Preface to his *Poems* of 1853.

Matthew Arnold, whose views on this matter were so far from Tennyson's that the two men might have lived on different planets,

248

took an extreme position but an illuminating one. What he wrote in 1853 might have been a deliberate refutation of Tennyson's aims. "The present age," he said, "makes great claims upon us: we owe it service, it will not be satisfied without our admiration"; and he thought that "commerce with the ancients" had a steadying and composing effect upon the judgments of those who constantly practised it. Such persons, he said, are like those

who have had a very weighty and impressive experience; they are more truly than others under the empire of facts, and more independent of the language current among those with whom they live. They wish neither to applaud nor to revile their age: they wish to know what it is, what it can give them, and whether this is what they want. What they want, they know very well; they want to educe and cultivate what is best and noblest in themselves: they know, too, that this is no easy task—χαλεπὸν, as Pittacus said, χαλεπὸν ἐσθλὸν ἔμμεναι, and they ask themselves sincerely whether their age and its literature can assist them in the attempt. If they are endeavouring to practise any art, they remember the plain and simple proceedings of the old artists, who attained their grand results by penetrating themselves with some noble and significant action, not by inflating themselves with a belief in the pre-eminent importance and greatness of their own times. They do not talk of their mission, nor of interpreting their age, nor of the coming Poet; all this, they know, is the mere delirium of vanity; their business is not to praise their age, but to afford to the men who live in it the highest pleasure which they are capable of feeling. If asked to afford this by means of subjects drawn from the age itself, they ask what special fitness the present age has for supplying them: they are told that it is an era of progress, an age commissioned to carry out the great ideas of industrial development and social amelioration. They reply that with all this they can do nothing; that the elements they need for the exercise of their art are great actions, calculated powerfully and delightfully to affect what is permanent in the human soul; that so far as the present age can supply such actions, they will gladly make use of them; but that an age wanting in moral grandeur can with difficulty supply such, and an age of spiritual discomfort with difficulty be powerfully and delightfully affected by them.

One may retort that Matthew Arnold was hardly the man to say some of these things: he was himself too greatly troubled with the spiritual discomforts of his age, too deeply afflicted with

> *this strange disease of modern life,*
> *With its sick hurry, its divided aims,*
> *Its heads o'er taxed, its palsied hearts,—*

yet he made poetry out of it. He laid great stress—and very wisely—on "the all-importance of the choice of a subject; the necessity of accurate construction; and the subordinate character of expression"; yet he, like Tennyson (and many if not most of his fellow English poets), often failed signally to meet these valid requirements. But his preoccupation with the right choice of subject and his belief that ancient subjects were better than contemporary subjects "dealing with the details of modern life which pass daily under our eyes," and that contemporary subjects offered actions less great, personages less noble, situations less intense than the ancient ones, were matters for Tennyson to ponder. Arnold exaggerated when he said that the subject was everything, and he overstated his case in insisting on subjects from antiquity; but he pointed a right direction by emphasizing the dangers of contemporary subjects for narrative and dramatic poetry. (This truth was brought home to Tennyson when 'The Promise of May' was performed.)

Now, theorizing apart, helpful as it may be, there remains the fact that nearly all the verses in which Tennyson dealt at any length with 'modern' subjects is inferior to his best: he did not succeed in making poetry out of them. It is a kind of tragic irony that the very principle he chose for guidance led him astray, and the irony is underlined by the part which his age played in this choice. His age placed him on that bad eminence of Interpreter General, and it gave him the gift of its own weakness, sentimentality in the serious concerns of daily life. It gave him the dangerous gift also of popularity—which at first unsought grew by what it fed upon. It recreated him in its own image and therefore in the end dominated him. It made him, to a large degree, or encouraged him to make himself, a mirror indeed, rather than a poet. Its own preoccupation with "the great ideas of industrial development and social amelioration," with its spiritual discomforts and its want of moral grandeur, would reduce him to an historical document. This of course was due partly to false doctrine and partly also to Tennyson's own lack of native energy, to the lack of poetic substance in his own endowment. Given a stronger personal endowment he might have dominated his age.

But there are signs of a contrary direction. More than half of Tennyson's later work was ostensibly not 'modern' at all: 'Idylls of the King' and the historical dramas; and the poems on classical subjects (though few) are honorable exceptions. In his search for subjects, subjects for the great justificatory poem, he turned to the Middle Ages and to the great crises of English history. Yet the 'Idylls' are frankly a kind of Ruskinian Gothic, at best a pageantry of mediæval trappings, at worst sentimentalized old tales. Tennyson did not attempt to depict the Middle Ages, but to use them as an escape background. More might be said for the tragedies, but their interest as contemporary comment on the Catholic question is slight, and though Tennyson may have turned to them as an expression of his hostility to Rome, the expression remained almost a private one. These are but negative examples. For those who expected him to be always interpreting his age they are almost derelictions; for the others they are, from this point of view, of small significance.

The Victorian mark on Tennyson's poetry took another form also. Four years before the Queen's accession Fox had told him publicly to "ascertain his mission and work his work"; and the age which Arnold found wanting in moral grandeur was greatly in need of a moral instructor. An age which concentrated on material prosperity (after the forties) and which saw its theological foundations overturned by the new science was in need of a prophet. Carlyle and his followers Ruskin and Morris raised their voices, and Arnold also, each with a different note; but they are prophets of a social divinity. The Church had its dissentions within and its difficulties both with Rome and with the Chapels. Atheism, always a terrible name, and agnosticism, its new brother, threatened. And after the great hymn (slightly ambiguous though it seemed to many) with which 'In Memoriam' opened, Tennyson became a new hope, a Christian leader whose position was the stronger because he was somewhat apart from ecclesiastical centers.[d] It might be debated whether his doctrine were truly Chris-

d That 'In Memoriam' was his patent may be shown also from a letter of the liberal Sidgwick. After "the struggle with what Carlyle used to call 'Hebrew old clothes'" had brought religious freedom, what, asked Sidgwick, "does re- ligious freedom bring us to? It brings us face to face with atheistic science; the faith in God and Immortality, which we had been struggling to clear from superstition, suddenly seems to be *in the air*: and in seeking a firm basis for this faith tian, but none doubted that he was a true religious teacher; and as the years multiplied he wore his robes of office with greater confidence. He became in turn teacher, prophet, seer, *vates sacer*—a high priest of the Victorian compromise religion, extra-ecclesiastical but ordained by public sanction. The garlands of the muses were his birthright; he also drew the bow of Apollo.

What was the effect of this vocation on Tennyson as a poet? This question confronts us with the old challenging problem of art and "morality." This is solved, if it ever is solved, by each of us according to his own light and temper. It need not be debated here; but in so far as it touches the position of Tennyson some attention to it cannot be avoided. A statement of the case from a late Victorian, who is a good witness because he was not always on the side of reverence, may serve as introduction. It is, oddly enough, in praise of Tennyson's Laureate successor:

He realizes, indeed, more clearly than any other modern English poet, that the value of poetry depends primarily on the comprehensiveness of the view of life, and the experience of life embodied in it. He realises, as Goethe realised consciously, as Shakespeare realised unconsciously, and as Rossetti did not realise at all, that the great poet must be a philosopher and a man of the world, besides being a man of song; that the gift of singing is subsidiary to what the song conveys; and what it conveys must be the soul of the world, not the soul of the artist's studio; . . .

The names of Shakespeare and Goethe are great names, and they must not be used to conjure with; but they suggest that the greatest have not been professed moral teachers. Both the moral and the intellectual directions of poetry are oblique. The works of literature which we are accustomed to call greatest and to rank highest were not written to give us comfort in sorrow or clarify our uncertainties about moral issues or inform us on matters of which we were ignorant or guide us through intellectual difficulties. Nor is this judgment invalidated by the two signal exceptions of the *Divine Comedy* and *Paradise Lost*, for we admire them artisti-

---

we find ourselves in the midst of the 'fight with death' which 'In Memoriam' so powerfully represents" (quoted in *Memoir* I, 302). Or as Hallam Tennyson said: "Men like Maurice and Robertson thought that the author [of 'In Memoriam'] had made a definite step towards the unification of the highest religion and philosophy with the progressive science of the day."

cally in spite of their original and apparent purpose. It is rather the writers of second rank, whose instincts are less for art than for uplift, whose impulses are less creative than homiletic and hortatory, that follow the lower and more dangerous ways of moral or other teaching.

Tennyson however was not often openly didactic; the question for him is one of emphasis. Since only abstract or decorative art is without some moral implication, and therefore those who hold the extreme oppositive view that art is or should be quite a-moral are left almost in a vacuum, there can be no talk of condemning his poetry because of its moral content: the point of attack or defence must be the quality and the appropriateness of the moral. If as in certain of the 'Idylls of the King' the moral is dubious, that is to say, narrow or temporary, or if as in 'The May Queen' and many another Idyll of the Hearth it is obtrusive, then the poem must suffer. If the poem seems to exist for the religious teaching it is so much the less a poem, no matter how profound the teaching may be. But if as in the opening stanzas of 'In Memoriam' or in 'Crossing the Bar' the religious ideas are transmuted (however loosely this word be understood) or if as in 'The Lotos-Eaters' the moral is left to stand for itself, there can be no ground of complaint.

Of the general moral ideas of Tennyson it will be enough to say that they were nearly all on the side of nobility and goodness as his contemporaries understood nobility and goodness. The more definitely Victorian these ideas are the more they are likely to seem to us muddled or queer. But on such points a cautionary suspension of judgment might be best. This moral teaching is everywhere pervasive, rarely overt, in Tennyson's work, and where it injured his poetry the damage is obvious. In Dr. Johnson's phrase, he often treated the Muses with ingratitude. It is, however, Tennyson's religious and 'philosophic' teaching which entitled him to the crown of *vates sacer*, and this claim must be examined more closely.

Tennyson's message to Victorian England, his philosophy, and his religion remain, after many commentators have tried to elucidate them, somewhat vague or general. His patriotism in the narrow sense, his admiration and love for an ideal England, is unquestioned. His hatred of many social evils of the time is plain. He had strong religious feelings but he was uninterested in dogmatic theology and cared little for organized Christianity. He was not a church-goer. The two primary principles of his religion were a belief in God—a God undefined, somewhat anthropomorphic, something between the deity of the Established Church and Arnold's Power-not-ourselves-that-makes-for-righteousness (the new stream-of-tendency God was abhorrent to him)—and a belief in the immortality of individual man. He had not a philosophic or speculative mind, and even his staunchest proponents do not claim for him any powers of intellectual analysis. A poet, they may well hold, is not a technical philosopher, but a philosopher in the sense that he sees life sympathetically and understandingly. When pressed, Tennyson would say: "Life is a mystery, death is a mystery"; and from his lips this was like the utterance of a prophet. The more curious in this matter should consult Masterman's little volume, *Tennyson as a Religious Teacher*, already mentioned, for the defence, and for the other side J. M. Robertson's essay.[16] For the present it is a question whether Tennyson was one of those who, as Emerson says, "live from a great depth of being" and translated this inner life into poetry.

IV

The 1830 volume contained five poems of an ethical cast, 'The "How" and the "Why," ' 'Supposed Confessions of a Second-Rate Sensitive Mind not in Unity with Itself,' 'Nothing will Die,' 'All things will Die,' and 'οἱ ῥέοντες.' These were either suppressed by Tennyson or classed as Juvenilia. In the second volume the principal poems of this kind are 'The Palace of Art' and 'The Lotos-Eaters.' The former has an explicit moral, characteristically Victorian (the compromise) and confused (because most of the poem is on art's side and the poet is not). But the latter is admirably dramatic: the poet is content to let the Lotos-Eaters express themselves without adding his private commentary: for anything in the poem itself this might be Tennyson's own philosophy. Most of the new poems of 1842 were narrative or idyllic, with one notable exception, 'The Vision of Sin'; and it is in this poem that Tennyson first comes forward as a serious teacher.

It "describes the soul of a youth who has given himself up to pleasure and Epicureanism. He at length is worn out and wrapt in the mists of satiety. Afterwards he grows into a cynical old man afflicted with the 'curse of nature,' and joining in the Feast of Death." Thus Tennyson. All this is in the form of an allegorical vision, beginning with heroic couplets, changing to trochaics, then diminishing to four-stress lines, and rhetorically pivotted on the thrice-repeated "Till"; followed by a group of heroic lines irregularly rimed. The Feast of Death section contains thirty-six short-line trochaic quatrains (which FitzGerald compared to Dr. Johnson's 'Long Expected one and twenty') ending—

> *Fill the cup and fill the can;*
> *Mingle madness, mingle scorn!*
> *Dregs of life and lees of man;*
> *Yet we will not die forlorn.*

These quatrains were meant to quicken the movement, but they hardly escaped jingling. "Then," adds the poet, "we see the landscape which symbolizes God, Law and the future life." The heroic couplets return; the "mystic mountain range" is visible again;

> *Below were men and horses pierced with worms,*
> *And slowly quickening into lower forms;...*
> *Then some one spake: 'Behold! it was a crime*
> *Of sense avenged by sense that wore with time.'*

Another says it was a crime of malice and another that "A little grain of conscience made him sour." Then one cried: "Is there any hope?"

> *To which an answer peal'd from that high land,*
> *But in a tongue no man could understand;*
> *And on the glimmering limit far withdrawn*
> *God made himself an awful rose of dawn.*

The answer is thus veiled in metaphor; for we are left faintly trusting the larger hope as in 'In Memoriam.' But certainly Tennyson had his fine flourish at the end, and the poem (already handicapped by a too mechanical structure) is all the better for not stating its moral baldly. 'St. Simeon Stylites' (in the same volume) was a fearful example of escape by mortifying the flesh; the Lotos Eaters escaped by denying the world; the youth who gave himself to the flesh and became a cynical old man teaches us that even after indulgence and sin there is hope. These make a kind of trilogy, to which may be added 'The Palace of Art,' where the danger of another kind of escape is shown.

But the narrative idyllic poems of this volume had their ethical lessons also, less overt but none the less pleasing to contemporary taste, and all wholesome. Even 'Ulysses,' we remember, taught in Tennyson's own view the necessity "of going forward and braving the struggle of life," though not all readers have read it in this sense. And the homely truths of 'Dora' and 'The Talking Oak' and 'Love and Duty' and their kind need no pointer. 'The Day-Dream,' indeed, was set out with a labelled *Moral* underlined by a slightly mocking apology—

> *. . . liberal applications lie*
> *In Art like Nature, dearest friend;*
> *So 'twere to cramp its use, if I*
> *Should hook it to some useful end.*

Yet the critics felt still that Tennyson was lacking in substance— "But what is wanting in Tennyson?" asked Mrs. Browning after the 1842 *Poems*—and that he possessed more beauty of the applied sort than energy in reading the riddle of the universe; so that Arnold (whose disapproval is well known) could complain to Clough in 1847 of "Tennyson's dawdling with its painted shell." 'The Princess' had not given satisfaction, for while it seemed to expound the position of woman as both equal to man and yet diverse—a shrewd verbal compromise—the levity of the early part undermined the seriousness of the great pronouncement and his burlesque picture of the female institute both irritated the believers and confirmed the sceptics: "so that later when a proposal for the establishment of a woman's college was put forward, Miss Elizabeth Sewell—and doubtless others also—said, a little scornfully, that it sounded like *The Princess*." [17] In 'In Memoriam,' however, Tennyson gave full measure.

'In Memoriam' established Tennyson as a religious teacher. Just as 'Locksley Hall' had stirred the breasts of Victorian youth, so 'In Memoriam' touched the minds and hearts of older men and women. It gave poetic voice not only to the eternal questions of death and afterlife, but to the present questions of the new science and religious doubt. Charlotte Brontë did not care for it. "It is beautiful," she said; "it is mournful; it is monotonous"; and she could not read it through. But men like Froude thought otherwise:

Tennyson's poems, the group of Poems which closed with *In Memoriam,* became to many of us what *The Christian Year* was to orthodox Churchmen. We read them and they became part of our minds, the expression, in exquisite language, of the feelings which were working in ourselves.

Judgments like this cannot be lightly discounted, and many similar ones might be adduced; but they must not be misunderstood, they must not be interpreted as praise of the poem, they must be recognized as tributes to its timeliness. They show that Tennyson's contemporaries read 'In Memoriam' as a beautiful representation of some of their own feelings. Yet even such a generalization as this is open to the suspicion of being a half-truth; for Matthew Arnold, whose poetry is almost a perfect foil to Tennyson's, could write in 1869, not without injustice:

My poems represent, on the whole, the main movement of mind of the last quarter of a century, and thus they will probably have their day as people become conscious to themselves of what that movement of mind is, and interested in the literary productions which reflect it. It might be fairly urged that I have less poetical sentiment than Tennyson, and less intellectual vigour and abundance than Browning; yet, because I have perhaps more of a fusion of the two than either of them, and have more regularly applied that fusion to the main line of modern development, I am likely enough to have my turn, as they have had theirs.[18]

It cannot be true that both Arnold and Tennyson reflect the main movement of mind in England at the middle of the century; rather, that each reflects a part of it. From one plausible point of view the truest interpreter of an age is the most popular writer, as measured by the sale of his books and the praise of contemporary reviewers. In this sense Dickens and Trollope, Reade and Wilkie Collins stand high; but so also do Mrs. Wood, Miss Broughton, and Ouida, and a little later Hall Caine and Marie Corelli: they pleased the common reader, they satisfied his tastes, they echoed his mind, they spoke for him better than he could speak for himself, they interpreted him to himself. In this sense also 'Festus' Bailey and Martin Tupper interpreted the readers of poetry, and especially Longfellow, who for many years was more popular in England than Tennyson and sold better. But this is clearly a narrow sense and not what Arnold meant or what the Tennyson enthusiasts mean. They claim for Tennyson an interpretation more profound than mere popularity, yet they have often mixed the two standards of measurement and perhaps Tennyson himself was confused when he dedicated his *Selections* of 1865 to the "Working Men of England."

In the next volume after 'In Memoriam'—*Maud and Other Poems*—Tennyson included two stanzas called 'Will,' which might almost have been written by Matthew Arnold. Long before, Arnold had written to Clough in advisory mood: "consider whether you attain the *beautiful*, and whether your product gives PLEASURE, not excites curiosity and reflexion." Tennyson for his part chose to give pleasure, but when he chose to write

> *O well for him whose will is strong!*
> *He suffers, but he will not suffer long*

he paid heavy tribute to reflective poetry and gave very little æsthetic pleasure. Better on his own line is the "brilliantly descriptive allegory" of "Life as Energy, in the great ethical sense of the word, —Life as the pursuit of the Ideal" in 'The Voyage,' published with 'Enoch' in 1864. This pleased Henry Sidgwick. "What growth there is in the man mentally! How he has caught the spirit of the age in *The Voyage!*" He quotes part of the ninth stanza:

> *Now high on waves that idly burst*
> *Like Heavenly Hope she crown'd the sea,*
> *And now, the bloodless point reversed,*
> *She bore the blade of Liberty.—*

and cries: "How sad—but a chastened sadness, our sadness—that of the second half of the 19th century—no 'Verzweiflung.'" Better, but still not good enough, for the poem ends:

> *Again to colder climes we came,*
> *For still we followed where she led;*

Now mate is blind and captain lame,
And half the crew are sick or dead;
But, blind or lame or sick or sound,
We follow that which flies before;
We know the merry world is round,
And we may sail for evermore.

Mrs. Tennyson entered in her journal for 1 December 1867:
"A. is reading Hebrew (*Job* and the *Song of Solomon* and *Genesis*):
he talked much about his Hebrew, and about all-pervading Spirit
being more understandable by him than solid matter. He brought
down to me his psalm-like poem, 'Higher Pantheism.' " The next
year he continued his Hebrew studies, chiefly attracted by the Song
of Solomon, which he called "The most perfect Idyl of the faithful
love of a country girl for her shepherd"; and wrote the 'Holy Grail'
idyll, in which he combined realism and symbolism, the natural
being made "to account for the supernatural"; and in 1869 joined
Knowles and Pritchard in forming the Metaphysical Society, in
which the pious and the sceptics could rub shoulders to mutual
profit. Tennyson's connections with the Society were never close;
he did not often attend the meetings, rarely spoke then, and he
resigned a few months before it was dissolved; but even his formal
interest in it is indicative of his quasi-mystical philosophic preoccu-
pations at this time. At its first meeting 'The Higher Pantheism'
was read but not discussed. Then he devoted himself to finishing the
'Idylls' and writing his plays, and it was not until 1880 that he pub-
lished another philosophical poem, 'De Profundis,' which had been
begun however in 1852. This was followed by 'The Ancient Sage'
in the 'Tiresias' volume, 1885, 'Vastness' in the same year (in *Mac-
millan's Magazine*), and 'By an Evolutionist' in the 'Demeter' vol-
ume, 1889. These five poems contain his later maturest "teaching."

Here surely we are no longer dawdling with the painted shell of
the universe. Here we are trying to penetrate the inmost mysteries,
and if we have learned very little it may be because the mysteries
are impenetrable. The simple commonplaces of truth sometimes
are enough; sometimes however men desire more and endeavor to
find satisfaction through the exercise of the speculative imagina-
tion. Many indeed appear to be satisfied with the exercise alone,
and call their work metaphysics. Others, equally passionate but less

disciplined, turn to mysticism, a kind of direct method of storming the unknowable by immediate converse with the supernatural sources of knowledge. These too enjoy the satisfaction of seeming to find truth, but they are unable to communicate their findings and can only recommend their method to others. Tennyson tried both ways. He was not by natural endowment or by mental discipline a thinker. He hardly aspired beyond the common results of what we call mature reflection on the phenomena; and when he did wish to go farther he resorted to the veiled language of poetry, which was his proper gift. There had been in him from youth a strain of apparently genuine mysticism, the product perhaps or the by-product of his melancholy moods. But the trance itself is an uncertain source of poetic inspiration and in its use by the poets it has probably always been mingled with the abstraction and ecstasy of composition, which though related is properly a different phenomenon. Tennyson in his later years tended to combine and confuse these two kinds of trance and also to combine and confuse them with his 'philosophical' meditations. The result was a mixture of the language of mysticism with ideas and beliefs which were not arrived at by the processes of the mystics.

'The Higher Pantheism' attempts to reconcile the old Pantheistic view of God in nature with the new scientific cosmology based on evolution, but the compromise seems to be achieved by juggling words rather than by compounding ideas.

> *Dark is the world to thee: thyself art the reason why;*
> *For is He not all but that which has power to feel 'I am I'? . . .*
> *God is law, say the wise; O Soul, and let us rejoice,*
> *For if He thunder by law the thunder is yet His voice.*

This was cruelly parodied by Swinburne:

What and wherefore and whence? for under is over and under:
If thunder could be without lightning, lightning could be without
>   *thunder. . . .*
More is the whole than a part: but half is more than the whole:
Clearly the soul is the body: but is not the body the soul?[e]

---

[e] Cf. 'The Ancient Sage':

Thou canst not prove that thou art body alone,

Nor canst thou prove that thou art spirit alone,
Nor canst thou prove that thou art both in one.

And Swinburne had some right to mock, for in 'Hertha,' published two years after Tennyson's poem, he had achieved "the most of lyric force and music combined with the most of condensed and clarified thought."[19]

Some of the same overreaching style appears in 'De Profundis'—

> *and the pain*
> *Of this divisible-indivisible world*
> *Among the numerable-innumerable*
> *Sun, sun, and sun, thro' finite-infinite space*
> *In finite-infinite Time—our mortal veil*
> *And shatter'd phantom of that Infinite One,*
> *Who made thee unconceivably Thyself*
> *Out of His whole World-self*

and

> *Hallowed be Thy name—Halleluiah!—*
> *Infinite Ideality!*
> *Immeasurable Reality!*
> *Infinite Personality!*
> *Hallowed be Thy name—Halleluiah!*

One doesn't like to call that poetry. And as for the thought, it is perhaps better obtained from Tennyson's paraphrase taken down by Wilfred Ward.[20] Tennyson's reading of this poem in his last years must have been impressive and memorable, an act of worship, liturgical in effect; but on the printed page this effect is wanting.

'The Ancient Sage' is Tennyson's benediction, both a personal last word and summary of his earlier doctrine and also an old man's answers to the hard questions of life. It has been wittily called 'The Two Voices Sixty Years After,' for it has the form of a dialogue between the old Sage (who speaks in blank verse) and the Youth (whose riming quatrains the Ancient reads and replies to); but it goes farther than the old solution of romantic-domestic love. Tennyson had been reading about Lao-Tsze,[21] whom he mistakenly placed "A thousand summers ere the time of Christ," but his Ancient Sage does not propound Taoism; rather, he sums up Tennyson's own ingathering of a long Victorian life. His Seer begins at once with a compromise: "Force is from the heights." The Youth's scroll asks

> *What power but the bird's could make*
> *This music in the bird?*

and the Sage replies that the Nameless exists in "the temple—cave of thine own self"—

> *For Knowledge is the swallow on the lake*
> *That sees and stirs the surface-shadow there*
> *But never yet hath dipt into the abysm,*
> *The Abysm of all Abysms, beneath, within*
> *The blue of sky and sea, the green of earth,*
> *And in the million-millionth of a grain*
> *Which cleft and cleft again for evermore,*
> *And ever vanishing, never vanishes,*
> *To me, my son, more mystic than thyself,*
> *Or even than the Nameless is to me.*

(Again the blank verse reminds one of Wordsworth's: Tennyson would hardly in 1842 have written a line like

> *And ever vanishing, never vanishes.*

Even more Wordsworthian is a later passage

> *for oft*
> *On me, when boy, there came what then I call'd,*
> *Who knew no books and no philosophies,*
> *In my boy-phrase, "The Passion of the Past."*
> *The first grey streak of earliest summer-dawn,*
> *The last long stripe of waning crimson gloom,*
> *As if the late and early were but one ...)*

The Sage echoes 'In Memoriam'—

> *The truths that never can be proved—*

with a more outspoken agnosticism—

> *For nothing worthy proving can be proven,*
> *Nor yet disproven: wherefore thou be wise,*
> *Cleave ever to the sunnier side of doubt,*
> *And cling to Faith beyond the forms of Faith*

and lauds the power

> *which knows*
> *And is not known, but felt thro' what we feel*
> *Within ourselves is highest*

(almost the God of Matthew Arnold); and when the Youth opines (speaking for evolution) that it is "the Years that make And break the vase of clay," the Sage counsels: "make the passing shadow serve thy will." The Youth, unsatisfied with this, insists on the destructive powers of time; he is told that this earth-life is but beginning and is further put off with the evasion

> *Who knows but that the darkness is in man?*
> *The doors of Night may be the gates of Light;*

man will develop "the last and largest sense" (evolution on the other side) which will dispel our present illusions

> *And show us that the world is wholly fair.*

(In his prose note Tennyson seems to regard this new sense as free will.) As a final argument the Sage alleges mystical revelation:

> *for more than once when I*
> *Sat all alone, revolving in myself*
> *The word that is the symbol of myself,*
> *The mortal limits of the Self was loosed,*
> *And past into the Nameless, as a cloud*
> *Melts into Heaven. I touch'd my limbs, the limbs*
> *Were strange, not mine—and yet no shade of doubt,*
> *But utter clearness, and thro' loss of Self*
> *The gain of such large life as match'd with ours*
> *Were sun to spark—unshadowable in words,*
> *Themselves but shadows of a shadow-world.*

Yet as though this were not enough, he ends on the practical homiletic note:

> *Let be thy wail and help thy fellow-men, . . .*
> *And more—think well! Do-well will follow thought, . . .*
> *But curb the beast . . .*
> *And leave the hot swamp of voluptuousness . . .*
> *And climb the Mount of Blessing, whence, if thou*
> *Look higher, then—perchance—thou mayest—beyond*
> *A hundred ever-rising mountain lines,*
> *And past the range of Night and Shadow—see*
> *The high-heaven dawn of more than mortal day*
> *Strike on the Mount of Vision! So, farewell.*

L'agnostique malgré lui, one might say. Has Tennyson learned nothing since 1850? The answer is still the same: honest doubt and faith. The faith is not more confident[t] and certainly the language is not more beautiful—though one would not have missed the fine phrase "we, thin minds, who creep from thought to thought."[22] 'The Ancient Sage' may be edifying, it may be "Useful and helpful and ennobling," it is a document in the history of Tennyson's development, but philosophically it is not interesting and poetically it is not impressive.

A few minor poems of Tennyson's last years close the account. In 'Vastness' he sums himself up as voice and interpreter and prophet of Late Victorian England. The old complaints of social wrongs are here, in slightly muffled tones; the old beauty is wanting and is not compensated by a particular incisiveness or brilliance of phrase, but the long roll of the eight-beat dactyllic lines gives dignity if not melody; and the leading ideas of the Laureate's mature judgment are repeated, with a new emphasis: the present evils—

Wealth with his wines and his wedded harlots; honest Poverty, bare to the bone;

and so on, with the present virtues also—

Household happiness, gracious children, debtless competence, golden mean

all "Swallow'd in Vastness," all "but a trouble of ants in the gleam of a million million suns," all our prosperity and our sins and desolation "a murmur of gnats in the gloom," insignificant and trivial except as preludes to the ultimate glory of the future. This future is not clearly prophesied and not, as it had been before, prophesied as an earthly culmination, but rather left, a bit cryptically, to the future life. The contemptible littleness of this life is asserted in eighteen and a half couplets, and the last line is set off by a row of dots as though a new voice spoke or the old one answered itself:

Peace, let it be! for I loved him, and love him for ever: the dead are not dead but alive.

[t] Tennyson said: "In my old age, I think I have a stronger faith in God and human good than I had in youth."

There was no suggestion before this of personal elegy and in the absence of any contradicting authority one must suppose that suddenly, in the midst of these depressing judgments on mortal life, comes the more than fifty-years-old memory of young Arthur Hallam, and the consolation won from that grief reasserts itself.[23] Tennyson himself glossed the final line: "What matters anything in this world without faith in the immortality of the soul and of Love." It is a somewhat negative view of things and very distasteful to many minds, but it was the profoundest of Tennyson's convictions, the foundation of his philosophy of life, and in 'Vastness' he worked it in with his earlier condemnations of the age and alongside his idyllic recordings of the domestic scene—a complete recapitulation.

Another prophetic note is sounded in 'By an Evolutionist.' "My father brought 'Evolution' into poetry," said the second Lord Tennyson with pride; this was chiefly in the fifty-sixth section of 'In Memoriam.' Now as an old man he adds a final comment, not meant as poetry in the old sense but as a colloquial self-communion. The first stanza is written almost with a chuckle—

> *The Lord let the house of a brute to the soul of a man,*
> *And the man said, 'Am I your debtor?'*
> *And the Lord—'Not yet; but make it as clean as you can,*
> *And then I will let you a better.'*

Then, if evolution has produced in the human body a superior medium of brutish pleasure which age now takes away, still old age thereby lightens him for the great ascent up "the ladder-of-heaven that hangs on a star"; and this single experience is generalized—

> *the Man is quiet at last,*
> *As he stands on the heights of his life with a*
> *glimpse of a height that is higher.*

Whether the better house on the higher height is an improved body in this world or hints at a bodiless existence in another world is not clear; and the moral implication, that a long life of "eighty years" is required to silence the "yelp of the beast," is a dubious idea to set before the young. But Tennyson always refused to be committed by implications—as he said of the three Queens: "They are and they are not." What in some might be called mental confusion was for him a poetical license. But a much finer review of life is 'The Oak,' which Tennyson cherished as "clean cut like a Greek epigram"—

> *Live thy Life,*
> *Young and old,*
> *Like yon oak,*
> *Bright in spring,*
> *Living gold;*
>
> *Summer-rich*
> *Then; and then*
> *Autumn-changed,*
> *Soberer-hued*
> *Gold again.*
>
> *All his leaves*
> *Fall'n at length,*
> *Look, he stands,*
> *Trunk and bough,*
> *Naked strength.*

By way of epilogue to these poems of an old man looking back reminiscently over his past and repeating somewhat Poloniusly his observations on life, might be added his 'Parnassus,' first published in 1889. It is a queer poem, introduced by a scrap of Horace's *Exegi monumentum* and beginning with a line which seems like a dactyllic hexameter—

> *What be these crown'd forms high over the sacred fountain?*

yet continuing

> *Bards, that the mighty Muses have raised to the heights of the*
> *mountain,*
> *And over the flight of the Ages! O Goddesses, help me up thither!*

and breaking down metrically to

> *These are Astronomy and Geology, terrible Muses!*

which suggests metrical burlesque; and ending with an eight-stress quatrain. The subject is serious, however: the poet reaches the summit, whence his voice goes forth

> *Sounding for ever and ever thro' Earth and her listening nations,*
> *And mixt with the great sphere-music of stars and of constellations,*

266

only to find there two shapes

Taller than all the Muses, and huger than all the mountain,

the terrible muses Astronomy and Geology. And, as he says, "the sight confuses" at first. But he consoles himself with thoughts of the Higher Immortality: if his lips were but touched with the true fire the mortality of this world will not harm him, for he looks ahead to other worlds—

Let the golden Iliad vanish, Homer here is Homer there.

V

Perhaps it is but an unworthy quibble which ensnares those who either praise or dispraise Tennyson as the interpreter of his age. As the Bard himself might have said: He is and he is not. But the question still has amusing and paradoxical by-plays illustrating—if nothing more—some of the looseness of critical thinking. For instance, Miss Anne Swanwick published a small volume in the year of the Laureate's death called *Poets the Interpreters of their Age,* and at the end of it Tennyson (the only living poet included) must have been gratified to read:

he has continued for upwards of sixty years

> *To fling abroad*
> *The winged shafts of truth;*

to denounce, with prophetic fire, our national sins; to pour forth, in impassioned strains, his enthusiasm for the Good, the Beautiful, and the True, and at the same time to delight his contemporaries with his stately music.

(This, which doubtless represents the common view, makes a pretty foil to Goldwin Brown's observation, made in 1855[24]—"Only on a theory that a moral purpose is indispensable to poetry, can it be denied that he is one of the greatest of poets. His works are perhaps the most exquisite intellectual luxury the world has enjoyed. His cynicism completes their exquisiteness; for the supreme luxury of an age like ours is a cynic.") But Miss Swanwick rather gave her own case away, three pages later, by adding that "in this preeminently sceptical and scientific age, two of the greatest minds of the

267

century [Tennyson and Browning] cherish a profound belief in the existence of God . . . and in the personal immortality of a human soul": which seems to show that Tennyson and Browning interpret their age by running counter to its preeminent characteristics. When then does *interpret* mean?

In 1890 an American professor could describe 'In Memoriam' as "that spiritual autobiography of our generation";[25] and Arthur Waugh concluded his volume (written while the Laureate was dying: the preface is dated 12 October 1892) with these words:

It was an age marked by a struggle between doubt and faith, from which faith rose conqueror. Every effort of the contest was recorded in Tennyson's verse. . . .
The task of the poet was to sift and combine the lesser voices of antagonism, to separate the tithe of truth from the mass of falsehood, and to fuse the many elements into one perfect amalgam. . . . Therefore it is that Tennyson is never with the revolutionist, nor yet with the dullard; he is never in the forefront, but always among the first to enter the stormed citadel. . . . With a calm strength and unbiassed judgment he took what good the age had to give, and threw aside the evil. And having proved the goodness of it, he proclaimed it from the housetops. Such was the poet: such too, was the man. . . .

Again, the *Edinburgh Review* remarked in 1895:

No country or period ever had a truer interpreter than the England of the Victorian age in the late Laureate. Lord Tennyson was English to the core . . . in his manly moderation, in his constant sobriety of judgment, Lord Tennyson reflects with absolute fidelity the character of his countrymen. . . . He has summoned poetry to the aid of statesmanship; and by the beauty of his language and the wisdom of his thought he has done much to fix and perpetuate and strengthen in men's minds the principles which they and he have held dear..
As with politics, so with religion. His poetry is instinct with the doubts and the hopes of thoughtful Englishmen of his day. . . .
The knowledge and love of nature in detail, so conspicuous in Lord Tennyson's poetry, are also eminently characteristic of our time.

And these are certainly partial truths. Set beside them the strictures of Matthew Arnold (already quoted) in 1853 and his comments on contemporary life in 'The Scholar Gypsy' and 'Thyrsis'; and among others, Pater's: "the modern world, with its conflicting claims, its entangled interests, distracted by so many sorrows, with many preoccupations, so bewildering an experience." It is a salutary corrective to Tennyson's preoccupation (so far as it went) with his own age.

And a curious corollary comes from a later contemporary, W. H. Mallock: "Tennyson under the Shadow."[26] The poet evokes from his age, says Mallock, "thoughts that were already existing, only existing unrecognized . . . he has not added them to it." He is "as it were, at once a mirror and a burning-glass." We must remember in fact "that be the genius never so great, it can grasp and assimilate nothing but what is present for it to assimilate; and that its nature, be it what it will, is subdued to what it works in." Well and good; but the 'shadow'? In reality Tennyson's genius "has not declined at all . . . it is the age that has changed, not he." In a word, a word not without its suggestiveness, the Victorian age, with which Tennyson set forth bravely in the eighteen thirties has been a disappointment, the materials which it offered his genius at the outset have changed in quality, and somehow have left him stranded.

The age has changed, but he has remained constant; and instead of being the impassioned exponent of contemporary thought, all he can now do is to bow his head and submit to it.

This is ingenious and not altogether wrong. It has also a note of pathos which Mallock did not intend. It bears out the much misunderstood complaint of Old Fitz, who even more definitely than Tennyson withdrew from the world about 1850 and watched his promising young friend with increasing detachment. But we are still left with a paradox, for it was just at the time when the Victorian age left its Laureate stranded that it most emphatically accepted him as its own. His successor in the Laureateship twenty-three years later had part of the answer ready in 1869: "he thinks of us with this particular day, feels with us of this day, and is the exponent of such poetical feelings as in this day we are capable of. But as far as poetry is concerned we and our day are not great, but little, and he shares our littleness with us."[27] This from Alfred Austin! And we of a still later day can add: Tennyson, when popularity overtook him, when he retired to Farringford and then to Aldworth, and became *vates Victorianus sacer,* more and more tuned his lyre to the conservative pitch of the common reader of whom and for whom he sang. He became a sort of *grand seigneur* comfortably savoring the sweet domesticities of love and of friendship, talking familiarly with his dependents, flattering their humble humanity and praising their simple nobility, and scolding them poetically for their shocking shortcomings. The less he was the more he seemed to be one of them. His very seclusion enhanced his popularity; for he was the visible *deus* descending from time to time *ex machina,* and it touched the hearts of his fellow men to see a god in their midst. If he did not mature intellectually he became, all the more, one with his tenants and beloved of them. He shared their simple doubts and their simple wonder. And thus the paradox comes full circle.

Yet as Mallock admitted: "It is given to no one man to understand his epoch completely, and there are doubtless forces at work in the world that have eluded Mr. Tennyson." Even he had limitations. The other poets added their color to the whole picture and the other great names cannot be utterly neglected if we are to know the Victorian age as in itself it really was.

When Paul Elmer More wrote on Tennyson apropos of the Eversley Edition in 1908 he centered his whole essay on the proposition "Tennyson is the Victorian age," and he made out the best case that can be made for that view. He saw "something typical of the heart of England" in Tennyson's childhood; "the surroundings of his early manhood" at the University "were equally characteristic"; later in life Tennyson "maintained in our modern prosaic society the conscious office of bard"—"turning its hard affairs and shrewd debates into the glamour of music before flattered eyes and ears"; and he gave expression to that great Victorian compromise of reconciling beauty and reality through prettiness and reconciling the new science and the ancient faith through acceptance of the one and a clinging to the other. Tennyson was on familiar terms with the great men of his day, discussed eagerly with them the great questions of the day, and when he spoke to the people he proclaimed "what may be called the official philosophy" of the day. Even in many unexpected ways he reflects his age—as in his cherishing of "that high comradeship of youth [Arthur Hallam] and those generous ideals" of his college years; and in having King Arthur "deplore the search for the Grail as a wild aberration." All this is true; and more of the same sort can be urged. But is it enough? It proves that Tennyson was a Victorian, not that he was "the Victorian age." Paul Elmer More a little weakened his position by asking if "the stoic resolve and self-determination of Matthew Arnold . . . have not really expressed the higher meaning of that age—though not the highest meaning of all—better than any official and comfortable compromise"; because, whether his characterization of Arnold is quite the best, he admits that the Victorians were not all compromisers and that the "age" was not all after one pattern. But More, representing conservative opinion in 1908 and acknowledging that Tennyson's glory was then "passing into a kind of obscuration," really used the Laureate's Victorianism apologetically and defensively to condemn "this weaker side of an admired writer who has so much noble work to his credit." And perhaps, if understood aright, this is the last word on the whole subject. Tennyson's extraordinary popularity during his last years (always remembering the dissenting voices) and the veritable *triumph* of his death can only mean that he represented a very large constituency and that his poetic voice declared their simple emotions and their confused understanding; and since popular taste is commonly bad Tennyson prejudiced his case with posterity to the extent that he and his works echoed it. But it is an unsound exaggeration either as history or as criticism to assert that Tennyson stood for the whole age—he merely partook of it—or that his artistic weaknesses were chargeable to his fellow citizens.

CHAPTER ELEVEN

Tennyson Living

IN ONE of his earlier essays Yeats pronounced a judgment on Tennyson which is illuminating and points a direction.

The poetry which found its expression in the poetry of writers like Browning and Tennyson, and even of writers, who are seldom classed with them, like Swinburne, and like Shelley in his earlier years, pushed its limits as far as possible, and tried to absorb into itself the science and politics, the philosophy and morality of its time; but a new poetry, which is always contracting its limits, has grown up under the shadow of the old. Rossetti began it, . . .[1]

Rossetti did not exactly begin it, for it was already in Tennyson (but had in some degree been driven out of him by the reviewers) and of course had existed long before Tennyson; but Rossetti was a distinguished exemplar in the nineteenth century and might well seem, from the point of view of Yeats and the æsthetic school, to be a new beginning. It was this in Rossetti which justified Mr. Gordon Bottomley in calling Rossetti (with all his limitations) "the most profoundly and essentially artistic creative force there has ever been in England." Rossetti had almost nothing to say, in verse, about the active world around him—in fact, he spoke privately with a certain disrespect of the "momentary momentousness" of quotidian affairs—its science or politics, its philosophy or morality. He was concerned only with art. It seems to many a very confined interest, narrow and even unnatural. He had no message for his fellowmen. He did not really belong to them. Tennyson, however, was so much a part of his time that when his time passed he was in danger of becoming a document, a monument of taste (as Pater would say) rather than a poet; and it is now therefore necessary to ask, not whether his contemporary interests were detrimental to his poetry, nor whether he has left any poetry which is independent of the tastes and concerns of his age, but just what part of his work deserves to survive for its own sake as poetry. On some points there has never been serious doubt or question: his lyrical excellence and his metrical virtuosity. His gifts were those of an artist, an artistic workman in small patterns. For the rest, there will probably always be doubt and debate, and on these questions each of us must form his own conclusions.

There are still persons who, for example, are moved to indignation when they hear Tennyson spoken of as less than a great thinker and intellectual leader. An article in the London *Times Literary Supplement* in October 1942, on the occasion of the fiftieth anniversary of his death, praised him for his satire, his nationalism, his mystic imperialism, and hinted disparagement of "the almost sugary lyricism" of "such occasional pieces" as 'The Lady of Shalott,' the songs in 'The Princess,' and even 'The Lotos-Eaters' (which the author misspelled). But this will pass. It is part of the latter Victorian tradition in which the Victorians praised and justified themselves, with its surviving prejudices which inclined them, like Macaulay, to a "triumphant glorification of a current century upon being the century it is," and by which the Victorians were not content with a national poet who was not also a divine prophet. A few years ago Mr. Harold Nicolson was severely reproved for calling Tennyson's mind commonplace.

It was occasionally said during Tennyson's lifetime that he lacked passion, but this meant only that he was deficient in the representation of the physical emotions. The charge could be pressed, however; for he is often deficient in that intensity of feeling the want of which cannot be compensated for by any amount of technical skill. And sometimes, even when he did feel deeply, as in parts of 'In Memoriam,' he was unable to distinguish between the emotions which we experience in daily life and the emotions which are translatable as art. It is never enough that a poet should be *moved* (or that he should *think*) or that he should have mastered the literary technique; it is necessary that he should amalgamate these two kinds of emotion, the real and the artistic, or in other words, that by possessing the one and knowing the other, the tech-

273

nique of translation, he should perform his miracle. But without first experiencing the emotion, either directly or by intuition, he cannot hope to achieve the representation of it in poetry. He produces a picture, a simulacrum, not a living thing. So it was with Tennyson. So 'Œnone' is a decorative piece of very fine writing, lyrically poetic, but not an emotional study; and this is not because of Tennyson's immaturity, for 'The Death of Œnone,' one of his last poems, is no more real. So Arthur and Guinevere are lay figures of a rather crude story (what in prose fiction are called types) overlaid with allegorical attributes, and only at rare moments coming to life. So "Even in *Maud,* where he sets out to present emotions which overpass the limits set by self-respect, he is more often creating songs than studying emotions."[2] That is, he was writing the "best poetry of which he was capable," but not transferring life into art, for the life was absent. In the real world *ex nihilo nihil fit* is true, in art the opposite is true—by the power of 'genius,' a genius which Tennyson often lacked. His own experience, actual and imaginative, was limited in scope: even for the numerous vignettes of simple life, so highly regarded by his contemporaries, the domestic idylls, he had enough technique to produce the illusion of reality, but not the passion which gives life. He was a master of what Yeats called "passionless sentiment," a kind of ready substitute, a circumstantial poetry—which pleased his middle-class readers because they recognized the circumstances—filled with things, but not with the spirit, filled with shapes, but not with great and deep dreams.

This circumsantial accuracy—a fine merit when it is not everything—has been imputed to Tennyson as one of his great qualities. He himself was proud of his careful use of botanical, historical, and scientific detail. He was near-sighted, and he corrected this handicap by the minute observation of little things; and he has been overpraised for it. For of course no one ever claimed that accuracy of this kind, or realism, is a poetic quality. It may be an asset or not. For those who enjoy it as a recognitive effect it is admissible, as it was for Mr. Holbrook with the black ash buds in March. Even for Tennyson himself it sometimes lost its savor, as with the "gummy chestnut buds" of 'The Miller's Daughter,' which he revised away at the sacrifice of a good line.

In fact a great deal of Tennyson's description of nature is external and pictorial, uninformed by the emotional meaning which raises description above the merely decorative; just as a great deal of his 'music' is music only, without the depth which distinguishes a melody from a mere tune. Such admired lines as

> *The mellow ouzel fluted in the elm*

> *The moan of doves in immemorial elms,*
> *And murmuring of innumerable bees—*

and there are many such, cherished by earlier readers—are mellifluous rather than musical; they suggest that art-for-art's-sake which Tennyson severely condemned (with the usual misapprehension).[3] Such mellifluousness is not immoral or "filthy," but it is not a high form of art; and even when cultivated for its own sake and exhibited with self-satisfaction it is harmless and a-moral except as it conduces to pride and the confusion of real beauty with an easy substitute. So in the description of Mount Ida—

> *The swimming vapour slopes athwart the glen,*
> *Puts forth an arm, and creeps from pine to pine,*
> *And loiters, slowly drawn. On either hand*
> *The lawns and meadow-ledges midway down*
> *Hang rich in flowers, and far below them roars*
> *The long brook falling thro' the clov'n ravine*
> *In cataract after cataract to the sea;*

and in the detailed series of 'Mariana'—

> *All day within the dreamy house,*
>   *The doors upon their hinges creak'd;*
> *The blue fly sung in the pane; the mouse*
>   *Behind the mouldering wainscot shriek'd,*
> *Or from the crevice peer'd about.*
>   *Old faces glimmer'd thro' the doors,*
>   *Old footsteps trod the upper floors,*
>   *Old voices called her from without;*

and still more deliberately in 'The Lotos-Eaters'—

> *A land of streams! some, like a downward smoke,*
> *Slow-dropping veils of thinnest lawn, did go;*
> *And some thro' wavering lights and shadows broke,*

275

> *Rolling a slumbrous sheet of foam below.*
> *They saw the gleaming river seaward flow*
> *From the inner land: far off, three mountain-tops,*
> *Three silent pinnacles of aged snow,*
> *Stood sunset-flush'd: and, dew'd with showery drops,*
> *Up-clomb the shadowy pine above the woven copse;*

the effect is rather of accumulated images for their own sake than of artistic composition. Yet this is only a step from the true mastery which Tennyson often commands, in forms ranging from the stark simplicity of

> *There twice a day the Severn fills;*
> *The salt sea-water passes by,*
> *And hushes half the babbling Wye,*
> *And makes a silence in the hills*

to the studied richness of

> *All in the blue unclouded weather*
> *Thick-jewell'd shone the saddle-leather,*
> *The helmet and the helmet-feather*
> *Burn'd like one burning flame together,*
> *   As he rode down to Camelot;*
> *As often thro' the purple night,*
> *Below the starry clusters bright,*
> *Some bearded meteor, trailing light,*
> *   Moves over still Shalott*

and to the magnificence of

> *There rose a hill that none but man could climb,*
> *Scarr'd with a hundred wintry water-courses—*
> *Storm at the top, and when we gain'd it, storm*
> *Round us and death; for every moment glanced*
> *Her silver arms and gloom'd: so quick and thick*
> *The lightnings here and there to left and right*
> *Struck, till the old dry trunks about us, dead,*
> *Yea, rotten with a hundred years of death,*
> *Sprang into fire: and at the base we found*
> *On either hand, as far as eye could see,*
> *A great black swamp and of an evil smell,*
> *Part black, part whiten'd with the bones of men,*
> *Not to be crost, save that some ancient king*

Had built a way, where, link'd with many a bridge,
A thousand piers ran into the great Sea.
And Galahad fled along them bridge by bridge,
And every bridge as quickly as he crost
Sprang into fire and vanish'd,

and so on for thirty lines more.

What Tennyson always needed was inspiration, that which could breathe upon his talent and transform it to genius. To a good subject, which stirred him and made him poetically alive, he could nearly always rise, but he was not readily stirred and good subjects did not spring up in his path. It is significant that he was afraid of the Holy Grail as a subject and put off the treatment of it, yet when it 'came' it mastered him and he composed the Idyll rapidly. The Idyll itself is but a qualified success, because the patterns were already determined and his mind unequal to the spiritual values of the subject, but his imagination was stirred. To say that Tennyson was deficient in imagination may seem oversimple. His imagination was often rich and soaring, but it was limited in its sources. For he lived a narrow and commonplace life which yielded him few experiences upon which to build, and after success came, that is, for the last forty years of his career, a calm, almost placid life, troubled only by occasional illness and by the 'mosquitoes' which were his critics. And to compensate for this emotional idleness he had nothing of the restless curiosity of Browning's mind or the roving imagination of Swinburne. He had but small experience and no substitute for experience. His emotions had no imagination. It was therefore not only natural but unavoidable that he should accept what came and write as well as he could about it, that he should frankly seize the opportunity of plain domestic subjects and direct appeal to his recognized readers and give them the easy beauty which flattered them and almost satisfied him. Almost—for he was not altogether deceived by his popularity—he called it "a bastard fame, which sometimes goes with the more real thing, but is independent of and somewhat antagonistic to it."[4] But that he was partly deceived by its origin only testifies to his honesty, while it does less credit to his intelligence. He did not purposely write down to his popular audience. He was really sincere in believing that both Enoch and Arthur were heroic figures. He followed his own bent, his own taste, rather than popular demand. But this relieves him of the charge of insincerity only to signal his limitation: his tastes and those of his large audience were one. And so his volume is crowded with pieces, early and late, like 'Love and Duty,' which illustrate that opposition of powers which has made it difficult to judge his merit. Such pieces, if they were another's, would stand forth as distinguished and superior writing. They can still be read with pleasure and would secure their author a place among those who are not to be dismissed as pretenders to Parnassus; but *as his,* however, they mark him as less than a great poet since they reveal his essential failure when he fails. For such poems exhibit his great talent unsupported by intellectual or spiritual strength. 'Love and Duty' itself is the work of a young man, but in this sense Tennyson hardly grew older, and there are pages and pages like it written throughout his long life which show the same mastery of language and the same absence of that fundamental energy which distinguishes talent from genius. Always a poet is to be judged by his best and not to be condemned too severely for his worst; but normally his inferior work is manifestly inferior, aside from its temporary attractiveness, whereas most of Tennyson's inferior verse is of such excellent workmanship that the distinction has been missed. Rightly, of course, we have blamed his choice of subject, but those unhappy choices were a symptom of what was false within, his own inability to recognize the true material which should justify the careful application of his skill. Yet it is this very level of his average, this general superiority of his, which has baffled criticism, for it marks him a minor poet of the first rank in such a large proportion of his verse and therefore, unfortunately, makes his great moments seem less great—as lofty peaks do not reveal their elevation when they rise above an already high plateau.

These are still generalities, but their import ought to be clear enough and their acceptance ready enough without specific argued examples. They amount to this: that besides Tennyson's handicap of Victorian popular taste, with which he was often in personal harmony, he was deficient in artistic energy. There was not enough inner power and impulse and too little external impulse. Without a good 'subject' to raise him out of and above himself he went on his own smooth easy way—a highly competent workman, with all the needed tools and the necessary skill to apply them, without the best materials for his trade. This accounts for his extraordinary success, at which some have expressed surprise, with occasional poems. He visits Sirmione, and his well-trained hand writes without effort the impromptu on

Sweet Catullus's all-but-island, olive-silvery Sirmio!

because his mind is already well-stocked with Catullan impressions, and he is too shrewd to blur the picture of the "Tenderest of Roman poets" with a hint of the other side of Catullus's poetry. Gollancz gets out an edition of the *Pearl,* and Tennyson obliges with a quatrain—

We lost you—for how long a time—
True pearl of our poetic prime!
We found you, and you gleam re-set
In Britain's lyric coronet,

which is felicity itself, though one misses a perception of the poem's deeper significance than is conveyed by "lyric." The Mantuans request some verses on the nineteenth centenary of their poet's death, and he delivers a perfect tribute, not imitating the Vergilian hexameter, but in long nine-beat couplets (divided into fours and fives) which suggest "the stateliest measure ever moulded by the lips of man"; not a cento of Vergilian echoes, but "golden" phrases which Vergil himself would have admired and enjoyed—

All the charm of all the Muses
often flowering in a lonely word:

as in

star that gildest *yet this phantom shore.*

He hears of Jebb's "Olympian" at Bologna, and sends three perfect stanzas in a new and specially fitting meter. In 1883 he wrote to Mary Boyle (Hallam Tennyson's wife's aunt): "I verily believe that the better heart of me beats stronger at 74 than ever it did at 18," and, proving it, he sent her a graceful poem of seventeen quatrains, personal and reminiscent and tender—almost a love poem—without one false or sentimental note.

Take, read! and be the faults your Poet makes
Or many or few,
He rests content, if his young music wakes
A wish in you

To change our dark Queen-city, all her realm
Of sound and smoke,
For his clear heaven, and these few lanes of elm
And whispering oak.

At this level Tennyson excels,—an Horatian Tennyson. It is far above 'light verse' and it is really above the falsetto grand manner of his 'poetic' style, for it is genuine and well composed within the scope of his unstrained talent of mastery.[a]

At this level, the verse which he liked to call "belle comme la prose," Tennyson is almost always at his best and almost always safe from the danger from which he was otherwise seldom free, where style degenerates into manner. Having inherited from the romantics a language of conscious beauty, in which the imagination is deliberately wooed and won, a Poetic Style which was to them what Poetic Diction was to the eighteenth century, and having developed this to its ultimate, there remained for him only the self-imitation which became a mannerism. Having achieved at the age of twenty-five the magic of

On one side lay the ocean, and on one
Lay a great water, and the moon was full

and

Nine years she wrought it, sitting in the deeps
Upon the hidden bases of the hills,[b]

he was continually haunted by the temptation to bring everything

a For further examples take the two poems to FitzGerald preceding and following 'Tiresias' and parts (at least) of 'The Daisy.' The list might be extended to include 'To E.L., on his Travels in Greece,' 'To the Rev. F. A. Maurice,' 'To the Rev. W. H. Brookfield,' 'To General Hamley,' and of course parts of 'In Memoriam.'

b The latter of these passages was greatly admired by Tennyson himself. The first won the special suffrage of Meredith, among many others. "Mr.

Meredith," says Mrs. Meynell, "speaking to me of the high-water mark of English style in poetry and prose, cited those lines as topmost in poetry." It was Mrs. Meynell who pointed most clearly to this weakness of Tennyson's: he possessed, said she, "both a style and a manner: a masterly style, a magical style, a too dainty manner, nearly a trick; a noble landscape and in it figures something ready-made" (Alice Meynell, "Tennyson," *The Dublin Review*, CXLVI (January 1910), 62-71; pp. 64, 62).

to this artificial height, to load every rift with magic. In the 'Small Sweet Idyl,' smoke from the cottage chimneys becomes the "azure pillars of the hearth"; in 'Lucretius' the sleeping dog

> *plies*
> *His function of the woodland;*

in 'The Last Tournament' an outside stair and the white arms of Isolt are transformed into

> *And when she heard the feet of Tristram grind*
> *The spiring stone that scaled about her tower,*
> *Flush'd, started, met him at the doors, and there*
> *Belted his body with her white embrace;*

(why more than one door?); and his Enoch poem is a mine of such beauties. Or for one last example of this mannered overrichness, take the contrast between Elaine's letter in Malory and in Tennyson. It has been used before but it will serve again.

And when the letter was written word by word like as she devised then she prayed her father that she might be watched until she were dead. And while my body is hot let this letter be put in my right hand, and my hand bound fast with the letter until that I be cold; and let me be put in a fair bed with all the richest clothes that I have about me, and so let my bed and all my richest clothes be laid with me in a chariot unto the next place where Thames is; and let me be put within a barget, and but one man with me, such as ye trust to steer me thither, and that my barget be covered with black samite over and over; thus father I beseech you let it be done. So her father granted it her faithfully, all things should be done like as she had devised. Then her father and her brother made great dole, for when this was done anon she died. And so when she was dead the corpse and the bed all was led the next way unto Thames, and there a man, and the corpse, and all, were put into Thames; and so the man steered the barget unto Westminster, and there he rowed a great while to and fro or any espied it. (XVIII, xix)

> *Then he wrote*
> *The letter she devised; which being writ*
> *And folded, 'O sweet father, tender and true,*
> *Deny me not,' she said—'ye never yet*
> *Denied my fancies—this, however strange,*
> *My latest: lay the letter in my hand*
> *A little ere I die, and close the hand*

Upon it; I shall guard it even in death.
And when the heat has gone from out my heart,
Then take the little bed on which I died
For Lancelot's love, and deck it like the Queen's
For richness, and me also like the Queen
In all I have of rich, and lay me on it.
And let there be prepared a chariot-bier
To take me to the river, and a barge
Be ready on the river, clothed in black.
I go in state to court, to meet the Queen.
There surely I shall speak for mine own self,
And none of you can speak for me so well.
And therefore let our dumb old man alone
Go with me, he can steer and row, and he
Will guide me to that palace, to the doors.'
  She ceased: her father promised; whereupon
She grew so cheerful that they deem'd her death
Was rather in the fantasy than the blood.
But ten slow mornings past, and on the eleventh
Her father laid the letter in her hand,
And closed the hand upon it, and she died.
So that day there was dole in Astolat.
  But when the next sun brake from underground,
Then, those two brethren slowly with bent brows
Accompanying, the sad chariot-bier
Past like a shadow thro' the field, that shone
Full-summer, to that stream whereon the barge,
Pall'd all its length in blackest samite, lay.
There sat the lifelong creature of the house,
Loyal, the dumb old servitor, on deck,
Winking his eyes, and twisted all his face.
So those two brethren from the chariot took
And on the black decks laid her in her bed,
Set in her hand a lily, o'er her hung
The silken case with braided blazonings,
And kiss'd her quiet brows, and saying to her,
'Sister, farewell for ever,' and again,
'Farewell, sweet sister,' parted all in tears.
Then rose the dumb old servitor, and the dead,
Oar'd by the dumb, went upward with the flood—
In her right hand the lily, in her left

The letter—all her bright hair streaming down—
And all the coverlid was cloth of gold
Drawn to her waist, and she herself in white
All but her face, and that clear-featured face
Was lovely, for she did not seem as dead,
But fast asleep, and lay as tho' she smiled.

Malory is at the same time simple and suggestive; he leaves the imagination to play freely over each detail. The last clause is a perfect example of those realistic touches by which Malory renders his most fanciful incidents plausible. Tennyson, on the other hand, adds unnecessary *beauty;* he underlines; he appeals to our emotions and lets us see that he is doing so; he allows us only a passive enjoyment of the picture, without dramatically sharing the whole scene with Elaine and her father and brothers—and the unwitting knights and ladies of Westminster.

In his later years Tennyson often sought to overcome this excess of zeal, in which the narrative moves like a stately procession through clouds of its own poetic dust, by a stronger and more dramatic style, as at the end of 'Balin and Balan' or the inserted passages of the Merlin Idyll. The intention is clear, but the effect both powerful and palpable. The *poetry* seems like a garment to put on or take off wherewith plain mundane things are made beautiful. But when he can fuse the inherent feeling of a situation with his applied beauty Tennyson is at his best.

The sudden trumpet sounded as in a dream
To ears but half-awaked, then one low roll
Of Autumn thunder, and the jousts began;
And ever the wind blew, and yellowing leaf
And gloom and gleam, and shower and shorn plume
Went down it. Sighing weariedly, as one
Who sits and gazes on a faded fire,
When all the goodlier guests are past away,
Sat their great umpire looking o'er the lists.
He saw the laws that ruled the tournament
Broken, but spake not; once, a knight cast down
Before his throne of arbitration cursed
The dead babe and the follies of the King;
And once the laces of a helmet crack'd,
And show'd him, like a vermin in its hole,

> *Modred, a narrow face: anon he heard*
> *The voice that billow'd round the barriers roar*
> *An ocean-sounding welcome to one knight,*
> *But newly-enter'd, taller than the rest,*
> *And armor'd all in forest green, whereon*
> *There tript a hundred tiny silver deer,*
> *And wearing but a holly-spray for crest,*
> *With ever-scattering berries, and on shield*
> *A spear, a harp, a bugle—Tristram—late*
> *From over-seas in Brittany return'd,*
> *And marriage with a princess of that realm,*
> *Isolt the White— . . .*

More perilously poised is the description of Arthur's dream in 'The Passing'—

> *Then, ere that last weird battle in the west,*
> *There came on Arthur sleeping, Gawain kill'd*
> *In Lancelot's war, the ghost of Gawain blown*
> *Along a wandering wind, and past his ear*
> *Went shrilling: 'Hollow, hollow all delight!*
> *Hail King! to-morrow thou shalt pass away.*
> *Farewell! there is an isle of rest for thee.*
> *And I am blown along a wandering wind,*
> *And hollow, hollow, hollow all delight!'*
> *And fainter onward, like wild birds that change*
> *Their season in the night and wail their way*
> *From cloud to cloud, down the long wind the dream*
> *Shrill'd; but in going mingled with dim cries*
> *Far in the moonlit haze among the hills,*
> *As of some lonely city sack'd by night,*
> *When all is lost, and wife and child with wail*
> *Pass to new lords; . . .*

and so on, till—

> *Then rose the King and moved his host by night,*
> *And ever push'd Sir Modred, league by league,*
> *Back to the sunset bound of Lyonesse—*
> *A land of old upheaven from the abyss*
> *By fire, to sink into the abyss again;*
> *Where fragments of forgotten peoples dwelt,*
> *And the long mountains ended in a coast*

> *Of ever-shifting sand, and far away*
> *The phantom circle of a moaning sea.*

Here, of course, he is—more than thirty years later—preparing for
and measuring himself by "the old *Morte*." The success demands
our wonder: at the thing done and at the man for having done it.
Yet the very ambivalence is damaging, for while we admire the
magician we are inclined to resent his ability to stir our admiration.

It is partly for this reason that all have agreed that Tennyson is
greatest by *moments*. "His genius lay in miniature," said Francis
Thompson; in miniature we expect the concentration without
being distracted by the artifice. Or, enlarging the image, his was
"a genius for experiencing, with astonishing sensibility," says Mr.
Lascelles Abercrombie, "and for rendering, with equally astonish-
ing nicety, that part of life which exists in moments."[5] Always pro-
vided, to be sure, that the moments are not too long. So his similes
are justly praised—though Tennyson himself thought that some of
them were not appreciated during his lifetime. They abound in his
work, from—

> *kisses, where the heart on one wild leap*
> *Hung tranced from all pulsation, as above*
> *The heavens between their fairy fleeces pale*
> *Sow'd all their mystic gulfs with fleeting stars;*
> *Or while the balmy glooming, crescent-lit,*
> *Spread the light haze along the river shores,*
> *And in the hollows,*

in 'The Gardener's Daughter,' to that of the "wild wave in the wide
North Sea" in 'Lancelot and Elaine' and that of the "slow-arching
wave" in 'The Last Tournament,' and that, with a slight difference,
in 'Demeter and Persephone'—

> *A sudden nightingale*
> *Saw thee, and flash'd into a frolic of song*
> *And welcome; and a gleam as of the moon,*
> *When first she peers along the tremulous deep,*
> *Fled wavering o'er thy face, and chased away*
> *That shadow of a likeness to the king*
> *Of shadows, thy dark mate.*

So also the familiar cameos scattered everywhere, the essential
Tennysonian magic, even in his lesser poems; for example—

A moonless night with storm—one lightning-fork
Flash'd out the lake; and tho' I loitered there
The full day after, yet in retrospect
That less than momentary thunder-sketch
Of lake and mountain conquers all the day,[6]

and

For knowledge is the swallow on the lake
That sees and stirs the surface-shadow there
But never yet has dipt into the abysm,

and

The first grey streak of earliest summer-dawn,
The last long stripe of waning crimson gloom,
As if the late and early were but one,

and

And then I crept along the gloom and saw
They had hewn the drawbridge down into the river.
It roll'd as black as death; and that same tide
Which, coming with our coming, seem'd to smile
And sparkle like our fortune, as thou saidest,
Ran sunless down, and moan'd against the piers.

and lastly,

Framing the mighty landscape to the west,
A purple range of mountain-cones, between
Whose interspaces gush'd in blinding bursts
The incorporate blaze of sun and sea.[7]

But there is no need to gather a bouquet of purple flowers; nor of single lines, such as

settled in her eyes
The green malignant light of coming storm

and

Not like the piebald miscellany, man

and

Tho' we, thin minds, who creep from thought to thought.[8]

There is one characteristic, however, of the Tennysonian magic which, besides its high visibility, its lacking the element of surprise, makes for inferiority. Ruskin put his finger on it in a suppressed passage of *Modern Painters*: "Tennyson's keen enjoyment of visible beauty belongs to him entirely as a poet of the second or emotional, not the first or creative class, and if he could conceive more he would describe less."[9] Arnold made a similar observation in a letter to Clough;[10] and a French critic who remarked: "Il manquait de vitalité intérieure"; and Dr. John Brown in a letter to Henry Taylor, that Tennyson was "more of a liqueur than of a wine"; and William Howitt, who asked: "You may hear his voice, but where is the man?" One is seldom aware in reading Tennyson of any depths of feeling or flashes of insight for which language has but a broken voice, of any high intense desire of the spirit towards which expression can only reach out, of any latent energies demanding release. One feels—such was his mastery—that for whatever he had in him he found the right words and the right tune. His grasp exceeded his reach. One hesitates to say that this uniform adequacy was a careful disguise, yet one hesitates to believe that this transcendent execution could possibly cover hidden depths or unscaled aspirations, and one is therefore forced to admit that unless he was greater than all other poets hitherto there would have to be an unsolved element, a residual force which resists all power of expression, that expressive force (which we sometimes call imagination) which moves us precisely because it declares the inexpressible, the unrealizable, because it testifies to the whole of which only a part can be disclosed, which

> *Spares but the cloudy border of his base*
> *To the foil'd searching of mortality.*

The truth is, that Tennyson wanted the power (in Donne's noble phrase) to contract the immensities and at the same time awaken in us recognitions which relate the immensities to our own little experience. Art performs two miracles, that of disclosing the beauty of our waking world and that of sweeping this too too solid flesh over the invisible boundary to the world of dreams, of the supernatural, of the divine. Only the former was Tennyson's gift. His was the magic of the magician, not that of the seer. "The most

peculiar and characteristic mark of genius," said Coventry Pat-
more, perhaps in unconscious self-defence, "is insight into subjects
which are dark to ordinary vision and for which ordinary language
has no adequate expression." What dark depths of the spirit or of
experience has Tennyson illumined for us?

In extenuation it must be urged that he did the best he could,
that he polished and perfected his given material, though it was
silver not gold; and also that through no fault of his own he was
touched by the idolatrous finger of a time which worshipped beauty
as a form of concrete goodness, of a generation who "troubled the
energy and simplicity of their imaginative passions by asking
whether they were for the helping or for the hindrance of the
world, instead of believing that all beautiful things have 'lain burn-
ingly on the Divine hand.' "[11] Tennyson and his contemporaries
pursued Truth like an army with banners flying, as though un-
aware that she cannot be captured in open battle. He was delib-
erately ethical and occasionally even hortatory. He had some of the
inclination and enjoyed some of the experiences of the true mystic,
but he was preoccupied with scientific and philosophical truth and
not content with mystic revelation.[c] Therefore the illuminative

[c] Tennyson's mysticism is a small mat-
ter, worth clearing up, perhaps, in a
footnote. His early experience of the
mystical trance, recorded in 'The Mystic'
(never reprinted from the 1830 volume)
has already been mentioned. And such
experiences continued throughout his
life. It was his custom to shut himself
in his room, frequently after dinner, for
meditation and unwritten composition,
and "when he came out from his room
on such occasions," says Knowles, "he
would often have a sort of dazed and
far-off dreamy look about him, . . . If
interrupted during his hours of seclu-
sion . . . his look of 'sensitiveness' was
surprising. He seemed ready to quiver
at the faintest breath, or sound, or move-
ment, as though suddenly waked up out
of a dream" (Nineteenth Century, xxxiii
(January 1893), 168). The poet himself
told Knowles: "Sometimes as I sit here
alone in this great room I get carried
away out of sense and body, and rapt
into mere existence, till the accidental
touch or movement of one of my own
fingers is like a great shock and blow
and brings the body back with a terrible

start" (ibid., p. 169). See also Memoir i,
320. The experience is described, briefly,
in 'Sir Galahad' and at the end of 'The
Holy Grail' and is hinted at elsewhere.
(The weird seizures in 'The Princess' are
not mystical.) Tennyson's most striking
use of the experience is in 'In Memoriam'
xcv (see Appendix), where he seemed
afraid of it. His general distrust of it is
implicit in the whole conception and
treatment of the Grail matter. In fact,
though he enjoyed the trance he brought
from it only a vaguely exhilarating sense
of touching the other world—no genuine
ecstasy, no revelation from a communion
with the Divine. He was therefore not a
true mystic, not even a novice, but at
best an amateur or a dilettante.—The
relation of the mystic's trance to the
trance state of poetic composition is a
problem not yet sufficiently explored.
    A special article, quite erratic, on
"Tennyson as a Mystic," by Reginald B.
Span, may be found in The Westminster
Review, clxxx (July 1913), 43-49. It is
not to be recommended. Mr. Span re-
gards "the well-known 'Lady of Shalott' "
as "replete with mysticism."

flashes by which poets 'reveal truth,' the swift phrases which dazzle with their light and penetrate the mysteries by

Their less than momentary thunder-sketch

are rare in his poetry. Therefore so much of his poetry is second-rate in spite of its felicities and its extraordinary skilfulness. Therefore so much of his magic is that of a magician—without depth or penetration, without power to touch the soul or move the spirit, in spite of his sincere and eager efforts. He was a teacher, yes; a seer, no.

Nevertheless, when all this is taken away there remains a large body of verse which is rewarding and pleasant reading and which will hold the attention of posterity for something more than historical interest. It is an irony that he staked his claim to immortality on the portraiture of an age which was not only deficient in moral grandeur and was afflicted with that strange disease of 'modern life,' but which was inimical to great poetry by reason of its concern with transitory values. He was absorbed in it. He liked its plush and cluttering bric-a-brac, its sentimentalism, its eagerness for improvement and culture. He was absorbed into it—its self-distrust, its peculiar blend of integrity and hypocrisy, of pride and conscious weakness. Its 'morality' interested him, its faults roused him to rhetorical outbreaks (though he was no satirist); and even when it moved beyond him—for he remained an Early Victorian to the end—he preserved the appearances of continued zeal, never grasping that the more he was for Victorian England the less he would inevitably be for all time.

When the object is to create beauty—rather than discuss a subject in verse or illustrate a moral—it becomes necessary for the poet to understand what elements of the complex living and visual world are congenial to his gifts. For it is obvious that neither we readers nor they the makers perceive the same beauty in the same things; since beauty does not exist until it is made. But the potential range is great, almost unlimited, and as one enchanter's wand differs from another in power, so the enchanter must know what it is whereof he can perform his miracle. The mere impulse or desire to 'make' is not enough, though with facility he may often deceive himself, and even his readers. But what each one needs is the true adjustment of desire and matter, together with the 'divine' gift which comes as mysteriously to him in the creation as to us in the enjoyment of it. The gift was undoubtedly Tennyson's, and nearly always the craftsman's skill. His failures, as they seem to us, are generally due to his misapprehension of what were *his* materials. There were times certainly when his intentions were impure, when he sought to make poetry out of subjects which came to him as ideas or incidents calling for expression but did not come to him as poetry. At such times he could only rely on his great practice in the forms, and perhaps trust that we should not see that the spirit was wanting. His greatest error, however, lay in not recognizing the distinction between the materials which he could mold with skill to the semblance of beauty and those which were his own because they were suited to his muse. The pathos of the May Queen, the heroism of Enoch Arden, the tragic weakness of Mary stirred something in his bosom, even kindled a flame, but they did not light the sacred fire, did not rouse an æsthetic passion. And he did not know the difference. (With Guinevere and the Holy Grail it was otherwise: they moved him deeply, but as we believe wrongly.) This was Tennyson's artistic failure.

What Tennyson needed—as he very well knew—was a good subject. After the first vernal impulses were exhausted, after he 'settled down,' and there came to be no emotional or other experiences in his private life to afford material for the muse, he was wholly dependent upon favorable or unfavorable fortune for his subjects; and being himself not an acute critic in such matters—admirable and fine as his taste often was in details—because he was unable to distinguish between poetic subjects and those which had other attractions, between those which were suited to his gifts and those which while proper to poetry were not for him, he often floundered in uncertainty and defeat. One of the most serious pitfalls was the popular (middle-class) subject. About these enough has already been said. They pursued him to the end. After he had exhausted the death of Arthur Hallam, and stretched it beyond its uses as elegy to its philosophic concomitants with which he was ill-fitted to cope, had in fact allowed it to become an omnium gatherum, he tried a melodramatic story of young love and incipient madness. The *plan* of 'Maud' was capital, and original, a monologue in various meters suited to the moods of the speaker, a series of scenes or speeches developed somewhat after the leap-and-linger method of popular ballads; but the story itself was commonplace and cheap; it gave him opportunity for purple passages as well as unfortunate flats, and with such he had to be content. 'Enoch Arden' and 'Aylmer's Field' betrayed him similarly. He might call Enoch "heroic," but only in the way of domestic tragedy. The Arthurian Idylls were like 'Maud' in that they allowed free play to his gifts of lyric adornment and fine writing but revealed his incapacity to plan and manage a large whole. 'Lucretius,' a splendid subject, failed him because he divided his interest between an effort to reproduce the pressure of the *De rerum natura* and the possibilities of a genuine pathologic study. For the group of late 'religious' poems he was insufficiently prepared both in intellectual grasp and in spiritual illumination. His temper was not fundamentally religious, nor had he the intellectual equipment for comprehending metaphysical problems.

In three notable instances however the later Tennyson found the right subject. 'The Northern Farmer' is apparently not in his 'line'; but it was congenial because it was native and came from his own soil. The poem is not one to satisfy æsthetes and is certainly not of the highest order. It is really a variety of domestic idyll, saved from the bane of its type by earthiness and humor. 'Rizpah' also is a variety of Tennyson's staple popular verse, and it is interesting to see how it transcends the typical product. (Swinburne's exaggerated praise is well known.) It has the melodramatic situation, the ready pathos, the tripping emphatic meter, and the familiar tricks of style—italics and dashes and dialect—which might have marked it for mediocrity. But it has also an energy suited to the macabre subject; and the background of eighteenth-century wildness and rough injustice shelters it from bathos. The third is a clear example of Tennyson's slow absorption and long gestation. He came upon the story of the *Revenge,* probably in Froude, who had written about it in the *Westminster* in 1852, and was attracted by it. He composed the first line long afterwards, hesitated for two years, and then finished his ballad rapidly.[12] His varied handling of the old measure is deftness itself, his ingathering of the vivid details from the accounts of Raleigh, Monson, and the English translation of

291

Linshoten, is sensitively skilful. His representation of English bravery and daring and pride is superb. If there had been only 'Rizpah' and 'The Revenge' in 1880, without the "Other Poems" that came with them; only the completed 'Tiresias' and the Catullus and Vergil poems in 1885; and only 'Crossing the Bar' in 1889 we should readily have overlooked 'The Cup' and 'The Promise of May,' and the last dozen years of his life would have been still memorable. We should have said that his mind was still clear and his hand steady; and we should have marvelled and also lamented that he had no more for us. But like Wordsworth he mistook the inclination to write for inspiration and we must both forgive (which is easy) and forget (which is more difficult).

The summing up is comparatively simple, though of course it is still temporary. It could almost be done by quotation, for as in the past Tennyson has been excessively praised so he has been needlessly censured, and for a balance one has only to choose and temper. The excesses, being now part of the dust of history, may be left where they lie; the judgments recorded in the preceding pages may be recalled rather than repeated; but a few observations remain.

Some of the best things to date were said about Tennyson apropos of the centenary of his most important volume and the semicentenary of his death. *The New Statesman and Nation* described him as an "Elisha draped in a velvet mantle" and speculated on what he might have been if he had gone south as he thought of doing in the thirties: he then "would have escaped the Laureateship and Jowett and Palgrave and Queen Victoria and Canon Rawnsley and, most important of all, Lady Tennyson."[13] This is clever as the nineteen-twenties understood cleverness, and means both that Tennyson was too deeply involved in Victorianism, especially in its characteristics which are least attractive to a later day, and that he left a name which even the sarcastic regret. But it is more important to recognize, not that Tennyson was a Victorian *pure et simple,* but that it was not his rôle, it was not in his character, to resent and repel, as others did, those Victorian traits which come under our disapproval. The most favorable aspect of the matter has been well expressed by Mr. Nicolson, and so for the present it may be left.

It is this, I think—this conviction that, although perhaps not very deeply rooted in eternity, Tennyson was very deeply rooted in his age—which in the end throws a real dignity, a feeling of something so inevitable as to be immune to transitory expressions of taste and bias, on the totality of his work and character.[14]

Mr. Nicolson, who had to his credit a volume on Tennyson (from which I have just quoted), a volume which is faintly apologetic and defensive, often eloquent, and frequently flavored, as he admits in an aside, with that other poisonous honey from France, the imaginative biography, and on the critical side suggestive and helpful and for its date very significant—Mr. Nicolson struck a deeper note for the semicentenary. Of Tennyson the man (who was to be sure of small interest except as he held the poet's pen) Mr. Nicolson said:

It is impossible to resist the impression that his fear of future exposure was due to morbid doubts regarding his own sincerity. . . . He knew instinctively that his genius was not attuned to the epic or the didactic, even as it was not attuned either to the optimism or the sentimentality of his age. . . . He enjoyed adulation, since it soothed his diffidence; . . . and yet there were times when he realized that his intellect was not sufficiently powerful to make him a teacher, . . . and that his faith was too uncertain to serve as a guide.[15]

A little earlier, Dr. Mackail summed up another side:

Much of his poetry is mannered and laboured; some is commonplace; not a little has been pronounced, by common consent, a failure. If we allow all this, it remains none the less true that in the lyric and the elegy he reaches supreme excellence; that he raised the standard of craftsmanship for English poetry; and that his mastery of phrase, both in melody and in delicate accuracy, is endlessly astonishing.[16]

And looking towards the final accounting, we may hear again some of the earlier critics. At the time of Tennyson's death the Quarterly reviewer, concentrating on the 'Idylls,' which then seemed more important than now, put it thus:

The Idylls lack strength and substance. Rich beyond comparison in details, they are weak in general impressiveness. They fail, in fact, where critics and lovers of Tennyson expect them to fail. . . . On smaller fields, in incidental touches, by vivid flashes, and through instantaneous strokes of illuminating criticism, he has more than once achieved a final rendering of elemental facts and primal truths concerning man and the universe.[17]

More briefly, Coventry Patmore wrote to a friend in July, 1893:

I know I may be wrong, but I cannot reckon T. with the truly great poets. He is, of course, immortal. No one ever wrote so well on his own line. But he did very little which seems to me to have been greatly conceived or passionately and deeply felt.[18]

So also in 1880 the *British Quarterly* reviewer concluded:

. . . wherever good work short of the very highest is prized; wherever men love the music of ordered words, the quiet loveliness of English landscape, the calmness, sometimes the commonplace, of our insular life; wherever they value a terse interpretation of the aspects of nature or scientific facts, a love for what is lovely, and a hopeful outlook on the future, will these works give delight.[19]

And Matthew Arnold, speaking more bluntly, in a letter to his sister, 17 December 1860:

The real truth is that Tennyson, with all his temperament and artistic skill, is deficient in intellectual power; and no modern poet can make very much of his business unless he is pre-eminently strong in this.

Finally, Emerson, having less to base an opinion on, but enough, said of the second volume of the 1842 *Poems:*

It has many merits, but the question might remain whether it has *the* merit. . . . It wants a little northwest wind, or a northeast storm; it is a lady's bower—garden spot; . . . And yet, tried by one of my tests, it was not found wholly wanting—I mean that it was liberating; it slipped or caused to slide a little 'this mortal coil.'[20]

Much remains, of course, and principally an appreciation of Tennyson's lyrical powers; but that is familiar ground—and enough for one time is enough. If the end was, unexpectedly or not, like the beginning, if the exit from the maze was close to the entrance, still the paths had to be traced again, even to find the exit. Tennyson, it has frequently been said, is coming back: but not the same Tennyson and not to the same place. "I shall go down, down," he once remarked to Barnes: "I am up now." And our *British Quarterly* reviewer began in 1880 where we begin in the 1940s: "Of the vast amount written on Mr. Tennyson's poetry but a small pro-

portion has been devoted to serious analytical criticism"; this is
our apology still.

"Criticism—or what is so termed—makes criticism necessary."
But this sarcasm merely declares the patient winnowing by means
of which posterity finds itself. An interim judgment, a transitional
sifting of previous errors, a gradual precipitation of crudities to
leave the fluid clearer—this is all that need be required of us. When
a poet has passed into the distance of recorded history and his back-
ground has settled into the vacuum of eternity, the temporary ele-
ments fall away and he remains a free-standing three-dimensional
figure. But the Victorians have not yet reached this distance. There
are too many among us who still remember the Queen, or at least
the stories about her. (A certain school of critics labor to recon-
struct the background and to project their poet against it. But this
is a vain thing, a contradiction of progress.) We are therefore con-
taminated still with their judgments, soiled with their dust; and
since it is partly also our dust we should brush it off tenderly lest its
removal reveal who-knows-what. The new Tennyson we bring to
light is surprisingly like the old Tennyson they knew, but divested
of their misplaced aura and their mistaken censures. He has di-
minished in magnitude and in grandeur, but his virtues are coming
into sharper focus. If he no longer stands among England's great
geniuses, he is certainly, ahead of Dryden and Pope, the greatest
talent in English poetry, with touches of genius which assure him a
more enduring laurel than Victoria's. The comparison may seem
infelicitous, for they wrote a different language and used particu-
larly a different poetic idiom. Dryden and Pope had keener minds
than Tennyson's: Tennyson had a feeling for beauty which they
lacked. All three share the gift of transcendent skill without great
depth or largeness of spirit. His admirers, and they are still numer-
ous, are not to be censured for praising him for reasons which do
not satisfy all of us, though their taste thereby comes to judgment;
nor a later day for disliking the large portion of his work which has
lost its savor. Looking at him now, not as a Victorian but as a poet,
we find him endowed with these qualities, deficient in those. We
find him disappointing as an intelligence: a man who strove dili-
gently to understand not mankind but the men of his day, to think
as they thought and tell what they were thinking; in philosophy a

dissatisfied rationalist, without faith or confidence in the irrational; in taste a middle-class Englishman, conventional and easily pleased with simple and obvious beauties; in temperament a latter-day romanticist carrying on the work of his predecessors with greater care for detail than was theirs, but without their strength and energy; in life raised to a false eminence by disastrous good-fortune—and by his diligence, his zeal for beauty as he knew it, his devotion to art as he understood art. Beyond all, we are puzzled and embarrassed to find that still, when we think of Tennyson, we see his limitations overshadowing his accomplishment. We admire, as profoundly as our elders did, his gift of language, his power of the swift and often brilliant phrase, his nearly perfect lyric style; we acknowledge his moments of insight; we feel his charm and wonder at his magic. Yet we seem unable to forget the "bad Tennyson," the drossy part. This is in some sense a judgment on him, because he chose to identify himself so closely with the peculiarly transient characteristics of his time, which we, and those who come after us, can comprehend only by means of the historical imagination and with which we can feel little sympathy. An unhappy irony. But it is also a judgment on us if we cannot—or until we can—dissociate his weakness from his strength and cherish the immortal part.

Appendix

Appendix

A NOTE ON 'ULYSSES'

Since 'Ulysses' is often regarded as one of Tennyson's best poems, it ought to justify careful analysis; and if (as was the case with the 'Morte d'Arthur') analysis reveals certain inherent flaws, there still remains the miracle, that by the power of incantation Tennyson had deceived us into believing it to be something more than it really is.

Besides the classical and the Dantesque elements 'Ulysses' contains, on the poet's own authority, a personal element: his personal feeling of "the need of going forward and braving the struggle of life" in the face of his private loss in the death of Arthur Hallam. How have these elements been fused? It would be a bold stroke, if successful, to make the aged Ulysses the mouthpiece of a young man's resolve to overcome despair, to say nothing of blending the Homeric, the mediæval, and the Victorian backgrounds.

The poem itself falls into three parts, clearly marked as paragraphs in the blank verse. The first (32 of the 70 lines) seems to be a soliloquy: Ulysses is speaking to himself, in part justifying himself for abandoning his wife and son and his countrymen, who have apparently degenerated during his absence. His hearth is "still," his land "barren crags," his wife "aged," and his people "a savage race." He has seen too much of life to be willing or able to adjust himself to them; he has outgrown his past. (There would be very little of Tennyson in this, save his leaving the rustic Arcadia of Somersby; and in 'In Memoriam' he shows real affection for his native heath and hearth.) Ulysses is, moreover, restless and eager for more experience: "I will drink Life to the lees." He has enjoyed and suffered greatly, both alone and with his friends. "Alone" is a puzzling word here. It hardly refers to the Homeric Ulysses. It might be an echo of Dante's "*sol* con un legno" misread or loosely remembered. It might reflect Tennyson's own solitary wanderings;

but these had hardly begun by 1834. Or it might suggest a somewhat Byronic romanticism; and this hint is strengthened as we follow the remainder of the soliloquy—Ulysses' pride, self-confidence, even boastfulness, his "hungry heart" for more "life" ("Life piled on life"), and his rather grandiose rhetorical language. It is almost as though he raises his voice in order to quiet his conscience. The personal and romantic notes are plain enough; the Byronic was probably not intended for our ears, perhaps not entirely clear in the poet's, but it is difficult to deny. It culminates in Ulysses' describing himself as "this grey spirit" yearning (with now a Faustian touch)

> To follow knowledge, like a sinking star,
> Beyond the utmost bound of human thought.

Here it is not more experience but more knowledge that Ulysses craves, knowledge tending towards the arcane and the unpermitted. The phrase "like a sinking star" is puzzling: does it modify "follow" or "knowledge"? Does it suggest something ominous and sinister: that knowledge betrays us to our death? or does it merely anticipate the purpose

> To sail beyond the sunset, and the baths
> Of all the western stars . . .?

What precisely is a *sinking* star? The characterization of Ulysses is thus Tennyson's own composite: there is no need to ask how many parts are Homer, Dante, Byron, or the youthful poet from Somersby, but only if it is interesting and consistent with what follows.

The second part is apparently addressed to a particular audience. One sees the accompanying gesture—

> This is my son, mine own Telemachus

But what audience? It cannot be the mariners, because when Ulysses speaks to them both he and they are aboard the vessel, and Telemachus remains on shore. We now turn back to wonder where Ulysses was during his preceding soliloquy. There is no easy answer. It may be that the poem consists of three quite separate dramatic fragments, the first a soliloquy *pure et simple*, the second a farewell speech to his countrymen, and the third a hortatory address to his fellow mariners. If this is so we should expect some indication in the text, or at least a plainer division in the printing, instead of consecutive paragraphs unspaced. Or it may be that throughout the poem Ulysses is standing on the deck of his vessel. Then *"this* still hearth . . . *these* barren crags" is for rhetorical vividness, and *"This* is my son" becomes something like an apostrophe, Ulysses still communing with himself but now explaining his disposition of home and country as before he explained his reasons for leaving them. Neither of these interpretations is quite satisfactory. Nor is the attitude of Ulysses in this part entirely clear. Taken by themselves the lines sound like an honest statement of the necessity for patient encouragement of the backward races, a sort of evolutionary humanitarianism, not really Homeric of course, and somewhat advanced from the Victorian point of view. But following as they do the soliloquy of Ulysses with his lofty tone and his eagerness to escape from an aged wife and

> *a savage race,*
> *That hoard, and sleep, and feed, and know not me,*

these lines hardly avoid the charge of inconsistency. He is diplomatic, at the very least, when he changes "savage race" to "rugged people." After his pride of participation ("Myself not least") in the civilized world of "councils, governments," his description of Telemachus as "Most blameless," devoted to "common duties," as "decent not to fail" in tenderness and in worship of "my household gods," has an air of condescension with a tinge of contempt. His words "the useful and the good" become almost a sarcasm. When he dismisses Telemachus with "He works his work, I mine," it is hard to miss the note of polite scorn. This would be unfortunate if Ulysses were merely soliloquizing still; if, as is possible, he is actually addressing his fellow Ithacans, he not only loses dignity, he reveals himself as πολύμητις, as wily, as πολυκερδής in the worst sense. So the question becomes one again of harmony or consistency. Has Tennyson carelessly queered the pitch in the interests of dramatic contrast? or has he tried to represent two conflicting elements in the character of Ulysses without quite fusing them? Has he prepared us for the real dignity and nobility of the next Ulysses, in the third paragraph?

> *There lies the port,*

says Ulysses now, and once we have discovered the meaning of "port" nearly all the rest is straightforward. Since his next words are: "the vessel puffs her sail," the mariners he is addressing must be on board: the "port" is probably, therefore, the harbor and town, a little distance away from the wharf. If the sails had not already begun to fill one might guess that both Ulysses and his men were somewhat inland, and his "Come, my friends . . . Push off" represents a further change of position. The former view seems more likely. The lights that twinkle from the rocks are the lights of the town set among its barren crags. There lies the port on one side, and on the other the dark glooming seas. When he says a little later "The long day wanes," he means *has* waned; when he says, before they have pushed off, "the deep Moans round with many voices," he is anticipating rather than describing what he hears. Thus at nearly all points the realism yields to the picturesque; the accuracy of descriptive detail is transcended by the romantic mood; and the spell is woven so securely that we rarely observe the contradictions. They are in a sense irrelevant; it seems almost indecent to take note of them. It is even bad taste to remark that neither Odysseus in Homeric times nor Ulisse in mediæval, would be likely to push off at nightfall, assuming a favorable wind then. We waive the improbability for the sake of the symbolism.

But is it still the same Ulysses speaking now, the same who a few lines back was restless and eager for fuller experience and for knowledge more than human, the same who left the blameless Telemachus to his work of subduing a savage race? Now he speaks of the "honour and toil" ahead, "Some work of noble note" to be achieved, even (with a slight anachronism, taken over perhaps from Dante) a new world to discover. The former impatience "How dull it is to pause") has left him and he speaks a higher language. He is even humble: we are no longer, he says, as vigorous as we were; our vessel may be lost in the ocean gulfs, but our hearts are still heroic and our will strong. We are "Made weak by time," he says truly, and, he adds, by fate: but certainly he is wrong there, for they are proving themselves untouched by the power of fate, they are able to challenge fate. Then he rises to a fine climax—

strong in will
To strive, to seek, to find, and not to yield.

This brings us back to the pride and confidence of our first Ulysses, but with a larger scope. The former had drunk delight of battle with his peers, the latter is one who strove with the gods themselves: and now he ventures to echo the very words of the fallen Archangel:

the unconquerable will . . .
And courage never to submit or yield.

(We were not supposed to catch this echo, or even to recognize the Byronic overtones. But there they both are.) It is here that we find Tennyson most clearly expressing "the need of going forward and braving the struggle of life." But it would be untrue to say that this need is implicit in the whole poem. One does not brave the struggle of life by craving fresh adventure and "new things" or by sailing beyond the sunset. One does not brave the struggle of life by abandoning one's wife or indulging one's desire of travel, by following knowledge like a sinking star, by resigning prudence, the useful and the good, the sphere of common duties, the offices of tenderness—to one's son. This is the philosophy of escape. We feel that Ulysses has somewhat deceived himself—or that Tennyson is confused about it. The magnificent language does not quite conceal the muddled thinking.

Nevertheless we bow before the miracle, the conjuring power of splendid imagery, wonderful phrases, lofty rhetoric. If the details are inconsistent, the point of view shifting, the reasoning specious, the whole a kind of brilliantly whited sepulchre, we yet yield to the potency of the charm and forgive the deception. We shall always call 'Ulysses' a fine poem, all purple, and go on quoting it. There is nowhere a better example of the triumph of rich color over bad drawing.

TWO NOTES ON 'IN MEMORIAM'

I

Section I of 'In Memoriam' is an admirable opening because it sets the tone and introduces the reader to one of the characteristic styles of the long poem. It raises questions and suggests answers.

I held it truth with him who sings
To one clear harp in divers tones,
That men may rise on stepping-stones
Of their dead selves to higher things.

The "him" is explained succinctly by the poet, in his Notes: "I alluded to Goethe's creed"; and in a letter to an inquirer he wrote, November 1891, "I believe I alluded to Goethe" (*Memoir* II, 391); or as Bradley puts it, "Tennyson in his later years believed he had alluded here to Goethe." But no one has identified the precise passage in Goethe; nor explained the sense of "one." There is no doubt that, as Tennyson said to Sidgwick, "Goethe is consummate in so *many different styles*," and therefore the "one clear harp" might of course be the harp of poesy; then the lines would seem to say that Goethe, or whoever, sang in poetry in divers tones that, etc.; i.e., rang the changes on the idea that etc.; or more simply and probably, that Goethe (whose poetry covered a wide range) held that, etc. "Stepping-stones" as a means of *rising* is not only rare (Bradley), but confusing. The "dead selves" is ambiguous. It might mean one's yesterdays, one's past experience during this life, or it might mean, especially in a poem devoted to personal immortality and the development of the race, one's improvement from incarnation to incarnation. To be sure, Tennyson is nowhere explicit about a series of incarnations, and usually he seems to assume (in harmony with orthodox Protestant Christian belief) that we attain sudden perfection in the first and only "landing-place" (XLVII, 15); but in the allegorical vision of CIII, where the familiar river-of-life image is elaborated, some gradual progress of the spirit after death might be intended. (Cf. "From orb to orb, from veil to veil" (xxx) and *Memoir* I, 321.) In the next stanza "the years" hints at the former meaning, and "time" at the latter. I suppose, however, the first and simple interpretation of "dead selves," phases of development within this life, is the right one; but the ambiguity is nonetheless suggestive.

But who shall so forecast the years
And find in loss a gain to match?
Or reach a hand thro' time to catch
The far-off interest of tears?

The image, "reach a hand thro' time" is very fine, but the imagination is baffled by a hand which shall catch the "interest" of tears: a mixed and strained metaphor. The passage from *Richard III* helps, but Tennyson's condensation is a kind of violence.

> *Let Love clasp Grief lest both be drown'd,*
> *Let darkness keep her raven gloss:*
> *Ah, sweeter to be drunk with loss,.*
> *To dance with death, to beat the ground,*
>
> *Than that the victor Hours should scorn*
> *The long result of Love, and boast,*
> *'Behold the man that loved and lost,*
> *But all he was is overworn.'*

The personifications of Love and Grief belong to quite a different style from that of the preceding lines, and one is left in doubt whether Love is to rescue Grief from drowning or *vice versa*. In the next line the reminiscence of Milton's famous mixed metaphor (*Comus* 251 f., noted by Bradley) is patent, but the contexts are very different. Milton first wrote "till she smil'd." Why does Tennyson not capitalize "darkness"? Does "to beat the ground" mean to hurl oneself in despair upon the ground, to beat one's head on the ground; or is it a Latinism merely repeating "To dance"?—a difficult choice. What are "the victor Hours"? Are they the same as

> *the far-famed Victor Hours*
> *That ride to death the griefs of men*

of the cancelled poem (originally cxxvii)? Are they the hours when death claims its victory over the body (with an echo of St. Paul), or more simply the passage of all-conquering time? (Bradley compares "the long result of time" in 'Locksley Hall,' but this is *time* in a different sense.) The last stanza seems, however, to mean that Time should say scornfully, Love has brought no result; and boastfully, the man who lost his loved one is exhausted, worn out. The last two stanzas would now mean: it is better to abandon oneself to grief than to suffer and have nothing to show for it. But this is certainly a meagre result for so many metaphors and divers tones, and the indirection verges on perversity. —The point I would make is that Tennyson has chosen to be deliberately cryptic and 'poetic' at all costs, and that, as in 'Ulysses' and the 'Morte d'Arthur,' he has deceived or charmed us into accepting a great deal of confused language as poetry.

XCV

As section I exhibits a strained style which is not natural to Tennyson outside of 'In Memoriam,' so section xcv exhibits, I believe, a weakness inherent in Tennyson's character and in his long elegy. For the purpose of this analysis it will not be necessary to quote the section entire, but I shall assume a general knowledge of the text. The scene is Somersby, the date some time between 1833 or 1834 and 1837. If the poem was written soon after the experience described it would be of relatively early date, though it stands well past midway of the whole elegy. The preceding sections contain pleasant memories of Somersby (LXXXIX), followed by a group of poems on communion with the dead. In xc the poet cries: "but come thou back to me." In xcI: "Come, beauteous in thine after form, And like a finer light in light." In xcII he deprecates "any vision" which may be only a delusion. In xcIII he says:

> But he, the Spirit himself, may come
> Where all the nerve of sense is numb;
> Spirit to Spirit, Ghost to Ghost—

or as one might say, a communion of two souls in a trance. In xcIV he tells us that the dead return only to those who are "at peace with all." Finally comes xcv, as a climax of this group; for the following sections are on a new theme. The Tennyson family ("we") are represented as gathered on the grass ("the herb was dry") at the end of a summer day—seemingly for a late tea; "the tapers burn,"

> And on the board the fluttering urn.

("Fluttering" is an odd epithet; since the tapers burn "unwavering" it must describe the audible bubbling of the kettle.) The distant brook can be clearly heard; and Tennyson's note—"It was a marvellously clear night, and I asked my brother Charles . . ."— testifies to the factual reality of the scene. The moths are described as "filmy shapes." The family sing old songs lustily; and the cows on neighboring knolls are "couch'd at ease." It is thus, for the first four of the sixteen quatrains a simple domestic idyll with poetical or fancy language. Then the family retire,

And in the house light after light
Went out, and I was all alone.

And he reads Arthur Hallam's letters ("those fall'n leaves which kept their green," he says prettily). The contents of these letters are given in two quatrains.

So word by word, and line by line,
  The dead man touch'd me from the past,
  And all at once it seem'd at last
His living soul was flash'd on mine,

And mine in his was wound, . . .

So read the early editions, until 1870-1880. This "troubled" Tennyson, however, "as perhaps giving a wrong impression," and he altered the first "His" to "The" and the second to "this," and glossed "The living soul" as "The Deity, maybe." The *maybe* is nothing less than shocking. If the poet did not know, who could be expected to know? This was a matter on which he was assuredly qualified to speak and on which we have a right to expect some sort of clear statement: either it *was* the Deity—for the purposes of the poem, of course—or it was not. It will not do to say that the poet's memory may have been at fault when he made his Note: this might be true as a biographical fact, but it is irrelevant to the poem. In looking back and trying to recall his impression of the moment described in the verses, Tennyson may have become confused as to the details of the Somersby incident; but there should be no doubt in his mind about such a crucial point in his poem. In the poem he has led up to a climax of desire for communion with Arthur Hallam "Spirit to Spirit"; the circumstances are all favorable, and in his trance state induced by the setting and by the words of Hallam's letters, the vision is vouchsafed. In the poem no other interpretation is possible: "His living soul" must be Hallam's soul. The word "seem'd" is of course ambiguous (as Bradley implies), but in the context it ought to mean not that there was an uncertainty but rather that the experience was by its nature a *seeming* in contrast to phenomenal actuality.[a] What was it then

[a] Bradley quotes Knowles' record rather than the Eversley edition Notes: that it was the soul "perchance of the Deity. . . . My conscience was troubled by 'His' "; and asks, "What was it that troubled his conscience?" For answer he relies on the other meaning of "seem'd" and supposes that Tennyson was in doubt "whether the soul that seemed to be flashed on his, and seemed to be Hallam's, *was* Hallam's";—a needless scruple, he adds, because Tennyson

that troubled Tennyson? His own trances are well attested. He was
not a mystic in the historical or technical sense, but on his own
testimony he enjoyed experiences similar to those of the religious
mystics. There is no reason therefore to question the genuineness
of the experience described in the poem. The truth must be that
he was confused himself about the *meaning* of this experience. As
he represents it—

> *And mine in his [this] was wound, and whirl'd*
> *About empyreal heights of thought,*
> *And came on that which is, and caught*
> *The deep pulsations of the world,*
>
> *Æonian music measuring out*
> *The steps of Time—the shocks of Chance—*
> *The blows of Death.*

That is, Hallam's soul was flashed on his soul and wound into his,
and then (if the language of the poem can be pressed) their united
souls were whirled into the empyrean, and what began as the com-
munion of his spirit with Hallam's became somehow a sort of
Beatific Vision. While it is dangerous, and presumptuous, to say
of any poet that he did not know what he was writing about, here
we seem to have a clear example, substantiated by the poet's own
admission: "The Deity, maybe." This is the more significant, not
because Tennyson may not naturally have been confused about his
own trance, but because he was induced to pervert his poem,
which demanded communion with Hallam and with Hallam alone.
For artistic purposes the findings of 'In Memoriam' purport to be
based on the poet's personal experiences; but both here and in
many other passages Tennyson has been unable to distinguish be-
tween this personal basis and the poetic fiction, between the priv-
ate record of his own emotions and the poem it was his chosen task
to create out of those emotions. This is then a plain and damaging
confession of the fault inherent in the whole elegy, of his inability
to grasp the simple artistic principle that the sole object of the poet
is to make a poem; otherwise he becomes a chronicler or expositor
in verse. The molds are hard to mix.

He continues—

---

never said it was Hallam's, but only that
it seemed to be. This interpretation ap-   pears to me quite trivial and perverse.

At length my trance
Was cancelled, stricken thro' with doubt.

It was a trance, to be sure, but Tennyson need not have given it its prose name; we knew what it was without the label. "The trance came to an end," Tennyson explains, "in a moment of critical doubt." This is curious, but it implies that he was able to doubt the genuineness of his trance *while* he was experiencing it: in other words, he did not even at the moment accept it as genuine, did not surrender himself completely to it, but reserved some part of his mind for critical detachment. This, in turn, can only undermine our faith in the record itself; and after he has sacrificed the integrity of his poem for the sake of the record, very little is left. Again his critical sense failed him. Then he adds, still disconcerting us, "but the doubt was dispelled by the glory of the dawn of the 'boundless day.' " And it is simply not true; it cannot be true. In the poem he says that words are inadequate to spell out and memory to report what he had seen and been, and then (playing on the word *doubt:* "the doubtful dusk") he describes the coming of dawn in splendid language, but in that language there is no evidence that the doubt which broke his trance has been dispelled. Rather, a new effect is produced and the beauty of his description is substituted for the lost, "cancell'd, stricken" glory of his vision. Once more Tennyson betrays his confused notions of his own work.

NOTE TO 'MAUD'

'Maud' is sometimes singled out as Tennyson's principal offering at the Spasmodic shrine; certainly it was a bid for popularity and the Spasmodics were much read and admired in the forties and fifties. Gosse, in fact, believed that Sydney Dobell's *Balder* (1854) "may be said to be one parent of 'Maud' as the Crimean War was the other."[a] Both poems are 'dramas of the soul,' both are in mixed meters (though most of *Balder's* seven thousand lines are blank verse), both are quasi-dramatic (though *Balder* is equipped with scene divisions and stage directions); the heroes of both are "egoistic, self-contained, and sophistical" (so Dobell in his Prefatory

[a] "The Centenary of a Spasmodist" (repr. from the *Sunday Times*), in *Silhouettes*, London, 1895, p. 335.

Note to the second edition); and both were supposed by contemporary critics to be autobiographical. But Balder, the embodiment of "a doubtful mind," stands for egotistic excesses of poetic genius and traces his dubious ancestry (according to the author) to Goethe, Keats, Haydon, and David Scott; whereas the hero of 'Maud' is a young man unbalanced by domestic misfortunes springing from social evils and stands (if for anything in particular) for the egotistic excesses of romantic love in conflict with society. Balderism is a late species of Byronism; the hero of 'Maud' is merely a victim of contemporary conditions, not of grandiose cosmological dreams. 'Maud' was written for readers of the sensational novel, and looks forward as well as backward; *Balder* was written (apart from its "moral purpose and import") for readers of Byron, Bailey, and the translations of Goethe. What Gosse calls "the extraordinary and temporary influence which he [Dobell] exercised over Tennyson" was rather general than particular; and I owe Gosse a grudge for obliging me to peruse the forty-two vapid scenes of *Balder* for such a negative reward, but I am grateful for having found these remarkable lines:

Ah! ah! ah!
Ah! ah! ah! ah! ah! ah! ah! ah! ah! ah!

in Scene xxxviii.

It is a fact that Sydney Dobell was one of the admirers of 'Maud' and planned a reply to some of the early hostile reviews.

Bibliographical Note

Notes

Index

Bibliographical Note

The fullest bibliography of Tennyson's works is that by T. J. Wise, 2 vols., London, 1908 (pr. pr.); it must be corrected however by reference to John Carter and Graham Pollard, *An Enquiry into the Nature of Certain Nineteenth Century Pamphlets*, London, 1934. For books etc. about Tennyson, see the lists in the *Cambridge Bibliography of English Literature*, III, 253 ff. There were various Collected Editions from 1870 onwards, the most important now being the Eversley Edition, 9 vols., with separate title pages, 1907-1908, and *The Works*, 1 vol., Macmillan and Co., 1913. Both of these contain Notes and Annotations by Tennyson and his son. To them must be added *The Devil and the Lady*, London, 1930, and *Unpublished Early Poems*, London, 1932, both edited by Sir Charles Tennyson. The Cambridge Poets Edition (Boston 1898, ed. by W. J. Rolfe) is not complete but contains in an Appendix selections from *Poems by Two Brothers*, 'Timbuctoo,' poems from the 1830 and 1833 volumes not reprinted by Tennyson, and "Other Discarded and Uncollected Poems"; and its notes contain partial collations to illustrate Tennyson's revisions, and also a condensed bibliography. The Oxford Standard Authors edition (ed. T. Herbert Warren, 1910) contains a useful list of the contents of the volumes issued before 1868, together with the poems first published in periodicals and annuals, in chronological order; and its Appendix contains "Poems not Included in the Author's Final Edition" through 1868.

Notes

CHAPTER ONE

1. This account is probably from the pen of Watts-Dunton (then only Watts), with details supplied by Hallam, the dying Laureate's son.

2. *The Spectator*, 8 October 1892, under 'News of the Week.' The next paragraph began: "M. Renan, the Voltaire *sucré* of modern France died on Sunday."

3. *Blackwood's Edinburgh Magazine*, CLII (Nov. 1892), 748-766.

4. From internal evidence alone I surmise that the author was Joseph Jacobs.

5. Edith Rickert, "Tennyson a Generation After," in *The Book News Monthly*, XXVII (1909), 819-821.

6. Edwin Ridley, "The Genius of Tennyson: the Poet and the Man!" in *Westminster Review*, CLXXII (1909), 511-514.

7. *Blackwoods*, CLXII (1897), 264-270.

CHAPTER TWO

1. *Memoir* I, XII ff.; also in Eversley ed., VII, 370-374.

2. Charles Tennyson, "Tennyson Papers," *Cornhill Magazine*, CLIII (1936), 302. Some further details of the poet's family and early years will be found in: W. D. Paden, *Tennyson in Egypt*, Lawrence, Kansas, 1942, pp. 111 ff. For a fuller version of Tennyson's father's experience in Russia, see W. Gordon McCabe, "Personal Recollections of Alfred, Lord Tennyson," *The Century Illustrated Monthly Magazine*, LXIII (March 1902), 722-737; pp. 734-735.

3. Cf. W. D. Christie, "The Cambridge 'Apostles,'" *Macmillan's Magazine*, xi (1864), 18-25; Frances Mary [Mrs. Charles Hallam Elton] Brookfield, *The Cambridge Apostles*, New York, 1906; and of course Carlyle's *Life of Sterling*.

4. They were to be married in September 1832, but the two fathers could not agree on a marriage settlement; cf. *Letters to Frederick Tennyson*, ed. Hugh J. Schonfield, London, 1930, pp. 27-31.

5. *Memoir* I, 95-96.

6. Cf. Edgar F. Shannon, Jr., "Tennyson and the Reviews, 1830-1842," *P.M.L.A.*, LVIII (1943), 181-194.

7. "He said he did not wish to 'obtrude himself on the great man at Rydal'"—thus apologetically the *Memoir* I, 155 n.

8. And so on for two pages. Cf. *Memoir* I, 158 ff. and T. Wemyss

Reid, *The Life, Letters, and Friendships of Richard Monckton Milnes,* I, 179 ff.

9. Cf. FitzGerald again: "With all his shattered nerves and weary gloom, he seems to have some sort of strength and hardihood. His tenderness is genuine as well as his simplicity; and he has *no hostilities,* and' is never active, as against people. He only grumbles" (quoted by J. C. Walters, *Tennyson: Poet, Philosopher, Idealist,* London, 1893, p. 142).

10. In his diary then Carlyle described Tennyson thus: "A fine, large-featured, dim-eyed, bronze-coloured, shaggy headed man is Alfred; dusty, smoky, free and easy. Swims, outwardly and inwardly, with great composure in an inarticulate element of tranquil chaos and tobacco smoke; a most restful, brotherly, solid-hearted man" (D. A. Wilson, *Carlyle on Cromwell and Others,* London, 1925, p. 122). The well-known later description by Carlyle is in *The Correspondence of Thomas Carlyle and Ralph Waldo Emerson,* Boston, 1899, p. 67, under date of 5 August 1844.

11. Quoted in J. W. Mackail, *The Life of William Morris,* I, 46.

12. Besides what is in the *Memoir,* a few details may be found in Hugh J. Schonfield, *Letters to Frederick Tennyson,* London, 1930, pp. 47 ff. A little of the bitterness of this episode is reflected in 'Sea Dreams.'

13. Wilfrid Ward, *Aubrey de Vere, a Memoir,* London, 1904, pp. 71 ff., 87 ff.

14. Cf. the *Memoir* I, 244 f., and see also *The Life of Edward Bulwer* by his Grandson the Earl of Lytton, London, 1913, ii, 69 ff. That the instinct to fight back metrically did not atrophy is evidenced by the story of a certain lady who, though admiring Tennyson's genius, ventured to remonstrate on his accepting the peerage. Tennyson replied with 'My Wrath.' "The entreaties of his friends prevented him from despatching it; but he kept it handy in a drawer" and would read it whenever her name was mentioned. Cf. George W. E. Russell, *Portraits of the Seventies,* London [1916], p. 286.

15. *A New Spirit of the Age,* World's Classics ed., p. 260.

16. So Emerson learned from Carlyle, in 1848, that "Tennyson dined out every day for months; then Aubrey de Vere . . . came up and carried him off . . . So poor Tennyson, who had been in the worst way, but had not had force enough to choose where to go, and so sat still, was now disposed of" *(Journals of Ralph W. Emerson,* Boston, 1912, VII, 404). In other words, "Carlyle describes him as staying in London through a course of eight o'clock dinners every night for months until he is thoroughly fevered" *(ibid.,* p. 447). For Emerson's description of Tennyson in 1848, see the *Journals,* VII, 444. In May 1847 FitzGerald reported Tennyson "at his very dirty hotel in Leicester Square: filled with fleas and foreigners. He looks thin and ill: and no wonder, from

his habits" *(Some New Letters of Edward FitzGerald,* ed. F. R. Barton, London, 1923, p. 137).

17. Ward, p. 154. See also *Memoir* I, 282, but the letter there is undated.

18. On the relations of Tennyson and Moxon, see Harold G. Merriam, *Edward Moxon Publisher of Poets,* New York, 1939, pp. 39 ff., 169 ff.

19. Perhaps the following half-jocular remark may be accounted an exception. "Tennyson names Mrs. Gordon as the model of his *Princess,* and according to Tom Taylor and Kinglake, reported by Mrs. Ross, Tennyson once 'burst out at dinner:—"I never loved a dear gazelle, but some damned brute, that's you, Gordon, had married her first" ' " (D. A. Wilson, *Carlyle at His Zenith,* p. 321).

20. "Memories of Tennyson," *The London Mercury,* v (December 1921), 144-155; p. 147.

21. Quoted in J. C. Walters, *Tennyson,* p. 138.

22. *The Heart of Hawthorne's Journals,* ed. Newton Arvin, Boston, 1929, pp. 242-245.

23. Mrs. Tennyson wrote to Woolner, 20 March 1856, " 'Merlin' goes on grandly"; and by 15 April it was "safely written down" (Amy Woolner, *Thomas Woolner, R. A., Sculptor and Poet. His Life and Letters,* London, 1917, pp. 111, 112).

24. *Memoir* I, 432-436.

25. Walters, p. 142.

26. *The Works,* p. 923, says that 'The Higher Pantheism' was written for the Metaphysical Society in 1869.

27. Letter to Palgrave, 24 December 1868.

28. "If I were at liberty, which I am not, to print the names of the speakers 'Gareth' 'Linette' over the snip-snap of their talk, and so avoid the perpetual 'said' and its varieties, the work would be much easier" (Tennyson to Knowles, 5 April 1872; *Memoir* II, 113 n.).

29. *Enoch Arden. A Drama in Five Acts,* by Arthur Matthison, 1869; and *The Home Wreck. A Drama in Three Acts. Suggested by Tennyson's Poem of 'Enoch Arden,'* by J. Stirling Coyne (and his son, J. Denis Coyne), 1870.

30. Cf. the letter to Swinburne, dated August 1891, in the *Catalogue of the Ashley Library,* VII, 156.

CHAPTER THREE

1. Both edited by the poet's grandson, Sir Charles Tennyson, in 1930 and 1931 respectively. A fragment of another play, with a Spanish setting is printed in the *Memoir* I, 23 ff.

2. This is based on the text in *Unpublished Early Poems.* There may of course have been an intervening version of 'Armageddon' closer to 'Timbuctoo.' The *Memoir* (i, 46) says that "unwillingly he patched

up" the old poem. A. J. Church (in *The Laureate's Country*, London, 1891, p. 75) alleges the poet's testimony that he merely "furnished [the old poem] with a new beginning and a new end."

3. Six lines of this ("The clear galaxy . . . wan sapphire") were added in 1829.

4. *Memoir* I, 45 n.

5. Charles Wordsworth, *Annals of My Early Life, 1806-1846*, 2nd ed., London, 1891, p. 73.

6. *Memoir* I, 47 n.

7. They may be read conveniently in the Appendix of Rolfe's edition and in the Oxford Standard Authors edition. For others of the same date, see *Unpublished Early Poems*, Part II, and the *Memoir* I, 56-60.

8. Published in December 1832, but dated 1833; usually referred to as of 1832, the former year.

9. Collins, *Early Poems*, p. 70. See also Stopford Brooke, pp. 113 ff., for a comparison of the two versions. A truer impression of the differences between the 'Œnone' of 1833 and the 'Œnone' of the 1842 can be gained from an attentive perusal of each version entire.

10. It is suggested by Professor A. C. Howell, in *Studies in Philology*, XXXIII (1936),507-522, that the poem expresses in some sense Tennyson's dissatisfaction with Trinity College, Cambridge, and the dons who "profess to teach, And teach us nothing, feeding not the heart." This view is developed in considerable and plausible detail. For a summary of other interpretations see Howell, p. 508, n. 3.

11. Possibly Tennyson was misled by a bad gloss on *wappe*. Even the scholarly edition by W. E. Mead, in the Athenæum Press Series, renders it 'lap.'

12. On the possible relations between 'Morte d'Arthur' and Tennyson's early reading, see W. D. Paden, *Tennyson in Egypt*, Lawrence, Kansas, 1942, ch. vi. In Faber's *The Origin of Pagan Idolatry* . . . (1816), a then admired work, Tennyson may have read of Arthur as a mystic Great Father, of his death as representing union with the Great Mother, of his sword as a phallic symbol, and of other Helio-Arkite mysteries. These and other connections must remain a matter of speculation, however, and at most a case not proven, though Professor Paden makes out the best case he can. That somehow the death of Tennyson's father in 1831 and of Arthur Hallam in 1833 are blended in the poet's mind with Arthur's death and that the poem "affords an oblique avenue for the poet's repressed conflict" (p. 87) seems highly probable—and important for those who like to study poetry as psychological revelation.

13. Tennyson said of 'Ulysses' that it "was written soon after Arthur Hallam's death," which means soon after September 1833; and to Knowles he said: "It was more written with the feeling of his loss

upon me than many poems in 'In Memoriam.' " This is not very pre-
cise, but suggests 1834 or possibly 1835. The 'Morte d'Arthur' was at
least partly written in May 1835 (*Works,* p. 896) and the whole poem
(without the framework) was read to FitzGerald in 1835 (*Memoir* I,
194). Two letters of 1833 (late) mention "the 'Morte d'Arthur,' " appar-
ently meaning Malory's work, not Tennyson's poem (*Memoir* I, 129,
131). Since 'Ulysses' reflects a certain mastery of his grief, I am inclined
to interpret "soon" liberally and assume that the 'Morte' was written
first. But the evidence is quite inconclusive.

CHAPTER FOUR

1. *Quarterly Review* CLXXVI (1893), 19.

2. There seems to be nothing in the early history of the poem to
account for these differences. Sir Charles Tennyson, after examining
two extensive manuscripts and some lesser fragments, believes that the
first six Parts were worked out together, beginning "not later than
1839" (*Cornhill Magazine* (1936), 672 ff.). Thus it was not a question
of having begun in one spirit and changed midway of the composition.
At one stage the Parts had separate titles with introductions describing
the different narrators (some of which were apparently Cambridge
portraits). The Interlude is therefore a vestigial remnant. The modern
setting was an afterthought, but there is an early version of the Pro-
logue. The manuscripts show considerable revision, to say nothing of
the changes in the first five editions. Accordingly, if Tennyson did not
'please himself,' it was not through haste; for he worked on the poem
nearly eight years before publication and six after.

3. Thomas R. Lounsbury, *The Life and Times of Tennyson,* New
Haven, 1915, p. 562.

CHAPTER FIVE

1. The quotations in this section are from Tennyson himself, either
the poem or his Notes, unless otherwise indicated. Cf. A. Gatty, *A Key
to Tennyson's 'In Memoriam,'* 3rd ed., London, 1885; and E. R. Chap-
man, *A Companion to 'In Memoriam,'* London, 1888.

2. See the edition of J. Churton Collins, pp. 9-10 and the *Com-
mentary* of A. C. Bradley, pp. 12 ff., both relying largely on the
Memoir and varying somewhat in their conclusions.

3. "Some were written in Lincolnshire, some in London, Essex,
Gloucestershire, Wales, anywhere I happened to be" (*Memoir* I,
305).

4. The sections which celebrate Hallam directly are CX-CXIII; to a
lesser degree XXII, LXXIV, LXXV, LXXXII, LXXXVII; and to a still lesser de-
gree XLII, LXIV, LXXXIX.

5. Charles F. G. Masterman, *Tennyson as a Religious Teacher,*
1900, p. 84. By organizing and translating into the conventional langu-

age of the subject Tennyson's fragmentary and sometimes confusing observations on religious philosophy, Masterman has done the poet more than justice. "In the narrower sense," he admits, Tennyson "was not a religious poet; in the wider sense he was not a teacher of religion. . . . He was too uncertain of himself." Yet Tennyson has had somehow a "wide-spread and increasing influence as a religious teacher." Which belongs to the history of Victorian ideas: I "point and pass."

CHAPTER SIX

1. This is Aubrey de Vere's version, quoted in the *Memoir* I, 379. Tennyson, in his own notes (Eversley ed. IV, 278; *Works*, p. 942) says merely: "Sir John Simeon years after begged me to weave a story round this poem, and so *Maud* came into being." For the other version see H. D. Rawnsley, *Memories of the Tennysons*, p. 122. On the relation of 'Stanzas' to 'Maud' II, IV, see J. C. Thomson, *The Suppressed Poems of Alfred Lord Tennyson*, p. 90.

2. *Memoir* I, 396. In the notes to the Eversley ed., IV, 270 f., these sentences are quoted as Tennyson's; in the *Memoir* they might be taken as Hallam's. In a letter to Dr. Mann, Tennyson qualified his unfortunate phrase "a little *Hamlet*": "not that I am comparing poor little 'Maud' to the Prince, except as, what's the old quotation out of Virgil, *sic parvis componere, etc."* (*Memoir* I, 406).

3. For a claim (which seems to me exaggerated) that Tennyson's poetic prescience enabled him to represent the abnormal psychology of his morbid hero with twentieth-century understanding see Roy P. Basler, "Tennyson the Psychologist," *South Atlantic Quarterly*, XLIII (1944), 143-159.

4. *Works*, p. 942. See *Memoir* I, 403 for a cancelled stanza of this section.

CHAPTER SEVEN

1. Morton Luce, *A Handbook to the Works of Alfred Lord Tennyson*, pp. 122, 123.

2. See W. P. Mustard, *Classical Echoes in Tennyson*, New York, 1904, ch.VI, pp. 65-83; and Ortha L. Wilner, "Tennyson and Lucretius," *The Classical Journal*, XXV (1930), 347-366. Tennyson's poem, says Miss Wilner, "repeats . . . the great scientific and moral doctrines of the six books of the *De Rerum Natura* in such a way as to leave a true impression of Lucretius, the poet, the scientist, the moralist. It does this by reproducing the original in ideas and in the expression of ideas, including brief turns of phrase so characteristically Lucretian as to be recognized by the most casual reader, and figures of speech, and actual translations of single lines and longer passages." See also her conclusion, in the text above.

3. First published as 'The Grandmother's Apology' in *Once a Week* for 16 July 1859.

4. For Woolner, see Chapter Two, pp. 56 f. On Adelaide Proctor, see Eugene L. Didier, "An Illustrious Plagiarist," in *Literary Era*, reprinted in *The Book-Lover*, II (1901), 374-376. Here it is claimed that Tennyson plagiarized Miss Procter's 'Homeward Bound' in *Legends and Lyrics:* "The plot, the treatment, the whole scope of the two poems are identical," though the language is "not very similar." 'Enoch Arden' was written in the summer of 1862, says Mr. Didier, and was not published until after the death of Miss Procter, 2 February 1864. In the next issue of *The Book-Lover*, p. 458, S. H. R. Capen draws attention to Mrs. Gaskell's short story in *Right at Last* (Harpers, 1860), "The Manchester Marriage," as apparently the source of both poems.

5. The fourth tale of the tenth day. Tennyson follows it closely, except that at the end the two men remain together as friends, and at the beginning they were not acquainted with each other. The names are entirely different. (In 'The Falcon' he keeps Boccaccio's names for the two principal characters.) One would guess that in his usual search for subjects Tennyson found the Boccaccio story, made a poem of it, and then saw that it would do as a conclusion to 'The Lover's Tale.'— See also William E. A. Axon, "Tennyson's 'Lover's Tale.' Its Original and Analogues," *Transactions of the Royal Society of Literature*, London, 1903 pp. 61-79.

6. The curious may be referred to a 32-page pamphlet by Eric Mackay, entitled: *Vox Clamantis. A comparison Analytical and Critical between the 'Columbus at Seville' of Joseph Ellis—Pickering. 1st Edition, 1869, 2nd Edition, 1876, and the 'Columbus' of the Poet Laureate. Kegan Paul & Co., 1880,* London [1887].

7. "I read the legend in Joyce' *Celtic Legends,* but most of the details are mine" (*Memoir* II, 255). Hallam Tennyson remarks, oddly, that his father "intended to represent in his own original way the Celtic genius, and he wrote the poem with a genuine love of the peculiar exuberance of the Irish imagination."

CHAPTER EIGHT

1. For a systematic study of the development of the 'Idylls' (following the method of Kuno Fischer on *Faust*) see Richard Jones, *The Growth of the Idylls of the King*, Philadelphia, 1895.

2. Only a few copies of this work were circulated. A reprint from that in the British Museum was made by A. C. Curtis, Guildford, 1902. In later versions the name of Nimuë was changed to Vivien. Lines 5-146 of the present text were added in 1874 (note the dashes), and there are other minor revisions.

3. The exact order of composition and the technical details of publication are rather complex. See T. J. Wise, *Bibliography of the Writings of Alfred, Lord Tennyson,* and *The Ashley Library*, VII. The

evidence seems to indicate that each of these Idylls was written just before its first printing, except 'Balin and Balan,' which was begun in 1872 but held over until the 'Tiresias' volume.

4. *Letters of Benjamin Jowett, M. A.* Arranged and Edited by Evelyn Abbott and Lewis Campbell, London, 1899, p. 172. The letter was addressed to Jowett's friend, Miss Elliot, and is dated "[1861]."

5. Mrs. Bradley reported Tennyson as saying in 1869 that "the key is to be found in careful reading of Sir Percivale's vision and subsequent fall and XIXth century temptations."

6. *Cornhill Magazine,* CLIII (1936), 534 ff.

7. Sir Charles Tennyson says (p. 547) that "The dialogue with Mark's messenger evidently suggested to Tennyson the theme of the 'Last Tournament,' which was written immediately after Gareth." So also the *Memoir* II, 104, says that 'The Last Tournament' was "just written" in May 1871.

8. Henry Alford, "The Idylls of the King," in *The Contemporary Review,* XIII (1870), 104-125. For a reply see "The Laureate and his 'Arthuriad,'" (already cited, note f). This article also reviews *The Works,* 10 vols., 1870 and contains some pungent observations on Tennyson's other poems; but it is particularly severe on "the clandestine articulations" of the new 'Idylls.' R. H. Hutton defended the unity of the 'Idylls' in the *Spectator;* cf. *Brief Literary Criticisms,* London 1906, p. 189.

9. One of the most thoroughgoing allegorists was Condé Benoist Pallen. He began with an article in *The Catholic World* for April 1885, which he amplified ten years later into a series of articles, in the same periodical, and later published in a small book. On receipt of the first article Tennyson wrote to him: "I thank you for your critique on the Idylls of the King. You see further into their meaning than most of my commentators have done." The focus of this insight seems to be: "The main purport of the Idylls is to show forth the kingship of the soul, and how only through that kingship the beast in man is subdued. Their message is a rebuke to the pride of the flesh, the crime of the sense becomes the crime of malice, the ancient rebellion against the spiritual and God" (*The Meaning of the Idylls of the King,* New York, [1904], p. 19).

10. The modern Christian view is expressed by P. Cameron, D.C.L., "Tennyson's Idyl of Guinevere," in *The Catholic World,* LXIII (June 1896), 328-342: "There have been many great poets, but of whom can it be said, as is true of the author of the 'Idyls,' that his words all have a good moral—nay, a religious bearing—and that no one idea is meretricious or doubtful in purity. . . . It was his delight to lift up poor humanity, bleeding and bruised, if it lay near him. If the Queen sinned, the Queen repented; *if Lancelot erred,* yet Lancelot at the end died a

holy man" (p. 329; the italics are mine). Cf. on the next page: "Tennyson was the greatest thinker in poetry England ever had, or perhaps the world ever saw or will see again."

11. Henry Elsdale, *Studies in the Idylls*, London, 1878, pp. 162, 163.

12. Says one of the defenders: the whole *Idylls* "is an elaborate picture of a great moral failure to subdue earthly circumstance to the highest will, but of a great moral failure in which there is more glory than in most success" (R. H. Hutton, *Brief Literary Criticisms*, London, 1906, p. 187.

CHAPTER NINE

1. Sir Richard Jebb, in *The Times*, 10 December 1884; reprinted in Eversley ed., IX, 433 ff.

2. "The play was a really enormous success," says Bram Stoker, *Personal Reminiscences of Henry Irving* (New York and London, 1902, 2 vols.) I, 242; "The public who had been waiting since early morning at the pit and gallery, could not contain themselves; and even the more staid portions of the house lost their reserve. It was like one huge personal triumph." This describes of course the opening night, 6 February 1893, less than four months after the author's death, and therefore the triumph was personal both to Tennyson and to Irving. 'Becket' was performed 112 times that season and 308 times in all (London 147, the provinces 92, America 69). Queen Victoria added a just word (to Irving) after the command performance at Windsor: "It is a very noble play! What a pity that old Tennyson did not live to see it. It would have delighted him as it delighted Us!" *(ibid., II, 220)*. A bit later, at the revival of 'Becket' in July 1894 William Archer said: "There is no rule that it does not break, no formula that it fails to set at naught. It is rambling, disjointed, structureless; its psychological processes take place between the acts; it overrides history for the sake of an infantile love-interest; its blank verse is 'undramatic,' and its humour is—well, unsophisticated. In short, it is nothing that it ought to be, and everything that it oughtn't. Literally everything: for it is most of all what it oughtn't to be—a success." And he credits Irving with the whole success; even "All Miss Terry's charm cannot make the *Rosamund* scenes very interesting to me" *(Theatrical World, quoted by M. J. Moses, *Representative British Dramas, Victorian and Modern*, Boston, 1925, p. 344.)

3. One testimony to the care which Tennyson lavished on 'Becket' is the unusual number of versions. Besides two notebooks (one containing first drafts of many parts of the play, the other a practically complete text of Act V) and a holograph manuscript (which is a fair copy, used by the printer, but with extensive additions, cancels, and alterations), there are two privately printed texts, both in 1879; the first tentative acting version, printed later in the same year; three

more acting versions (one of them by Hallam Tennyson) printed with a view to satisfying Irving; the published edition, December 1884, which was based on a revision (not earlier than 1882) of the first privately printed texts; besides Irvings's acting version. This last was published and sold at the time the play was produced: "Becket A Tragedy In a Prologue and Four Acts By Alfred, Lord Tennyson As Arranged for the Stage by Henry Irving and Afterwards Submitted to the Author." That is, besides the first drafts, with many revisions in manuscript, the play was twice set up in type for Tennyson's use in making the published edition in 1884; and four attempts at an acting version were printed and submitted to Irving before the final acting version was arrived at. This version, as the title page indicates, was not strictly the result of collaboration. See the unpublished dissertation by Dr. Mary Poteat, Duke University Library.

4. Tennyson himself named "Becket's letters, and the writings of Herbert of Bosham, Fitzstephen, and John of Salisbury" as best for background; and he added: "Bishop Lightfoot found out about Rosamund for me"—which is certainly curious. He had of course J. C. Robertson's biography of Becket, 1859, and after 1875-85 the two volumes of the *Chronicles and Memorials*.

5. So, for example, William Archer: "If Tennyson had taken to drama earlier in life, and had been at the pains of studying its laws, I believe he had in him the makings of a great playwright" (*The Old Drama and the New*, 1923, p. 51).

CHAPTER TEN

1. Arthur Waugh, *Alfred Lord Tennyson*, pp. 309-310.
2. *The Critic*, x (1887), 1-2.
3. Osbert Burdet, *The Brownings*, Boston, 1929, p. 88.
4. *New Monthly Magazine*, XXXVII (1833), 74.
5. N.S., VII (1833), 41.
6. *The Life and Letters of Benjamin Jowett*, by Evelyn Abbott and Lewis Campbell (2 vols., 1897), I, 367.
7. *Letters of Benjamin Jowett*, ed. by Evelyn Abbott and Lewis Campbell, London, 1899, p. 235.
8. F. R. Leavis, *New Bearings in English Poetry*, London, 1932, p. 15.
9. This is less startling than it sounds. The notes to *Poems by Two Brothers* show that Tennyson was acquainted with Sir William Jones' works (apparently in the six-volume edition of 1799). Cf. E. Koeppel, "Tennysoniana," *Englische Studien*, XXVIII (1900), 397-406; and Sir Alfred Lyall, *Tennyson*, 1902, pp. 49-50 and n. I have used the London, 1783 edition: *The Moallakat, or Seven Arabian Poems, which were Suspended on the Temple at Mecca; with a Translation, and Arguments*. Five of the seven poems begin with a nasîb or "amatory and

elegiack" passage which resembles the opening lines of 'Locksley Hall'; and the first one, by Amriolkais (Imra-al-Kais), ends, like 'Locksley Hall,' with a storm. Jones' argument to this poem runs: "The poet, after the manner of his countrymen, supposes himself attended on a journey by a company of friends; and, as they pass near a place, where his mistress had lately dwelled, but from which her tribe was then removed, *he desires them to stop awhile* [italics in original], that he might indulge the painful pleasure of weeping over the deserted remains of her tent. They comply with his request, but exhort him to show more strength of mind, and urge two topics of consolation; namely, *that he had before been equally unhappy,* and *that he had enjoyed his full share of pleasure:* thus by the recollection of his passed delight his imagination is kindled, and his grief suspended. . . ." The first four couplets, in Jones' translation are:

"Stay—Let us weep at the remembrance of our beloved, *at the sight of* the station *where her tent was raised,* by the edge of yon bending sands between Dahul and Haumel.

"Tudah and Mikra: *a station,* the marks of which are not wholly effaced, though the south wind and the north have woven the twisted sand."

Thus I spoke, when my companions stopped their coursers by my side, and said, "Perish not through despair: only be patient."

A profusion of tears, *answered I,* is my sole relief; but what avails it to shed them over the remains of a deserted mansion?

This is not very close, obviously, to Tennyson, but the influence is strengthened, according to Koeppel, by the presence of the "comrades" in 'Locksley Hall,' who are soon forgotten, and by the Pleiades couplet (23);

It was the hour, when the Pleiads appeared in the firmament, like the folds of a silken sash variously decked with gems.

Cf. 'Locksley Hall,' lines 9-10. There is some resemblance also between Tennyson's 8-stress trochaic couplets (thought however to be his own invention, though they are a simple variation of the $abcb^4$ quatrain printed as two lines) and the Arabic "long verse":

Amator puellarum miser sæpe fallitur
Ocellis nigris, labris odoris, nigris comis.

It may be added that the Arabic poems, after their amatory and elegiac opening have a varied subject matter, which loosely parallels Tennyson's method of interlarding a commentary on the times with his love-story.

10. *Letters,* ed. Kenyon, New York, 1898, I, 339.

11. H. V. Routh, *Money, Morals and Manners as Revealed in Modern Literature,* London, 1935, p. 27.

12. Mortimer Dyneley, "Locksley Hall and Liberalism," *The National Review,* VIII (1887), 641-647; see 643, 644.

13. Lord Lytton, as quoted in *Memoir* II, 330.

14. "'Locksley Hall' in Youth and Age," in *Criticisms on Contemporary Thought and Thinkers Selected from the Spectator*, 2 vols., London, 1894, pp. 204-205. The poems have been learnedly defended, with citations from Condorcet, J. B. Bury, and Morris Fishbein, by Robert K. Richardson, "The Idea of Progress in *Locksley Hall*," in *Transactions of the Wisconsin Academy of Science, Arts and Letters*, XXVIII (1933), 341-361. This paper ends by saying (in true academic English) that 'Locksley Hall' is "a magnificent embodiment of the factors historically and logically inherent in the idea of progress; of the emotional and mental atmosphere so vitally connected with the idea; and, by implication and inference, of the definition of the idea as producible by a generalization based on its several components."— Cf. also Gaetano Negri, "Tennyson e Gladstone," in *Segni dei Tempi*, Milano, 1893; I have seen only the authorized translation in *Die Gesellschaft*, Leipzig, 1898, II, 762-771.

15. Cf. Henry Van Dyke's impressions, with an analysis of the content and a record of the variant readings, in *Poems of Tennyson*, Boston, 1903, pp. 439 ff.

16. "The Teaching of Tennyson," in *Browning and Tennyson as Teachers*, London, 1903. This is written of course from the rationalist's point of view; the language is sometimes strong and the attitude impatient; the reasoning is not always too clear, or at least not clearly expressed; but the general result is interesting.

17. Amy Cruse, *The Victorians and their Reading*, Boston, 1935, p. 341.

18. To his Mother, 5 June 1869; *Letters*, II, 10.

19. Swinburne to Stedman, *Letters*, Bonchurch ed., XVIII, 184-185. The thought may not be perfectly clarified, but it is there; and the language is more lyrically powerful than Tennyson's.

20. Reprinted in *Works*, p. 970-972, and more fully in *Tennyson and His Friends*, pp. 475-480.

21. John Chalmers, *Speculations . . . of 'The Old Philosopher' Lao-Tsze*, London, 1868.

22. For a more enthusiastic restatement of the new creed see (in addition to Ward's version) Henry Van Dyke, p. 446.

23. Cf. *Memoir* I, 321; II, 105, 457; and the Prologue to 'In Memoriam.'

24. *Saturday Review*, I (3 November 1855), 14-15.

25. James T. Bixby, "Alfred Tennyson and the Questionings of our Age," *The* [Boston] *Arena*, II (1890), 57-71; p. 59.

26. *Atheism and the Value of Life*, London, 1884, pp. 83-146; originally a review of Tennyson's 1880 volume, *Edinburgh Review*, CLIV (1881), 486-515.

27. *Temple Bar*, XXVI (1869), 191.

CHAPTER ELEVEN

1. "Ideas of Good and Evil (1896-1903)," in *Essays*, New York, 1924, p. 234.

2. A. E. Powell, *The Romantic Theory of Poetry*, London, 1926, p. 7.

3.   Art for Art's sake! Hail, truest Lord of Hell!
            Hail Genius, Master of the Moral Will!
            "The filthiest of all paintings painted well
            Is mightier than the purest painted ill!"
            Yes, mightier than the purest painted well,
            So prone are we toward the broad way to Hell.

(*Memoir* II, 92) These verses certainly do Tennyson no credit as artist of any sort. They are rather more reprehensible *as verse* than their sentiment is as criticism. Swinburne took offense at this "doggerel" when he saw it in the *Memoir* and about 1900 expressed himself vigorously in "Changes and Aspects": "And whenever Tennyson himself was not serving this lord of hell, the law which compels every artist to do his very best in his own line, and not allow the very noblest intention or instinct or emotion to deflect or distort or pervert his hand, he drivelled: he drivelled as pitifully as in this idiotic eructation of doggerel" (Clyde K. Hyder, "Swinburne: *Changes of Aspect* and *Short Notes*," *P.M.L.A.*, LVIII (1943, 223-244; 231 ff.; 233).

4. This is from Locker-Lampson's account of his tour in Switzerland with Tennyson in 1869. Locker-Lampson adds: "He appears to shrink from his own popularity" (*Memoir* II, 80). Cf. Tennyson's petulant impromptu *Memoir* II, 157; and Lecky's observation (*ibid.*, 204) in 1874: "The popularity of his poems sometimes seemed to bewilder him, and I have heard him gravely express his belief that it was largely due to his official position as Laureate." As the poet himself would say, it was and it was not.

5. *Revaluations*, London, 1931, p. 67. Mr. Abercrombie cites 'Maud' and 'Lucretius' with approval—which I should call more than moments.

6. From 'The Sisters.' Tennyson notes: "What I saw myself at Llanberis, in North Wales."

7. The first two, of these four, are from 'The Ancient Sage,' the last is from 'The Lover's Tale,' Part I; the third is from 'Queen Mary,' II, iii. Many of the 'good things' in the plays are vitiated by their obvious Elizabethanism.

8. The first two are from 'The Princess,' the third from 'The Ancient Sage.'

9. *Modern Painters*, Part IV, ch. xvii (Library ed., v, 362 n.).

10. *The Letters of Matthew Arnold to Arthur Hugh Clough*, ed. Lowry, London, 1932, p. 63.

11. W. B. Yeats, "Ideas of Good and Evil," p. 139. Yeats was actually speaking of "poets of a better time [than Blake's]—Tennyson and

Wordsworth, let us say." On a later page (232) he noted "that 'externality' which a time of scientific and political thought has brought into literature."

12. Some of the details are still unclear. Cf. *Memoir* II, 142; also a series of letters to the *Times Literary Supplement* for 15 October, 22 October, 17 December, 31 December 1931. It would seem that Tennyson caught fire from Froude's account, which was a composite of the early sources, and then having got the sources themselves from Arber's reprint was moved to composition. Something by way of incentive may have been due to Gerald Massey's poem, 'Sir Richard Grenville's Last Fight.' Cf. *Memoir* I, 405.

13. XXIV, no. 607, 10 October 1942, p. 241.

14. Harold Nicolson, *Tennyson,* London, 1923, p. 11.

15. *The Spectator,* 9 October 1942, p. 334.

16. J. W. Mackail, *Studies of English Poets,* London, 1926; based upon lectures in Australia in 1923.

17. *Quarterly Review,* CLXXVI (January 1893), 37-38.

18. Basil Champneys, *Memoirs and Correspondence of Coventry Patmore,* London, 1900, II, 267.

19. *The British Quarterly Review,* CXLIV (October 1880), 290-291.

20. *Journals,* VI, 218-219 (1842).

Index

INDEX